Network
Exchange Theory

Network
Exchange Theory

EDITED BY
David Willer

PRAEGER

Westport, Connecticut
London

Library of Congress Cataloging-in-Publication Data

Network exchange theory / edited by David Willer.
    p. cm.
   Includes bibliographical references (p.) and indexes.
    ISBN 0–275–95377–7 (alk. paper).—ISBN 0–275–95378–5 (pbk. :
alk. paper)
    1. Social networks. 2. Exchange theory (Sociology) 3. Social
exchange. 4. Social structure. I. Willer, David.
   HM131.N452 1999
   301'.01—dc21   98–56070

British Library Cataloguing in Publication Data is available.

Library of Congress Catalog Card Number: 98–56070
ISBN: 0–275–95377–7
     0–275–95378–5 (pbk.)

First published in 1999

Praeger Publishers, 88 Post Road West, Westport, CT 06881
An imprint of Greenwood Publishing Group, Inc.
www.praeger.com

Printed in the United States of America

∞

The paper used in this book complies with the
Permanent Paper Standard issued by the National
Information Standards Organization (Z39.48–1984).

10 9 8 7 6 5 4 3 2 1

To
Jan, Bill, Ann, Fred, and Robb
my daughters and sons

It is the grand object of all theory to make these irreducible elements as simple and few in number as possible, without having to renounce the adequate representation of any empirical content whatever.

—Albert Einstein, The Herbert Spencer Lecture,
Oxford, 1933

Contents

Preface

If understanding the powerful effects which social structures have on human behavior is not the central issue of sociology, it should be. As Network Exchange Theory shows, human social behavior is shaped by the social relations in which it occurs. In turn, social relations are conditioned by the structures within which they are embedded. When a social relation is embedded in one type of structure, people produce one kind of behavior. When the same relation is embedded in a second type of structure, another kind of behavior is produced. Theory which links structures and relations to behavior is at the core of this book.

This is the first book to trace the development of a formal social theory from its first concepts to its most recent formulations. I begin with basic concepts that were first developed in the early 1980s. These basic concepts are still in use today and form the core of "Elementary Theory." That theory deals with exchange, conflict, and coercive structures. Since 1987, Elementary Theory's research has concentrated on exchange structures, and as the exchange component grew it gained its own name: Network Exchange Theory. For brevity, Network Exchange Theory is sometimes shortened to NET. Of course, the basic concepts of Elementary Theory are also the basic concepts of NET.

Chapter by chapter, this book traces a theory development that extends scope to more and more kinds of structures. Looking more closely, we find that this theory work has also had its share of setbacks and blind alleys. The presentation here is not an artificial reconstruction; both progress and regress are covered. Furthermore, no theory develops in an unbroken line. In the development of Elementary Theory/Network Exchange Theory, important relations and structures have been jumped over which should have been studied. I point to them in the hope of enlisting the reader in the process of theory development and testing.

What passes for theory in sociology is not at all like Network Exchange Theory. What some call theory is no more than untested pronouncements on the nature of the social world, pronouncements grounded only in the method of authority. By contrast, scientific theories, like Network Exchange Theory, are formulations and procedures for generating explanations and predictions. This is tested theory and, as it is offered in this volume, it is theory for use. The reader can use it for generating new explanations and predictions. To learn how to use the theory, follow how models are drawn, how experiments are designed, and how hypotheses are generated and tested in experiments. Applications of Network Exchange Theory are not limited to the laboratory. For investigations outside the lab, models are built which correspond to historical and institutional social structures and which explain their dynamics.

The explanatory power of Network Exchange Theory is a result of its theoretic methods. Most of the theoretic methods used here are borrowed from two sources. First, by beginning with fundamental concepts and combining them to form more complex, derived concepts, we extend methods of theory construction used by Karl Marx and Max Weber. Oddly, their use of theoretic methods remains unnoticed in histories of sociological theory. Central to our extension is the use of network geometry to represent fundamental and derived concepts. Using network geometry, we picture social relations and structures, resulting in vivid and precise theoretic models.

The second source is theoretic methods used in physical theory. Physical theories are also built up by combining fundamental concepts to form more complex, derived ones. Physical theories also use a geometry to represent these fundamental and derived concepts and in model building. In physical theories, principles and laws are applied to theoretic models to generate dynamics. Dynamic theoretical models are powerful tools; they predict and explain events in the world. Although every beginning student in physics knows how to apply principles and laws to models, these procedures are little understood in the social sciences. They are explained in detail here.

Network Exchange Theory did not grow out of *social* exchange theory, and Chapter 1 of this volume shows that it did not. It examines social exchange theory and finds it to be reductionist. Social exchange theory attempted to find the cause of social structures inside individuals and failed in that attempt. With origins clarified, Chapters 2 and 3 give the basic concepts of Elementary Theory which Network Exchange Theory shares. Five of the eight chapters to follow first appeared in journals and annuals. I introduce each of these chapters with a preface explaining the question motivating the investigation and relating the study to the evolution of the theory.

Most works in sociology are read passively. Terms and facts are memorized. This volume is better read actively. An active reading means working with the theory, using new formulations as they are introduced. Designing and running experiments, either as demonstrations or as tests, are excellent ways to learn how to use theory. Experiments do not require complex and expensive instrumentation. All Elementary Theory experiments, through Chapter 4, were face-to-face experiments. In the face-to-face experimental paradigm, subjects were seated facing each other and negotiated over poker chips. Networks were built by using simple office dividers to block eye contact. Dividers were placed between subjects not connected by exchange relations. Before office dividers were available, slabs of plywood and portable blackboards were used. In fact, all of the experiments reported here could be replicated using the face-to-face paradigm, and much would be learned from those replications.

Today, most experiments are run in advanced electronic laboratories where subjects interact through networked PCs. Electronic laboratories have traditionally been expensive instruments. The development of specially designed and programmed software that allows experimental subjects to interact intuitively has been one major expense. The cost of hardware, such as dedicated PCs and Hubs, has been a second major expense. As a result of high costs, very few labs have been built.

Nevertheless, we are now on the brink of a major development in social science. Work is now under way to put the software for network exchange experiments onto an active web site. Call that web site a *Web-Lab*. With the Web-Lab, anyone with access to one or more PCs that connect to the World Wide Web can run experiments and demonstrations by logging into the Web-Lab. A computer classroom, for example, would be an excellent setting. The software of the Web-Lab is user friendly. Using a mouse, we can set initial conditions for experiments. With initial conditions specified, the PCs are interconnected in the designated network, subjects are instructed, the experiment is conducted, and data is recorded, including a complete event history of subject interactions. If only a single PC is available, the investigator can run networks with simulated actors. Information on the Web-Lab is available from the author at Willer@garnet.cla.sc.edu.

Certain of the chapters to follow were written with Michael Lovaglia, Barry Markovsky, and John Skvoretz. There is no doubt that the development of Network Exchange Theory is very much due to the excellence of their work. Travis Patton, Brent Simpson, and Shane Thye have also made important contributions to the theory, and I am very fortunate that some of their work is included here. I have learned much about how to do science from working with these six. Sharee St. Louis drew the figures found throughout this volume; her work required not just a steady hand, but also an intimate understanding of the workings of the theory. Many thanks to her for the excellent work. I also thank Linda Karr for her excellent work preparing the indexes for this book. I want to thank the National Science Foundation (NSF) for continued support. With the exception of Chapter 4, all of the research reported here was funded by NSF. I would also like to thank the University of South Carolina for seed money funding the beginning of the laboratory here. Finally, my thanks to Patricia Powell Willer. Without her nothing could have been done.

Chapter 1

Network Exchange Theory: Issues and Directions

David Willer

This book traces the growth of the Elementary Theory of Social Structure from basic concepts through its most recent models and predictions. As noted in the Preface, this is the only book to trace the development of a formal social theory from inception through tests and extensions to its current state. Because it has been developing for more than 15 years and because its parts are scattered in time and across journals and books, even those who specialize in Network Exchange Theory are not always aware of all of Elementary Theory. Here I draw together all of the theory in a single work and show how it forms a coherent whole.

There are other network exchange theories, and they will also be discussed. They include "expected value" (Friedkin 1992, 1993), "power-dependence" (Emerson 1972a, 1972b; Cook et al. 1983; Cook and Yamagishi 1992a), an application of the "core" (Bienenstock and Bonacich 1992, 1993), and "identity theory" (Burke 1997). These network exchange theories deal only with exchange; they successfully predict power outcomes for an array of structures. Elementary Theory is also successful in predicting power outcomes for exchange structures, but offers predictions for coercive structures as well. It also applies to normative structures and property systems. Only Elementary Theory has links to Status Characteristics Theory, which allows it to predict power due to influence and influence due to power. Applications across the whole scope of Elementary Theory are found in this book.

Since social science began, a central question for theory has been how to link human activities to the social structures in which they occur. Network exchange theories are the first to succeed in rigorously predicting activities from structure and actor conditions. A core concern of these theories has been to predict a particular type of activity, called a "power exercise." The exercise of power is indicated by the movement of valued resources among people, by the control of one person by another, or by both. Generally, people who exercise power gain more and give less than those over whom power is exercised. Because power is about gaining and losing and about the control of some by others, the direction of power and the amount exercised is a vital concern to people in society.

Granted that people in society are concerned about power, how commonly are power relations encountered? To answer this question we need to know how to identify power relations. At one time it was believed that power relations were distinguished from relations of other kinds by the presence of communications, like orders or commands. That is to say, a power event occurs only when a command is sent by one person and obeyed by another. By this measure, few relations in a society like the United States today would be power relations.

But the idea that power is reliably indicated by particular communications is flawed. When power structures are well established, very few orders or commands will occur. There will be few commands because, when conditions favor the exercise of power, people in high power positions need only make suggestions. When suggestions are sufficient to direct the activity of others, they are generally preferred to commands. It follows that orders and commands may indicate, not the presence of power, but its imminent failure.

A better measure for the presence of power begins with the power relation itself. Social relations are power relations when people's interests and motives are mixed. As Weber put it, in power relations, interests are opposed but complementary ([1918] 1968). For example, interests are opposed in economic exchange because buyers want the lowest price possible, whereas sellers want the highest price. Interests are also complementary: both buyers and sellers have an interest in completing exchanges. Interests are also mixed in coercion. States coerce citizens to extract taxes. The state wants to collect as large a measure of taxes owed as possible, whereas each citizen wants to pay as little as possible. Both want to avoid the costs of legal sanctions. In game theory terms, exchange and coercion are mixed-motive games; in both, interests are opposed but complementary.

All relations with mixed motives, including economic exchange and coercion, are power relations. Note that the presence of a power relation is determined only by the mixed motives of the relation and not by motivations or beliefs unique to individuals. In a later chapter I report on an experiment which shows that power exercise requires no special "Will to power." The exercise of power requires no special motivations because it occurs through the rational pursuit of interests. For example, when a buyer tries to gain a favorable price and does so to some degree, that buyer has exercised power. The outcome is a power exercise by the buyer because (1) the buyer gains the favorable outcome (2) in an exchange relation where motives are mixed. Power is about gaining and losing, but for a social relation to be a power relation it is not necessary that one person gain more than the other. When motives are mixed but the outcome benefits people similarly, the relation is a power relation and its state is "equipower."

Research on power over the last 15 years has clearly linked an array of structural conditions to power exercise. But the study of exchange did not begin from a structural perspective. To the contrary, the "social exchange perspective" of the 1960s and 1970s denied any role to structure. Elementary Theory of Social Structure did not grow out of the social exchange perspective. It grew in opposition to that perspective, yet the two are frequently conflated. To clarify this intellectual history, here I will draw a line of demarcation between Elementary Theory and the earlier social exchange perspective.

The part of Elementary Theory that focuses on structures of exchange is called Network Exchange Theory (with capitals). By contrast, network exchange theory (no capitals) is a field of study which, as mentioned above, contains a number of theories. Frequently, it will be convenient to abbreviate Elementary Theory of Social Structure as "ET" and Network Exchange Theory as "NET."

ET and NET share the project of relating structure to activity with the classical theories of Marx and Weber. By contrast, the social exchange perspective is "reductionist." Social reductionist perspectives claim that everything which happens in society is a consequence of properties of individuals. If some people are powerful, it is because they have powerful personalities. If some people are rich, it is because they economize. The social exchange perspective adds that social structure is an "incidental by-product" of human activity. Structures are produced by human activity but have no effect on human activity. I show this reductionism to be false.

Experiments reported throughout this volume show that "exclusion" produces power in the exchange networks. Exclusion is a property of social structures. Since exclusion is not found in individuals, showing that power is the result of exclusion falsifies the reductionism on which social exchange perspective was based.

The working of exclusion is not limited to small social structures built up in the laboratory. Later in this introduction, I show how exclusion produces power in larger social structures identified by Marx and Weber. Then I trace the two meanings of power from classical theory and show how the reductionism of social exchange "theory" requires that the two be ripped apart and opposed in a single relationship. The resulting paradoxes and contradictions are noted, and it is shown how both are avoided when the role of structure is central in theory.

CLASSICAL FOUNDATIONS

Network exchange theories were not the first to seek relations between human activities and social structures. In each generation, scholars return to Marx and Weber because both made substantial progress in linking activity to structure. When comparing the form and structure of theory, these classical works could hardly be more different from the network exchange theories of today. Marx and Weber's theories are largely discursive. Network exchange theories are formally stated. Marx and Weber focused on historical examples, and their conclusions are embedded in the cases for which they were drawn. At times, their terminology is little removed from ordinary language. By contrast, at their best, network exchange theories use fully abstract terms to express the content of theory and conclusions drawn from it. These conclusions are testable and are not limited by particulars of time and place. That is, network exchange theories have made a substantial step toward the kind of testability and universality that are expected and required of science.

Nevertheless, as I show later in this introduction, for all of these formal differences, there are important substantive similarities. For anyone interested in explaining the effects of social structure on what people do, there is much to be learned from Marx's *Capital* and Weber's *Economy and Society*. For example, both Marx and Weber recognized *exclusion* as a condition of structural power. This recognition is significant because exclusion is undoubtedly the single most important structural condition producing power. Its importance is underlined by the fact that the vast majority of network exchange research has focused on the effects of exclusion.

Thus it is accurate to say that network exchange theories have confirmed, in an array of experiments, an important structural power condition already recognized by Marx and Weber. Structure also affects power in coercive relations. Later I show what kinds of structural conditions affect coercion and explain the context in which the two classical scholars recognized those conditions. In fact, Elementary Theory has tested and experimentally confirmed the relation between structure and coercion found by Marx and Weber. But I do not mean to imply that network exchange theories are simply redundant restatements of ideas first found in Marx and Weber. It is important to recognize that the two were right about exclusion and coercion. But their comments on these structures were incidental, almost offhand. The conditions of power which they favored, value theory for Marx and legitimacy for Weber, remain untested.

Progress is made in science because it is self-correcting. Errors are always being made in theory and being sifted out by empirical tests. Knowledge cumulates as a result of this interplay of theory and research. Judged only by insights about structural conditions of power, the theories of Marx and Weber are still broader in scope than all but one network exchange theory. But Marx's insights on structure are found in a few passages mixed into a very large discourse. Exactly the same is the case with Weber. Neither offers an empirical method of testing that would sift one part of the theoretical discourse from another.

In science, theory designs experiments. Later chapters will show how models drawn from formal theory are the blueprints for study design. The need for formal theory to design research has limited tests of Marx and Weber. Controlled tests of Marx and Weber's theories—or any part thereof—were not possible because their theories are not well enough formed to design experiments. Today some of their insights can be rigorously tested, however, by coupling them to a theory that can design experiments. An example was already mentioned. Marx and Weber asserted that exclusion produces power in structures: experiments designed by Elementary Theory demonstrate the efficacy of that condition.

Elementary Theory builds small social structures with theoretically known properties, predicts power exercise from those structures, and experimentally tests the predictions. Each of these steps, from building structures through experiments as tests, is examined later in this book. Elementary Theory is grounded in classical theory. But the result of this stream of research is that, today, theory makes exact predictions, confirmed by careful research, which simply cannot be imagined from a classical perspective.

Precision is important, but I believe that the most important contribution of network exchange theory has been to bring social structure back to the center of social science theory and research. From Weber's death in 1920 to well past mid-century, little or no progress was made in relating social structure to human activity. Instead of searching for the effects of structure, the emphasis was on presumed motives internal to individuals. Human beings were either assumed to be individually autonomous, being driven by inner motives only, or were treated as such by default. As a result, network exchange theory's inferences from structure to behavior are a major revolution in thinking about society.

Elementary Theory was initially designed to capture, formalize, and test the structural insights of Marx and Weber. So, from its inception, it was engaged in predicting activity from structure. As the theory has grown, new conditions of power have been discovered. Conditions such as ''inclusion'' and ''hierarchy/ mobility'' (see Chapter 3) were not suggested by Marx, Weber, or any other previous theory. These new discoveries are the result of formal methods in theory which allow a step-by-step development from old to new ideas. But many new discoveries are due to competition between Elementary Theory and other theories of exchange networks, a competition that could occur only because all the theories are stated formally.

I now turn to the social exchange perspectives of the 1960s and 1970s to draw the line of demarcation between their reductionism and the structural understanding which is at the core of Elementary Theory and its exchange component, Network Exchange Theory. Central to the social exchange perspective is a presumed ''truth'' about the social world on which its point of view toward society is centered.

REDUCTIONIST PERSPECTIVES

The ''truth'' which the social exchange perspective asserts is that social structures do not determine behavior. This is a strongly ''reductionist'' position which maintains that social structure contains nothing that is not a quality of individual humans or a consequence of individual qualities. But the social exchange perspective goes further than previous reductionist positions which denied the existence of structures. It asserts that social structures are real but that they are an *incidental by-product* of the everyday activity of individuals. Social structures are produced by individual behavior but have no effect on behavior. For the leading reductionist, George Homans, there are no general laws that are specifically social. Only "psychological general propositions" are needed to explain human activity (Homans 1971, p. 376).

In the following pages I show that reductionist social exchange contributed to its own falsification. It was the belief that structure is produced by behavior, not the inverse, that led Richard Emerson to develop "a theory of social exchange in which *social structure* is taken as the dependent variable" (1972, p. 58). Emerson's power-dependence theory was initially reductionist, but, unlike Homans and other reductionists, Emerson was not content with ungrounded claims. So power-dependence theory was applied experimentally. But the result of that application was that its perspective reversed out of reductionism toward a more structural view. When science is intensively pursued, errors are corrected. The reversal of the power-dependence perspective illustrates well the self-corrective quality of scientific knowledge.

Reductionist social exchange perspectives claim that *all* social structures are a consequence of qualities of individuals, but only *one* example was ever put forward, exchange in a "unilateral monopoly." A unilateral monopoly is a structure in which one position is connected to two or more others that have no alternative to the monopolist. Monopolies are covered in neoclassical microeconomics under the "theory of the firm." The theory of the firm asserts that any business firm which is a monopolist should put its products on the market at a price incrementally higher than the price which would be received in a perfectly competitive market. For neoclassical microeconomics, monopolists are advantaged relative to their exchange partners. The social exchange perspective also saw monopolists as advantaged. Because they reached a similar conclusion, many believed that the social exchange perspective was supported by economic theory. But was it?

To follow social exchange thinking, imagine a simple monopoly like that given in Figure 1.1a, where *B* is central to three peripheral *A*s. The social exchange perspective assumed that, when things are exchanged, actors in the *A* and *B* positions are subject to "satiation." By satiation I mean that, as more and more of something is received, each new unit is valued less and less. For example, I would like one steak very much, and to eat a second now would be nice, but I will not eat a third steak until next week. Satiation simply asserts that, for limited time periods, humans and other organisms have limited capacities and thus limited desires for particular things. Assume that the *A*s are sending *B* similar things. Since *B* exchanges with three *A*s, *B* becomes satiated three times as fast as any *A*. As exchange continues, if the *A*s want to receive as much now as before, all three must send more and more to *B*. As *B* becomes more and more satiated, however, eventually each *A* will get less and less. In other words, the exchange ratio between B and the As changes over time. This change imposes higher and higher costs on each A. The change does not benefit B more, however. B is gaining larger and larger amounts but, through satiation, wants each unit less and less. B's gross benefit either flattens out or declines.

This hypothetical example was to be the opening wedge in the proof that all qualities of society grow out of qualities of individuals. Certainly the example is generally consistent with operant psychology's understanding of satiation in organisms like people and pigeons. A starved pigeon will peck a lever to receive corn seeds but stops when hunger is satisfied. The example contains no evident internal contradictions; assuming all people are satiated by similar amounts, eventually the As should send more and get less. But a hypothetical example, however plausible it may be, cannot prove anything about the world. It must be shown that the events of the hypothetical example actually ever happen. Is monopoly pricing based on differential satiation? Is power in centralized networks?

The satiation example and the economist's monopoly pricing are not alike. A monopolist is a seller, not a buyer, so monopolists sell goods and receive money. But people are not satiated by money. Money does not produce satiation in people because (1) it is not a particular thing and (2) is not consumed on the spot. In fact, money is not consumed at all. It is because money is exchanged for the preferred bundle of consumer goods, or saved—or given to charity—that money, unlike steaks and candy bars, does not satiate. Moreover, the monopolist of neoclassical microeconomics is not a person but a firm. People and pigeons are biological organisms. The corporate firm is a legal fiction. Since firms are not biological organisms, they do not satiate regardless of the kind of thing input. The economist's theory of the firm, from which monopoly pricing is derived, has nothing to do with operant psychology's satiation.

Nevertheless, those in the social exchange perspective insisted on equating terms from operant psychology to terms from neoclassical microeconomics. For example, when the economists' marginal utility declines, the curve describing utility increases at a decreasing rate. These utility curves and satiation curves have similar shapes. But the conditions producing a decline in marginal utility and the conditions producing satiation are not the same. Monopolistic firms do not peck levers for corn until they are satiated. The social exchange perspective is not supported by economic theory.

POWER IN CENTRALIZED NETWORKS

According to Emerson's social exchange theory, satiation produces changes in exchange ratios and thus power in unilateral monopolies. In 1977, Stolte and Emerson designed an experiment to test Emerson's satiation-based theory. The experiment could have supported the relation which the social exchange perspective believed to hold between satiation and power. But we now can see that the 1977 experiment was the first experimental demonstration that structure produces power.

Networks and Experiments

The Stolte–Emerson experiment was the first to build and investigate small social structures. It is pivotal because, quite apart from the operant theory that inspired it, it actually demonstrated the effect of structure on activity under controlled laboratory conditions—and was the first to do so. To see how this was done, some detail concerning their design is needed.

Figures 1.1a and 1.1b are diagrams for exchange networks which Stolte and Emerson built in their laboratory. A, B, and C are nodes which are positions in the network, each occupied by a person acting as an experimental subject. Social theories call persons "actors." So the 3-Branch of Figure 1a contains four positions, occupied by four actors. The convention is to assign different letters to different kinds of positions. For example, the 5-Line of Figure 1.2 contains three different kinds of positions: the As at the end of the line, the Bs adjacent to the As, and the C in the center. There are three kinds of positions, but five positions in all, and each of the five is occupied by a different actor making its own decisions. The Figure 1.1b "All-to-all" network is symmetrical, so its four positions are identical and are given the same letter, but in the experiment each of the four C positions is occupied by a different experimental subject. Most diagrams of this book follow these conventions. Letters like A, B, and C are used to designate both positions and actors. When a letter is mentioned, whether it designates an actor or a position will be given by context.

The relations of the Figure 1.1 and 1.2 networks are "resource pool relations" that have important similarities to exchange relations. As displayed in the diagrams, a pool of 10 resources is placed *between* each pair of positions. Initially, the resource pools do not belong to any actor, but agreements produce flows of resources from the pool to the actors in the adjacent positions. Only when a pair agree on a division will each receive the agreed upon number from the pool. All resources so received are appropriated by the actor in the position and are the payoff to the actor. Resources received cannot be retransmitted to other actors distal in the network. Actors not agreeing on a division do not divide any pool and they receive no payoff.

The placement and movement of resources in exchange relations is not like that of resource pool relations. In exchange relations each actor initially holds the resources it owns. For example, initially Bill owns a Miata sports car and Ann has money. When exchange occurs, there are two resource flows: Ann buys the Miata, sending $10,000 to Bill, while Bill signs the Miata's title over to Ann. Each actor appropriates the resource received. Unlike payoffs from resource pools, resource flows like money and Miatas can, at some future time, be sent on to some other actor.

Resource pool relations are substituted in experiments for exchange relations because *payoffs* of the two are analogous. The analogy is easily seen. Agreements result in positive payoffs for both actors, whereas failure to agree results in both gaining zero. For example, in the Miata sale, Bill has an alternative offer

Figure 1.1
Two Exchange Networks Like Stolte and Emerson

a. Monopoly

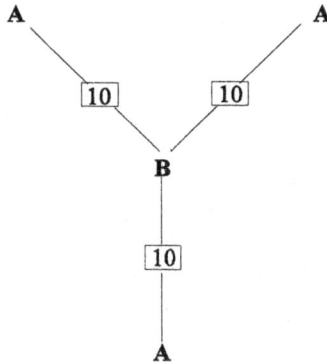

b. All-To-All

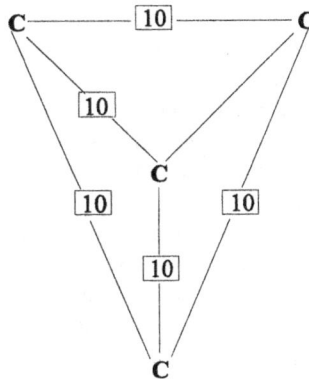

of $9,500, while Ann can get a similar car for $10,500. At the selling price of $10,000, both have gained $500 relative to their alternatives. If they fail to agree on the price, however, the exchange does not occur and their relative gain is zero. Similarly, when a resource pool is divided, both actors benefit. If Ann and Bill equally divide a pool of 10 resources, each gains 5. If they fail to agree on a division, however, both gain zero. The payoffs for resource pool and exchange relations are both examples of opposed but complementary interests. For the game theorist (as I show in Chapter 2), the payoffs of the two define exactly the same kind of mixed-motive game. Nevertheless, resource pool relations are found only in network exchange experiments, and, because they are not identical to exchange relations, results from experiments must be carefully interpreted when brought to bear upon exchange networks outside the laboratory.

Here are the core *initial conditions* for the Stolte–Emerson experiment. The networks of Figure 1.1 were actually built for the experiment, and people acting as experimental subjects were placed in each network position to negotiate and divide resource pools with each other. Each resource in the pool was given a money value, and subjects were paid by resources gained. Only subjects connected by exchanges were allowed to communicate. One run of the experiment was a session, and each session had a number of rounds for negotiations. Each round began with the resources of the network renewed. Within each round, each subject was limited to, at most, a single exchange. The aim is to predict resource divisions, which are usually reported as averages across rounds.

The Stolte–Emerson Experiment: From Satiation to Exclusion

For the monopoly, Stolte and Emerson reported that *B* gained far more resources per exchange than did any *A*. By contrast, in the All-to-all network, divisions were equal. Then as now, the division of resources within each relation indicates power and its direction. So Stolte and Emerson found only *B* to be high in power and, the *A*s to be low in power, whereas the *C*s of the All-to-all network were power equals. A study by Cook and Emerson one year later agrees (1978). Whereas these results are consistent with Emerson's 1972 satiation model, neither study asserted that power was due to satiation.

We know today that power in the Stolte–Emerson experiment was due not to satiation but to exclusion. *Because exclusion is a quality of structures, not of individuals, this experiment was the first step toward the falsification of reductionism.* Recall that one of the experimental conditions limited each subject to at most a single exchange—a condition now called the "1-exchange rule." The 1-exchange rule does not block a satiation interpretation of power in the monopoly. Regardless of the number of exchanges allowed, *B* is central and exchanges three times as often as any *A*. Thus, if satiation occurs, *B* satiates three times as fast.

But the 1-exchange rule allows a very different explanation—one in which exclusion comes to the fore. Since each position exchanges maximally once, *B* must *exclude* two of three *A*s from exchanging. The two excluded *A*s gain zero points. Only the one *A* exchanging with *B* receives any points. The Stolte–Emerson experiment sharply limited information such that the subject in *B* knew all offers, but each *A* knew only the offers ongoing in its relation to *B*. Although *A*s could not know what others were offering to *B*, each did know that s/he was being routinely excluded. Recent studies have shown that after exclusion people adjust their offers, asking for less. I suspect that the excluded subjects in the *A* positions asked for less and less, producing the high payoffs to *B* which indicated that *B* was high in power.

Here is why we now know that power differences in the Stolte–Emerson experiment and the Cook–Emerson experiment were due to exclusion and not satiation. Four years after Stolte-Emerson, Brennan (1981) studied the Figure 1.1a monopoly network without exclusion. For Brennan's experiment, the central position was allocated three exchanges and each of the *A*s one exchange. Satiation theory again predicts that *B* will gain more resources in each exchange, but that prediction proved false. Observed resource divisions indicated equal power. Because there was no exclusion, the equipower outcome is the one expected by Network Exchange Theory (see Chapter 3). Brennan's study was to be a critical test between reductionist and structural theories. Further critical tests are reported in Willer, Markovsky, and Patton (1989).

Exclusion in Strong, Weak, and Equal Power Networks

That exclusion produces power in networks like those investigated by Stolte and Emerson was further confirmed by the recent discovery of "weak power." Weak power stands between the strong power of the Figure 1.1a monopoly and the equal power of the Figure 1.1b All-to-all network. That is, higher power positions in weak power structures gain higher payoffs than those lower in power, but their payoffs never approach the extreme of strong power structures.

Payoffs in strong power structures approach extreme values because exclusion drives them toward the extremes. The Figure 1.1a monopoly is strong power under the 1-exchange rule because *B* is never excluded and two *A*s are always excluded. More generally, in all strong power structures, there is one or more high power positions which are never excluded and two or more low power positions, at least one of which is always excluded. As in Figure 1.1a, low power positions are connected only to positions high in power and all exchanges occur between the two types.

In some equal power networks, no position is excluded, as in the All-to-all network and Brennan's 3-Branch. In the rest, all positions face exclusion with the same probability. For example, add one more position to the Figure 1.1b network and connect it to the other four. We now have an All-to-all network with five positions. Under the 1-exchange rule, two pairs of positions will exchange and one position will always be excluded. But all face the possibility of exclusion with the same probability: each is excluded one-fifth of the time for a probability of .20. Since the probability of exclusion is the same for all positions, none is advantaged and resource divisions will be equal—as they are in all equal power networks.

In weak power networks, some or all positions face exclusion with *different*

Figure 1.2
Simple 1-Exchange Networks

a. 2-LINE

b. 3-LINE

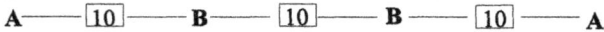

c. 4-LINE

d. 5-LINE

A———[10]———B———[10]———C———[10]———B———[10]———A

likelihoods. The 4-Line of Figure 1.2 is a weak power network. The first step in predicting power in networks like the 4-Line is to calculate the likelihood of exclusion for each position. Positions more likely to be excluded like the *A*s gain proportionally less than positions less likely to be excluded like the *B*s. Resulting resource divisions vary between—but not inclusive of—the equal divisions of equal power networks and the extremes of strong power networks. In later chapters two general procedures are offered. The first assigns likelihoods of exclusion to positions, and the second uses those likelihoods to calculate predicted payoffs.

Not all relations in weak power networks are unequal. For example, in the 4-Line, because the two *B* positions are identical, they must have the same probability of exclusion. The *B*s are equal in power and will exchange equally. Weak power networks are unique in containing both differential power and equal power relations. By contrast, strong power networks contain only strong power relations, while equal power networks contain only equi-power relations.

I use the line networks of Figure 1.2 to show how the three different kinds of networks are constructed. For the discussion assume that all nodes exchange only once. The 2-Line is a dyad: its two positions are identical; since neither has an alternative to the other, they must be equal in power. Adding a position to the dyad gives the strong power 3-Line of Figure 1.2b where one of the two As is necessarily excluded. The 3-Line is a simpler version of the Figure 1.1a monopoly. Both are strong power networks because their positions can be sorted into two connected sets: high power positions which are never excluded and low power positions at least one of which is always excluded.

Adding a position at the end of the strong power 3-Line results in the weak power 4-Line. The 4-Line cannot be strong power: if each A exchanges with its B, all are included. Yet A–B power cannot be equal because, when the Bs exchange, the As are excluded. Adding a position to the end of the 4-Line gives the 5-Line of Figure 1.2d, which is a strong power structure. Why is the 5-Line strong power? Two As plus one C are three positions that have only two Bs as exchange partners. No B is excluded, whereas one of the set of A, A, and C is always excluded. The 5-Line is significant in the development of network exchange theories because Cook et al. (1983) used it to show that high power positions (the Bs) need not be central.

That power in the Figure 1.1 and 1.2 network structures is due to exclusion falsifies social exchange's reductionist position and supports the position that structure affects behavior. This is a falsification because exclusion is a result of structure alone; it is not a quality of individuals. Other structural conditions of power such as "inclusion" and "hierarchy/mobility," which are taken up in later chapters, are like exclusion in that they cannot be reduced to qualities of individuals. Reductionism was once the opinion of some prominent scholars. Its rejection here is not an opinion. Reductionism has been experimentally tested and shown to be false.

To reject reductionism is not to assert "structuralism." Structuralism is the position which asserts that social events are due wholly to structural condi-tions: individual conditions do not effect events. For structuralism, it matters not whether people are rational, act habitually, or react to emotions. Whatever the basis for action, structures are claimed to produce exactly the same events.

Elementary Theory does not take a structuralist perspective. To the contrary, Elementary Theory is a multilevel theory which predicts events from conditions at structural and individual levels. As Markovsky (1987) demonstrated, a purely structuralist perspective cannot explain power in exchange networks. So theo-retic formulations for actors are central to the theory. In many cases, Elementary Theory operates as a rational choice theory using actors that seek to optimize on well-ordered preference sets. In other applications, backward-looking actors that adjust their behavior in light of experience are used.

EXCLUSION AND CLASSICAL CONCEPTIONS OF STRUCTURAL POWER

Marx and Weber identified exclusion as a structural condition of power, but neither developed a theory of power that is formally stated like those found later in this book. Neither used the term "exclusion" or any term like it. Nevertheless, both recognized that exclusion produces power in particular structures that they were analyzing.

Exclusion can operate only in structures where people are "separated" from positions. When separated, people have no ownership rights to their positions and can be excluded. I first consider Marx's separation of the workers from the means of production and then Weber's separation of bureaucrats from the means of administration. I conclude by showing that both Marx and Weber recognized structural conditions analogous to exclusion in coercive structures, like slavery.

To analyze the labor market under capitalism, Marx made a simplifying assumption: that the market is not differentiated by the skills or education of workers. His term "industrial reserve army" refers to those presently unemployed who are actively seeking work. According to Marx:

Taking them as a whole, the general movements of wages are exclusively regulated by the expansion and contraction of the industrial reserve army, and these again correspond to the periodic changes of the industrial cycle. They are, therefore, not determined by the variations of the absolute number of the working population, but by the varying proportions in which the working-class is divided into active and reserve army. (Marx [1867] 1967, p. 596)

Imagine a market with capitalists buying and workers selling labor. The total number of jobs is the number of the working class who are actively employed, and each is connected to a capitalist by an exchange relation. The reserve industrial army is *excluded* from the exchange of labor for the wage. Marx's specific contention is that the proportion of exclusions determines the rate of exchange of labor for the wage.

The labor market is a strong exchange structure, as long as the proportion of the reserve industrial army is nonzero. It is strong because the structure can be divided into two connected sets: *the capitalist class*, the members of which are never excluded, and *the working class*, at least some of whom are always excluded. Workers work only for capitalists. In this strong structure, each capitalist is high strong power and each worker is low strong power. Marx and Elementary Theory agree that exclusion produces power in the form of differential benefit favoring capitalists. Elementary Theory predicts the equilibrium rate of exchange for any strong structure to be the extreme favoring the capitalist power positions.

Now it is possible to see why separation is a power condition. Because members of the working class are separated from the means of production, they have no ownership rights in the position of being employed: they are hired and fired.

By contrast, capitalists own the physical means of production; therefore, they own their positions as capitalists. Capitalists cannot be hired and fired by workers. If there is a reserve industrial army, capitalists are high power and workers are low. But the converse is not the case. When there is a shortage of labor, capitalists are inconvenienced but they are not excluded from their positions as capitalists. There is never a reserve industrial army of capitalists.

Whether or not positions are owned is the central distinction in Weber's analyses of bureaucracy and other organizations ([1918] 1968). In premodern patrimonial administrations, positions in civil and military organizations could be purchased, and once purchased were owned. Since the official who purchases his position cannot be discharged, promoted, or demoted, he cannot be excluded from benefits. So patrimonial administrations have no structural condition of power. Though hierarchical, they lack an effective chain of command, and power centralization is ineffective.

By contrast, power in bureaucracy is based on the separation of officials from the means of administration. Bureaucrats can be excluded from benefits, so bureaucracies have a structural condition of power. Officials are hired, promoted, and discharged at the pleasure of the head of the organization. But the converse is not the case. The head of the organization cannot be hired or fired by any official below. Modern bureaucratic organizations are strong power structures, with the head who is high in power which extends through the structure.

Under feudalism all positions were owned from birth. Since no one was separated, no one could be excluded. Feudalism was not a strong or weak power structure and should not be analyzed as an exchange network. There were power differences between levels of feudal structures, but these differences stemmed from coercion. The power of the monarch over any baron rested on ownership of resources which funded a greater military force; the power of the baron over any lord had the same basis in military force and similarly to the bottom of the feudal hierarchy.

The separation of workers, officials, and others from positions is largely a modern phenomenon which distinguishes modern from premodern power structures. If and only if people do not own their positions can exclusion be a condition of power. Since the rise of capitalism and centralization of the state, power differences occur more and more in exchange relations and are due to structural exclusion. For premodern societies, the ownership of position precludes exclusion but not coercion: so power through coercion is paramount.

In slavery, coercion and a structural condition analogous to exclusion produce strong coercive structures (see Chapter 3). In strong coercive structures, the maximum is extracted from those subject to the coercion. Both Marx and Weber recognized these highly exploitative slave structures. They saw that the effect of easy and cheap slave replacement on the structure of slavery was to maximize exploitation. Marx compared slavery in Jamaica "where annual profits often equal the whole capital of plantations" to the less profitable slavery of the United States where slave importation was illegal ([1867] 1967, p. 254). Weber linked the fall of the Roman Empire in the West to the changed exploitation of slaves. As long as Rome expanded, slaves were cheap, and "The ancient plantation consumed slaves like the modern blast furnace consumes coal" ([1896] 1976, p. 398). With the end of expansion, the slave market dried up, and coercive exploitation declined, as did cities and eventually the Empire.

THE CONCEPT OF POWER EVENTS: WHO GETS WHAT, WHEN, AND HOW

When people interact, two kinds of events indicate that power is being exercised. First, A is exercising power over B when A *benefits* more than B. This is the kind of power event of the last two sections. Second, A is exercising power over B when A *controls* B more than the contrary. Laswell (1936) captured both kinds when he defined power as "Who gets what, when, and how." In this section, I trace the two meanings of power—benefit and control—from classical theory to network exchange theory today. At the end of the section I show that, though analytically separable, there is reason to suppose that in large structures the two types of power are linked, albeit at times quite indirectly.

I then turn to the quandary faced by the social exchange perspective in developing its concept of power. The problem stems from the fact that power is asymmetrical, but the exchange relation is symmetrical: it does not favor either actor. Power occurs in exchange relations because it is produced by conditions outside the relation—conditions like exclusion which are in exchange structures. But the social exchange perspective asserts that structures do not affect behavior. Thus they have the insurmountable problem of finding the source of power within the exchange relation where power cannot be produced. I show that their "solution" produced a concept of power that is self-contradictory.

Classical and Contemporary Conceptions: Power as Benefit

The concept of social power can be traced to Hobbes but takes its current form with Marx and Weber. For Hobbes, "The Power *of a Man* . . . is his present means to obtain some future apparent Good" ([1651] 1968, p. 150). For Hobbes, people are more or less powerful as individuals, and their power results from personal qualities like intelligence and eloquence or social advantages like wealth and reputation. The shift of meaning away from power as a quality of individuals toward power in social relations occurs with Marx and Weber. Marx contributed the concept of power as differential benefit, whereas Weber contributed the concept of power as differential control.

For Marx, power as differential benefit is called exploitation. A has power over B to the extent that A benefits by extracting valued resources from B ([1867] 1967, p. 304). In exchange, the question of "Who benefits?" is linked to "Who suffers the loss?" Marx's focus was on capitalist exploitation in relations between capitalist and workers where labor is exchanged for the wage.

These relations are power relations because capitalists seek to extract as much labor as possible in exchange for as small a wage as possible and workers seek the reverse. As wages go up profits go down and vice versa, so the interests in these relations are opposed. Interests are also complementary: unless capitalists and workers reach agreement, no value is created and both profits and wages are zero. Since coercive relations, like those between master and slave, also have opposed but complementary interests, the question "Who benefits?" also applies. Therefore, I extend application of the term "exploitation" beyond exchange where Marx confined it to include "coercive exploitation."

To use the concept of power as benefit today, the theorist needs to know when power is equal and when it is not. At first glance, it seems simple enough to define equal power as occurring when two actors' benefits are equal. As I now show, however, to assert that A's benefits are equal to B's means that the theorist has compared the utility of A with the utility of B, a comparison that is disallowed in social theory and for good reason.

The measure of any actor's benefit is a joint function of the utility of each resource to the actor, μ times the number of resources gained, r. So the benefit for actor i is equal to $\mu_i \times r_i$. Expressions like "$\mu_i \times r_i$" make sense when they are used to compare the relative value of things for i because theory assumes that actors know relative worth. For example, let $(\mu_i \times r_i)j$ be i's utility when exchanging with j and $(\mu \times r_i)k$ be i's utility when exchanging with k. Then $(\mu_i \times r_i)j = (\mu \times r_i)k$ means that i gains equally when exchanging with j as when exchanging with k. Setting the two utility factors equal to each other is legitimate because the utilities being compared are *within* the i actor. Direct comparisons of utility within actors is quite common in all exchange theory.

Because no one has devised a utility scale that can span between actors, however, the theorist cannot directly compare i's utilities to j's utilities. Therefore, the equation, $\mu_i \times r_i = \mu_i \times r_j$, which directly equates i's and j's utilities, is *not* the correct way to find the equal power point, even when power is defined as relative gain (Heckathorn 1983).

Moreover, the $\mu_i \times r_i = \mu_j \times r_j$ equation has counterintuitive, even ludicrous results precisely because it makes utility comparisons between actors. We cannot know actors' relative valuation of resources. So assume that A asserts that she values each resource twice as much as does B. Then the two make a 5–5 resource pool division. By A's assertion she gained more than B, so the 5–5 division was a power exercise by A over B. What then if B disagrees and asserts that he values each resource twice as much as A? Has B also exercised power over A? If so, then actors exercise power simply by asserting that self-interest per unit received is greater than other's interest. Since any actor can make that claim, power becomes a matter of opinion and opinions can and will contradict themselves.

Equal power in exchange can indeed be found but not by comparing utilities. Finding equal power rests on the insight that *perfectly isolated exchange relations contain no internal or external power condition.* Therefore, the exchange ratio for the isolated dyad is the equal power ratio. Then deviations from that ratio which disproportionately benefit *A* over *B* indicate that *A* is exercising power, and conversely. This solution does not require that an exchange relation actually be found which is perfectly isolated. Frequently, an empirical solution is not possible, nor is it needed. With the introduction of "resistance equations" in Chapters 2 and 3, the exchange ratio at equal power for any relation can be theoretically calculated, a calculation that does not require utility comparisons.

Classical and Contemporary Conceptions: Power as Control

For Weber, power is control: " 'Power' (*Macht*) is the probability that one actor within a social relationship will be in a position to carry out his own will despite resistance, regardless of the basis on which this probability rests" ([1918] 1968, p. 53). When power is well established, as between a boss and subordinate, Weber calls it "domination." Domination is defined as "the probability that a command with a given specific content will be obeyed" (p. 53). For both power and domination, the question of "Who controls?" is central. That question pervades all of Weber's sociology.

Weber preferred the concept of "domination" to "power" because he found power to be "amorphous." By amorphous he meant that practically any quality of a person or circumstance could produce a power exercise. By contrast, Weber believed that domination was easily identified because it was always linked to "the actual presence of one person successfully issuing orders to others" ([1918] 1968, p. 53). Since the conditions producing power are practically unlimited, Weber intended to gain precision by linking control to orders.

As seen earlier in this introduction, however, there is no necessary relation between orders and power exercise. When the subordinate is ambitious and future promotion is at stake, the boss's suggestion will control the subordinate's action. Sometimes even suggestions are not needed. "Management by Objectives" asks subordinates to set their own goals for the coming year. Subordinates infer (1) what their boss wants done and (2) what other competing subordinates will offer. Ambitious subordinates offer more. Here power as control is exercised in the complete absence of directives. So Weber was wrong to attempt to infer power as control from orders and commands.

It is a discovery of network exchange theory that, contrary to Weber, the conditions producing power are not practically unlimited. As will be seen, only a small number of structural conditions produce power as control—though those few can take a variety of forms in practice. The issue is not an unlimited number of qualities or circumstances. All that is needed is knowledge of a few theoretically formulated structural conditions. Therefore, Weber's concern that the concept of power is "amorphous" is unfounded for network exchange theory—and perhaps more generally for any theoretically driven analysis of social structure.

Power as Benefit and Control

The meanings of power as control and power as benefit have both persisted in social theory but for the most part independently. For example, Lukes defines power in terms of the distribution of benefit: "A exercises power over B when A affects B in a manner contrary to B's interests" (1974, p. 34). Dahl defines power in terms of control: "A has power over B to the extent that he can get B to do something which B would not otherwise do" (1957, pp. 202–3). In the United States, Weber has generally had greater impact than Marx. The most influential formulations, from Goldhamer and Shils (1939) through French and Raven (1968) and Wrong (1979), have defined power exclusively in terms of control. With the rise of network exchange theories, however, power as benefit has gained significance.

Just as the two meanings of power were introduced independently, for a given relation embedded in a given structure, it is possible for either power event to exist independently from the other. Power as control is common in civil and military agencies of governments where a chain of command from top to bottom is emphasized. Valued resources are not being produced in government agencies, and the power exercised over subordinates by higher administrators does not distribute benefit between them. Within these organizations there is no exploitation in Marx's sense, and they largely escape a Marxist value analysis.

Similarly, power as benefit without control is also found. In the capitalist firm, workers employed on piece rates are motivated to work by the desire for earnings, and the capitalist will profit without the need to supervise the labor process. Outsourcing is a pure case of exploitation without domination. When work is contracted out, organizations do not exercise control directly, and they largely escape a Weberian analysis.

Nevertheless, there is reason to suppose that power as benefit and power as control are necessarily related. For example, if control is never costless, there must be an interest to motivate it; the distribution of benefit provides that interest. That is, A controls B in order to benefit from B. The link between the two types of power need not be immediate. In the larger society, the two can be in different institutions. To exploit workers, the capitalist need not exercise immediate control but must have private property. Private property is produced by the state and takes the form of power as control. Because the state cannot live on power as control, it is funded by value produced in capitalist firms. So power as differential benefit and power as differential control are in separate institutions, but the two institutions are linked.

The Social Exchange Perspective on Power: Power as Control through Benefiting Others

Because the social exchange perspective denies the efficacy of structure, power in exchange must result from conditions *within* the exchange relation. This poses a difficult problem for theory, and the solution offered was to *oppose* control and benefit. For Homans, power is only control and never benefit. It is produced by "the principle of least interest" (1974, p. 73). Homans' definition is:

When A's net reward—compared, that is, with his alternatives—in taking action that will reward B is less, at least as perceived by B, than B's net reward in taking action that will reward A, and B as a result changes his behavior in a way favorable to A, then A has exerted power over B. (1974, p. 83 [italics removed])

The sense of this awkwardly stated definition is quite simple: *A* controls *B* because *B* benefits more than *A*—at least as believed by *B*. Homans is quite clear about the relation between benefit and control: "the person who has greater power in the relationship with another person is the one who gets the least out of the exchanges taken as a whole" (1974, p. 73).

Sharing Homans' social exchange perspective, Blau and Emerson also define power as control and find its cause in the greater benefit of the person over whom power is exercised. For Blau, "power refers to all kinds of influence . . . when one induces others to accede to his wishes by rewarding them for doing so" (1964, p. 115). Here the principle of least interest becomes the principle of no interest. "To achieve power over others" requires that "he remain indifferent to the benefits they can offer him in exchange for his" (p. 121). Emerson's exchange theory is more formal, yet he also reaches the conclusion that high power actors benefit less and low power benefit more. "(T)he exchange approach leads to the important insight that the less powerful party in a relationship is the one who derives the largest benefits from the exchange relation" (1981, p. 59).

Homans, Blau, and Emerson have ripped benefit and control apart and opposed them in a single relation—with only power as control called "power." The result is self-contradictory because power is separated from its motivational basis. Why would anyone exercise power as power is defined by Homans? All rational actors prefer being subject to power because being controlled gives greater benefits. Why would anyone exercise power as defined by Blau? Since the high power actor is *indifferent* to benefits from the low power actor, no one can have any interest in power exercise. The same is the case for Emerson. Therefore power events cannot occur. Yet Homans, Blau, and Emerson claimed to offer theories of power.

There are further contradictions. Suggestions in Homans and assertions in Emerson imply that power tends to equality: "To have a power advantage is to *use* it; and to use it is to *lose* it" (Emerson 1972, p. 67). For power to tend to equality, there must once have been power events. But as seen above, power events will never occur. So power cannot tend to equality. For Homans' definition, it is sufficient that the low power actor believe that she is gaining greater benefits. Real benefits are unneeded. As quoted above, "When A's net reward . . . is less, at least as perceived by B, than B's net reward." Therefore, power is a matter of opinion. But opinions can contradict. Let both *A* and *B* believe that self benefits more than the other. Then both are low in power and so neither controls. Yet being low in power, both are controlled by the other—clearly a contradiction in theory.

Theories that make contradictory inferences necessarily make false predictions. Such theories must make false predictions because, if one inference is not false, the one that contradicts must be and conversely. The social exchange perspectives make contradictory inferences. Therefore, they are falsified.

The social exchange idea of power where control and benefit are opposed does not survive in any network exchange theory today. Even power-dependence theory, which traces its origins to Emerson, does *not* classify experimental subjects who earn less as high in power or those who earn more as low in power (Cook et al. 1983). Furthermore, network exchange theories do not assert that power tends to equality. Instead, a central implication of network exchange theories is that power events in society persist because the structural conditions producing them persist.

The line of demarcation between network exchange theory of today and the earlier social exchange perspective should now be clear. Network exchange theory recognizes the efficacy of structure and focuses its investigations on finding the conditions in structures that produce different behaviors. The social exchange perspective denies the efficacy of structure and focuses its polemics on those who claim that structure determines behavior. Denying the effect of structure leads directly to self-contradictory ideas like power based on least interest. When put to the test, reductionist social exchange actually demonstrated its opposite: that structures produce power.

Chapter 2

Actors in Relations

David Willer

Social structures do not directly affect activity. Instead, structures affect activity through the social relations within which activity occurs. When structures affect relations, the activities that occur in the relation are quite different from the activities that occur when the relation is isolated. In this chapter, I show how to predict activity in social relations first when the relation is isolated from structural effects. Then I show how to calculate the effects of conditions outside the relation on activity in the relation. Finding the effect of outside conditions is the first step toward discovering how structures affect activity through the relations.

At the core of Elementary Theory is a "modeling procedure" that is used to build models for properties inside the actor, like preferences and beliefs, and for properties outside the actor, like social relations and social structures. These are theoretic models for actors in relations in structures, and they begin with simple elements, "sanctions" that are connected to generate preferences, beliefs, and relations. The work of this chapter goes forward at two related levels. At the level of the actors, the focus is on decisions, decision procedures, and their relation to conditions inside and outside the actors. At the level of relations, the focus is on the activity that results from the ways actors are linked and decide. The next chapter adds structure as a third level of analysis

The logical structure of Elementary Theory is displayed in the organization of the chapter. I first show how to construct theoretic models for actors and relations. In fact, the modeling of actors and relations is the first step in any application. I then introduce the theory's principles and laws and infer activity. In any application, once actors and relations are modeled, principles and laws are applied to generate predicted activity. Thus the organization of the chapter follows the steps taken in application of the theory.

Figure 2.1
Types of Sanctions

a. Positive Sanction

b. Negative Sanction

SANCTIONS

"Sanctions" are the elements out of which actors, relations, and structures are composed. A sanction is a social action transmitted by one actor and received by another, which alters the "preference state" of the actor receiving the sanction. Given in Figure 2.1 are the nodes A and B, which are actors. The nodes are connected by arcs, which are acts by A oriented to B. These arcs have signs next to the actor receiving the sanction. These are "reception signs." Only arcs with reception signs are sanctions. Only the transmitting actor decides whether or not the sanction is sent. So, in Figure 2.1, only A can decide whether either sanction is sent.

Two types of sanctions are displayed, and they are differentiated by the direction of "preference state alteration" of the receiving actor. In Figure 2.1a, B is receiving a positive sanction and experiencing a "positive preference state alteration." In Figure 2.1b, B is receiving a negative sanction and experiencing a "negative preference state alteration." Said somewhat differently, the first sanction is positive because B wants to receive it, and the second is negative because B does not want to receive it. More generally, all actors prefer positive sanctions to no sanctions and no sanctions to negative sanctions. Sanctions may also have signs at the transmission end which indicate that the preference state of the transmitting actor is also being altered. But an act is a sanction if and only if it affects the preference state of the receiving actor.

The things that can be positive sanctions are extremely varied and include goods and valued services. From a network perspective, the fundamental difference between a good and service is how far either can move. A good received from one actor can be sent on to another actor who may send it further again. So goods can move to points distal in the network. If you give me a pen, I can pass it to another who, in turn, sends it further and similarly to the end of the network. By contrast, services are consumed as they are received so they cannot be retransmitted. After you give me a hair cut, I can give a hair cut to another— but I cannot give *your* hair cut to another.

Because goods and services are things, they are "material" positive sanctions. Though what counts as a positive sanction is to some degree culturally determined, a great many things that are material positives in one culture are material positives in many other cultures. Many Germans like BMWs and so do I. "Symbolic" positive sanctions are communications. Complements are symbolic sanctions and, like services, they cannot be retransmitted. Symbolic positives vary more between cultures than do material positives. What counts as a complement in one culture may very well be an insult in another. A Frenchman can affectionately call his wife "My little cabbage," but, being in the United States, I would be unwise to do the same. Material negative sanctions are always "negative services." A blow to the head is a negative sanction, and it cannot be retransmitted. Like material positives, a great many material negatives maintain their negativity cross culturally. Whether a blow is received by an American in the United States or a Chinese in China, it is a material negative.

Negative and positive sanctions are *not* "punishments" and "rewards." A negative sanction is an *act* that has negative consequences. A punishment is a negative consequence that may or may not be an act. An actor can be punished by a negative sanction sent (a blow to the head) or by a terminated ongoing positive sanction ("You're fired"). Reward is a positive consequence. Like punishments, rewards may or may not be acts. A reward may be produced by reception of a positive sanction, for example, a gift of money. But a reward may also be produced by terminating a negative sanction, for example, being let out of jail. Because rewards and punishments are defined only in terms of psychological effect, the acts and termination of acts that produce them have nothing in common.

Elementary Theory works with models for action, and in those models sending and not sending a sanction are clearly differentiated states. It follows that there are two ways to increase the preference state of any actor: (1) transmit a positive sanction to the actor or (2) terminate the transmission of a negative sanction. Similarly, there are two ways to lower the preference state of any actor: (1) transmit a negative sanction to the actor or (2) terminate the transmission of a positive sanction. In ET models, terminated positive sanctions are just that—terminated positive sanctions and similarly for negative sanctions. Unlike rewards and punishments, a sanction always links an objective act with a subjective effect, allowing social relations like exchange and coercion to be accurately identified.

SOCIAL RELATIONS

Sanctions are *paired* in social relations because each actor's decision affects the other's preference state. For example, in Figure 2.2a, B wants to receive the positive sanction, but A decides whether or not B receives a sanction. Exactly

Figure 2.2
Three Types of Social Relations

a. Exchange

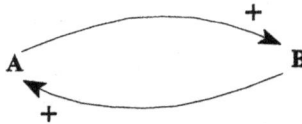

b. Coercion

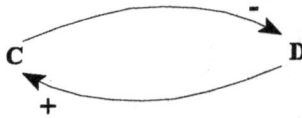

c. Conflict

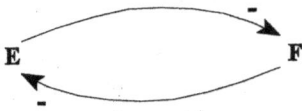

the same is the case for the sanction from B to A. A wants to receive the positive, but only B decides whether or not to transmit it. Here and in the other two relations there is a separation between a preference effect and the decision to act. This separation occurs routinely in the society. Sanctions are preeminently social acts: actors connected by sanctions always have an interest in affecting the decisions of the other. Figure 2.2 presents an exhaustive list of social relations which have two sanctions: they are exchange, coercion, and conflict. In exchange both sanctions are positive; in conflict both sanctions are negative; and in coercion one sanction is positive and the other negative.

One advantage of using sanctions to define relations is that the social relations found in society are simply and accurately sorted into distinct types. For example, exchange is a relation in which two actors have positive sanctions. When actors exchange, they transmit sanctions for which the other always gains. This meaning singles out an array of phenomena ranging from economic exchanges to mutual gift giving, and these phenomena share important qualities. For example, exchange, as defined by sanctions, is central to modern industrial societies, and, as Gilham (1981) has shown, modern forms of exchange grew incrementally out of earlier ones.

By contrast, defining exchange as mutual rewards includes exchange as just defined and relations in which negatives are terminated. The mugger has now stopped hitting me (a reward), so I give him my money (another reward). But mugging is not just a particularly clever way of doing business, and the mugger is not a businessman who has found how to get something for nothing. The state and its legal system will not treat mugging as exchange, and sociological theory should not confuse the two. Mugging is coercion, but the line between exchange and coercion cannot be drawn using terms like reward and punishment.

Coercion is a relation in which one actor has a negative sanction and the other has a positive sanction. The actor with the negative is the coercer, and the actor with the positive is the coercee. Coercers use threat of transmission of the negative to extract the positive from the coercee. It follows that, in coercion, typically only one sanction flows. For example, when a coercer's threat is effective, the coercee sends the positive to the coercer and the coercer does not send the negative to the coercee. When the threat fails, the coercee does not send the positive, so the coercer sends the negative.

Two states of coercion are centrally important to analyses: "agreement" and "confrontation." The two states correspond to the transmission of the positive and the transmission of the negative, respectively. Agreement occurs when *both* adopt the rule that the coercee will transmit the positive *and* that the coercer will not transmit the negative. Actors are both driven toward agreement because the decision of the other affects the preference state of self. Confrontation occurs when an agreement is not reached. In coercion, when an agreement is not reached, the negative sanction is transmitted. Later in the chapter, the formulations for agreement and confrontation will be quantified so that coercers and coercees can be modeled as reaching agreements on numbers of positive sanctions. The quantification will show that the specific agreement reached is a function of the *costs of confrontation* to coercee and coercer.

The conflict relation also has states of agreement and confrontation. In conflict, because the two sanctions are negative, neither actor benefits when the sanction of the other is transmitted. Therefore, agreements are concerned with the conditions under which no sanctions flow. When an agreement is not attained, the relationship is in confrontation and both actors transmit their negatives. Frequently, the outcome of conflict is coercion. Carneiro's "Theory of the Origin of the State" (1970) asserts that states arise when conflict intensifies and escape is impossible. Tribes that win conflicts disarm tribes that lose and coercively extract taxes in kind. Great Britain engaged in wars to establish colonies from which positives could be extracted through favorable rates of exchange. When actors recognize opportunities that result from coercion and exchange, engaging in conflict relations becomes a means to an end.

Agreement and confrontation are also centrally important to exchange. In exchange, both actors benefit when the sanction of the other is sent and agreements are about the number of sanctions each actor sends. When counting quantities sent by the two actors, agreements can be expressed as ratios of one sanction flow to the other. These are *exchange ratios*. Prices are exchange ratios. Confrontation occurs when A and B cannot agree on an exchange ratio. Then no exchange occurs, and no sanctions are transmitted or received. In exchange, the states of confrontation and agreement are importantly related. Later in the chapter, I show how costs of confrontation affect exchange ratios on which actors agree.

Displayed in Figure 2.3 are two different exchange relations. For each, both sanctions have two signs. These sanctions are "bisigned" arcs, and by convention transmission signs are always enclosed in brackets. Though unnecessary for isolated relations, the convention is useful for structures in which many sanctions are incident to a node.

The economic exchange relation is composed of "negative–positive sanctions." The negative sign at the transmission end of the sanction indicates that transmission is costly to A. When A sends a positively valued resource to B, that transmission is a loss that is reflected in the negative transmission sign. B positively values the resource, so its reception is a gain and the reception sign is positive. Exactly the same is the case for the sanction linking B to A. So negative–positive sanctions are loss–gain relations, and, in economic exchange, actors positively value both resources moving between them. Empirical cases of economic exchange relations are well known. The exchange of money for a commodity is an economic exchange. When I buy a house, the money paid is a loss, whereas receiving the deed is a gain. For the seller the money is the gain and the house is the loss. So both sanctions are negative–positive, and the relation is an economic exchange.

Whereas economic exchanges occur between people who are socially distant, social exchanges occur between people who are socially close. In the social exchange of Figure 2.3, that A wants to send the positive sanction to B is indicated by the positive sign of transmission. B also wants to receive it. Sanctions like these have been called "friends' favors" (Hansen 1981). Erling willingly helps build Mads' house. Later, Mads returns the favor by helping Erling dig his garden. At the bar, I want to buy my friend a beer and do so. At a later time, my friend is pleased to reciprocate. But not all social exchange relations have reciprocity. Social exchanges are not mixed-motive games: within the relation there is no opposition of interest between the actors. Parents who send their children to college know that sustained one-way flows can and do occur in social exchange relations.

Figure 2.3
Two Types of Exchange

a. Economic

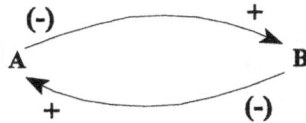

b. Social

SOCIAL ACTORS

Social actors contain decision procedures, preferences, and beliefs, which I introduce in that order. The introduction of decision procedures begins with Principle 1, which asserts that social actors act rationally. Two types of rationality are discussed; "parametric" from economics and "strategic" from game theory. Later in the chapter, "resistance" quantifies strategic rationality. Principle 1 asserts only that theoretic *actors* are rational. It asserts nothing about people's mental processes, and it is indifferent concerning the mental heath of those to whom the theory is applied. That Principle 1 asserts nothing about people does not thwart the application of ET for testing and prediction. When ET is applied, its predictions are about activity. Applications do not compare thought processes between theoretic actors and real people.

Preference systems are the values held by actors. Looking ahead to Figures 2.5 and 2.6, we can see that preference systems, like relations, are constructed using sanctions. For example, in Figure 2.5, the coercive relation is divided into three system states: positive sanction, negative sanction, and no sanction. The preference system is built by ordering the three states for each actor. This way of building preference systems means that actors' preferences only occur in and are a function of the relations in which they are engaged. Outside relations social actors have no value systems.

The anchoring of actors' value systems to relations is quite unlike mainstream approaches in fields as diverse as sociology and economics. In sociology, discourse frequently gives the impression that people are full of norms that are values carried about from one interaction context to another. Apparently, one explains the activity of "normative man" by first measuring norms and then waiting until an interaction context triggers one off. Can normative man economize? If not, it is difficult to imagine how normative man would act in the economic exchange relation of Figure 2.3.

By contrast, when neoclassical economics assumes rationality, two very different things are asserted: (1) actors maximize when selecting among alternatives and (2) maximizing is always economizing. Economic man carries about the values of economizing and always seeks to maximize gains and minimize losses. Is it rational to have friends? If not, it is difficult to imagine how economic man would act in the social exchange relation of Figure 2.3.

Since ET and NET locate values in relations, Principle 1 carries no economizing or normative baggage. ET/NET social actors economize in economic relations, act altruistically in social exchange relations, exploit in coercive relations, and so forth. Social actors have norms but only when they are in normative structures (see Southard 1981). ET and NET also model actors' beliefs using sanctions.

Rationality and Decisions

To generate models and predict behavior, I need to specify the principles that govern actors decisions and actions. Elementary Theory's first principle is:

P₁ ALL SOCIAL ACTORS ACT TO MAXIMIZE THEIR EXPECTED PREFERENCE STATE ALTERATION.

The first social science to assume rationality was economics. Its formulation for rationality assumes that "economic man" optimizes among given alternatives. The kind of rationality that is limited to selecting between given alternatives fixed by the environment Elster calls "parametric" (1986: 7). Good science always demands simplicity. Since market price can be found by assuming no more than optimizing between alternatives, quite properly economists have preferred to limit economic man to parametric rationality. I separate parametric rationality from more elaborate forms in the following way: parametrically rational actors do not attempt to infer what other actors will do. Under some conditions, for example, when information is limited, the social actors will always be parametrically rational.

Since the invention of game theory by von Neuman and Morgenstern (1944), "strategic rationality" has become increasingly central to social theory. Strategic rationality means that "each player's best choice of action depends on the action he expects the other to take" (Schelling 1970: 86). Players of game theory act strategically: social actors of Elementary Theory can be strategically rational as well.

Since readers may not be familiar with strategic rationality as it is employed

Figure 2.4
Prisoner's Dilemma Game

	C	D
C	2,2	0,3
D	3,0	1,1

in game theory, I will give an example. The example uses a game called the "prisoner's dilemma," an instance of which is displayed in Figure 2.4. The game is given in "normal form." The players select one of two alternatives labeled C and D. A box is selected when both players select an alternative. Within each box are two numbers; the number to the left is the payoff of Player 1, while the number to the right is the payoff of Player 2. If both players choose C, both receive 2, but if Player 1 chooses C while Player 2 chooses D, then C receives zero and D receives 3—and similarly for the remaining boxes. Game theory's "default assumptions" are that (1) players do not communicate, (2) or make binding agreements, and (3) choose without prior knowledge of the other's choice. These default assumptions are called the conditions of noncooperation.

To be strategically rational under conditions of noncooperation requires first that a player determine whether the other player's choice can be inferred and, if so, what it will be. Here the inference is straightforward because each has a "dominant strategy." Whether Player 1 has a "dominant strategy" in this game is found in the following way. Assume that Player 2 chooses C. Then Player 1 should choose D because a payoff of 3 is preferred to a payoff of 2. Now assume that Player 2 chooses D. Again, Player 1 should choose D: 1 is preferred to zero. So regardless of what Player 2 chooses, Player 1 should always choose D: that means that D is Player 1's dominant strategy. The game is symmetrical. Therefore, Player 2 also has a dominant strategy: always choose D. The choice "D, D" is called the "dominant strategy equilibrium."

The prisoner's dilemma game is unique among two-person games in that the dominant strategy equilibrium is not "Pareto optimal" (Rapoport and Guyer 1966). A joint selection is Pareto optimal when it gives the highest joint payoff. In the prisoner's dilemma, however, when the players select D, D, they do not receive the highest joint payoff. By both choosing D, each player gains only one. Had both chosen C, both would have gained two: C, C is Pareto optimal. As we have seen, however, the choice of C is not strategically rational. More precisely, C, C is not strategically rational if two players play the game with each other only once.

When the game is played together more than once, strategies that bridge between games are possible. For example, Axelrod (1984) finds the strategy called "tit-for-tat" effective. In tit-for-tat, players cooperate in the first game and then do what the other did in the previous game. When both players play tit-for-tat, both cooperate in the first round by choosing C. Then in the second round each chooses C because the other chooses C in the first round—and similarly through further rounds. What should I do if I believe that the other player is playing tit-for-tat? I should also play tit-for-tat to gain the Pareto optimal "2,2" payoff each round.

Values and Beliefs

Actors' preferences and beliefs, like social relations, are built out of sanctions. Figure 2.5 gives preferences for the coercive relation. To build preference systems like these, the theorist assumes that either one sanction is transmitted, the other is transmitted, or neither is transmitted. This treatment, which generates three system states, is consistent with the discussion of agreement and confrontation in coercion. The system states become a preference system when they are ordered from most to least preferred. Figure 2.5 displays two different cases. Each gives P_C, the preferences for the coercer, and P_D, the preferences for the coercee.

Here the particular preferences displayed are selected because they result in interesting inferences and are consistent with the meaning of positive and negative sanction. To be consistent with the meaning of negative sanction, in Figure 2.5 actor D always ranks the reception of the negative sanction lower than not receiving the sanction. The ranking of some system states is not determined by the meaning of the sanctions, however. For example, in Case 1, D ranks transmitting the positive sanction higher than receiving the negative sanction, but in Case 2, D ranks receiving the negative sanction higher than transmitting the positive sanction. Both rankings are possible given meanings assigned to positive and negative sanctions.

Actors may have accurate or inaccurate beliefs. ET and NET always assume that actors know their own preferences. So, for isolated dyads like those analyzed here, the only relevant initial condition for which actors can have beliefs is the preferences of the other. For the analyses of coercion to follow, I will assume that both actors have accurate beliefs. When B_i is any actor i's beliefs, for coercion I assume $B_C (P_D) \equiv P_D$ and $B_D \equiv (P_C) \equiv P_C$: the beliefs of each actor about the preferences of the other are the other's preferences. When we turn to models for structures in the next chapter, actors' beliefs can also include initial structural conditions.

Looking ahead, in the conflict relation of Figure 2.6, the actor E is modeled as having false beliefs. That is to say, $B_E (P_F) \equiv P_F$. Since E's beliefs are not accurate, the specific preferences E believes about F must be specified. It is immediately obvious that, because further specifications are needed, models with inaccurate beliefs are more complex than models where actors' beliefs are accurate. As the number of initial conditions increases, as when multiple actors are in large structures, models with inaccurate beliefs become unwieldy. To avoid complexity when possible, ET/NET take accurate beliefs as the default assumption.

SOCIAL INTERACTION

Threats and Offers in Coercion

Coercive relationships include mugger (the C) and victim (the D), master (the C) and slave (the D), and state (the C) and citizen (the D). All coercive relations are alike in that all oppose one actor's positive sanction to the other's negative sanction. Nevertheless, initial conditions for action can vary, and, as they do, so do predicted outcomes. Among the initial conditions of relations are actors' preference systems: Between Case 1 and 2 of Figure 2.5, I vary the preferences of both actors and, as a result, produce contrasting outcomes.

The analysis of the coercive interaction will have the following steps. First, generate all offers, orders, and threats that are possible for the relation. These "rules" are generated by linking two or more system states using "v" which is "exclusive or." All rules possible for the coercive relation are SS2 v SS3, SS1 v SS3 and SS1 v SS2. Second, find whether an actor has an interest in adopting one or more rules and, if so, determine which one is optimal. Whether a rule is optimal is found by mapping the rule on to the preference order of the other in order to determine its result and then mapping that result back onto the actor's own preferences. This mapping treats the other as parametrically rational. That is to say, the other actor is assumed to act on the rule and its own preferences only. Having evaluated rules for both actors, the third and last step infers outcomes.

Case 1 displays the coercee D's preference order as SS1 > SS2 > SS3 and the coercer C's as SS2 > SS3 > SS1. Interests are opposed because the ordered system states for the two actors do not correspond. Because SS2 > SS3 is common to C and D, however, interests are also complementary. C knows, as we do, that, if C does nothing and D is parametrically rational, D will select its highest ranked system state, SS1, and do nothing. This results in C being in its lowest ranked alternative. If C hopes to receive D's positive sanction, SS1 must be blocked.

The threat SS2 v SS3 blocks SS1. If D tries to select SS1, C transmits the negative sanction transforming SS1 into SS3 Let D be parametrically rational. Then the threat leaves D with only the choice of SS2 and SS3. Since SS2 is preferred, it will be selected. In fact, SS2 is C's best system state. Therefore, SS2 v SS3 is C's optimal rule, and it is adopted by C and communicated to D. In words, the coercer has selected a threat like "Your money or your life" and expects to receive the money, which the coercee values less than life.

At issue now is whether there is a rule for D, the outcome of which is better

Figure 2.5
Preference Orders for Coercion

Case 1

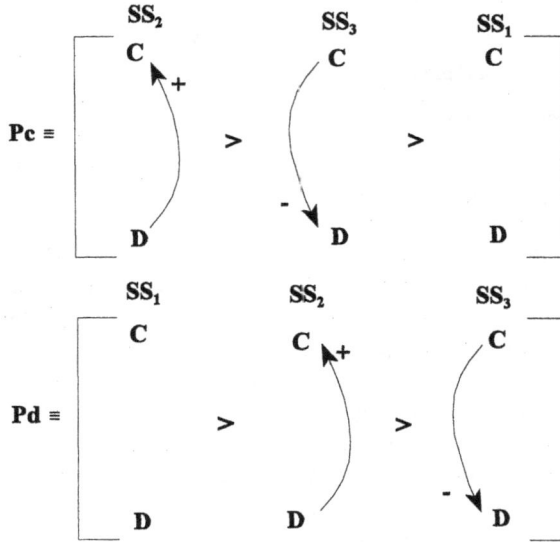

Case 2

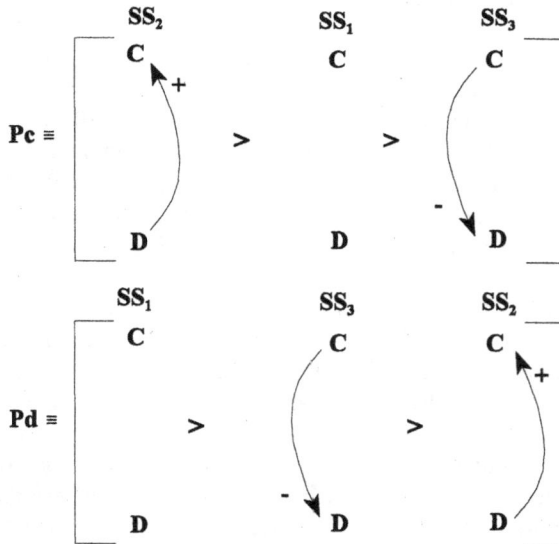

for D than C's threat. A possible candidate is SS1 $\underline{v}$ SS3. Communicated by D to C, this says "Transmit the negative or not." This statement of defiance rules out transmission of the positive sanction and blocks C's best state (i.e., SS1 $\underline{v}$ SS3 $->$ $-$SS2.). But D knows, as we do, that C acting parametrically will transmit the negative sanction—which puts D in its lowest ranked world. Because C's threat gives D a better outcome, it is accepted. D transmits the positive sanction, and the interaction is concluded.

The analysis of Case 2 proceeds similarly and illustrates why coercers do not always succeed. The preferences of C and D have been changed. Interests are still opposed, but now they are not complementary. In C's preferences, SS1 $>$ SS2 suggests that C will be less aggressive, while D's preference ordering of SS3 $>$ SS2 implies that D will be more resistant. Now D has an interest in adopting the rule SS1 $\underline{v}$ SS3 because D knows, as we do, that, given that rule, a parametric C will not transmit the negative sanction. On the other hand, C no longer has an interest in adopting the threat, SS2 $\underline{v}$ SS3, because it will not result in D transmitting the positive. So C's best ranked system state is impossible, leaving C with the choice between SS3 and SS1. Since SS1 is preferred, C adopts D's rule and the interaction ends with no sanction transmitted.

Conflict and Types of Rationality

Initial conditions for a conflict relationship are given in Figure 2.6. Standing outside the system, we know that E and F are "peace lovers." Both rank SS1 highest, preferring that vacuous system state to any system state in which negative sanctions flow. However, if any sanctions were to flow, each would prefer to transmit a negative sanction, then conflict, and then receive the negative of the other without the transmission of a negative in return. If both actors had full and accurate information, both would choose their highest ranked system state and no sanctions would be transmitted.

But E's belief concerning F's preferences is false. E believes that F is aggressive, ranking transmission of the negative sanction highest, then engaging in conflict, and so forth. There is no threat which E believes will block the conflict. For example, E could threaten to transmit a negative only if F did the same. But mapping that threat onto the believed preferences, a parametric F will simply choose its preferred system state and transmit the negative. So E can only choose between its third- and fourth-ranked system states, between conflict and receiving F's negative. Preferring conflict, E selects the third and transmits the negative sanction, expecting F to respond similarly. F's only rational response is to act similarly, and so conflict occurs.

This interaction exhibits many theoretically interesting characteristics. E is strategically rational and prefers no conflict. Yet E's belief concerning F makes conflict inevitable. Using Merton's ([1949] 1968) terms, E's belief is a self-fulfilling prophecy. It is also an example of the "Thomas Theorem." The Thomas Theorem asserts that what is believed to be true is true in social interactions.

Figure 2.6
Preferences and Beliefs for Conflict

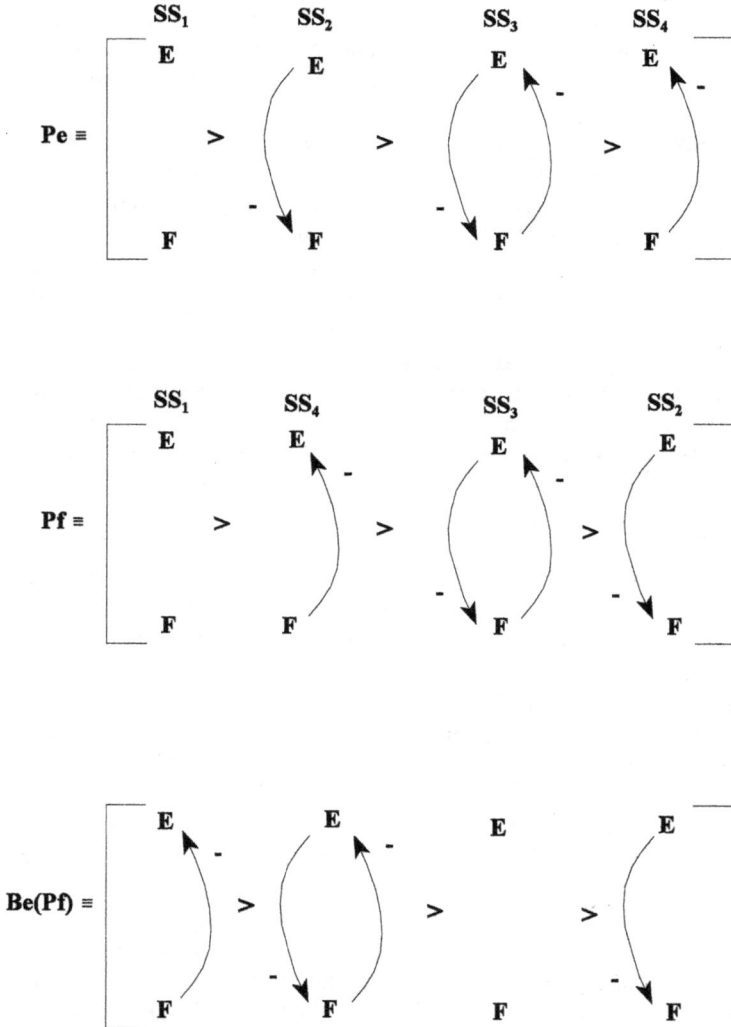

Note that F's subsequent transmission of the negative to E does nothing to dispel E's initial belief that F is aggressive; if anything, it tends to confirm it. At the same time, F will assuredly believe that E is aggressive, whereas we know that E acted defensively. People who routinely err in belief attribution as did E, if mentally ill, are paranoid. Mentally ill or not, as we have seen, E's selection of action was rational.

Figure 2.7
Three Social Relations

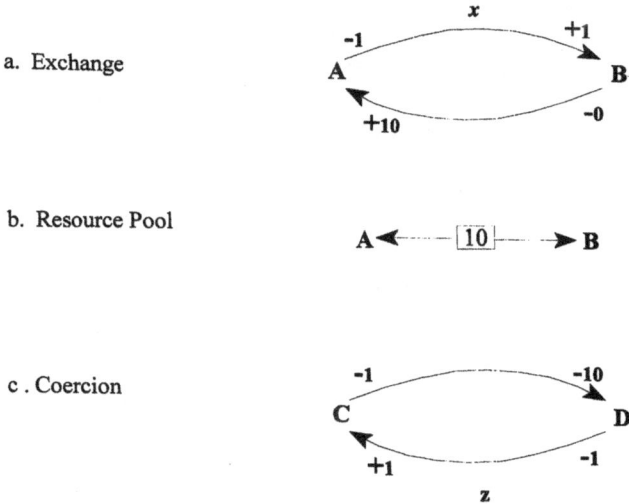

a. Exchange

b. Resource Pool

c. Coercion

We know that E is a peace lover, but E has taken the first step toward conflict. Given that act, F takes the second step by transmitting its negative sanction and conflict occurs. But note that the conflict occurred only because E was strategically rational. If E and F are only parametrically rational, both act only on their own preferences and conflict does not occur. Interestingly, as illustrated here, strategic rationality does not always produce results which are superior to parametric rationality.

QUANTITY AND SANCTION FLOW

This section introduces sanction flows, which vary quantitatively. Previously, actors' value systems were preferences composed of ordered system states. Now, with the introduction of quantities of sanction flows, value systems can be expressed quantitatively as functions of flows. When sanctions flow and/or resource pools are divided, the preference state alteration for each actor will have a numerical value. For actor i, the value of the preference state alteration is "Pi." Pi is called i's "payoff."

Sanctions and Payoffs

Figure 2.7 presents three relations for which actors' payoffs vary quantitatively. The Figure 2.7a exchange relation displays the value per unit flow of each sanction for each actor. As indicated, each unit sanction transmitted by A represents a loss of one to A and a gain of one to B. Each sanction transmission by B is costless to B and gives a payoff of ten to A. Assume that B has one sanction to transmit and x is the number of sanctions transmitted by A. Then Figure 2.8a is the payoff matrix for the relation. P_A which is A's payoff and P_B which is B's payoff vary inversely for the range $1 \le x \le 9$. This range of flows is also the array of agreements possible for A and B in the relation. When A and B cannot agree, they are in confrontation. In confrontation, no sanctions flow; therefore, both P_A and P_B will equal zero.

A "negotiation set" is the array of agreements over which negotiations can range. The payoff matrix displays the negotiation set and is constructed in the following way. Assume that A's resources are lumpy in units of one. No actor will exchange if the payoff is the same as confrontation. Thus, if exchange occurs, both A and B will transmit at least one sanction. When both transmit just one, $P_A = 10 - 1 = 9$ and $P_B = 1 - 0 = 1$. A's payoff is nine and B's is one. Since at confrontation B's payoff is zero, we have found one extreme of the negotiation set. At the other extreme, A transmits nine positives to B and receives one: $P_A = 10 - 9 = 1$ and $P_B = 9 - 0 = 9$. A's payoff is one and B's is nine. Having found the two ends of the negotiation set, filling in the middle is straightforward.

These payoffs indicate that the exchange relation is a mixed-motive game. On the one hand, the payoff matrix shows that A's and B's interests are opposed. The more gained by A in the exchange, the less gained by B and conversely. When A gains seven, B gains three, but when B gains eight, A gains two—and similarly for the remaining values of Figure 2.8a. On the other hand, both prefer all displayed agreements to confrontation where $P_A = 0$ and $P_B = 0$. The resource pool relation of Figure 2.7b is also a mixed-motive game, and its payoff matrix is exactly the same as that of the exchange relation. The pool contains 10 resources, so if $P_A = 7$, then $P_B = 3$, and if $P_A = 2$, then $P_B = 8$, and similarly for the other possible divisions. Payoffs at confrontation are also identical to those for exchange: If A and B do not agree to a division, both $P_A = 0$ and $P_B = 0$. As games, the profit pool relation is identical to the exchange relation.

Figure 2.7c gives a coercive relation and displays the value per unit flow of each sanction for each actor. Whereas C's negative sanction costs one to transmit, C gains one from each positive sanction transmitted by D. When receiving the negative sanction, D's loss is ten while each sanction transmitted to C represents a unit loss of one. At issue in coercion is the number of D's positive sanctions which C can extract by threatening to transmit the negative. If an agreed-upon number of positives is sent, the negative sanction is not transmitted, but if agreement is not reached, the relation is in confrontation and C transmits the negative sanction. So $P_D con = -10$. When z is the number of positive sanctions transmitted by D, Figure 2.8b gives the payoff matrix for the coercive relation. Note that P_D is always negative, but that $P_D = -9$ is preferred to $P_D con = -10$.

That the payoff matrix for coercion is similar to that of exchange can be seen by adding ten to all of D's payoffs. With the addition of ten, P_D now ranges

Figure 2.8
Payoffs at Agreement

a. Exchange

x	Pa	Pb
1	9	1
2	8	2
3	7	3
4	6	4
5	5	5
6	4	6
7	3	7
8	2	8
9	1	9

b. Coercion

z	Pc	Pd
1	1	-1
2	2	-2
3	3	-3
4	4	-4
5	5	-5
6	6	-6
7	7	-7
8	8	-8
9	9	-9

from one through nine for agreements and $P_D\text{con} = 0$, just as in the exchange and resource pool relations. Since games are unaffected by adding or subtracting constants, the addition of the constant of ten here indicates that the coercion game is much like the exchange game. That is, coercion is also a mixed-motive game. Exactly the same kind of resistance analysis that predicts points of agreement for exchange and profit pool relations also applies to coercion.

Sanction Flows and Payoff Functions

Let x be the quantity of any sanction flow and v the valuation per unit of the flow by the receiving (or transmitting) actor. As previously, P is the payoff of the flow for the actor. For any one sanction flow for i, P is a function of x, the quantity of the flow, and v, the value per unit of flow. For any actor either receiving or transmitting one sanction flow,

$$P_i = f(v_i, x_i)$$

and the simplest expression of that function is $P_i = v_i x_i$. In Figure 2.7a each actor can transmit one type of sanction and can receive a second type. When the effect of transmissions and receptions is independent, and when the subscripts t and r represent transmission and reception, then Elementary Theory's first Law is stated as

$$\text{L1: } P_i = v_{ri} x_{ri} + v_{ti} x_{ti}$$

The Law links preference change for any actor to the events of the relationship. Removing the restriction on numbers of flows, when all preference alterations are independent, we observe that T is the index set of sanctions transmitted and R is the index set of sanctions received,

$$\text{L1: } P_i = \sum_{i \in R} v_i x_i + \sum_{i \in T} v_i x_i$$

For the Figure 2.7a exchange and 2.7c coercive relations, there are only two sanctions, and the simpler, first expression for L1 can be used. The exchange relation and coercive relation will carry over to models for structures and for experiments of the next chapter. For those examples, I will continue to treat the quantitative value of the v term as a constant for the range of x quantities considered. However, these expressions can be given a more general interpretation with the introduction of parametric equations relating variations in the value of v to variations in x.

The x terms of the first Law are always either zero or positive. The sign of the v terms and their value are the signs and values of the sanctions displayed in Figure 2.7. For example, when an actor is in an economic exchange relation and sanctions are negative–positive, the sign of that actor's v_t is negative and the sign of v_r is positive. For coercees, both v_r and v_t are negative and similarly for other relations. In Figure 2.7a, that v_{tA} is negative does not mean that A disvalues the transmitted sanction. As we have already seen, a negative sanction transmission sign means a loss to A; and a thing sent that is a loss is positively valued. By contrast, a negative v_r term always means that the received sanction is disvalued.

Because there is no common scale for utility between actors, care must be taken when "P" and "v" terms are interpreted. From the payoff matrix for the exchange relation, it is easy to infer that A's and B's payoffs are inversely related: in fact, $P_A + P_B = 10$. The equation only asserts that when P_A decreases by one *for A*, P_B increases by one *for B*. The equation and its interpretation are legitimate because neither requires a common utility scale. But now consider an A–B agreement, the numerical value of which is equal: for example, $P_A = 5$ and $P_B = 5$. Since $P_i = v_i x_i$, the values of v for two different actors are implicated in these and all other P_A and P_B values. Since we have no common scale on which v terms from A and B can be compared, we cannot know whether or not A's and B's *benefits* are equal. So no assertion about equality of benefits between actors can be justifiably made. We will return to this issue on page 44 under the discussion of equal power.

Initial Conditions: *Pmax* and *Pcon*

To predict the point of agreement in any relation, two terms are needed: $P_i$con and $P_i$max. $P_i$con, which we have already encountered, is the payoff to i at confrontation—when i and j do not agree on a settlement. $P_i$max is i's best payoff for the given relation. $P_i$con and $P_i$max are "initial conditions" of the relation in the following sense. These are conditions given by the relation which affect actors' negotiations and settlements. For two-person isolated relations, these two initial conditions are constant through the interaction. I now show how to employ Principle 1 to find $P_i$con and $P_i$max.

Let us consider the Figure 2.7a exchange relation first. Principle 1 asserts that actors seek to maximize payoffs, which means that *actors must be induced to act*. The exchange relation of Figure 2.7 is isolated and, at confrontation when no exchange occurs, $x = 0$ for both actors. Using L1, $P_A$con $= 10 \times 0 - 1 \times 0 = 0$ and $P_B$con $= 1 \times 0 + 0 \times 0 = 0$. Therefore, for any exchange in which the P_A is zero, A will not exchange—and similarly for B. For example, A will not send 10 sanctions to B in exchange for B's one sanction, for then $P_A = 10 \times 1 - 1 \times 10 = 0$ and for zero gain A selects confrontation. Similarly, B will not send a sanction to A without receiving something of value. So applying L1 confirms the negotiation set inferred above. Since the range of A's transmissions is $1 \leqslant X \leqslant 9$ (which is the range displayed in the Figure 2.8a payoff matrix), it follows that $P_A$max $= 10 - 1 = 9$. That is, $P_A$max occurs when P_B is minimal: that is, when B gains just enough to be induced to exchange. Similarly, $P_B$max $= 9 - 0 = 9$ when P_A is minimal: B receives nine sanctions from A and transmits one in return.

When resources are similarly lumpy for the resource pool relation, it will have the same Pmax and Pcon values as the exchange relation. $P_A$max $= 9$ and P_B max $= 9$, while $P_A$con $= 0$ and P_B con $= 0$. Thus the relation between P_A and P_B will be the same as that displayed in the Figure 2.8a payoff matrix for the exchange relation. Network exchange experiments have traditionally used a resource pool of 24 points, which are also lumpy in units of one. For that relation, since Pcon $= 0$, Pmax $= 23$ and for any pair of subjects. So all agreements fall at or between 23–1 favoring one subject and 1–23 favoring the other.

Principle 1 similarly applies to the coercive relation of Figure 2.7c, but in this case confrontation occurs when C transmits the negative sanction. So, $P_D$con $= -10$ and $P_C$con $= -1$. Since a cost is associated with the negative sanction transmission, it is possible for C and D to agree that D sends no positives to C *and* for C not to transmit the negative. When D's resources are lumpy in units of one, the range of agreements is $0 \leqslant z \leqslant 9$, which is just slightly wider than displayed in Figure 2.8b. $P_D$max $= 0$ when no sanctions flow, and $P_C$max $= 9$ when D agrees to transmit nine sanctions to A.

Exactly the same procedures are used to find Pmax and Pcon in other relations. For example, in Chapter 1, "Ann" was buying a Miata sports car from "Bill." Ann can buy an equivalent car for $10,500, so that price is Ann's point of confrontation and the most Bill can hope to receive is 10,499. Bill has an alternative deal which is $9,500; this defines his point of confrontation and the minimum price at $9,501. Thus for Bill Pmax $= 10,499 - 9,500 = 999$. For Ann, Pmax $= 10,500 - 9,501 = 999$. There is no gain at confrontation when agreement cannot be reached, so Pcon $= 0$ for both.

Since exchange occurs only when both actors gain, $P_A > 0$ and $P_B > 0$ is necessary. I now show that that condition is not satisfied if the value of v terms is symmetrical for both actors: that is, $v_r = -v_t$ for A and $v_r = -v_t$ for B. For these values, if the same number of sanctions are sent and received, $P_B = v_{rB} x_{tB} + v_{rB} x_{rB} = x_{tB} - x_{rB} = 0$ and similarly $P_A = 0$. So A and B will not exchange for equal numbers. Alternatively, if A sends fewer than are received, $P_A > 0$, but $P_B < 0$ and B will not exchange. Similarly, if B sends fewer than received, $P_B > 0$ but $P_A < 0$ and A will not exchange. Therefore, there is no condition in which A and B will exchange. By extension, only ''v'' values that satisfy the following inequality allow exchange:

$$v_{rA} v_{rB} - v_{tA} v_{tB} > 0$$

Note that the size of the factor is proportional to the range of the negotiation set: as the factor increases, so does the range of agreements that are possible for the relation. Given that range and the lumpiness of resources, the *number* of possible agreements is determined. For example, plugging in the values for the Figure 2.7a exchange relation, $v_{rA} v_{rB} - v_{tA} v_{tB} = 10$: between zero and ten there are nine possible agreements. Now increase the reception value to A of the sanction transmitted by B from 10 to 24. Now the factor equals 24, and the number of possible settlements is 23—and similarly for other exchange relations.

The possibility of coercion is determined by the ratio of ''v'' values for the coercee. When D is the coercee

$$\frac{v_{rD}}{v_{tD}} > 1$$

and the larger the factor, the greater the range of positive sanctions that can be extracted from the coercee. Note that if the threat succeeds, only the positive sanction flows from D to C. It follows for any coercer that when the threat succeeds, always $P_C > 0$. Therefore ''v'' terms for the coercer never determine whether or not coercion is possible.

In general and for all social relations, the sanction flows that produce Pmax for one actor produce a state just slightly better than confrontation for the other. For the exchange relation of Figure 2.7a, when A is gaining maximally at $P_A = P_A$max $= 9$, B is gaining minimally at $P_B = 1 > 0 = P_B$con. Similarly, when B is gaining maximally at $P_B = P_B$max $= 9$, A gains minimally at $P_A = 1 > 0 = P_A$con. Exactly the same holds in the coercive relation. When $P_C = P_C$max $= 9$, then $P_D = -9 > -10 = P_D$con; and when D is gaining maximally at $P_D = P_D$max $= 0$, then $P_C = 0 > -1 = P_C$con. That the sanction flows which produce Pmax for one actor produce a state just slightly better than confrontation for the other is quite general across many relations that are mixed-motive games. For example, these relations between Pmax and Pcon also hold for the profit pool relations used in experimental research.

At issue now is how to predict the settlement at which agreement will occur. Principle 1 asserts that actors seek to maximize. But Pmax settlements are at opposite ends of the range of possible agreements. Actors that are only capable of maximizing can only make opposed Pmax offers to each other, and, as just seen, these offers are as far from each other as is possible for the relation. Principle 1 fails to generate agreements for actors because it does not fully reflect the interest situation in mixed-motive relations. It ignores actors' interests in avoiding the costs of disagreement. The formulation that predicts agreements from actors' interests in maximizing *and* in avoiding confrontation is resistance.

RESISTANCE, THE SECOND LAW AND PRINCIPLE 2

Resistance is the second law of the theory. It systematically relates costs of confrontation to the distribution of value at agreement. A's resistance is:

$$R_A = \frac{P_A \max - P_A}{P_A - P_A \text{con}} \tag{2.1}$$

The resistance factor to the right in Equation (2.1) relates agreement and confrontation *within* the actor A in the following way. The numerator of the resistance factor is A's interest in gaining a better payoff. For example, when A's best payoff, $P_A\max = 9$ and A is considering an agreement with a payoff of only $P_A = 1$, then A's interest in gaining a better payoff $(9 - 1 = 8)$ is large. Whereas if a payoff of $P_A = 7$ is being considered, A's interest in a better payoff $(9 - 7 = 2)$ is substantially smaller. In general, as A's payoff deviates from $P_A\max$, the interest in a better agreement is greater and, as it approaches $P_A\max$, the interest in a better agreement approaches zero.

The denominator of the resistance factor is A's interest in avoiding confrontation. When $P_A\text{con} = 0$ and A is considering a payoff of only one, A's interest in avoiding confrontation $(1 - 0 = 1)$ is small. When $P_A = 7$, however, A's interest in avoiding confrontation $(7 - 0 = 7)$ is substantially larger.

The agreements that actors will reach are predicted by relating their resistances in the following way. Principle 2 of Elementary Theory asserts that:

P2: AGREEMENTS OCCUR AT THE POINT OF EQUAL RESISTANCE FOR UNDIFFERENTIATED ACTORS IN A FULL INFORMATION SYSTEM.

The principle asserts that actors reach agreements when the benefits of maximizing and costs of avoiding confrontation are mutually balanced. Therefore, to find the point of agreement we set $R_A = R_B$, and

$$R_A = \frac{P_A \max - P_A}{P_A - P_A \text{ con}} = \frac{P_B \max - P_B}{P_B - P_B \text{ con}} = R_B \qquad (2.2)$$

To apply resistance to the exchange relation, recall that $P_A\max = 9$, $P_A\text{con} = 0$, $P_B\max = 9$, and $P_A\text{con} = 0$. Therefore, substituting,

$$R_A = \frac{9 - P_A}{P_A} = \frac{9 - P_B}{P_B} = R_B$$

Furthermore, $P_A + P_B = 10$; thus $P_B = 10 - P_A$ and substituting,

$$\frac{9 - P_A}{P_A} = \frac{P_A - 1}{10 - P_A}$$

Solving, we find that $P_A = 5$ and $P_B = 5$. We now have payoffs for A and B and need to find the sanction transmissions to which they correspond. Using the first law, $P_A = 5 = -x + 10$ and $x = 5$. So, at the point of equiresistance, A sends five sanctions to B and B transmits its sanction to A. Since the initial conditions for the resource pool relation of Figure 2.7b were the same as for exchange, $P_A = 5$ and $P_B = 5$ for that relation as well. These ''P'' values occur only when the to pool is divided evenly at 5–5.

Resistance is applied to the coercive relationship in exactly the same way as to exchange. Recall that, for the coercive relationship, $P_C\max = 9$ and $P_D \max = 0$ while $P_C\text{con} = -1$ and $P_D\text{con} = -10$. Therefore,

$$P_C = \frac{9 - P_C}{P_C - (-1)} = \frac{0 - P_D}{P_D - (-10)} = R_D$$

Since sanctions sent by D are received by C, for any agreement D's losses are C's gains and $P_C = -P_D$. Substituting and solving, we find $P_C = 4.5$ and $P_D = -4.5$.

I now use resistance to find the agreement at which the exercise of power by two actors is equal. With equal power found, the direction and amount of power exercised for all other agreements can be determined. As already seen in Chapter 1, exchange relations have no condition of power within. It follows that when an exchange relation is completely isolated, it must be equipower. For all isolated exchange relations, $P\text{con} = 0$ for both actors. Therefore, power is equal at equal resistance when $P_i\text{con} = 0$ and $P_j\text{con} = 0$. But exactly the same agreement is predicted by $P_i\text{con} = 0$ and $P_j\text{con} = 0$, and by $P_i\text{con} = P_j\text{con} > 0$. *Therefore, power is equal at equal resistance when $P_i\text{con} = P_j\text{con}$.* It follows that, when $P_i\text{con} < P_j\text{con}$, i is exercising power over j and when $P_j\text{con} < P_i\text{con}$, j is exercising power over i.

Confrontation is never equal in coercive relations: it is always smaller for the coercer. Therefore, all coercive relations are power relations, and the coercer is higher in power than the coercee. Nevertheless, in some coercive relations, like that of Figure 2.7, there is a limiting condition when no sanctions flow. For that limiting condition only, the exercise of power is equal at zero.

We find equipower for resource pool relations by setting Pcon $= 0$ and solving for equal resistance. For the 10-point pool, equiresistance occurs at the 5–5 division which is equipower. But note that this division is equipower because of resistance calculations only. It does not matter that the numerical value of resources going to the two actors is equal. To assert that the 5–5 division is equal power because the two actors earn the same asserts that they benefit equally and makes interpersonal utility comparisons. These comparisons should be avoided because they produce contradictions in the following way. Let power mean relative benefit and A and B make utility comparisons. A claims that she benefits more than B at the 5–5 settlement and B agrees. Now power exercise is a matter of opinion. But opinions need not agree. Now A claims to benefit more at 5–5, but B disagrees and claims that he gains more. Because both gain more, A and B are exercising power over each other, which is self-contradictory.

Power exercise is defined only for agreements, and so its range is the negotiation set. For confrontation, the amount of power exercised is undefined. Why it is undefined is easy to see. In exchange, at confrontation, when A and B fail to agree, no sanctions flow, so there is no power exercise to measure. In coercion, at confrontation, C transmits the negative to D: the coercer has failed to extract positive sanctions. Since no positives flow, there is no power exercise to measure.

Figure 2.9 gives resistance curves for the exchange relation. These curves suggest how negotiations lead to agreements. For isolated dyads like the ones considered here, negotiations take the form of bargaining. In bargaining, the offers of actors begin at sharply divergent points and move successively toward a common medial offer which is the point of agreement. Acting on Principle 1, actors initially make their Pmax offers to the other; A's offer is one sanction in exchange for B's, whereas B asks for nine. Because A's offer is $P_A$max, A's resistance is zero, and for that offer B's resistance is maximal at 8. Thus $R_B \gg R_A$. Similarly, for the P_B max $= 9$ offer, $R_B = 0$; but R_A is maximal at 8: $R_A \gg R_B$. Both actors know that the resistance of the other is too high, which precludes agreement. To lower the other's resistance, each makes better offers. As actors alternate making a sequence of better and better offers to the other, they slide down the resistance curves to meet at the intersection. The curves intersect at equal resistance when $x = 5$ which, as calculated above, is the point of agreement.

When bargaining is determined by resistance, it should be quite similar across all exchange relations not affected by structures. It should be similar because, although payoffs will vary, the shape of the curves remains the same. For the same reasons, bargaining in coercion will be similar to bargaining in exchange.

Figure 2.9
Resistance Curves

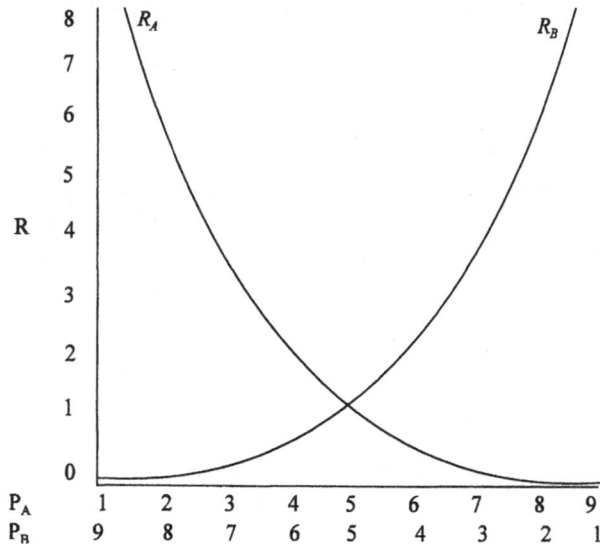

This follows because (1) the payoffs of the coercive relation can be transformed into those of the exchange relation by addition of a constant and (2) thus the coercive relation will have resistance curves like the exchange relation.

The Effect of Added Negatives and Positives on Power in Exchange

The flexibility of the resistance analysis is best illustrated by changing initial conditions and calculating consequences. Here I show how adding negative and positive sanctions to exchange affects the equiresistance point. To show that all exchange relations are affected similarly, the examples used in the discussion are quite general.

I begin by predicting the effect of added negatives on the point of equiresistance of the exchange relation. In Mario Puzo's *The Godfather* there is a passage in which the Godfather breaks a contract then current between his Godson and a band leader. The Godfather offers the band leader a new contract which stipulates a modest money payment in exchange for releasing the Godson from the current contract. The band leader immediately rejects these terms of exchange: the money is too little compensation. At this point the Godfather pulls out his gun and says, ''Either your name or your brains will be on that contract in ten seconds.'' The contract is signed. The threatened negative produced an exercise of power.

Adding a negative to any exchange relation results in a power relation (1) because now Pcon < 0 for one of the actors and (2) because it produces a shift in the point of equiresistance which favors the actor making the threat. For the exchange dyad, A's threat increases the size of the denominator of R_B, which reduces R_B's numerical value. Since agreement occurs at equal resistance, as R_B declines so must R_A. Since $P_A$max and P_A con are fixed by A's initial conditions, R_A can decline only if P_A increases. Therefore, adding a negative sanction to exchange increases the payoff of the actor making the threat.

Consider now the quantitative effect of negatives on exchange. I explore that effect by assuming a given shift in the point of agreement and seeking the size of the threatened negative that produces it. Let the shift be one-half the distance from equal power to Pmax. What is the size of threat which produces this shift? Let Pmax be the same for two actors. When exchange resources are infinitely divisible, the payoff at equal resistance and no threat is at equal power: it is Pmax/2 for both actors. Moving the payoff one-half of the way from Pmax/2 to Pmax gives a payoff of 3/4Pmax to the actor with the threat. Correspondingly, the payoff to the actor receiving the threat will move from Pmax/2 to Pmax/4. Let x be the size of the negative sanction needed to produce this shift: x is Pcon of the threatened actor. Then

$$\frac{P\text{max} - 3/4P\text{max}}{3/4P\text{max}} = \frac{P\text{max} - P\text{max}/4}{P\text{max}/4 - x}$$

and $x = -2P$max. That is, to move halfway to Pmax requires a threat, the absolute value of which is twice Pmax. So Puzo was right. When negative sanctions are appended to exchange relations, the actor with the negatives will gain more than would have been received without the threat.

Now consider the effect of an outside offer, which is an exclusive alternative for one actor. If A has an exclusive alternative and B does not, we expect that the exchange ratio will shift from the equal power point to one more favorable to A. To see how outside offers affect points of agreement, I find how large such an offer will be to have the same effect as the threat considered above— that is, to move the payoff to 3/4Pmax while the payoff for the actor without the alternative is Pmax/4. Let the size of the alternative offer be y. The offer y has two effects. First, the payoff at confrontation for the actor with the offer is now y. Second, the actor without the outside offer must meet it or be excluded. Since that offer is y, the best payoff for the actor without the outside offer is now Pmax $- y$. Therefore,

$$\frac{P\text{max} - 3/4P\text{max}}{3/4P\text{max} - y} = \frac{(P\text{max} - y) - P\text{max}/4}{P\text{max}/4}$$

and $y = P$max/2. In fact, y^2 occurs in the solution, so two y values satisfy the equality: Pmax/2 and Pmax. But for $y = P$max, both resistance factors are negative. Resistance factors are never negative, so $y = P$max is ruled out.

Size for size, the outside offer has greater efficacy than the threat. Both had the same effect: the high power actor gained $3/4P$max. But the negative was $-2P$max, whereas the outside offer was only Pmax$/2$. Although both had exactly the same effect, the absolute value of the negative threatened was *four times* larger than the outside offer. This is a novel result. Sociologists frequently assert that negatives have greater effects than do positives. Here resistance predicts the contrary.

Testing Resistance

Extensive experimental research supports structural formulations of elementary theory, but resistance predictions for dyads are not directly supported. There is no direct support because dyad research has not been completed. There is indirect support for central predictions, however. I briefly mention that support here, keying it to later discussions. In the next chapter, "null" connected exchange networks are investigated. When relations are null connected, the structure has no effect on exchange outcomes. That is, exchange relations in null connected networks are independent, so each relation is like an isolated dyad. Experimental subjects bargain to compromise at medial rates, and those rates correspond well to resistance predictions here (also see Chapter 8 of this volume, as well as Skvoretz and Willer 1991). The next chapter also reports on coercive structures where the coercive relations are independent. Again, rates are like those predicted here for coercive dyads.

The absence of dyad research is a gaping hole in the theoretical research program supporting ET and NET. Programs should begin with the simplest theoretic formulations and move to more complex ones only after those are investigated. ET/NET jumped past dyads to focus first on simple and then on increasingly complex structures. Of course, experiments on these structures provide extensive support for resistance. The success of that research, however, only points to the significance of dyad research and offers further reason why it should be done.

Chapter 3

Relations in Structures

David Willer

In this chapter I show how structural conditions of power affect actors' behavior. The effect is not direct, from structure to actor, but indirect. Structures affect actors' behavior by modifying interests that are produced in relations.

In exchange and coercion, actors have an interest in gaining Pmax, their best hope. Pmax is an initial condition. When the relation is isolated from structural effects, Pmax is constant. But some structures affect Pmax of related actors differentially: for one actor Pmax is unchanged, but for the other it declines. As Pmax declines, the actor's aspirations sink lower and lower, such that resistance is reduced. As a result, less and less favorable offers are accepted, and power is being exercised over the actor.

Structures also change resistance by altering Pcon, the actor's cost/benefit at confrontation. Pcon is initially determined by the relation and, like Pmax, is constant when the relation is isolated from structural effects. When Pcon of related actors is differentially affected, it remains constant for one actor and increases or decreases for the other. When Pcon increases, so does the actor's resistance such that better and better deals are gained. Then the actor is exercising power over others. For other types of structures, Pcon decreases and the effect is reversed. Poorer deals are made indicating that the actor is subjected to others.

Some structures have twofold effects. The interests of actors at both ends of its relations are affected such that the resistance of one increases and the other declines. This twofold effect results in large power differences. All of these effects are a result of the way relations are "connected" at positions.

Three types of connection are studied: exclusion, null, and inclusion. I define these types in the section that follows and analyze exclusive and null connected exchange "branches" first. A branch is a network with a single central position connected to two or more peripheral positions that are not connected to each other. In exclusive branches, power is centralized, but null branches are equipower throughout. Resistance predicts their contrasting processes and outcomes. Experiments on null and exclusive branches support predictions from resistance. Exclusion takes different forms in different structures. In hierarchies, exclusion takes the form of competitive mobility. Examination of this condition shows that, in hierarchies with mobility, subordinates compete to move to positions at a higher status. Experiments on hierarchy/mobility structures show power differences like those produced in exclusionary branches.

Resistance also infers the distribution of power in inclusively connected branches, a distribution that is quite unlike that of exclusion. Whereas exclusion centralizes power, inclusion decentralizes power. In inclusively connected branches, peripherals exercise power over the central position. Relative to the program of research, the discussion of inclusion here is slightly out of order. It was studied three years later than the other structures of this chapter, and experimental results were published two years after the research of the next chapter was published. Nevertheless, inclusion is best discussed here precisely because, for structures otherwise identical, the direction of its effect is exactly opposite to exclusion.

Types of connection are defined only for exchange networks, but there are coercive networks whose processes and outcomes have contrasts like those of two exchange types. Resistance shows why some coercive branches are structurally equivalent to null connected exchange branches and others are structurally equivalent to exclusively connected branches. In branches, a coalition is formed when two or more peripheral positions are allowed to associate. I investigate resistance's prediction that coalition formation countervails structural power. Experiments supporting these applications of resistance are noted.

Branches are "simple structures" because they have only one centrally located position, and only that position is connected to multiple relations. Looking ahead to the figures of this chapter, we can see that the longest path in any branch is only two steps, from a peripheral position to the single central position to any other peripheral. Since no path returns to any node, all branches are trees. In fact, branches are "maximally compact" trees because no path is longer than two steps.[1] The branches investigated here are simple in a second sense: all connected relations are identical. I will build exchange structures and coercive structures but no structures with both exchange and coercive relations.

By studying simple structures, the effects of contrasting types of connection are seen in their theoretically purest form. After each of the structures is built and predictions are generated, I explain how experiments test the predictions. The same experimental procedures were employed for all experiments. Contrasting experimental conditions are produced by varying types of connection. To cover a range of theoretical predictions, experiments investigate exchange networks and coercive structures.

Figure 3.1
A 2-Branch

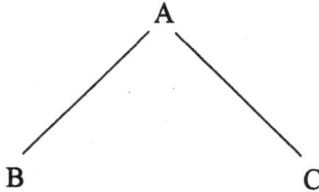

THREE TYPES OF CONNECTION

This section introduces the three types of connection. I begin with the 2-Branch of Figure 3.1 and introduce the types using sentential connectives from symbolic logic. Then the connection types are generalized to nodes with any number of connected relations.[2]

The 2-Branch and Three Types of Connection

Here concepts from symbolic logic are used to define types of connection in the 2-Branch of Figure 3.1. Specifically, I apply the three sentential connectives—the conjunctive "and," the disjunctive "exclusive or," and the disjunctive "inclusive or"—to the connection between $A–B$ and $A–C$ relations in Figure 3.1. That application gives three types of connection, which are:

1. *Exclusion*: A exchanges with B or C but not with both.
2. *Null*: A exchanges with B or C or both.
3. *Inclusion*: A exchanges with both B and C.

Now I apply Principle 1 to find conditions for each of the three types. A is exclusively connected when A benefits from exchanging in either of its two relations, but not in both. For example, when A is interested in making only one exchange but wants to consider options in two relations, A is exclusively connected. A is null connected when A benefits from exchanging in either or both relations. Null connection means that A benefits independently in each relation. A is inclusively connected when A benefits if and only if exchanges are completed in both relations.

A great many different empirical conditions produce connection types. For example, the need to match two different kinds of resources produces inclusive connection. If A wants bread only with butter and buys bread at the bakery and butter at the dairy, then A's two purchases are inclusively connected. Note that resource differentiation alone does not produce inclusion. If A wants either bread

Figure 3.2
An Equipower Branch Null Connected at A

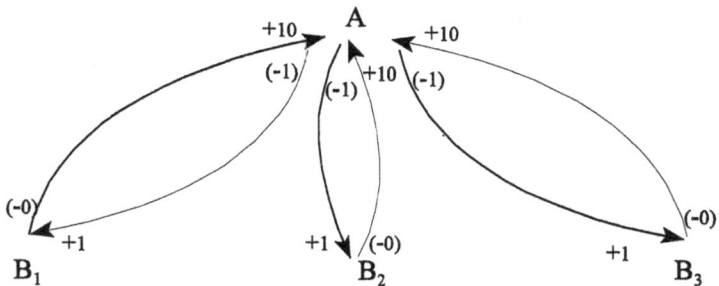

or butter or both, then the two purchases are null connected. When A can afford only bread or butter, the connection is exclusive. Alternatively, the conditions for connection may be time dependent. For example, A is exclusively connected if, for the time t_0 to t_1, A exchanges with only one and chooses between B and C. If, for t_1 to t_2, again A can exchange with B or C but not both, then A is again exclusively connected and similarly for further time periods.

The three types of connection are easily produced in experiments. Let a subject have two exchange relations like A–B and A–C. Exclusive connection is produced when all subjects are limited to maximally a single exchange. Null connection is produced when the subject in A is allowed to make as many as two exchanges, while B and C have one each. Inclusive connection is produced when the A subject is (1) allocated two exchanges while again B and C have one, but (2) the A is paid only when both exchanges are completed.

The Typology and N-Branches

I now extend the three types of connections to "N-branches." An N-branch is a branch in which the central node is connected to N exchange relations. Links between N, "M" and "Q" are used to generalize network connections to larger branches. Let the set of exchange relations connected at i be i's "potential network," and let its size be N. Then i will exchange in all, some, or none of Ni. For the 3-Branch of Figure 3.2, $N_A = 3$ and $N_B = 1$. That is, A's potential network is size three, while each B has a potential network of size one. M is the size of the largest network in which i benefits from exchanging, i's "maximum possible network." For example, when A of Figure 3.2 can benefit from exchanging with two of its three Bs, then $M = 2$. Let Q be the size of the smallest network in which i must complete all exchanges to benefit from any one. This network of size Q is i's "minimum necessary network." For example, if A must complete exchanges with all three Bs, then $Q = 3$ (see Willer 1984, 1987, 1992; Patton and Willer 1991).

N is the number of relations connected at a node: N is M's upper bound, and

M is Q's upper bound. That is, $Ni \geqslant Mi \geqslant Qi$. Stated somewhat differently, i can make as many as M exchanges and will always have N alternatives among which to choose. Similarly, i must exchange Q times and will always have M opportunities to exchange and N alternative exchange relations among which to select. Then

- i is exclusively connected when $Ni > Mi \geqslant Qi = 1$
- i is null connected when $Ni = Mi > Qi = 1$
- i is inclusively connected when $Ni = Mi = Qi > 1$

Finally, when $Ni = Mi = Qi = 1$, i is singularly connected. Since the Bs of Figure 3.2 are connected only to A, they are all singularly connected.

First, apply the three types of networks to the 2-Branch to find whether they generate the conditions of null, exclusive, and inclusive connection as defined by sentential connections. For the 2-Branch, null connection is $N_A = M_A = 2 > Q_A = 1$: A exchanges with B or C or both, which is null connection as defined by "inclusive or." For the 2-Branch, exclusion is $N_A = 2 > M_A = Q_A = 1$. That is, A exchanges with B or C, but not with both, which is exclusive connection as defined by "exclusive or." For the 2-Branch inclusion is $N_A = M_A = Q_A = 2$. A exchanges with both B and C, which is inclusive connection as defined by "and."

Null, exclusive, and inclusive connection types are exhaustive for the 2-Branch. A 2-Branch network is null only if $N = M > Q$; it is exclusively connected only if $N > M = Q$; and it is inclusively connected only if $N = M = Q$. The intersection of the three conditions is $N \geqslant M \geqslant Q$: therefore, the three are exhaustive for the 2-Branch. When $N > 2$ relations are connected at a node, the three types are not exhaustive, however. Two more types are needed, and they are introduced later in Chapter 8.

Although I have introduced exclusion, null, and inclusion only for the branch, the typology is quite general and applies to any exchange network. In the branch when i is central, Ni, Mi, and Qi are necessarily 1-step networks from i. More generally, N, M, and Q are 1-step networks from any node in any network. Branches are simple networks. Complex networks have more than one node with two or more connected relations. To define conditions of connection for a complex network, N, M, and Q are specified for each multiply connected node.

Since the branch has only one multiply connected node, its structural conditions are given by the ordered triple "NMQ." When "Br" means "branch," Br531 means $N = 5$, $M = 3$, and $Q = 1$. Br531 is an exclusively connected branch, Br551 is a null connected branch, Br 555 is an inclusively connected branch, and similarly for branches of any size. Note that for a given "N" sized branch, there is exactly one that is null connected and one that is inclusively connected, but there are $N-1$ which are exclusively connected.

The formulations that follow and associated experiments test the "empirical import'' of the typology: whether the different types correspond to real differences in the world. This typology is valuable if and only if it has empirical import. If it does, exclusively connected branches like Br531 and Br311 will behave similarly and will *not* behave like Br551 null connected or Br555 inclusively connected networks. This chapter begins the test of the typology, which continues in later parts of the book, especially Chapter 8.

I now apply resistance to generate predictions for each type and review the results of experiments that test the predictions. These experiments test whether the typology has empirical import; they also test the predictive power of resistance.

NULL AND EXCLUSIVE EXCHANGE BRANCHES

Let Figure 3.2 be Br331, a null connected branch. Its three exchange relations are identical to the exchange relation analyzed in Chapter 2. A initially holds resources that are each a loss of one to A and a gain of one to the B receiving it, while each B holds a single resource that is costless to transmit and worth 10 to A when received. Figure 3.3 is a Br531 exclusively connected branch constructed with the same exchange relations. Applying resistance, I now show that the null branch is equipower and that the exclusive branch is a strong power structure.

Null Connected Branch

It will be remembered from Chapter 2 that agreements occur when the resistance of actors is equal. For a single A–B relation,

$$R_A = \frac{P_A \max - P_A}{P_A - P_A \text{ con}} = \frac{P_B \max - P_B}{P_B - P_B \text{ con}} = R_B \tag{3.1}$$

For a null branch in which A is connected to N peripherals, all of A's payoffs are increased by N. Therefore, A's resistance in any null connected branch is

$$R_A(\text{null}) = \frac{NP_A \max - NP_A}{NP_A - NP_A \text{ con}} = \frac{P_B \max - P_B}{P_B - P_B \text{ con}} = R_B \tag{3.2}$$

Canceling Ns, it follows that $R_A(\text{null}) = R_A$: the resistance of A in any null branch is exactly the same as the resistance of A in a single exchange relation.[3] Therefore, the payoffs for each position are predicted to be exactly the same as for the isolated exchange relation. I repeat the initial conditions of the exchange relations that were given in the last chapter: The 3.2a network has three exchange relations and for each the initial conditions are:

$$P_A\text{max} = 9 \qquad P_B\text{max} = 9$$
$$P_A\text{con} = 0 \qquad P_B\text{con} = 0$$

Therefore,

$$R_A = \frac{9 - P_A}{P_A} = \frac{9 - P_B}{P_B} = R_B$$

Since the total payoff in each relation is 10, $P_B = 10 - P_A$. Substituting, we find that $P_A = 5$ and $P_B = 5$: each B transmits its sanction to A and receives five of A's sanctions in return.

A conclusion reached from this application is quite general for all null branches. Since (1) the exchange ratios for the null branch and dyad are predicted from the same equation and (2) use the same initial conditions, and since there is no power in the exchange dyad, *there is no power in any null branch.* This prediction is independent from the distribution of resources in the branch. For example, when the relations are reversed, such that A holds B's relations and each B holds resources like A, resistance again predicts for each relation that $P_B = 5$ and $P_A = 5$. So reversing the relations leaves A's and B's payoffs in each relation unchanged.

The social exchange theorists discussed in Chapter 1 asserted that central positions in unilateral monopolies are powerful. The reason cited was satiation effects. The opinion that centrally placed actors are powerful is frequently encountered across the social sciences, although the reason given is not always the effects of satiation. Contradicting this opinion, resistance analysis offers the surprising conclusion that the central position is equal in power with those at the periphery when the unilateral monopoly is null connected.

Power is equal, but remember that power is measured relation by relation. That is, A is equal in power when exchanging with B_1, equal in power when exchanging with B_2, and again equal in power when exchanging with B_3. It follows that payoffs for the structure as a whole are not equal between A and any one B. Since A exchanges with three Bs, A's total payoff is three times as large as each B's: A gains 15 for the structure as a whole, whereas each B, exchanging only once, gains only 5.

The Design of Face-to-Face Experiments: Results for the Null Branch

The "face-to-face" experimental design was used to test resistance predictions just calculated for the null branch. Using the same procedures and with only minor modifications of initial conditions, it tested predictions for the rest of the structures investigated in this chapter. Initial conditions of the structure governed the experimental design. For the null connected 3-Branch, one subject in the A position faced three subjects in B positions. These subjects were seated in chairs and given different colored poker chips, blue for A and white for B. Instructions read by subjects prior to the experiment explained the values of the chips, values that corresponded exactly to those given as initial conditions and in Figure 3.2. Blue chips initially held by A were worth one to A and one to B, while B's white chip was worth nothing to B and 10 to A. The layout of the experimental room allowed subjects to see the shape of the structure. Since it was assumed that subjects in peripheral positions act independently, the three B positions were separated by plywood barriers to prevent eye contact. Because the resistance analysis assumes rational actors and because rational actors can optimize only in a full information environment, the face-to-face design allowed subjects to hear the offers and counter-offers of others.

Each experimental session was divided into rounds and periods, and in each round subjects negotiated and exchanged poker chips. For the investigation of null connected branches, the subject in the central position was given three exchange opportunities and enough resources to complete all. Rounds lasted 3 minutes and 20 seconds: subjects were warned when 3 minutes were up. Subjects bargained hard, and frequently the last of the three exchanges was completed with only seconds to go in the round. At the end of the first round, counters were redistributed, and a second round exactly like the first was begun.

The experiment was a repeated game. After four rounds, the first period was completed and all subjects rotated: each one moved to a new position. The subject in the A position moved to B_1, B_1 moved to B_2, and so forth, with B_3 becoming the new A. Then a second period began exactly like the first. Each experiment had as many periods as subjects. The experiments on null branches had four subjects, so there were four periods and each period had four rounds in which subjects negotiated and exchanged. Since each subject occupied each position for one period, mean earnings by position could not be a consequence of idiosyncratic qualities of any subject.

The Br331 network was the first experimentally investigated. Four sessions were run, each with a different group of subjects. On the average, A paid 6.9 resources for each resource of the Bs: $P_B = 6.9$ and $P_A = 10 - 6.9 = 3.1$. This is a substantial deviation from the predicted 5–5 earnings and indicates that the Bs were exercising power over the A. Some years later, Szmatka in Poland investigated this network. For three sessions he found $P_B = 5.5$ and $P_A = 10 - 5.5 = 4.5$ (Willer and Szmatka 1993). The Polish results are closer to resistance predictions. Still, both experiments indicate that the peripherals were exercising power over the center, though the amount exercised in Poland was small.[4]

Exclusion and the Branch

In "strong power" networks, power is produced by exclusion. A network is strong power if and only if (1) its positions can be divided into one or more high power positions that are never excluded, (2) two or more low power positions, at least one of which is always excluded, and (3) low power positions exchange only with high power positions (see Chapter 10, Part 2). In branches, only the central position can be high strong power; when it is, all exchanges must occur between it and low power positions at the periphery because only they are connected. Any branch is strong power when $N > M$ for the central position and $N = M = 1$ for all peripherals. That is, the central position exchanges with as many as M but not all N peripherals. Since the central position is never excluded and $N - M > 0$ peripherals are always excluded, the central position is high power and the peripherals are the low power positions.[5]

As seen in Chapter 2, negotiations in equal power structures like the dyad and null branch take the form of "bargaining." Actors began at opposed extreme offers and, sliding down the resistance curves like Figure 2.9, their offers moved toward each other to compromise at equiresistance. In equal power structures, the equal power point occurs where agreements are medial between the Pmax values of the actors paired in the relation. Initial negotiations in strong power structures may also be bargaining, but a transition occurs when the high power position has received its first M offers.

Because the central position can exchange with only M peripherals, the Mth + 1 peripheral faces exclusion. That peripheral will assuredly be excluded unless the central position prefers to exchange with it and not to exchange with one of the M peripherals considered earlier. The central position will have that preference iff the Mth + 1 peripheral makes a better offer to the center. So the peripheral makes that offer, and the first "iteration" begins. This and later iterations are composed of negotiations between the center and M peripherals.

More generally, when the first M offers are medial, the offers of the first iteration move off-center to favor the high power actor. These new offers are more favorable to the center because the peripherals know, as we do, that they will be excluded unless the central actor is induced to exchange with them and not in one of the previously negotiated exchanges. When the first iteration ends, a new subset of low power peripherals face exclusion. Therefore, the second iteration begins with offers even more favorable to the central high power position. Iterations continue, with subsequent offers moving toward and finally reaching the extreme favoring the center. Then the central actor is gaining its Pmax and will continue to do so in future exchanges.

Iteration is not bargaining. Bargaining occurs between two actors: over time their offers approach each other at medial values. Iteration in the branch occurs between the one actor in the central high power position and the N low power peripherals. Peripheral actors, seeking to avoid exclusion, make better and better offers to the center. Iteration is a power process because the high power actor benefits maximally. This inequality suggests that low power actors are controlled. But it is clear that control of those low in power is not the result of a special exercise of will by the high power actor. Instead, those low in power are controlled by the way that structure mediates their interests and those of the high power actor. I now show how a series of linked applications of resistance models the effects of structure in this power process.

Resistance predicts the effect of exclusion in strong power structures and, as a part of that prediction, traces power development through the iteration process. The application of resistance here is quite different from its application to null connected networks. In null connected networks, Pmax and Pcon are constants given by the relation: they do not change from their initial values. By contrast, in strong power networks, resistance asserts that the Pmax values of actors in low power positions and the Pcon values of actors in high power positions vary as part of the negotiation process.

When $M = 1$ for all positions, the Figure 3.1 2-Branch Br211 is the simplest strong power structure, and it is used to show how power develops. Let the $A–B$ and $A–C$ relations each contain 10 valued resources that are infinitely divisible, and let the smallest noticeable difference, $\Delta \rightarrow 0$. Thus initially,

$$P_A\text{max} = 10 \qquad P_B\text{max} = 10 \qquad P_C\text{max} = 10$$
$$P_A\text{con} = 0 \qquad P_B\text{con} = 0 \qquad P_C\text{con} = 0$$

For the demonstration, I assume that A, B, and C are engaging in a series of exchanges beginning at t_0 and ending at t_n. I also assume that all actors act independently. Let A begin negotiations at t_0 with B:

$$R_{Ab} = \frac{10 - P_A}{P_A - 0} = \frac{10 - P_B}{P_B - 0} = R_B$$

and since, for any agreement $P_A + P_B = 10$, we solve for $P_A = 5$ and $P_B = 5$ and the first exchange occurs at equal power. This exchange alters initial conditions for the first iteration.

At t_1, A begins negotiations with C knowing that $P_A = 5$ can again be gained by exchanging with B. Since A gains five from B, if agreement cannot be reached with C, $P_{Ac}\text{con} = 5$. Furthermore, C knows that P_C max $\neq 10$ because C cannot hope to gain more than was gained by its rival B. Since $P_B = 5$ at t_0, $P_C\text{max} = 5$ at t_1. Therefore,

$$P_A\text{max} = 10 \qquad P_C\text{max} = 5$$
$$P_A\text{con} = 5 \qquad P_C\text{con} = 0$$

$$R_{Ac} = \frac{10 - P_A}{P_A - 5} = \frac{5 - P_C}{P_C - 0} = R_C$$

substituting and solving, $P_{Ac} = 7.5$ and $P_C = 2.5$. A's exchange with C completes the first iteration. In that iteration, by shifting from B to C, A's payoff has moved one-half of the distance to $P_A\text{max}$.[6] At equal power $P_A = 5$, but now $P_A = 7.5$: this is a substantial power exercise by A over C. Crucial for this power exercise is the change of initial conditions: Pcon for A increases, while Pmax for C decreases.

As A returns to B for the next exchange, the values of Pcon and Pmax change again, now determined by the A–C exchange. If no agreement is reached at t_2, A will exchange with C gaining 7.5: thus P_{Ab}con $= 7.5$. Now B cannot hope to gain more than has just been gained by C: thus $P_B$max $= 2.5$ and for the initial conditions,

$$P_A\text{max} = 10 \qquad\qquad P_B\text{max} = 2.5$$
$$P_A\text{con} \; = 7.5 \qquad\qquad P_B\text{con} \; = 0$$

$$R_{Ab} = \frac{10 - P_A}{P_A - 7.5} = \frac{2.5 - P_B}{P_B - 0} = R_B$$

Substituting and solving $P_A = 8.75$ and $P_B = 1.25$. Power has increased again and has moved closer to the maximum of $P_A = P_A\text{max} = 10$. As in the first iteration, in the second P_A has again moved one-half of the way to $P_A\text{max}$. The shape of the iteration curve is already clear. When "Δ_t" is the size of the increment of the tth iteration, $\Delta_t = \Delta_{(t-1)}/2$. Therefore, Pmax of the central high power actor is approached as the limit of the iteration process. Since each step halves the distance to maximum power, an infinite number of iterations is required to reach the extreme.

We can call this series of applications the "equiresistance model" of power development: each exchange occurs at equiresistance as conditioned by the previous exchange. Note that the number of iterations is very large because the smallest noticeable difference is zero. When resources are minimally nonzero lumps, however, iteration becomes finite. As lumpiness increases, the number of iterations declines in the following way. Assume that early increments are larger than resource lumps. Then the increments of early iterations are unaffected by lumpiness; but, as iterations continue, the increments between them decline. When increment size declines to the size of resource lumps, further increments do not grow smaller. From that point, each new iteration spans one lump, and Pmax of the high power actor is reached in finite iterations.

The equiresistance model has been presented as a series of exchanges, but it can be expressed another way. Let exchange occur only at the end of the iteration process. Then each iteration is a set of tentative agreements conditioned by agreements negotiated in the iteration just before. So iteration proceeds *across agreements*. Iteration ends when $P = P$max for the high power actor: only then do exchanges occur and only at maximum power.

In generalizing the equiresistance model to any branch, I focus on iteration across agreements, not exchanges. A is central in a branch with N peripherals and M exchanges. For example, Figure 3.3 is a Br531: A is central to five Bs

Figure 3.3
A Strong Power 5-Branch with *A* Exclusively Connected

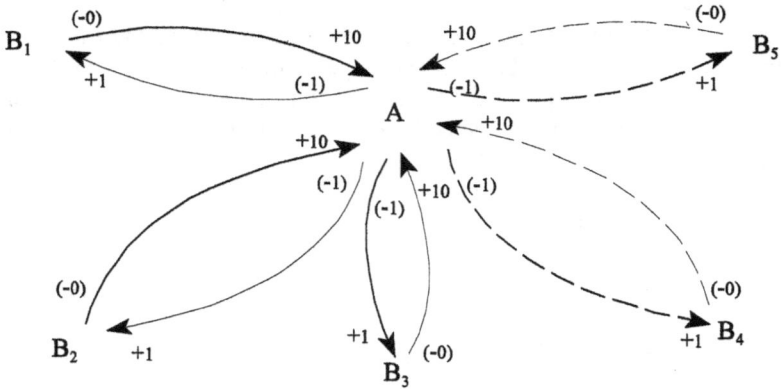

and exchanges maximally with only three. Let A negotiate agreements at equiresistance—but not exchange—with M peripherals. Completion of the Mth negotiation ends t_0. The Mth $+ 1$ negotiation begins t_1, first iteration, and is logically similar to the first iteration above: $P_A$con at t_1 is P_A at t_0, and the Mth $+ 1$ peripheral's Pmax at t_1 is P for any peripheral at t_0. Then t_1 concludes when M new deals are negotiated.

Note that unless $N_A \geq 2M_A$, during t_1 A will return to some peripheral(s) to negotiate a new, more favorable agreement. For example, in Br531, the first iteration begins when A has tentative agreements with three Bs. Now A negotiates with the fourth and fifth B; the t_1 iteration is completed when A returns to one of the first three Bs and renegotiates their earlier agreement. As t_1 concludes, t_2 begins, M new agreements even more favorable to A are negotiated, and similarly until $P_A = P_A$max where A exchanges at maximum power.

Let Ei^{t-1} be the payoff to actor i at $t - 1$ and Pi^t the payoff at t. When A is central and X is any peripheral, and R(ex) is resistance for any exclusive branch, for any iteration of M peripherals offers are:

$$R_A(\text{ex}) = \frac{P_A\text{max} - P_A^t}{P_A^t - E_A^{t-1}} = \frac{E_X^{t-1} - P_X^t}{P_X^t - 0} = R_X(\text{ex}) \qquad (3.3)$$

The limit of Equation (3.3) as t increases is Pmax for the central actor and $P = \Delta$ for any peripheral. If there are no costs or time limits on negotiation, it is in A's interest to exchange only at the conclusion of the process when power is maximal.

Whereas the equiresistance model emphasizes the role of the central actor over a series of iterations, I now introduce the "zero resistance" model, which emphasizes the role of peripherals. Now iteration takes the form of a series of bids from low power peripheral Bs to the high power central A. For this model let resources be lumpy: one resource is the smallest unit. I first examine A's interest situation at the beginning of any iteration to show that only bids at least one unit better will be accepted. I then show that peripherals have zero resistance to offers that are exactly one unit better than those of the previous iteration.

Consider first A's interest situation at time t_0 and after its first M agreements are completed. For those agreements payoffs are P_A for A and P_B for each of M peripherals. We know for t_1 that $P_A\text{con} = P_A$ at t_0. Therefore, were the Mth + 1 peripheral B to make the same offer as offers made previously, $P_A - P_A\text{con} = 0$, the denominator of A's resistance factor becomes zero, and $R_A \rightarrow \infty$. That is, at t_1, A's resistance to any new offer that is the equal of previous offers is infinite: all such offers will be rejected. Therefore, the smallest offer A will consider is $P_A + 1$. This conclusion is quite general. For each new iteration, the smallest offer A will consider is one unit better than that of the previous iteration.

What is the resistance of any B to the smallest incremental offer A will consider? This offer is also the smallest decrement to B. Call the Mth + 1 peripheral B_X. Now let P_A and P_B be the payoffs at the last iteration. We have just determined that the smallest increment which A will consider for this iteration gives $P_A + 1$. Therefore, the most which B_X can hope to receive is one less than P_B. That is, $P_{BX}\text{max} = P_B - 1$. The smallest decremental offer for B_X is also $P_B - 1$. So,

$$R_{BX}\,(\text{ex}) = \frac{(P_B - 1) - (P_B - 1)}{P_B - 1} = 0$$

Since B_X's resistance to the offer is zero, it will be made immediately. More generally, at each iteration, M peripherals will make the better offer at zero resistance. Iterations continue until A receives $P_A\text{max}$ offers from M peripherals, and the process concludes at maximum power. Figure 3.4 displays the paths for the two models of power development. The slope of the line for the zero resistance model is determined by the smallest unit difference. Here, the smallest unit is one and the slope is one. But if the smallest unit were two, the slope would be doubled, and $P\text{max}$ for the high power actor is attained in exactly one-half as many steps.

The zero resistance model makes the seemingly paradoxical assertion that high power actors in a strong power structures exercise power maximally by simply letting low power actors make better and better offers. It claims that power exercise and activity are separated. That claim rests on the fact that low power actors are rivals: only some can exchange, and the rest will be excluded. The scramble to avoid exclusion leads them to bid making better and better offers to the central high power actor. A variety of experiments support the idea that actors lower in power are more active. Elsewhere I discuss experiments which show that a simulated actor capable only of accepting best offers

Figure 3.4
Iteration Paths for Power Development[a]

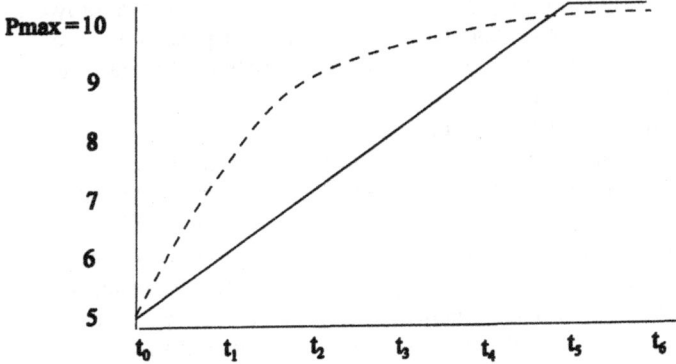

Note: [a]P is the payoff to high power actor: The dashed line traces the equiresistance path, while the solid line traces the zero resistance path. $P = 5$ is equipower.
Equiresistance: $t_0 = 5$, $t_1 = 7.5$, $t_2 = 8.75$, $t_3 = 9.378$, $t_4 = 9.6875$, $t_5 = 9.84375$, $t_6 = 9.9219$.
Zero resistance: $t_0 = 5$, $t_1 = 6$, $t_2 = 7$, $t_3 = 8$, $t_4 = 9$, $t_5 = 10$.

exercises power as effectively as subjects in high power positions (Willer and Skvoretz 1997).

At issue is which path power development will take. Will it follow the curve of the equiresistance model? Or will the line of the zero resistance model be traced? Because early increments are larger, small resource lumps favor the equiresistance model. But if negotiation time is proportional to resistance, the zero resistance model takes precedence in the following way. Let A be connected to B, C, and D in a Br311: I pick up the interaction after A has concluded an equipower agreement with B. Now C and D face exclusion. Let A turn to C to begin bargaining to the new equiresistance settlement. But before bargaining can proceed, D has already sent a better offer to A than B's and B has bettered D's. Iteration has taken off, forcing C's hand. Instead of protracted bargaining, C tops B's offer and iteration continues. Because zero resistance bids interrupt bargaining, power development follows the zero resistance line.[7]

The model that dominates is the one that is fastest. Iteration at zero resistance is fast. By contrast, bargaining to equiresistance is too slow. Before bargaining can go forward, zero resistance offers preempt it, at least early in the process. Nevertheless, speed of iteration is not constant for the equiresistance model. When the time duration of each iteration is proportional to resistance, as iteration goes forward, $P_A \text{con} \rightarrow P_A$ and $P_B \max \rightarrow P_B$. The numerical value of resistance for both A and the Bs declines rapidly, as does the duration of each iteration, and the speed of the process picks up. Thus a very large number of iterations is not a barrier to reaching maximum power at $P_A \max$. Finally, when power is maximal, equiresistance and zero resistance models are the same: all exchanges then occur at zero resistance for both actors.

Resistance hypothesizes that the availability of information by position affects the speed at which power develops. In some experimental designs, only the central position knows competing offers. For that design, the zero resistance model stalls because the peripherals' Pmax does not change as competing offers are made. The equiresistance model is only slowed, however, for it is still driven by the increase of the center's Pcon. The power process is slowed because (1) each step of the iteration is smaller and (2) all settlements occur at higher resistance values than under full information conditions. These implications from resistance are hypotheses and have yet to be tested.

The Figure 3.3 Br531 strong power network was investigated experimentally. Both models predict that exchanges will begin at equal power payoffs of $P_A =$ 5 for the center and $P_B = 5$ for peripherals and move to $P_A$max $= 9$ and $P_B =$ 1 for the three peripherals not excluded. Four sessions were run. For the whole of the experiment the mean and mode for A were 7.8 and 9, respectively.[8] That the overall mean was lower than the mode that was at the extreme reflects the fact that (1) power developed from lower values earlier in the experiment and (2) reached the extreme favoring A later in the experiment. There was a satisfactory fit between models and data, but no attempt was made to find which model offered the better fit.[9]

Hierarchy/Mobility and Power

This section brings ideas of strong power in exclusionary networks to bear on formal organizations like historical and contemporary bureaucracies. These hierarchical organizations are built so that policy set at the top can be carried out by those at the bottom. Stated somewhat differently, bureaucracies are built to be power structures. When effective, power relations link each pair of levels so that control extends, beyond adjacencies, to span multiple levels in an unbroken line linking top to bottom. Explaining power of this kind also explains power centralization.

In this section I explain power in organizations in terms of formulations for strong power. Admittedly, large organizations in the field do not resemble the small networks studied in the lab. Nothing like the formal organizational chart of Figure 3.5 has been encountered. Nor does exclusion appear to be present in all hierarchies. Dismissal is a form of exclusion, but dismissal is absent in Japan's major corporations where people take jobs for life. Furthermore, in the exchange networks modeled in the last section, the exercise of power was limited to adjacencies. In formal organizations like that of Figure 3.5, however, A exercises "power-at-a-distance" over D, E, F, and G. In these and many other regards, the small exchange networks modeled for experiments are not like large, complex organizations. Nevertheless, the same theory will explain power in both.

Figure 3.5
Formal Organization

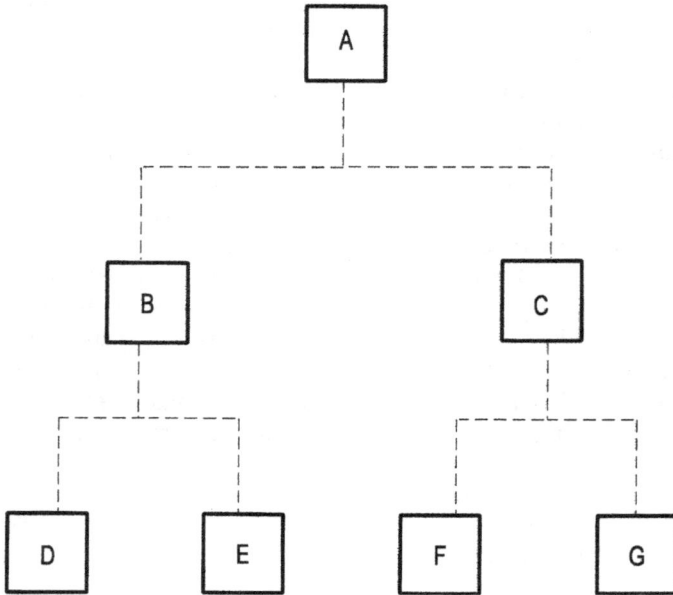

In the hierarchies of historical and contemporary bureaucracies, each position is assigned a salary as well as perquisites and privileges, which are graded according to rank. The top positions have the highest salaries, the most perquisites, and the greatest privileges, whereas the bottom positions have the lowest salaries, fewest perquisites, and least privileges. Each pair of levels as between *A* and *B* or *B* and *D* in Figure 3.5 is similarly stratified. We can call the bundle made up of salary, perquisite, and privilege the status of a position. Then positions can be graded by status from top to bottom so that, when effectively designed, status differences between pairs of levels are well beyond "just noticeable differences." Let the statuses in the hierarchy of positions be the only values of a set of actors called "officials," and let us assume that occupying even the bottom position is better than having no position. Then all officials prefer all higher to all lower positions, and all prefer any position to no position. Put somewhat differently, all officials have interests in upward mobility.

Now I introduce two further conditions. First, there is a system of evaluation, as in Figure 3.6, through which officials in higher positions decide which lower ranked officials will be promoted. A necessary condition for promotion is that officials in lower positions always be obedient. Second, no official appropriates any position and all positions are filled from below. Then there is a system of promotion like that shown in Figure 3.7. The effect of upward mobility at higher levels cascades, opening positions for mobility at levels below. That is, advance-

Figure 3.6
Evaluation System

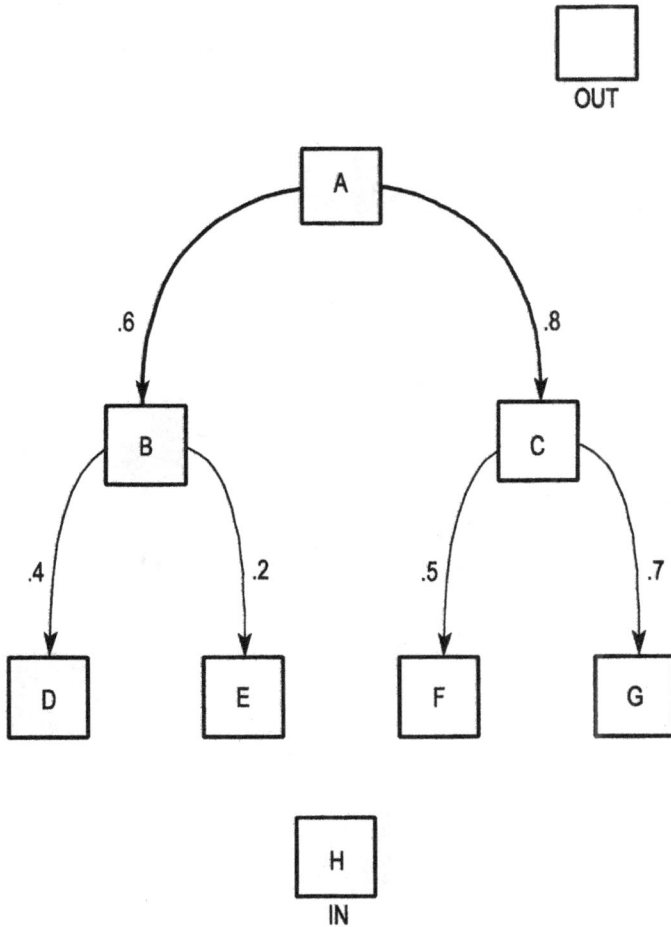

ment produces a vacancy chain that extends to the bottom (White 1970). These conditions link the interest in upward mobility to an interest in obedience. Since all hierarchies are branching trees, there are fewer positions at each higher level: at any point in time, only some, not all, officials can be upwardly mobile.

The interest in mobility and the shape of the structure produce competition to move up. Since obedience is a necessary condition for promotion, all officials offer high and higher levels of obedience to their superiors. In this way, hierarchy/mobility produces power relations from superiors to subordinates.

These kinds of hierarchies are strong power structures in which exclusion does not take the form of "exclusion from exchange" but of "exclusion from

Figure 3.7
Vacancy Chain

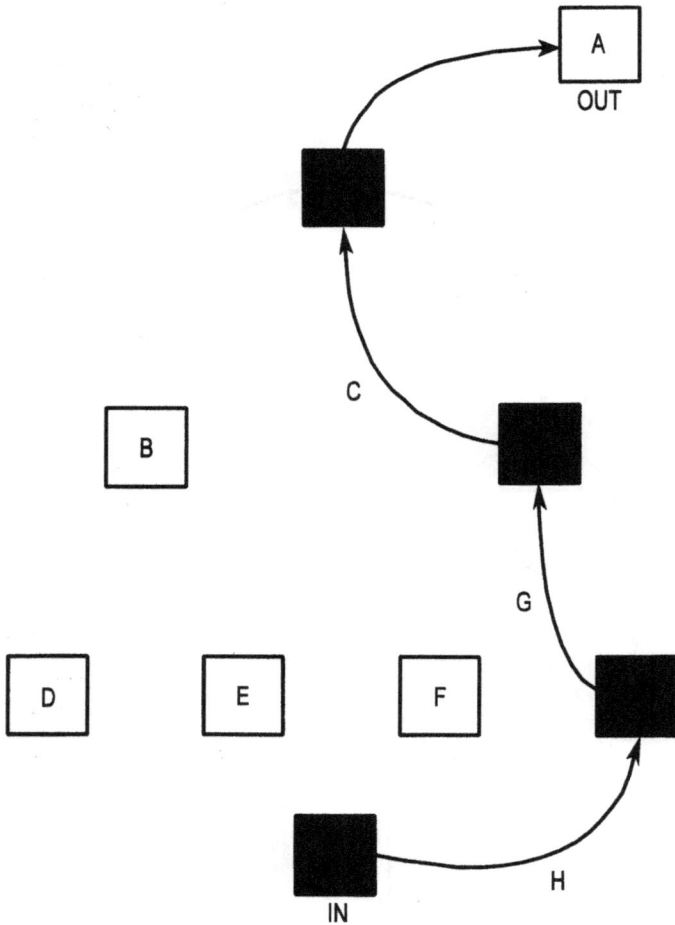

mobility.'' The identity between the two forms of exclusion is easily seen. Exclusionary structures like Figure 3.3 have two statuses: the higher status of exchanging and the lower status of being excluded. Any peripheral B who is excluded prefers the status of exchanging. And those who are exchanging prefer to avoid the lower status of exclusion. Exclusionary structures maximize power differences; therefore, hierarchy/mobility structures will maximize obedience. Figure 3.8 combines the ideas of Figures 3.5 through 3.7 to display the fundamental dynamics of hierarchy/mobility structures.

For hierarchies with mobility to be strong power structures, it is only necessary that officials compete for higher positions. It does not matter whether or

Figure 3.8
Hierarchy/Mobility Structure in Formal Organizations

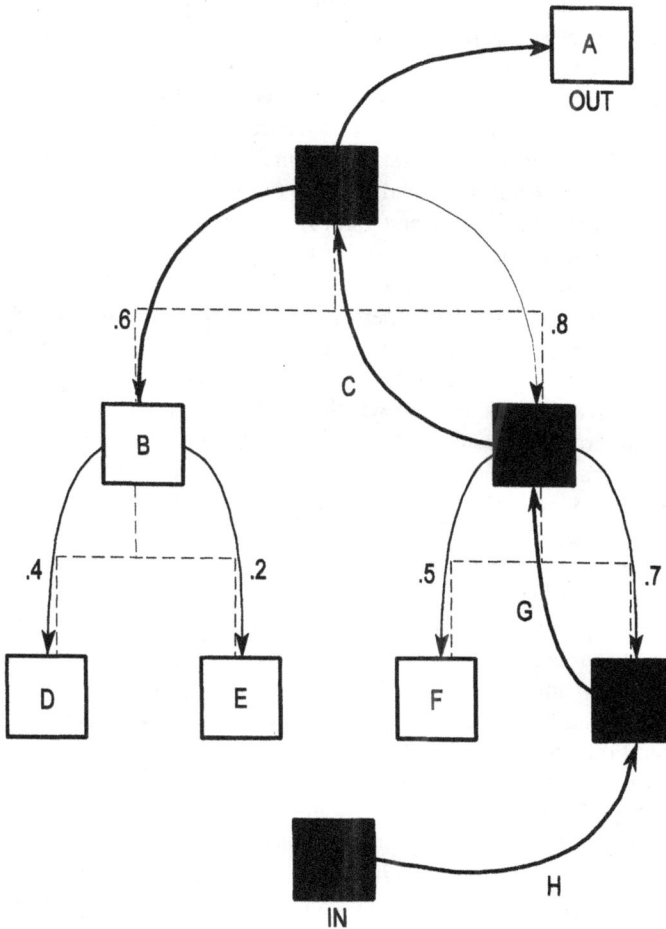

not officials who fail to move up are dismissed. If those who fail to move up are also dismissed, then the hierarchy is doubly strong: hierarchy/mobility and dismissal, both strong power conditions, are working together to produce power relations between levels. This double strength occurs in the U.S. military. Army officers who, after a given term, do not reach the rank of captain must resign their commissions. In turn, captains have a term to attain major, and similarly for higher levels.

The relation between hierarchy/mobility and power has been tested quite directly by building simple 2-level hierarchical structures in the laboratory. For each experiment, there were four positions at the lower level and two at the higher level, all occupied by B subjects connected in exchange relations to a central A subject. The same exchange relations were used here as were employed in the models for strong and equipower structures above. Unlike the experimental structures discussed earlier, no B was excluded. All Bs could and did exchange with the A.

A's power exercise is indicated in two ways: (1) by an extreme exchange ratio favoring A which indicated power as differential benefit, and (2) by brief and one-sided negotiation processes which indicated power as control. That is, the A was powerful when it gained its best rates by demand, and the Bs were obedient when offering their worst (and A's best) rates to A. The absence of power is also indicated in two ways: (1) by a medial rate of exchange and (2) by protracted two-sided negotiation processes indicating a balance of interests.

The 2-level hierarchies were experimentally produced in the following way. The Bs' payoffs from exchanges were ordered: the last four exchanges were required to be for two points less than the exchange completed first. As a result, there are two payoff levels, both of which could vary but with an experimentally determined minimum distance between the two points. For example, if the first B to exchange gained six points, the second B could gain as many as six. But the last four Bs to exchange could gain no more than $6 - 2 = 4$ points.

Mobility between the two levels was attained by stipulating that any B could exchange first, any B second, and so forth. The first A–B exchange was simply the first deal struck between A and one of the Bs. As a result, B subjects were given "equal opportunity" to occupy either the higher or the lower level.

Knowing that those who exchanged later received less, the Bs competed to exchange first. To attract A's attention, each B made better and better offers. As a result, payoffs at both levels declined. This is an iteration process that is very like the iteration processes theorized and observed in strong power branches with exclusion. But this structure had no exclusion. Here strong power was due solely to mobility between the two differentially privileged levels.

The end point of this iteration process was the extreme favoring A. At the extreme, the first B to exchange gained only three as did the second, while the last four gained only $3 - 2 = 1$ point each. This extreme indicated "power as benefit" with the A as high and the Bs as low in power. These negotiations were brief and one-sided, indicating A's control over the Bs. The observation of both forms of power, benefit and control—or in the terms of classical theory exploitation and domination—confirmed that hierarchy/mobility produces strong power in exchange networks.

If mobility is a necessary condition for strong power, then hierarchies without mobility should not be strong power structures. The 2-level networks without mobility were investigated. These "fixed" networks were identical to the hierarchical structure above except for the absence of mobility. As above, two levels were established by the rule that the last four exchanges were for no more than two less than the first exchange. But now the two high-status positions were reserved for two designated subjects. That is, two subjects were allowed to appropriate the two advantaged positions, while the four remaining *B*s were fixed in the lower status. Blocking mobility eliminated competition for higher status. As a result, exchange ratios were medial, and negotiation processes were protracted and two-sided: *A* and each *B* bargained hard. Neither form of power was observed, confirming that the 2-level fixed networks are not strong power structures.

The experimental structure had only two levels, but in large hierarchies in the field, the structural power of the 2-level mobility network is repeated between each pair of levels. For a hierarchy of n levels, the conditions of power are repeated $n - 1$ times, and our model asserts that power will be concentrated at the top. There are also large fixed hierarchies, like feudalism, in which power is not concentrated through mobility. Feudal structures contain power differences, but the experiments on hierarchies suggest that they cannot be strong power structures. A king with a feudal hierarchy cannot hire, promote, or fire, and thus he cannot dominate through the hierarchical structure itself. Since power differences in fixed hierarchies are not structurally produced, they stem from other conditions, for example, differential access to resources (Korpi 1985). The king's power was based on holding more land with more wealth which supported more troops than the barons who, in turn, held more land with more wealth and more troops than the lords at the next level and similarly to the bottom of the hierarchy.

Here the concept of structural exclusion has been extended to competitive mobility in hierarchies. This extension suggests that the models for strong power structures have quite general implications. As we have seen, organizations with systems of hierarchy/mobility do not resemble the simple exclusionary exchange structures investigated earlier. Nevertheless, both are strong power structures, and both operate similarly.

INCLUSIVE BRANCH

When an actor must complete two or more exchanges to benefit from any one, that actor is in an inclusively connected position. If *A* wants bread only with butter, buying bread at the bakery and butter at the dairy, then *A*'s two purchases are inclusively connected. Manufacturing firms are inclusively connected to suppliers. When Volvo buys wheels from one supplier, headlights from a second, tires from third, bearings from a fourth, water pumps from a fifth, and so forth, Volvo is inclusively connected in a very large number of relations. In this section, I show how resistance is applied to purely inclusively connected branches. In purely inclusively connected branches, $Ni = Mi = Qi > 1$.[10]

In inclusively connected branches, peripherals are singularly connected. Each benefits when its exchange is completed. It does not matter whether the center has completed all of its Q exchanges. Therefore, the resistance factor for peripherals is unchanged from the form it takes in the dyad.

By contrast, the inclusively connected central position must exchange with all peripherals. In the B–A–C branch, once A has exchanged with B, the value associated with that exchange is lost if A fails to complete an exchange with C. This added jeopardy of inclusive connection modifies A's resistance factor in the following way. For A's first exchange, there is no value from a previous exchange to lose and inclusion has no effect. Employing here the same exchange relation as used above, for the first exchange,

$$R_A = \frac{9 - P_A}{P_A} = \frac{9 - P_B}{P_B} = R_B$$

and $P_A = 5$, $P_B = 5$. For the A–C exchange that follows, A can lose the value gained in the A–B exchange. Therefore,

$$P_A\text{max} = 9 \qquad\qquad P_C\text{max} = 9$$
$$P_A\text{con} = -5 \qquad\qquad P_C\text{con} = 0$$

$$R_A \text{ (inc)} = \frac{9 - P_A}{P_A - (-5)} = \frac{9 - P_C}{P_C} = R_C$$

Since for any settlement $P_A + P_B = 10$, we solve for $P_A = 4.13$ and $P_B = 5.87$. Now add D to the branch. We now have a Br333, and A stands to lose both the five from the A–B exchange and the 4.24 from the A–C exchange: so $P_A\text{con} = -(5 + 4.13) = -9.13$. Now,

$$P_A\text{max} = 9 \qquad\qquad P_B\text{max} = 9$$
$$P_A\text{con} = -9.13 \qquad\qquad P_B\text{con} = 0$$

$$R_A \text{ (inc)} = \frac{9 - P_A}{P_A - (-9.13)} = \frac{9 - P_D}{P_D} = R_D$$

and $P_A = 3.65$, $P_D = 6.35$.

More generally, when bi is the ith peripheral and A has exchanged with $j = i - 1$ peripherals,

$$P_{Abi}\text{con} = -(P_{Ab1} + P_{Ab2} + P_{Ab3} + \ldots P_{Abj}) = -\sum_{i=1}^{j} P_{Abi}$$

and

$$R_A \text{ (inc)} = \frac{P_A \text{ max} - P_A}{P_A + \sum P_{Abi}}$$

P_{Abi}con increases in a negative direction with each subsequent exchange; therefore, the peripheral exchanging last gains the best settlement. In the Br333 just solved, B exchanged first and gained five, but C exchanging second gained almost six and D exchanging last gained more than six. This trend is quite general. For example, when one more peripheral, E, is added to the branch, P_{Abi}con $= -(5 + 4.13 + 3.65) = -12.78$. Again A is disadvantaged more, and E, exchanging last, will gain more than any other peripheral.

This pattern of changing payoffs implies a pattern of interaction for inclusion, interactions that are not like those found in exclusive or null branches. Let all peripherals be rationally self-interested and let a series of exchanges occur between A and the peripherals. Soon the peripherals will know, as we do, that the one exchanging last gains the most. Since peripherals are seeking maximal payoffs, all attempt to exchange last. The effect is that all peripherals initially avoid negotiating with A. By contrast, A knows that all Q exchanges must be completed to benefit. From the outset, A actively seeks to exchange. This pattern of interaction has two important implications.

First, the low power A in the center is more active than the high power peripherals. Something like this was seen for exclusion earlier in the chapter. For exclusion, power is at the center, not the periphery as it is here. Nevertheless, the same relation between high activity and low power also holds. Low power peripherals actively made better and better offers, while the high power center need only accept its best to maximize power. Is there a general relation between power and activity? Both inclusion and exclusion support the proposition that power and activity are inversely related.

The second implication is that the peripherals, by individually attempting to exchange last, will all exchange at effectively the same time. For example, in inclusive experiments when each round of negotiation is time limited, all exchanges occurred in the last moments of the round. As a result, exchanges are effectively simultaneous; therefore, all peripherals will gain the same, and P_A is the same in all relations. This allows a simplification of A's resistance factor. Remember that A is connected to $N = M = Q$ peripherals. For any one peripheral, A exchanges with $Q - 1$ others. Therefore, $P_A$con $= (Q - 1) P_A$ and

$$R_A \text{ (inc)} = \frac{P_A \max - P_A}{P_A + (Q - 1) P_A}$$

simplifying,

$$R_A \text{ (inc)} = \frac{P_A \max - P_A}{QP_A}$$

Table 3.1 assumes simultaneous exchanges and gives P_A values at equal resistance for various Q values. The table shows that, as Q increases, P_A decreases but at a decreasing rate. Note that P_A values for simultaneous exchanges are not

Table 3.1
The Payoff to the Central Actor, P_A by Q, the Number of Inclusively Connected Relations When the Resource Pool = 10

Q	1	2	3	4	5	6	... 10
P_A	5	4.24	3.81	3.52	3.30	3.14	2.70

the same as P_A values for sequential exchanges. For example, in Br222, when simultaneous, P_A = 4.24 for both exchanges, but when exchanges are sequential P_A = 5 for the first exchange and P_A = 4.13 for the second. For small branches, the central position benefits more when exchanges are sequential. But for larger branches, overall payoff is greater when exchanges are simultaneous.

Experiments reported by Patton and Willer (1990) offer partial support for these formulations. They studied inclusively connected 3-Branches and 5-Branches. These experiments used exactly the same designs as employed in the null and exclusionary branches reported earlier but for the condition needed to produce inclusive connection. Inclusive connection was produced by requiring the central position to complete exchanges in all relations before points were gained. In the 3-Branch the central A needed to complete three exchanges to score points, and in the 5-Branch A needed to complete all five. Since, as in all designs, subjects were paid by points earned, the inclusively connected central position had a strong incentive to complete all exchanges.

As predicted, the peripherals gained more favorable exchange ratios than the center. Also as predicted, the effect of inclusion was greater in the 5-Branch than in the 3-Branch. Furthermore, in all experimental runs, the low power central subject was more active than the high power peripherals. Although the inclusively connected central subject continually tried to engage them, peripherals initially refused to negotiate. Then, with only a few seconds remaining, all exchanges were completed at nearly the same time. Since exchanges were effectively simultaneous, in Br333 resistance predicts P_A = 3.81, but the average P_A = .281 was observed. In Br555, resistance predicts P_A = 3.30, but mean P_A = .265 was observed. In both cases, the observed effect of inclusion was greater than the predicted effect. This discrepancy may have been due to use of the face-to-face design. Chapter 8 reports results for inclusion experiments where subjects interacted using networked PCs. In those experiments exchange ratios much closer to predictions were observed.

By altering type of connection at the central position, a full range of contrasting effects has been shown. For the inclusive branch, power is at the periphery. For the exclusive branch, power is centralized. The null connected branch is equal power throughout. These contrasts show that there is no *general tendency* for power centralization in unilateral monopolies. More generally, no necessary association exists between shape of structure and power. The distribution of power is not determined by one structural condition but by two acting together. Shape and type of connection jointly determine power. As seen in later chapters, this joint determination holds, not just for simple branches, but across all exchange networks

Furthermore, altering the type of connection at the central position has effects that differ in degree. The effect of inclusion is substantially weaker than exclusion, while null has no effect at all. Exclusion has the greater effect because (1) the resistance of *both* central and peripherals are affected and (2) iteration sequentially produces greater and greater effects on both. As a result, exchange ratios become more and more extreme. The effect of inclusion is weaker because (1) only the resistance of the central and not the peripherals is affected and (2) there is no iteration. Unlike exclusion, the history of earlier negotiations or exchanges has no effect whatsoever. Null connection is different from both inclusion and exclusion. There is no null effect because the resistances of central and peripheral are unaltered from the dyad.

STRUCTURAL POWER AND COERCION

Unlike exchange, where power must be structurally produced, coercive relations are power relations. Whereas isolated exchange relations are equipower, isolated coercive relations have high and low power positions. Muggers, who are coercers, exercise power over their coercee victims, gaining valuable resources through force threat. In Chapter 2, it was seen that coercive relations are power relations because confrontation is more costly for the coercee than for the coercer. Resistance relates the specific difference in Pcon values to the coercer's ability to extract a particular quantity of value from the coercee. Coercive relations are power relations, but structures can affect power in coercion.

This section uses resistance to show how the conditions of the coercive relation and the conditions of structures *interact* to affect the amount of power exercised. Three kinds of centralized coercive structures are modeled here. In the first model, the structure does not affect the amount of power exercised. This kind of coercive structure is *structurally equivalent* to *null* connected exchange branches. The second model is a strong coercive power structure in which structural conditions increase the amount of power exercised. Strong power coercive structures are *structurally equivalent* to strong power exchange structures, and the two have similar processes. In the third model, relational power and structural power work in different directions. These are "coercee central structures" where the power of the coercive relation is decreased by the structure. These are also structurally equivalent to strong power exchange structures.

Coalitions form to oppose power exercised in structures. The final part of this section examines the effect of coalition formation on coercive power. Low power actors in strong power structures can act together to reduce or eliminate

Figure 3.9
A Centralized Coercive Structure

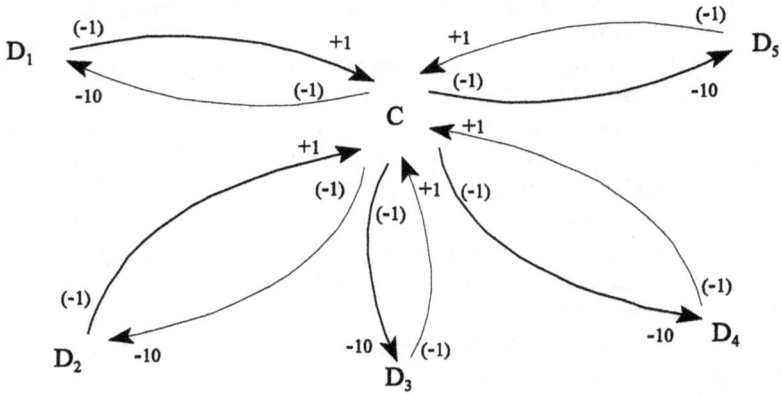

the power exercised over them. A central question for research on coalition formation is whether collective action countervails only structural power or whether relational power is also affected.

Power in Null and Strong Coercive Structures

To build the coercive structure shown in Figure 3.9, five of the coercive relations introduced in Chapter 2 were connected at C, the coercer's position. The negative sanction acts independently in each relation: it eliminates the value of all D's 10 resources at a cost of only one to C. The initial conditions for each of the relations are:

$$P_C\text{max} = 9 \qquad\qquad P_D\text{max} = 0$$
$$P_C\text{con} = -1 \qquad\qquad P_D\text{con} = -10$$

$$P_C = \frac{9 - P_C}{P_C - (-1)} = \frac{0 - P_D}{P_D - (-10)} = R_D$$

and $P_C = -P_D$. So $P_C = 4.5$ and $P_D = -4.5$. That is, resistance predicts that the coercer's threat to transmit the negative sanction results in the coercee sending 4.5 positive sanctions to C, almost one-half of its resources. Since the negative works independently in each relation, the solution for the dyad holds for each relation in the structure. This independence is structurally equivalent to the null exchange branch. We can call it the null coercive structure.

I now define the rate of coercive exploitation. The ratio of resources sent to the cost of receiving the negative can be termed the rate of coercive exploitation or Cx. Since the size of the threat was -10 and the value of resources sent was -4.5, $Cx = -4.5/-10 = .45$.

How many negative sanctions does C need to extract $Cx = .45$ in the five relations of the Figure 3.9 structure? Since five relations are connected, C holds five negative sanctions, one for each peripheral. But are all five needed? Assume that C negotiates first with D_1, reaches an agreement, and gains four to five positive sanctions. Now C turns to D_2, negotiates, and again gains four to five. Now only three Ds remain, but C still holds all five negative sanctions—certainly two more than needed. More generally, as long as C's threat is believed, resistance asserts that any D will transmit four to five sanctions and the negative is not transmitted. Because the pool of negative sanction resources is not used up, in theory C needs only one negative sanction to extract the resources from five Ds.

Experiments support the assertion that C does not need five negative sanctions to effectively extract positives in the five relations of the null coercive structure. In the 5-Branch null coercive structure, the C was allocated only two negative sanctions. Yet an average $Cx = .538$ was observed for 5-Branch null coercive structures—slightly higher than the $Cx = .45$ predicted by resistance. In the experiments, coercer and coercees bargained to compromise at the medial Cx value. Thus the interaction process in the null coercive structure was like the interaction process in the null exchange structure. Would C have been as successful with only one negative sanction? That question was not investigated, but it is worthy of future study.

Now the null coercive structure is changed into a strong coercive structure by changing confrontation of the coercer from a cost to a benefit. Above $P_C$con $= -1$: there is a cost of one to transmit the negative sanction. Now let $P_C$con $= 9$ so that the C initially holds two negatives, each of which gives a payoff of nine when transmitted. In the experiments, this payoff was produced by allowing the C to confiscate the 10 positives held by the D who received the negative. That is, $P_C$con $= 10 - 1 = 9$: C gained the 10 valued resources by confiscation at the cost of one for transmission of the negative. Since confrontation is affected by confiscation, we can call this the con-sanction. For the Ds, however, the effect of receiving the con-sanction is to lose the value of the 10 resources held. Note that the effect on D of the con-sanction is exactly the same as the effect of receiving the negative sanction of the null structure.

We now have a strong coercive power structure because each D knows, as we do, that the C is indifferent between transmitting the con-sanction and receiving nine positives. But the D prefers to transmit the nine and retain one than to receive the con-sanction and retain nothing. As a result, there is an iteration process, with Cx moving to the .9 extreme favoring C. Note that Cx was measured only in the relations in which the con-sanction was not transmitted.

The strong power coercive structure is *structurally equivalent* to the strong power exchange structure. In exchange, the central position chose which two of five of the peripherals would receive zero from exclusion. It was this choice that produced rivalry among the peripherals; they competed to avoid exclusion. In coercion, the central position also chose which two of five peripherals would

Figure 3.10
A Coercee Central Structure

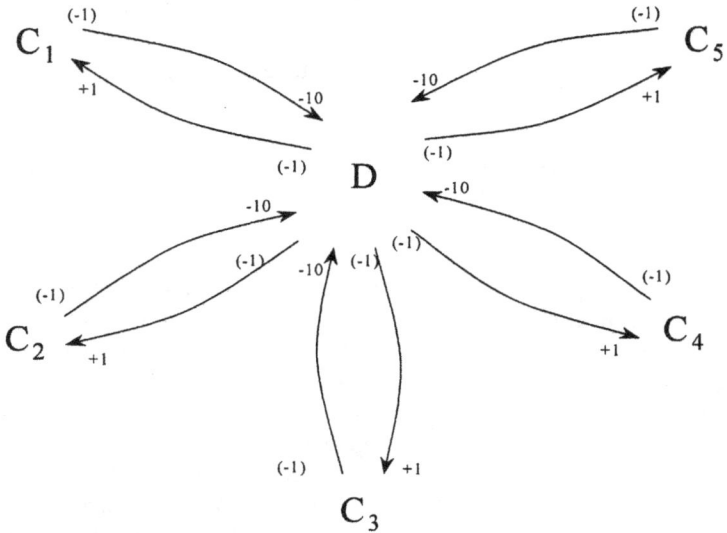

receive zero, but now from receiving the negative. This choice also produced rivalry among the peripherals, which competed to avoid receiving the con-sanction. These are the similarities that generated the iteration process through which power was driven to the maximum in both structures.

There is a difference between the two. In the strong power exchange structure, the central position had to exclude two peripherals and that exclusion was cost-less. In the coercive structure, the C could choose whether to send the negative, but, if it was sent, the C gained. In another design for a strong coercive structure, the C did not gain from transmitting negatives but was required to transmit a minimum of two. Here the coercive structure is again equivalent to the strong exchange structure. And for this design the central position's payoffs at agree-ment and confrontation are like those of the central position in the exchange structure.

The strong power coercive structure was investigated in the lab. The mode, median, and mean Cx were, respectively, .9, .9, and .85, with the mean being lower because there was a short iteration process. Again these values indicate that the coercive structure was strong.

Now consider strong coercee central structures. Here relational power and structural power work in different directions. As a result, Cx, the rate of coercive exploitation, is decreased by the structure. An example is displayed in Figure 3.10. Relative to the previous figure, the coercive relations have been reversed such that there is now just one central D and five peripheral Cs. For this struc-ture, D can make deals with only three of the five Cs, and none of the Cs can transmit negatives to the D until D agrees to enter their "domain of coercion." A rational D will negotiate agreements with three Cs and only then enter their domains of coercion. Since two of five Cs are excluded, the coercee central network is structurally equivalent to the strong exchange structure and to the strong coercive structures above. For experiments on these structures, Cx values approached the minimum of zero, which was optimal for the central D.

News of coercee central structures is heard almost every day when capital uses its mobility to exploit political states. For example, when the automotive company BMW announced that it planned to build an assembly plant in the United States, state governments competed for it to be located within their boundaries. South Carolina's winning bid abated state and local taxes and added a number of special services, including an expanded airport. Whereas now BMW is subject to the coercive power of the state, BMW's negotiations prior to arriving negated and even reversed the state's power of coercion. Such is the power of strong central coercee structures. The power of capital over the state is not new. According to Weber, the power gained through mobility by capital was a necessary condition for the rise of capitalism in Europe ([1918] 1968, p. 352).

Collective Action and Countervailing Power

Here I focus on the effect collective action has on the strong coercive power structure.[11] In that structure there is a collective good, which the Ds could receive. The good is the difference between the payoffs received when Ds do not act collectively and the payoffs when they do. For example, assume that, when acting collectively, each D sends only five positive sanctions to C, not the nine sent when acting individually. Then the collective good, $Gc = -5 - (-9) = 4$. Because only five, not nine, sanctions are sent, each D benefits by four points. The four are a *collective* good because they are gained only if the Ds act collectively.

All experiments had two parts. The first part was already discussed above. Experimental conditions isolated D subjects from one another blocking collective action and power developed to the maximum. In the second part, one of two forms of collective action were allowed, each in a different set of experiments.

In "Collective Resistance" the Ds are allowed to share information. By sharing information, Ds are able to develop a common policy for dealing with C. For example, the Ds could agree upon the number of positive sanctions each would give to C if C agreed not to send con-sanctions. This policy blocks iteration, changing the coercive structure from strong to null. But there is no assurance that the Ds will succeed, for they have no way to enforce this agreement within the group. Without enforcement, some D may free ride and make a better offer to the C. If more Ds free ride, better and better offers are made, and the structure iterates to the maximum power exercise by the C. *Here, free riding and iteration are the same processes.*

To predict the rate of coercive exploitation, I assume that the Ds' collectivity has blocked iteration such that they will bargain to compromise with the C. Given their unity, I aggregate five Ds to form a single actor, but I assume that the C can negotiate in sequence with one and then another D. Since C negotiates in sequence, its two con-sanctions are not used up. As a result, the two have the effect of five on the Ds. The aggregated conditions are:

$$P_C\text{max} = 45 \qquad\qquad P_D\text{max} = 0$$

$$P_C\text{con} = 18 \qquad\qquad P_D\text{con} = -50$$

$$R_C = \frac{45 - P_C}{P_C - 18} = \frac{0 - P_D}{P_D + 50} = R_D$$

and since $P_C = -P_D$, for the aggregated actors, $P_D = -29.22$ and $P_C = 29.22$. Dividing by five, for each D, $P_D = -5.84$ and $Cx = .584$. The collective good is the difference produced by the collective action: $C_G = 9 - 5.84 = 3.16$. Each Ds retains 3.16 more resources as a result of acting collectively. The rate of coercive exploitation is decreased from the maximum because collective action has blocked iteration.

Normative Resistance offers more effective modes of organization to the Ds than did Collective Resistance. Ds can again share information to develop a common policy toward C. But now two further capabilities are added. First, Ds are allowed to pool resources after all C–D negotiations are competed. Pooling allows Ds who receive the con-sanction from C to be compensated so that they do not earn zero that round. Nevertheless, this compensation is not required by the experimental design. Sanctioned Ds will be compensated only if the other Ds choose to do so. Second, after C–D negotiations are complete, each D can send a negative sanction to another D. When any D receives negatives from *two* other Ds, the resources held are eliminated. The effect of the sanctioning condition could be to enforce agreements to suppress free riding in C–D relations and to institute resource sharing. But the experimental design requires no D to send negatives. So agreements will be enforced only if at least two Ds choose to do so.

The Normative Resistance group is much better organized than the Collective Resistance group, and now C's two con-sanctions can do only the work of two. Again I aggregate the Ds to a single actor, and the new initial conditions are:

$$P_C\text{max} = 45 \qquad\qquad P_D\text{max} = 0$$

$$P_C\text{con} = 18 \qquad\qquad P_D\text{con} = -20$$

$$R_C = \frac{45 - P_C}{P_C - 18} = \frac{0 - P_D}{P_D + 20} = R_D$$

and since $P_C = -P_D$, for the aggregated actors, $P_D = -19.15$ and $P_C = 19.15$. Dividing by five, for each D, $P_D = -3.83$. The rate of coercive exploitation here is $Cx = .383$, which is lower than $Cx = .584$ for the Collective Resistance group because, being better organized, the Ds confront the C together and not in sequence.

Should the Ds negotiate with the C, compromise, and send an average 3.83 positive sanctions each, or should they send nothing? The predicted loss to the five Ds at equal resistance, $P_D = -19.15$, is very close to $P_D = -20$, which is the loss suffered if the Ds were to send nothing but receive the C's two con-sanctions. When the Ds send nothing, $Cx = 0$. Sending nothing can be termed the revolutionary policy. The payoff difference between compromise and revolution is very small. If the Ds are indifferent, groups are balanced on a knife edge. Some groups will compromise and $Cx = .383$ is predicted, while others will revolt and $Cx = 0$ is predicted.

Experiments were divided into two parts. The first part where collective action was blocked was reported above: mean observed $Cx = .85$ overall. An average rate that high means that the $Cx = .9$ maximum power of C over the Ds was attained well before the end of the first part. In the second part, one of the two types of groups could form. For the Collective Resistance group, mean observed $Cx = .588$, which is very close to the predicted $Cx = .584$. For Normative Resistance, one group pursued a purely revolutionary strategy. The Cs sent no positive sanctions, and the C always transmitted both con-sanctions. So $Cx = 0$. In a second group, the Ds compromised with C on the first round and then changed to a revolutionary strategy. For that experiment as a whole, mean $Cx = .044$. Two other groups bargained to compromise in early rounds and later were revolutionary: their mean $Cx = .233$.

These results indicate that collective action countervails power in strong coercive power structures. Collective action based on information sharing only—Collective Resistance—was able to block iteration such that the structure was changed from strong to null. Bargaining replaced iteration. Power was still exercised by the C, but that power exercise was relational power, not structural power. The better organized Normative Resistance groups also changed the structure from strong to null and blocked iteration. In addition, some groups chose the revolutionary strategy, a strategy that also eliminated relational power. That relational power was completely blocked is clearly indicated by the fact that no positive sanctions were sent in spite of C's threats. C gained nothing from the Ds in the second part of the experiment. And C would have gained nothing at all but for resources confiscated by sending the two con-sanctions.

CONCLUSION

In this chapter, resistance and types of connection are employed to predict activity in simple branch networks. Different types of connection produce very different effects. When branches are exclusively connected, power is centralized.

Exchange ratios move to the extreme favoring the central actor. When branches are null connected, relations are unaffected. Since exchange relations in isolation are equipower, null connected branches are equipower throughout. Inclusive connection reverses the power distribution of exclusion. For inclusion, power is at the periphery such that exchange ratios favor peripherals over the central actor.

For each type of connection, resistance predicts distinct dynamics. In exclusive branches, power increases through iteration. In iteration peripheral actors, seeking to avoid exclusion, make better and better offers to the center. The effect is to drive the exchange ratio to the extreme of maximal power exercise of the center over the periphery. From the outset, the resistance of central and all peripheral actors at agreement is numerically lower than resistance of corresponding actors in the null structure, and, as the iteration process goes forward, resistance declines to reach zero when power is maximal. These values suggest that time taken for agreements will initially be short and will become shorter and shorter as iteration moves exchange ratios to the extreme. Resistance also predicts that iteration will be more rapid when information is complete than when it is restricted. Furthermore, when all actors know the deals in all relations, the low power peripheral actors are more active in this power process than is the high power central actor.

In null connected branches, central and peripheral actors bargain to compromise at medial exchange ratios. Exchange ratios are never near the extreme, and resistance is not successively dissolved here as it is in exclusive structures where iteration is observed. To the contrary, at the point of compromise, the resistance of all actors is much higher than in exclusively connected branches. High resistance implies extended negotiations. Experiments show that bargaining in null branches takes substantially longer than iteration in exclusive branches. Actors in null branches exchange at equal power: activity is high at both center and periphery.

Negotiations in inclusively connected branches tend to stall. The reason that they stall is not a heightened value of resistance. To the contrary, resistance at the point of settlement is lower here than in null branches. So bargaining should take less time. But the interest situation across peripherals ensures that bargaining will be delayed. A deadlock occurs when peripherals learn that the one who exchanges last gains the best deal. Seeking to exchange last delays bargaining to the end of the negotiation period. In face-to-face experiments, peripherals simply did not respond to the entreaties of the center until the last seconds. Like exclusive branches, high activity is associated with low power. Here power is at the periphery; the central is low power and is far more active.

Coercive relations are power relations, as are some coercive structures. The coercer central in a branch, which is structurally equivalent to a strong power exchange branch, has both relational power and structural power. Illustrating their equivalence, the strong power coercive branch also has an iteration process. As a result of that process, the rate of coercive exploitation moves to the extreme. Collective action affects power in strong coercive power branches. The least cohesive collectivity eliminated the effect of structural power but were still subject to relational power. The more cohesive collectivities at their best eliminated both structural and relational power. When both relational and structural power were eliminated, low power coercees sent no positive sanctions and the rate of coercive exploitation was $Cx = 0$.

Two further coercive structures were considered. One was structurally equivalent to null connected exchange branch. As predicted by resistance, experiments showed that the null coercive branch had relational power but no structural power. For the last structure considered, the relation was reversed such that there was one coercee in the center and five peripheral coercers. This was a strong coercee central structure. The coercee made deals with only three of five, and two coercers were excluded. Here relational power and structural power worked in opposite directions so that the rate of coercive exploitation declined toward $Cx = 0$.[12]

Taken together, the investigations of exchange and coercive structures suggest that the problem of predicting outcomes in structures, even substantially more complex structures, may be generally tractable. Here the complexity faced in generating predictions was *not* proportional to the size of the structure. For example, structures that contain multiple relations are not substantially more difficult to solve than individual relations. That difficulty in theory does not increase with size is a remarkable quality. By contrast, in game theory, as von Neuman and Morgenstern gloomily point out, "The combinatorial complications of the problem . . . increase tremendously with every increase in the number of players" (1944, p. 13). Even today, three-person games are much more complex than their equivalent two-person counterparts, and four-person games are substantially more complex than three. That the same does not appear to be true for NET/ET suggests that a general theory of social structures is possible.

In this chapter two formulations were central to generating predictions: type of connection and resistance. At the level of structure, type of connection specifies conditions that span relations at a node. Each connection type has clear implications for the application of resistance. At the level of relations, resistance predicts processes and outcomes that are generated by actors in pursuit of their interests. Spanning levels of analysis, connection and resistance offer an array of predictions that have been supported by experiments.

Elementary Theory is distinguished from other social theories by the development of formulations at different levels—structure, relation, and actor—which form an integrated whole for prediction and explanation. In Markovsky's terms, Elementary Theory together with its exchange component, Network Exchange Theory, is a *multilevel* theory (1987). It is also a *modular* theory: new formulations can be plugged in at any level.

Alternatively, one set of formulations can be unplugged and different formulations plugged in. For example, the actors considered up to now have been forward-looking. They are rational maximizers who compromise at equiresistance. Unplug those and plug in backward-looking actors. Let the backward-looking actors make offers better to self when included and offers better to others when excluded. Markovsky's "X-Net," a network simulator, uses backward-looking actors (see Markovsky 1995). X-Net gives exchange ratios for an array of exclusive and null connected networks, which are quite similar to ratios predicted with resistance for forward-looking actors. Why they are similar is yet to be explained.

The following chapter extends Network Exchange Theory beyond branches to an array of complex equipower and strong power networks. Complex networks contain more than one node which has multiple relations. In complex networks, type of connection alone does not determine which positions are advantaged and which are not. For example, when all nodes exchange only once, the 5-Line A–B–C–B–A has three adjacent exclusively connected positions. All three cannot be high power positions. The next chapter develops the Graph-theoretic Power Index (GPI) to locate advantaged and disadvantaged positions in complex networks.

NOTES

1. In network terms, all branches are "trees" because they contain no "cycles." A cycle is a path from a node which returns to that node.

2. This presentation parallels Willer (1992). Barry Markovsky suggested the use of sentenial connectives in defining the types.

3. Chapter 4 introduces the idea of network "domains" between which exchanges are independent. Null connected nodes like A in Figure 3.2a are at the boundary of network domains. Each null connected node is in as many domains as it has connected relations. For the null connected 3-Branch, this means that A's three relations are all in different domains. With the introduction of the concept of domain, resistance is applied independently in each domain. In the 3-Branch of Figure 3.2, each of the three relations is treated as a dyad and solved independently by setting R_A equal to R_B. Since each relation is solved independently, R_A (null) is no longer used. Nevertheless, R_A (null) = R_A in the branch is consistent with—and supportive of—the idea that exchanges between domains are independent.

4. It was suggested elsewhere (Willer 1987) that face-to-face experiments are affected by "symbolic sanctions" employed by subjects. Peripherals in these experiments asserted that the one acting in the center was "greedy" and "selfish." This "negative convergence" is a means of enforcing norms, which Southard (1981) also finds in tribal societies. Competitive bidding in the strong exchange branches tended to follow blocked negative convergence. There outcomes were much more favorable to subjects in the center, but no one asserted that they were selfish or greedy. The ExNet system used in Chapter 8 also blocked negative convergence, and there exchange ratios for null connected branches were very close to predicted values.

5. Branches can be strong power when peripherals exchange more than once. More generally, any branch is strong power iff the sum of M exchange opportunities for peripherals is greater than M for the center. This is a more general specification than any given in the opening paragraph of the section. For example, it is now possible that no

peripheral is entirely excluded, but it is necessarily the case that some peripheral(s) will not be able use all exchange opportunities with the center. Thus there is still exclusion and, consequently, competition among peripherals to exchange with the central position.

6. This result is like that found for the outside offer late in Chapter 2.

7. The "time" referred to here is clock time. This is not the same as "t" above, which refers to steps of the iteration process. For example, in Figure 3.4 equiresistance takes fewer iterations and thus initially rises more rapidly than zero resistance when measured across t iterations. Yet equiresistance takes longer in clock time. Any process that takes longer in clock time can be preempted by the alternative process that takes less time.

8. Experiments in Poland, prior to the revolution, gave a mean of $P_A = 7.6$ and a mode of $P_A = 8$. Power developed more rapidly in Poland but did not stay at the extreme as consistently as in the United States.

9. For an analysis of different rates of power development, see Brennan (1981).

10. Inclusion can be mixed with exclusion or null. Chapter 8 explains how predictions are generated for these compound connections and reports later research on inclusive-exclusive and inclusive-null branches.

11. The research from which this discussion is drawn is reported in Willer (1987). There the effect of Collective Resistance and Normative Resistance groups on two types of strong coercive power structures and one coercive null structure are detailed. As in the discussion here, the main effect of both types of collective action was to eliminate iteration changing structures from strong to null.

12. One type of structure not considered places the coercer in the center of an inclusively connected branch. The coercer must complete deals with all peripherals in order to profit from any one. The prediction from resistance is straightforward. Here Cx will be smaller than in the coercive structure, which is equivalent to the null exchange branch. Experiments on this structure would add to the scope in which Elementary Theory has been tested.

Chapter 4

Power Relations

Preface
David Willer

When two theories have similar scope but offer competing predictions, empirical evidence alone may not be enough to resolve the dispute in favor of one or the other (Lakatos 1970a, 1970b). Evidence can be explained away. But if it can be shown that one theory offers predictions that are self-contradictory and its competitor does not, the dispute is resolved in favor of the competitor. Galileo ([1638] 1954) was the first to resolve a dispute between two theories by showing (1) that predictions from his theory of falling bodies were superior to predictions from Aristotle's and (2) that some of Aristotle's predictions were self-contradictory. In this chapter, a dispute between two theories is resolved in exactly the same way.

At this point in the development of Network Exchange Theory, the research focus changes in two regards. The first change concerns the kinds of networks investigated. Previous work focused on simple N-Branch networks where only one position has multiple connections to others. Now "complex" exchange networks where two or more positions have multiple connections are also considered. For example, the $A–B–C–B–A$ (L-5) network is complex: three positions, B, C, and B, are each connected to two others.

Second, the networks now being studied do not have sanction flows. Here we follow Stolte's design where the division of a pool of resources is substituted for exchange. Each pair of connected positions has a pool to divide. Experimental applications of power-dependence theory were always to profit pool networks. Stolte's design is adopted here so that the "Graph-theoretic Power Index" (GPI), a new formulation of Network Exchange Theory, can be tested against power dependence's "Vulnerability."

Furthermore, in Stolte's design, a condition here called the 1-exchange rule limits each position to dividing, at most, a single pool. Power-dependence theory did not consider the effect of variations from the 1-exchange rule on the distribution of power. In the chapter that follows, however, the scope of the Graph-theoretic Power Index is not limited to 1-exchange networks. By applying and testing it where some positions exchange twice, the effect of the 1-exchange rule on the distribution of power is found.

Structural-level procedures predict resource pool divisions by locating power positions. Power-dependence theory's Vulnerability is the first structural-level procedure (Cook, Emerson, Gilmore, and Yamagishi 1983). The Graph-theoretic Power Index, being also a structural-level procedure, competes with Vulnerability. When research considered only simple networks, no structural-level procedure was needed. In N-branches only the central position can be high power, and the central position will be high power if it excludes any peripheral. In complex networks, however, that a position can exclude others is only a necessary condition of power: it is not sufficient. Thus arises the need for a structural-level procedure.

Power Relations in Exchange Networks
Barry Markovsky, David Willer, and
Travis Patton

Many theories address the problem of how a social structure affects the experiences and behaviors of its members. This section offers a network exchange theory designed to solve this problem. Previous research has shown that the nature and outcomes of negotiations among individual or corporate actors can be inferred from their network positions. The impact of this research has been limited because its theory does not enable the researcher to locate power positions in networks. We offer a theory that is both consistent with all previously reported experimental research and is generalized to conditions not considered by other formulations. In addition to supporting derived hypotheses pertaining to network-based power, our experiments demonstrate, among other things, that certain unstable networks break down to form stable substructures and that some networks contain overlapping but autonomous domains of power and exchange.

INTRODUCTION

Although no single exchange theory dominates the social sciences, a fairly coherent social exchange perspective exists. In this perspective, social structures and processes impinge on and emerge from resource and sanction transfers between individuals and/or collectivities.[1] Recently, some theories have moved beyond two-party exchange contexts to focus on networks of exchange relations. As structural theories, network exchange theories attempt to explain how macro-properties bear upon micro-units within structures. Concretely, they try to show how network structures affect the power of actors to extract valued resources in their exchanges with others.

We propose and test a theory that predicts relative power for network positions. In so doing, we address several structural phenomena, including the breakdown of larger networks into smaller parts and the emergence of positions that simultaneously have one level of power in one part of the network and a different level in another. Our theory is further intended to provide higher levels of rigor, power, and specificity than are found in earlier approaches. We find that each such technical advancement produces a manifold increase in the array of potential applications.

Whenever a person or group negotiates with another person or group over the allocation of valued resources, a minimal social exchange network exists. More elaborate (i.e., nondyadic) structures form when one member is involved in two or more such relations. For example, college students Al, Bea, and Cleo each want to date, and norms prohibit them from dating more than one person at a time. Suppose that Bea and Cleo both vie for Al's attention and have no other prospects, while Al would be happy to date either Bea or Cleo. This creates a B–A–C network, where A(l) may "negotiate" with B(ea) and C(leo), but only date one of them. Such circumstances actually do tip the balance of power (People 1979) in dating relations: A is able to make greater demands than his chosen partner and generally has greater influence in the relationship. But if B or C develops dating interests with a responsive D, A loses his structural advantage.

This type of analysis is applicable in other areas such as international, auctioneer-bidder, retailer-consumer, and manufacturer-retailer relations. A good example is the control that a manufacturer may impose upon retailer marketing strategies (Skinner and Guiltinan 1986). Suppose Ascii Ugetty (A) is the sole manufacturer of a line of computer games. Big Bytes (B), Chips-R-Down (C), and Data Dump (D) are independent retailers that want to carry the line. Even with fixed wholesale prices, A's position affords it power over B, C, and D. Skinner and Guiltinan found that retailer activities such as advertising expenditures, sales force training, and credit policies were under manufacturer control to a greater extent when retailers had no alternative suppliers. So if D can obtain the product from E-Z Access (E), A loses its ability to control D's policies. A may have to "outbid" E just to keep D's business.

Our purpose is to understand the structural logic manifested in all such exchange networks—a logic unbounded by empirical content. If the experiences of actors depend on their positions, this suggests a structural determination of behavior. At issue in this chapter is the logic of that determination.

AN EARLIER APPROACH

Recent work by Cook, Emerson, Gillmore, and Yamagishi (1983) clearly overlaps with our own in scope.[2] They showed that their approach could anticipate power distributions in some cases where alternative measures failed. Based on Emerson (1972b), Cook et al. (1983) defined *exchange network* as

(1) a set of actors (either natural persons or corporate groups), (2) a distribution of valued resources among those actors, (3) for each actor a set of exchange opportunities with

other actors in the network, (4) a set of historically developed and utilized exchange opportunities called exchange relations, and (5) a set of network connections linking exchange relations into a single network structure. (p. 277)

The set of exchange relations is a subset of exchange opportunities, and actors in the system are assumed to be committed to exchanging within their relations, to the exclusion of alternative opportunities. The concept of *connection* permits networks to be considered from relations. Formally

Two exchange relations between actors A–B and actors A–C are connected to form the minimal network B–A–C to the degree that exchange in one relation is contingent on exchange (or nonexchange) in the other relation. (a) The connection is positive if exchange in one relation is contingent on exchange in the other. (b) The connection is negative if exchange in one relation is contingent on nonexchange in the other. (p. 277)

A negative connection exists if *B* and *C* can substitute as providers of *A*'s resources. The authors cite as examples dating and friendship networks. In the case of a positive connection, *A* cannot benefit without exchanges from *B and C*. This is true if *A* is a brokerage agent or if *B* and *C* are assembly-line workers who must exchange their labor for pay before the firm (*A*) can benefit.

Cook et al. (1983) define *power* as "In any dyadic exchange relation $A_x:B_y$ (where A and B are actors, and x and y are resources introduced in exchange), the power of A over B is the potential of A to obtain favorable outcomes at B's expense" (p. 284). *Dependence* is given as: "The dependence of A on B in a dyadic exchange relation is a joint function (1) varying directly with the value of y to A, and (2) varying inversely with the availability of y to A from alternate sources" (pp. 284–85).

By *informally* applying power-dependence ideas, Cook et al. developed several hypotheses predicting relative power for positions in several types of negatively connected networks. Toward the end of their paper, a network *vulnerability* (V) method was suggested as a first step toward a formal procedure for predicting positions' relative power.

To determine *V* for the *B–A–C* network, assume that related actors negotiate over the division of 24 resource points and a 1-exchange rule creates the negative connection: *A* may exchange with *B* or *C* but not both in a given round. First, the maximum resource flow (MRF) for the network is calculated. *MRF* = 24 since, by the 1-exchange rule, only 24 points may be distributed per round. Next, the reduction in maximum flow (RMF) is calculated for each position by noting the effect of its removal on MRF. If *B* or *C* is removed, RMF = 0, since *A* may still exchange with the other. However, *RMFa* = 24. The network is the most vulnerable at *A*, and *A* is declared a power node.

Discussion

This general approach has been corroborated in several experiments, including those published by Cook et al. (1983), Stolte and Emerson (1977), and Cook

Figure 4.1
A "T"-Shaped Network (a), GPI Values (b), and GPI Values After the Break (c)

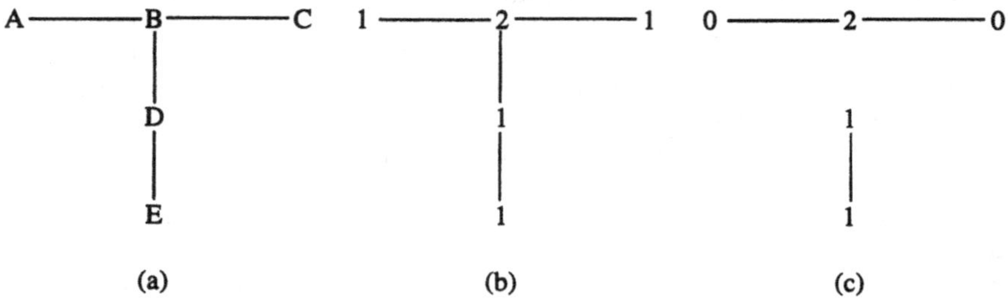

```
A ——— B ——— C    1 ——— 2 ——— 1    0 ——— 2 ——— 0
        |                  |                  |
        D                  1                  1
        |                  |                  |
        E                  1                  1

       (a)                (b)                (c)
```

and Emerson (1978). However, V has not been systematically tested. Moreover, Willer (1986) determined that V produces untenable predictions for some relatively simple networks such as that in Figure 4.1a. V predicts high power for B, D, and E. But under Cook et al.'s experimental conditions, high profit for D would entail low profit for B, E, or both. Although Cook, Gillmore, and Yamagishi (1986) described V as only "a preliminary notion," it still provided the only explicit basis for deriving hypotheses. Without it, predictions were informal and not fully determined by the theory.

Cook et al. (1986, p. 447) later proposed a modified V-measure. Network-wide dependence (D_N) weighs a position's RMF by the factor $(1 - CRMF)$, where CRMF is "no. of lines that need to be removed [for a position] to exercise power at its potential" divided by the number of lines connected to the position. By this measure, B in Figure 4.1 has higher power than D, and D higher power than A, C, and E. Although these predictions are tenable, they diverge from test results reported later in this chapter and their derivation is indeterminate.[3]

Many of Cook et al.'s methodological choices were neither necessitated nor precluded by their theory. For instance, negotiations took place over a series of rounds; each relation had its own resource pool; each pool was replenished before every round; exchange consisted of mutually agreed on pool divisions; there was a 1-exchange rule; resources did not move through positions; coalitions were prohibited; and actors had no information on negotiations in which they were not directly involved. At issue is whether the approach might have been falsified under alternative methodological conditions. Later we demonstrate that very different results are obtained under slightly different conditions.

A GRAPH-ANALYTIC THEORY

In his recent elaboration on the work of Cook and her associates, Marsden (1987) succinctly offered as unsolved problems several of the implications that may be drawn from our theory:

The difficulty in developing a more general measure is that an alternative exchange partner may be exploitable for two reasons: It may have few alternative relations or all of its alternatives (irrespective of how many in all are available) may be in a position to exploit others. The second condition of exploitability can lead to consideration of quite distal features of network structure. (p. 147, note 5)

Building on an earlier exchange formulation (Willer and Anderson 1981; Willer 1987), our graph-analytic approach recognizes both types of "exploitability" and specifies conditions under which distal network properties will influence proximal outcomes. We first present $p(1)$, an index for power in 1-exchange networks. This allows us to test our predictions against those of Cook et al. (1983, 1986). Next, $p(e)$, a generalized version, will be explicated and tested.

Conditions of Exchange

Power and resource distributions are affected not only by network shapes but also by the conditions under which exchanges transpire. The theory provides scope statements encompassing relatively broad conditions, some of which are later relaxed, others of which await future tests, theoretical extensions, and refinements. Scope conditions are not assumptions about human nature or frequencies of empirical circumstances. They are statements that, if satisfied (or approximated), commit the theory to critical examination and, if not satisfied, relieve it of any explanatory imperative (Walker and Cohen 1985).

Several important concepts must first be defined: *actors* are decision-making entities (e.g., organisms, collectivities, or even computer programs). *Positions* are network locations occupied by actors. A *relation* between two positions is an exchange opportunity for actors in those positions. In short, *actors* occupy *positions* linked by *relations*.[4] We will index both actors and positions using upper case letters and at times refer to them interchangeably.

Actor Conditions. Four conditions delimit actors' behavior: (1) all actors use identical strategies in negotiating exchanges; (2) actors consistently excluded from exchanges raise their offers; (3) those consistently included in exchanges lower their offers; and (4) actors accept the best offer they receive and choose randomly in deciding among tied best offers.

Condition 1, requiring identical strategies, is nearly always implicit in exchange theories. In tests and applications, however, it is generally sufficient that actors adopt functionally *similar* strategies. Condition 1 also asserts that actors negotiate, i.e., they make offers and adjust their subsequent offers in light of counter-offers they receive. Conditions 2 and 3 require that actors seek to enter exchange if previously denied and to improve outcomes beyond those previously obtained. Finally, condition 4 rules out a range of strategies that may drive up the offers of excluded parties.[5]

Position Conditions. These apply to positions and their relations: (5) each position is related to, and seeks exchange with, one or more other positions; (6) at the start of an exchange round, equal pools of positively valued resource units

Figure 4.2
A Seven-Position Network

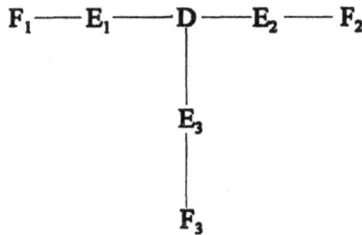

$$F_1 \text{———} E_1 \text{———} D \text{———} E_2 \text{———} F_2$$
$$|$$
$$E_3$$
$$|$$
$$F_3$$

are available in every relation; (7) two positions receive resources from their common pool if and only if they exchange; (8) each position exchanges with at most one other position per round.

Since isolates cannot exchange, Condition 5 omits them from consideration. Condition 6 reflects conditions in most prior research: a pool of *profit points* resides in every relation and is replenished with each new round. Condition 7 indicates that two actors will not exchange unless both benefit. Condition 8, relaxed later, asserts that actors may complete at most one exchange per round. This creates negative connections in a way that is consistent with all previously cited experimental research and Cook et al.'s (1983) simulations. It assumes that, for whatever reasons, actors only require a single exchange or are only able or permitted to complete a single exchange in a given round.[6]

The Graph-theoretic Power Index

Building upon simple arithmetic procedures, our Graph-theoretic Power Index (GPI) determines relative power for all positions in any network that meets the scope conditions.[7] As also implied in the work of Kuhn (1974), Cook et al. (1983), Bonacich (1987), Marsden (1983, 1987), and others, power is assumed to derive from the availability of alternative exchange relations, the unavailability of their relations' alternative relations, and so on. *Power* is then conceived as an unobservable, structurally determined potential for obtaining relatively favorable resource levels. *Power use*, as manifested in resource distributions, serves as an indicator of power. So while we theorize about potential power, we test our theory by observing its use.

The procedure for determining GPI involves counting path lengths. Thus network *B–A–C* has two one-paths, *A–B* and *A–C*. *B* and *C* are linked by a two-path. As explained later, path counting is greatly simplified by only counting the number of *nonintersecting* paths of each length stemming from a given position. Nonintersecting paths stemming from position *X* have only *X* in common. In Figure 4.2, for example, three nonintersecting two-paths stem from *D*, but only one nonintersecting two-path stems from E_1 (connecting with either E_2 or E_3).

An implication of this procedure is that it does not matter for X whether a position m steps away "branches" to one or a hundred positions $m + 1$ steps away. All that matters is *whether or not* there is a position $m + 1$ steps from X. This is a subtle, possibly nonintuitive, but incontrovertible assertion within our framework. The following example therefore bears careful study.

Imagine removing A and C from the Figure 4.1a network. D benefits greatly from the resulting three-actor chain: B and E must try to engage D, offering ever more favorable deals to D. *Now restore A.* B now has an alterative to bidding against E, but with E not bidding against E, D's advantage dissolves. Although D still has two alternatives, it cannot play B and E against each other and so all positions are on an equal footing. *Now restore C.* B now benefits because A and C will try to outbid each other for B's exchange. This presents no further disadvantage for D, however, who may still exchange with E on an equal basis.

Note that A and C are on intersecting two-paths from D. The creation of one of those two-paths changed the minimum relative power in D's relations from high to equal. *But the creation of the second two-path had no effect on this minimum.* If we further attached F, G, and H to position B, these added two-paths from D would still not affect the minimum relative power that D would enjoy. This shows why only one nonintersecting path of a given length is counted.

It may now be apparent that X's odd-length nonintersecting paths are advantageous, and even-length nonintersecting paths are disadvantageous. *Advantageous paths* either provide direct exchange alternatives (in the case of one-paths) or counteract the advantage-robbing effects of *disadvantageous* paths.

The GPI simply tallies the number of advantageous paths and subtracts the number of disadvantageous paths to determine each position's potential power. Position i's GPI under the 1-exchange condition is calculated as[8]

$$p(1)_i = \sum_{k=1}^{g} (-1)^{(k-1)} m_{ik} \qquad (4.1)$$
$$= m_{i1} - m_{i2} + m_{i3} - m_{i4} + \ldots \pm m_{ig}$$

and i's power relative to j is

$$p(1)_{ij} = p(1)_i - P(1)_j.$$

The function $(-1)^{(k-1)}$ produces $+$ signs for advantageous paths and $-$ signs for disadvantageous paths. These are attached to the m_{ik} values—the number of position i's nonintersecting paths of length k. For now we may suppress the number-of-exchanges parameter for $p(l)_i$ and refer to the index simply as p_i.

The values for g and m are obtained as follows:

m_{i1} is the number of one-paths stemming from position i, which is the same as the number of i's relations. In Figure 4.1a, for example, $m_{D1} = 2$.

m_{i2} is the number of nonintersecting two-paths from i. As shown in the earlier example, D has only one nonintersecting two-path, so $m_{D2} = 1$.

m_{i3} is the number of nonintersecting three-paths stemming from i; $m_{D3} = 0$.

The largest path of length k for which $m_{ik} > 0$ is the diameter (g) of the network. In Figure 4.1a, three-paths link A to E and C to E, hence, $g = 3$.

The final step is to combine the m_{ik}s: take m_{i1}, subtract m_{i2}, add m_{i3}, and so on. We find that $p_D = 2 - 1 + 0 = 1$. Figure 4.1b shows this value and the p_i values for the other four positions.[9]

Axioms and Theorems

In the statements below, "power" refers to p_{ij}, with i and j related.

AXIOM 1: given by Equation (4.1) above.

AXIOM 2: i seeks exchange with j if and only if i's power is greater than j's, or if i's power relative to j equals or exceeds that in any of i's other relations.

AXIOM 3: i and j can exchange only if each seeks exchange with the other.

AXIOM 4: if i and j exchange, then i receives more resources than j if and only if i has more power than j.

In Axiom 2, "i seeks exchange with j" means that i makes competitive offers to j (i.e., offers that compete with others that j receives). A more psychological interpretation would be "i makes offers that j seriously considers." The axiom first claims that this occurs if i's power is greater than j's. Further, even if i's power is less than j's, i will seek exchange with j if i's relative power is even lower in its other relations.[10] Note that Axiom 3 *does not* imply that two actors will exchange if they seek exchange with each other; actors may negotiate without exchanging. Finally, Axiom 4 asserts that potential power determines the use of power (i.e., GPI predicts final resource distributions).

Some of the theorems that can be derived from these axioms include

Theorem 1: If i has no alternative relations, then i seeks exchange with j.

Theorem 2: If i does not seek exchange with j *or* if j does not seek exchange with i, then i and j do not exchange.

Theorem 3: Actor i does not seek exchange with j if and only if i's power is less than j's or equal to j's and i has a better alternative to j.

Theorem 4: If i's power is less than or equal to j's and i has a better alternative to j, or if j's power is less than or equal to i's and j has a better alternative to i, then i and j will not exchange.

More intuitively, Theorem 1 claims that an actor in a position with only one relation will seek exchange via that relation, whatever its relative power. Theorem 2 is a logical variant of Axiom 3. Theorem 3 specifies the conditions under which an actor will not seek exchange via one of its relations. Theorem 4 predicts when a network will break at the i–j relation. It reveals that certain relations are expected to remain unused, leading some complex networks to break apart into smaller, stable subnetworks. When such a break occurs, power indices are recalculated within the resulting subnetworks. This is demonstrated in some of the applications below.

Applications

We have applied the GPI, axioms, and theorems to a large number of networks of varying shape and size. This small sampling demonstrates the use of the theory.

For the A–B dyad, $p_A = p_B = 1$. No position has a structural advantage. The same is true for positions on any even-length chain, as verified in computer simulation research (Markovsky 1987b). In general, however, the longer the chain, the more rounds transpire before the predicted power relations stabilize.

For the B–A–C network, $p_B = p_C = 1 - 1 = 0$ and $p_A = 2$. A's power advantage is 2 in both of its relations, while $p_{BA} = p_{CA} = -2$. For odd-length chains of any length, $p = 2$ for even positions and $p = 0$ for odd positions; low and high power positions alternate. This conforms with Cook et al.'s predictions and experimental results for the five-position chain and with our computer simulations for longer chains.[11] Similarly, in Figure 4.2, $p_F = 1 - 1 + 1 - 1 = 0$, $p_E = 2 - 1 + 1 = 2$, and $p_D = 3 - 3 = 0$. Thus the center and periphery have low power, and the off-center positions have high power. This also conforms with Cook et al.'s predictions and simulation results.

Returning to Figure 4.1, we find that a decomposition is predicted. Figure 4.1b shows the p_i values as initially calculated. Applying Theorem 4, however, since D's index is less than B's, and since E is a "better" alternative for D (because $p_E < p_B$), D and B are predicted not to exchange. Finally, Figure 4.1c shows the final p_i values recalculated for the resulting subnetworks.

Experiment 1

Since the scope of our theory appears to overlap with that of Cook et al., we compare our predictions with those derived from their measure. We tested the Figure 4.1 network. Based on our analysis, D–E will form an equal power dyad, the B–D relation will break, and B will have power over A and C. In contrast, Cook et al. (1986) order $B > D > (A, C, E)$ with no breaks predicted.

Method. Subjects were undergraduates at a large university. Before being taken to the laboratory, participants in a given session met as a group, received written instructions, and had any questions answered. In the research room connections among network positions were clearly marked, and, to limit collusion, temporary barriers separated positions among which exchange was prohibited. The setting minimally restricted the availability of information about the structure and the actions of others.[12]

Twenty-four counters were placed between related positions. These served as resources to be divided by mutual agreement, each valued at one profit point and worth 3 cents. Each position was limited to one agreement per round. Before starting, we emphasized that exchanges could only occur by mutual agreement between related positions, and long-term strategies were prohibited.

Experiments were organized by rounds, periods, and sessions. In all, five sessions were run, each with a different group of subjects. There were five periods per session, allowing each subject to occupy each position for one period before the session was over. Each period contained four negotiation rounds, each with a three-minute time limit. Each position's scores were announced after every round. At the close of a session, participants were paid according to points they obtained—around $5.00 on the average. This design produced a total of 100 rounds of negotiation.

Hypotheses. Below we present hypotheses derived from our theory, those obtained from Cook et al.'s (1986) D_N procedure, and the null hypothesis.

1. Our theory predicts that the network will break at the *B–D* relation, eliminating exchange between *B* and *D*. D_N provides no hypothesis in this regard. In contrast, if exchanges are distributed randomly in the network, *B* will turn to *D* one-third of the time, but half of those times *D* will turn to *E*. The null hypothesis, then, predicts .333 $\times$ .500 $\times$ 100 = 16.667 exchanges between *B* and *D*.

2. *B* will exercise power over *A* and *C*, so *B* will receive more points per exchange than *A* and *C*. The D_N hypothesis also predicts $B > (A, C)$. The null hypothesis predicts no difference in the point accumulations of *B*, *A*, and *C*.

3. The GPI indicates that *D* and *E* have equal power, and so should have a 12–12 division of points. D_N predicts that *D* will obtain higher profits than *E*. Our prediction can be falsified either by $D > E$, as D_N predicts, or by $E > D$.

4. *E*'s profits will exceed those of *A* and *C* since *E* is in an equipower dyad and the others are low power positions. The D_N and null hypotheses predict no profit differences among *E*, *A*, and *C*.

Results. In 100 negotiation rounds across five sessions, only three exchanges occurred between *B* and *D*.[13] The difference between this number and the null hypothesis of 16.667 was assessed with the *z*-test for proportions. The result, $z = 3.666$, $p < .0003$, supports Hypothesis 1 and refutes the null hypothesis.

Table 4.1 shows the average number of points per session for each position. *B* clearly obtained favorable exchange rates, above 19–5 in all but one session. The *t*-tests show that in every session, *B*'s mean profits were significantly above 12 (and, by necessity, *A*'s and *C*'s significantly below). The null hypothesis is rejected, and Hypothesis 2 and the D_N prediction are supported.

Table 4.1 shows that the mean *D–E* exchange rates for each session differed

Table 4.1
First Experiment: Profit by Position

	Position					TEST	
Session	E	D	A	B	C	t*	p
1	12.55	11.42	4.29	19.10	5.09	7.85	<.0005
2	12.45	11.58	8.56	15.33	8.25	2.01	<.025
3	12.00	12.00	3.29	20.95	3.29	3.50	<.0005
4	12.05	11.95	3.75	21.55	3.75	11.15	<.0005
5	11.80	12.20	4.17	19.16	4.17	5.77	<.0005

*The reported tests are for position B's actual profit points versus the null hypothesis of 12 profit points.

only slightly from the 12–12 split; t-tests indicate that none of these differences was statistically significant. Therefore, Hypothesis 3 is also confirmed and the D_N hypothesis rejected.

As for Hypothesis 4, the mean point total for position E was 12.12, A's was 4.81, and C's was 4.91. Combining session means for the latter two positions and testing against E's scores, $t = 7.552$, $p < .0005$. Hypothesis 4 is supported and the null and D_N hypothesis refuted.

In sum, this study provided strong support for the $p(1)$ measure as tested against its null hypotheses and the revised Vulnerability measure. In the next section we present $p(e)$, a generalization for *multi-exchange* networks, that is, networks in which actors exchange more than once per round.

DOMAINS OF POWER AND MULTI-EXCHANGE NETWORKS

Identifying Domains

The concept of *domain* simplifies GPI calculations in multi-exchange networks. Domains are independent subnetworks—independent in the sense that structural changes in one cannot affect power in another.

First, let e be the maximum number of *unique exchanges* that positions can make in a given round. Two exchanges are unique for i only if they involve different relations. To identify domains, we will need to distinguish e^+ positions and e^- positions: e^+ positions have more than e relations, and e^- positions have e or fewer. In Figures 4.3–4.5, e^+ positions are boxes, and e^- positions are circles.

There are two types of domains. A *dyadic domain* is two related e-positions. A *power domain* is a set of one or more related e^+ positions, along with all e^- positions related to any member of this set. Formally,

> DOMAINS: Given the set V of all positions on a path between i and j, i and j are in the same domain if and only if there exists a path such that either (1) $V = \{\}$, or (2) all members of V are e^+ positions.

Figure 4.3
Single Domain Lines

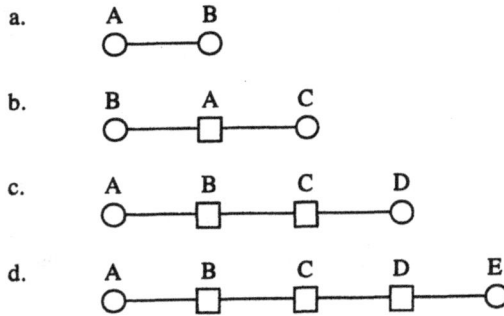

a.
A   B
○—————○

b.
B   A   C
○————□————○

c.
A   B   C   D
○————□————□————○

d.
A   B   C   D   E
○————□————□————□————○

For example, both positions in the one exchange network of Figure 4.3a are in the same domain since the set of positions (V) on the path connecting them is empty. They form a dyadic domain. Network 4.3b, in which $e = 1$, forms a single-power domain: all pairs of positions are either related or can be reached through a path containing only e^+ positions (boxes). Network 4.3c is also a single-power domain, and, as noted earlier, no position has a structural advantage. This shows that being an e^+ position is necessary but not sufficient to produce high power (Willer and Patton 1987). Network 4.3d also forms a single-power domain.

By comparing 4.3c to 4.3d, we can see how change in one part of the power domain can have distal effects. Note that 4.3d is the 4.3c network with E added to the D position. In 4.3c, A was in an equipower relation with B. But A becomes a low power position when E is attached. In fact, the relative power positions in all relations in the network change when E is added.

We can draw two implications at this point. (1) If there is differential power in a domain, then there is an e^+ position. This yields the useful contrapositive assertion: the absence of e^+ positions implies no power differentiation. So for power to exist in a domain (or in a network, for that matter), at least one position must have an excess of available partners. (2) All 1-exchange networks form single domains. The reason will be clear as we next show that when $e > 1$ a network can have multiple domains.

When $e > 1$, by the unique-exchange restriction, a position can exchange e times only if it has e or more relations. Some positions—those with fewer than e relations—can have effective maxima less than e. Since $e = 2$ in Figure 4.4a, for example, A can exchange twice, but B and C have effective maxima of one.

In Figure 4.4a, B–A–C now has two dyadic domains, (AB) and (AC); there is no core of one or more e^+ positions. By the assertion given above, since there are no e^+ positions, there is no power differentiation. This is reasonable since neither B nor C is excluded from exchanging with A in a given round. No

Figure 4.4
Multidomain Networks

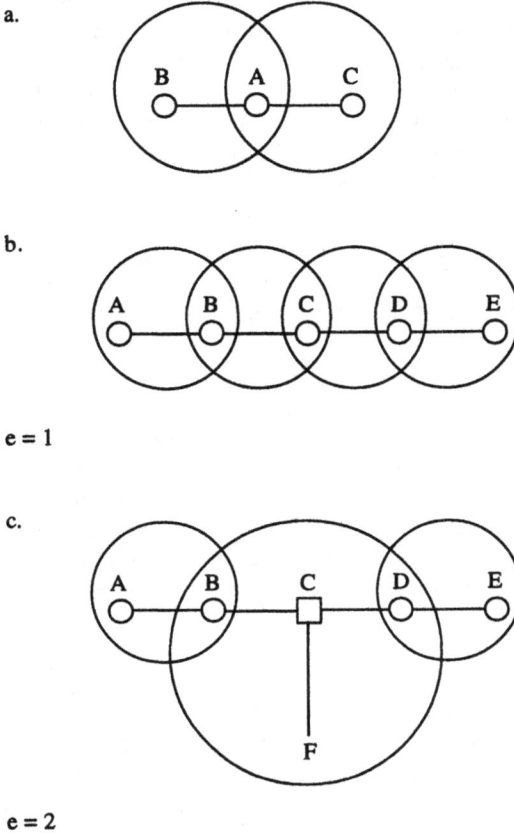

a.

b.

e = 1

c.

e = 2

position has excess exchange opportunities, and no position may garner favorable profit divisions. The same logic holds for chains of any length, including the 4.4b network. This network contains four dyadic domains.

The manifestation of distal effects depends on the extent of domains. For instance, since *B* and *C* in 4.4a are in different domains, neither removing *C* nor adding new relations to *C* can affect *B*'s power, and vice versa. The same is true for any two positions, e.g., *B* and *D*, lying in different domains in the 4.4b chain. In contrast, 4c shows that attaching *F* to the center of the 4.4b chain changes *C* from an e^- to an e^+ position—from a circle to box. This creates a (*BCDF*) domain. *C* now has power over *B*, *D*, and *F* since it can exclude one of them in each round. Attaching a new position to *D* would remove *C*'s power and benefit *B*, further demonstrating that *B* and *D* are in the same domain.

Calculating $p(e)$

Every position in a multi-exchange network will have a p index for each of its domains: p_{id} (e_d) is position i's power in domain d, under the condition that i can make e_d exchanges per round within this domain.

Let m_{idk} be the number of nonintersecting paths of length k from position i in domain d, and h the longest such path from i in that domain. Only paths within a domain's boundaries are counted. As illustrated in the graphs, each path begins and ends with circles, between which there are either no positions or only boxes. Position i's GPI within the domain is[14]

$$p_{id}(e_d) = [1/e_d] \sum_{k=1}^{h} (-1)^{(k-1)} m_{idk} \qquad (4.2)$$

$p(e)$ is closely related to $p(1)$ and is similarly calculated. Multiplying the summation by $1/e_d$ simply places $p(e)$ and $p(1)$ values on the same scale.

Let us apply Equation (4.2) (which now substitutes for Axiom 1) to network 4.4a, with $e = 2$. The two dyadic domains are indicated by (AB) and (AC) subscripts. We see that $p_B = p_C = p_{A(AB)} = p_{A(AC)} = (1/1)(1) = 1$. Each position has, in each of its domains, exactly one-path and one exchange. Therefore, A has no power advantage in either of its domains. Similar results obtain in Figure 4.4b.

The 4.4c network has (AB) and (DE) dyadic domains and power domain $(BCDF)$. Again $p = 1$ for members of dyadic domains. However, for the power domain we calculate $p_{C(BCDF)} = (1/2)(3) = 3/2$, and for B, D, and F, $p = (1/1)(1-1) = 0$. Thus C has a power advantage in both of its exchanges, E and D have low power in one of their exchanges and equal power in the other, A and E have equal power in their one exchange, and F has low power in its one exchange.

We may also calculate an *average power* index, p_i, as the mean of i's indices across domains. In 4c, $\bar{p}_C = 3/2$; $\bar{p}_A = \bar{p}_E = 1$; $\bar{p}_B = \bar{p}_D = (1 + 0)/2 = .5$; $\bar{p}_F = 0$.

The Figure 4.5a network is the same as Figure 4.2 but redrawn using the circle and box notation. When $e = 1$, the network is a single domain and only the Es are high power positions. In 5b, where $e = 2$, the situation is drastically altered. Only D has power advantages, with the Es all having low power relative to D. Furthermore, the $E-F$ relations form three equipower dyadic domains.

The 5a and 5b networks tested the GPI generalization. The two networks have *identical* shapes. Only the number of exchanges per round differs. Cook el al.'s (1983) simulations found the Es to be high power positions in this network; $p(e)$ concurs but *only* for the special case of $e = 1$.

Figure 4.5
Single and Multidomain Networks

a.

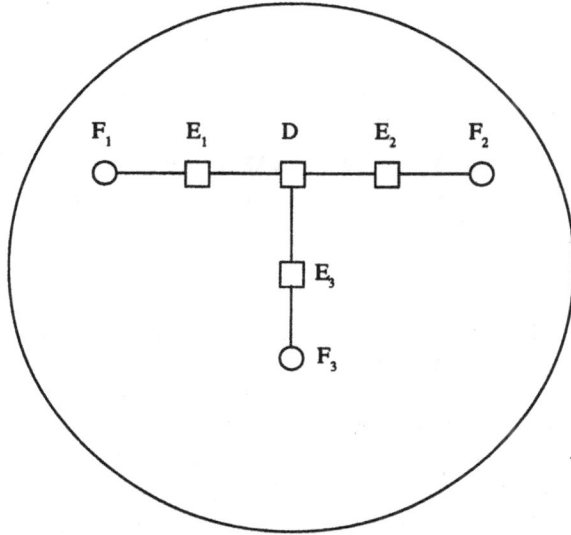

e = 1

b.

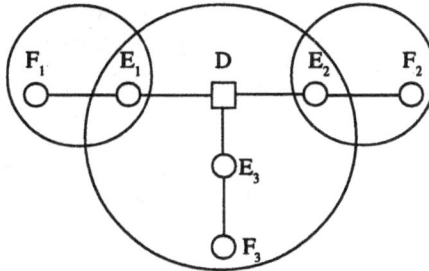

e = 2

Experiment 2

Experiment 2 tests the Figure 4.5 networks under $e = 1$ and $e = 2$ conditions. In spite of their identical shape, our analysis indicates that these networks should exhibit radically different profit distributions.

Method. The procedures for this experiment were similar to those used in Experiment 1. In this case, however, each subject negotiated from the different network positions under both 1-exchange and 2-exchange conditions, controlling for any personal characteristics of subjects that might confound the test.

Table 4.2
Second Experiment: Profit by Position, 1-Exchange Condition

	D	E_1	E_2	E_3	F_1	F_2	F_3
				Position			
mean profit	4.93	18.77	17.89	18.17	5.25	6.52	6.08
s.d.	4.55	4.58	4.82	4.64	4.56	4.86	4.65
t	13.65	15.53	12.91	13.87	13.65	10.64	11.66

Note: All tests significant at $p < .001$, 1-tailed.

Instructions for the 1- and 2-exchange conditions were identical, save for the number of exchanges allowed per round. In the 2-exchange condition only, D and E could exchange with up to two different partners in the same round.

Four groups were run. Each group had seven subjects, one for each of the seven network positions. Two of the groups had the 1-exchange condition first, followed by the 2-exchange condition. The other two groups had the order of conditions reversed. As in the previous experiment, each subject occupied each network position over a series of four negotiation rounds. The design produced a total of 224 negotiations, 112 under each exchange condition.

After completing both parts of the experiment, subjects were paid according to the number of points they had accumulated, around $7.00 on average.

Hypotheses. The following hypotheses apply to the Figure 4.5 networks. All are tested against the null hypotheses that every relation would average 12–12 divisions.

1. In the 1-exchange condition, the Es will exercise power over the Fs and D, and so all the Es will receive higher point totals than the others.

2. In the 2-exchange condition, only D will exercise power. D will obtain higher point accumulations than the Es.

3. In the 2-exchange condition, Es exchange in two domains. In the power domain, they will receive unfavorable profit divisions with D. In their respective dyadic domains, they will receive 12–12 divisions with the Fs.

Results. Table 4.2 and Figure 4.6a show the mean number of profit points obtained by each position under the 1-exchange condition. The position labels for Figure 4.5a are also the column headings of Table 4.2: The Es clearly obtained favorable profits, around an 18–6 split on the average. The t-tests show that the Es' profits were significantly greater than a 12–12 split. Moreover, the Es exercised power over both D and the Fs. Hypothesis 1 is supported.

Table 4.3 and Figure 4.6b show results for the 2-exchange condition. Now the power relationships have been reversed from the 1-exchange condition, with

Table 4.3
Second Experiment: Profit by Domain and Position, 2-Exchange Condition

Power Domains	$D - E_1$	$D - E_2$	$D - E_3$
mean profit	18.05	18.12	17.43
s.d.	4.61	4.50	4.65
t	11.66	11.63	9.77

Note: D's profit shown, E's profit = 24 − D's. All results significant at $p < .001$, 1-tailed.

Dyadic Domains	$E_1 - F_1$	$E_2 - F_2$	$E_3 - F_3$
mean profit	12.15	11.90	12.08
s.d.	1.46	1.46	.73
t	1.05	.72	1.17

Note: E's profit shown, F's profit = 24 − E's. No significant test results.

the Es losing power and D gaining. As was the case for the Es under the 1-exchange condition, D was able to gain approximately 18–6 profit divisions—significantly greater than the 12–12 split. Hypothesis 2 is confirmed.

Hypothesis 3 predicted equipower relations between the Es and their adjacent Fs under 2-exchange conditions. The Es and the Fs should then have 12–12 profit-point divisions. As Table 4.3 shows, the 12–12 split was approximated. None of the differences was significant. Hypothesis 3 is also supported.

In sum, this experiment provided strong support for the hypotheses testing the GPI generalization to multi-exchange networks. The presence of domains within the larger network under the 2-exchange conditions strongly influenced the exchanges transpiring within those domains. As far as we know such phenomena are not anticipated by alternative network exchange theories.

NEW THEORETICAL DIRECTIONS

In addition to making its predictions more precise, the formality of our theory has made it easier to develop extensions. We briefly note five extensions that are in varying stages of development and corroboration.

M-Exchange Networks

After developing the $p(e)$ model, we discovered that, with no loss of precision, different positions may seek different maximum numbers of exchanges per

Figure 4.6
Results for Seven-Position Network under 1-Exchange and 2-Exchange Conditions

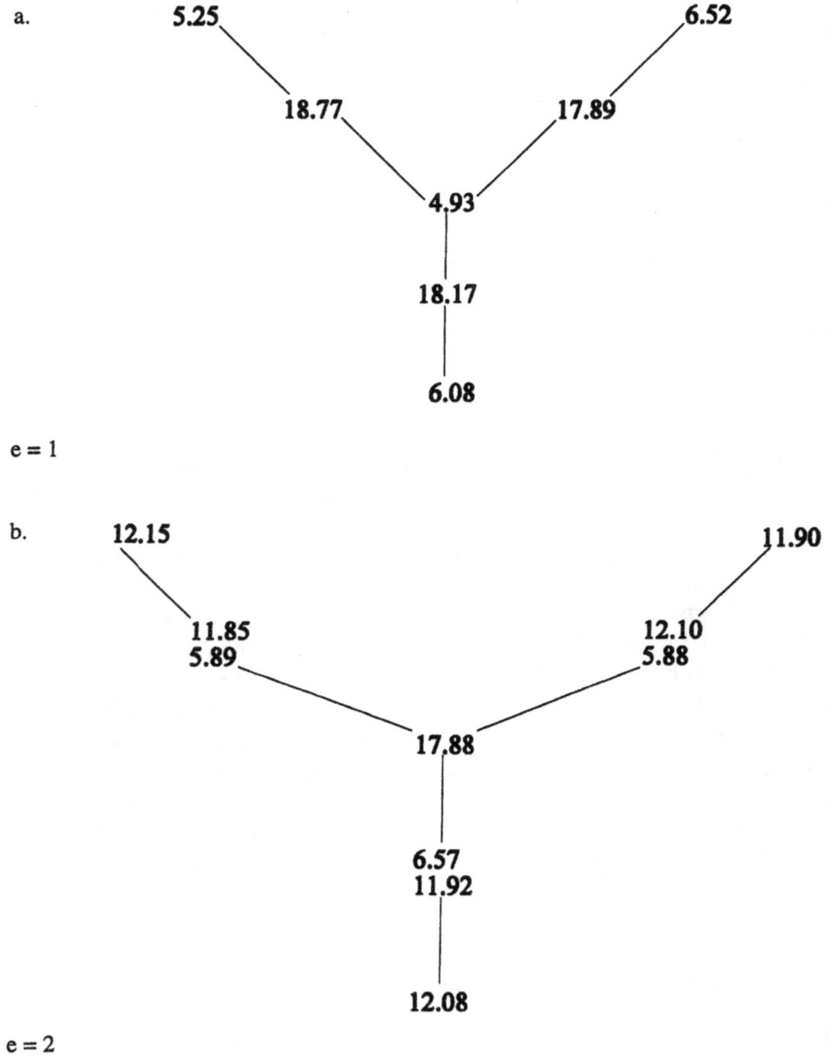

a.

5.25   6.52

18.77   17.89

4.93

18.17

6.08

e = 1

b.

12.15   11.90

11.85   12.10
5.89   5.88

17.88

6.57
11.92

12.08

e = 2

round—what we call the *M-Exchange* condition. This admits networks in which actors may seek exchange in one, some, or all of their relations. No reformulation of the GPI is needed to deal with this extension. The analysis predicts a new class of previously unanticipated power shifts.

No-Round Exchange

Allowing nonunique exchanges lets positions exchange more than once per round *within relations*. This effectively eliminates the need for exchange rounds. This is the *M-Exchange No-Round* condition. Now i may exchange up to e times or until those to which it is related have exchanged up to their limits. Although this is a more complex situation, it is still true that only $e-$ positions can have low power and only $e+$ positions can have high power.

Resource-Pool Values

If resource pools are different sizes in different relations, then there is another source for network breaks (Willer and Patton 1987). For example, in the 1-exchange B–A–C network, let B and A negotiate over the division of 30 points, while A and C negotiate over 10. At first A will benefit from the bids of B and C. Eventually, C will offer 9 points to A, keeping 1. Then B will offer 10 to A, keeping 20. C cannot meet this bid and still receive profit. Therefore, exchange should continue exclusively between B and A, with C excluded from the network. With the loss of C, only an A–B dyad remains, and profits should reach a 15–15 split. Thus power relations can be affected by variations in resource-pool values.

Flow-Networks

So far, we have focused on exchange conditions under which resources cannot transfer across relations. We have done so primarily because this is the condition under which most of the relevant research was conducted. However, as others have indicated (Marsden 1983; Bonacich 1987), it is worthwhile to relax this restriction and consider networks with transferable resources—those in which resources may flow through positions.

A consequence of extending into the realm of flow-networks is that positions may have power over others to which they are not related, depending on the initial distributions of resources and on which actors seek which resources. This is similar to Marsden's view. The foremost difference between that view and our approach is that we incorporate explicit assumptions about individual negotiation strategies and the conditions of exchange factors that affect exchange outcomes, breaks, and domains.

Positive Connection

Although negative connections place an upper limit on the number of exchanges in which a "hub" position may engage per round, positive connections place a lower limit on the number of exchanges in which the position must engage to realize a profit (Patton 1986). An example is the manufacturer who must obtain *all* components for a synthetic product before that product becomes a viable source of revenue. New research shows that the exchange dynamics that occur in positive connections differ markedly from those in negatively connected networks, and power advantages belong to peripheral positions in branches such as *B–A–C* (Patton and Willer 1987). This work on positive connections only begins to uncover a range of phenomena at least as broad and interesting as those associated with negative connections.

CONCLUSION

Our findings indicate that by only focusing on the effects of networks per se, alternative network theories do not recognize that power and resource distributions depend as much on prevailing exchange conditions as they do on configurations of positions and relations. We introduced a model that considers both structural form and exchange conditions, anticipating and explaining such phenomena as relative power, network breakage, power reversals, and domain-specific effects. The studies we described are only the first of many that could investigate stability and instability in exchange networks.

Future developments aside, we have found the present incarnation of the theory quite useful for understanding many real-world power struggles in exchange networks—from international disputes over geographical control to toddlers' negotiations over the sharing of playthings. Whatever the application, the theory directs us to specify the relevant actors and resources, identify other pertinent relations in which the actors are engaged, observe who seeks exchange with whom, identify which actors risk exclusion from valued resources, consider temporal constraints such as ultimatums or deadlines that create exchange rounds, and, in general, determine the extent to which the exemplar departs from the idealized scope conditions of the theory.

Our work also has implications for two very general questions that are relevant to structural approaches: (1) what is the appropriate unit of analysis for structural theories: and (2) how are characteristics of structures and the social units within them mutually determined?

Regarding the first question, we eschew the designation of one unit of analysis as, in general, more or less appropriate than another. Our theory explains certain actor and network behaviors. In any given instance, the network may be an organization, as may the actor. It follows that actors may or may not be individual persons. All that matters is that the units considered have the necessary properties. Therefore, no unit of analysis is generally most appropriate for structural approaches.

We can offer no universal solution to the question of how social structures and constituent units each determine properties of the other. Our approach does, however, point to *excludability* as a linchpin securing individual and network realms. That is, structures and exchange conditions at times bar some actors from procuring the resources they value and desire. Thus power *happens* to those whose positions allow them to dodge the struggle to avoid exclusion.

As the foregoing review of extensions-in-progress implies, we do not claim that our theory is finished or unimprovable. Nor do we claim that it explains all phenomena within the purview of alternative formulations. It is, however, consistent with the findings of *all* previous experimental research on exchange networks. Moreover, it addresses a range of conditions and generates predictions that are either beyond the range of alternative formulations or simply contradict them, depending on how one interprets their scope. Our long-term goal is to continue incremental extensions and systematic tests of increasingly refined network exchange models.

NOTES

1. Theoretical statements have been provided by Thibaut and Kelley (1959), Blau (1964), Gergen (1969), Homans (1974), Ekeh (1974), Heath (1976), Blalock and Wilken (1979), Burgess and Huston (1979), and Cook (1987). Emerson (1976), Bredemeier (1978), and Turner (1986) have written reviews. Applications involving ethnographic, institutional, and historical analyses are provided by Polanyi (1944), Elkin (1953), Sahlins (1972), Earle and Ericson (1977), and Emerson (1981). Recent applications of *network* exchange theories to interorganizational relations, backward and forward integration of the firm, community structure, historical development of modern exchange relations, and exchange processes in antiquity are given by Hansen (1981), Loukinen (1981), Gilham (1981), Galaskiewicz (1985), Skinner and Guiltinan (1986), Lind (1987), and Willer (1987).

2. Comparisons among these theories are hindered by their lack of explicit scope conditions. Although some scope conditions can be inferred, at times it is not clear when theories are competitors (Wagner and Berger, 1985) with divergent predictions testable in the same empirical settings.

3. Using their model, we could not reproduce Cook et al.'s predictions. The authors stated "This measure is relevant only when RMF is not zero" (p. 447). But RMF = 0 for positions A and C, apparently making D_N inapplicable. Further, the expression "exercise power at its potential" is not defined, and it is not stated whether the removed lines must stem from the position whose D_N is being assessed. Following the Cook et al. examples, it appears that in the 1a network, two lines must be removed from B to reduce the maximum flow of network resources, and one relation must be removed from D. The result is $CRMF_B = 1/3$, $CRMF_D = 1/2$, $D_{NB} = 8$, and $D_{ND} = 12$. D should be higher than B, contradicting Cook et al.'s prediction. In either case, the predictions diverge from those we will obtain from our model.

4. The reason for distinguishing actors and positions is that actor properties (e.g., decision strategies) and position properties (e.g., number of relations) may affect power independently (Markovsky 1987a).

5. These conditions allow a variety of more determinate rational or quasi-rational strategies. For example, resistance theory (Heckathorn 1980; Willer 1981, 1987) provides an elegant model of joint-bargaining decision making. Resistance is given as the ratio of an actor's interest in gaining a better exchange to the actor's interest in avoiding conflict. The conditions do, however, rule out strategies such as coalition formation (Kahan and

Rapoport 1984; Shubik 1982; Willer 1987), in which some actors temporarily accept reduced resources while receiving increasingly favorable offers from others.

6. We treat negative connection the same way as Cook et al. (1983), but we diverge from Emerson's (1972a, 1972b) original usage (Willer, Markovsky, and Patton forthcoming). In the earlier formulation, for an actor with multiple relations, exchange in one reduces the value of exchange in others because the actor's satiation level increases with each exchange. Exchange rates across the actor's relations are then negatively correlated, but as an *outcome* of the exchange process, not as an *initial condition*.

7. See Harary, Norman, and Cartwright (1965), Harary (1969), and Fararo (1973) for discussions of a variety of graph-theoretic tools.

8. Readers familiar with our unpublished reports should note that we have referred to this measure as C_N (i), position i's centrality when allowed N exchanges. The present notation more accurately reflects our concern with power rather than centrality and adheres to the convention of displaying variable indices and parameters as, respectively, subscripts and parenthetical elements.

9. Exchange in one relation will often temporarily alter the relative power of nearby positions. This dynamic is captured through an iterative application of the GPI. In Figure 4.2, for example, p_i is first calculated for all positions in the network. In a given round of negotiation, if E_1 and F_1 exchange first, p_i is recalculated for the network with E_1 and F_1 removed. The new p_i values are then in force until the next exchange occurs or until the end of the round. In the relatively simple network examined in this chapter, initial p_i values provide accurate predictions for power use. In more complex networks, however, the iterative application of the GPI is required to obtain accurate predictions (Markovsky, Willer, and Patton 1987).

10. After a sufficiently extended series of exchanges, an actor with $p = 0$ should seek exchange in *all* of its relations, regardless of power differences. That is, to avoid complete exclusion, the actor will offer to keep just one resource unit and relinquish the balance of the pool to any other that is willing to exchange. This seems to violate Axiom 2; however, this actor is no longer engaged in negotiation. This violates the first actor condition and makes the theory inapplicable. This is hardly a limitation of the theory, however, for when exchanges reach this point of nonnegotiability, the system (or subsystem) has run its course, exchange rates will remain fixed, and the theory is "finished" with its predictions for the application.

11. Cook et al. had a "low profit" relation between the two end points of the chain. While this places a lower limit on the profit that these positions can receive, it does not affect the relative power of positions in this network.

12. Having information on negotiations other than one's own is expected to accelerate the use of power but not affect relative power. For a more extended discussion of effects, see Willer and Markovsky (1986).

13. The three B–D exchanges occurred in three different experimental groups, on second, third, and fourth rounds. In two cases, B received 12 points, and in a third case, 11. This indicates that the Bs were checking their alternatives but quickly found no reason to continue such explorations.

14. For clarity, i subscripts have been suppressed for the e and h variables, d is suppressed for h, and p_{id} (e_d) will be written as $p(e)$ or p. Note that Axiom 1 is now comprised of the more general Equation (4.2).

Chapter 5

The Discovery of Weak Power

David Willer

INTRODUCTION

"Weak power" is so-called because it stands *between* the extremes of equal power, where actors benefit similarly, and power of the extreme type observed by Stolte and Emerson (1977), Cook and Emerson (1978), Brennan (1981), Cook et al. (1983), Willer (1987) and Markovsky, Willer, and Patton (1988). Since weak power was discovered, power of the extreme type has been called (fittingly) "strong power." We now say that these six experimental investigations, all published prior to 1990, studied strong power and equal power. We must be very careful, however, not to interject our current understandings into works published earlier. Publications prior to 1990 give not the slightest evidence that anyone engaged in network exchange research suspected that weak power existed. Certainly none of the networks considered, whether investigated experimentally or merely drawn and discussed, would prove to be a weak power network. Since the existence of weak power was not then suspected, none of the six publications qualified power differences as "strong."[1]

Insofar as observable outcomes are concerned, weak power poses no mystery. The presence of weak power is indicated by resource divisions that are intermediate to and between those of equal power and strong power. What may be difficult to grasp now—and what was obscure before its discovery—are the structural conditions that produce weak power events. In the section that follows, I demonstrate that weak power networks can be constructed by weakening the power conditions of strong power networks. I also demonstrate that weak power networks can be constructed beginning with equal power networks: I add or remove relations to eliminate the equivalence of positions that made power equal. These two demonstrations illustrate a quite general point: the structural conditions of weak power networks are intermediate to and between the structural conditions of strong and equal power networks. It follows that resource divisions of weak power networks are between those of strong and equal power networks *because* the power conditions of weak power networks are intermediate to the power conditions of strong and equal power networks.

Having shown how networks produce weak power, I turn to how the phenomenon of weak power was discovered. The discovery of weak power owes something to theory competition and to use of Markovsky's X-Net simulation. As to who discovered what and the order of events, the record of published papers makes some of this clear; the rest I have cross checked with those involved in the discovery.

Once the phenomenon was discovered, the problem for theory was to solve weak power networks. By "solving" networks I mean inferring resource divisions from network conditions. In experiments, the researcher builds network structures prior to the experimental run. So network structures are initial conditions, and the resource divisions that result are the observed final conditions. Once theory can solve weak power networks, initial network conditions are used to predict observable resource divisions. So experimentally testing a theory's solutions is a straightforward task. I trace the early steps taken in Network Exchange Theory toward solving weak power networks.

By 1992, four theories offering competing predictions were brought together in a special edition of the journal *Social Networks* (1992, 14: 3–4) which I edited. This was a fortuitous time to introduce new theories such as Bonacich and Bienenstock's application of the core and Friedkin's expected value theory. Unlike strong power, where resource divisions are always extreme, and equal power, where divisions are equal, weak power varies in degree. Since metric predictions are possible, theories will inevitably be evaluated by how closely their predictions correspond to observed resource divisions. The problem of precise metric predictions required that existing theories like NET and power dependence be extended.[2] Later in the chapter, I will discuss some of the basic formulations of the core and expected value theory. This discussion leads directly to Skvoretz and Willer (1993) in Chapter 6: they test the four competing theories against each other.

The following definitions are useful for a fuller understanding of the next section.

- All strong power networks have two and only two sets of positions; in the first set no position is ever excluded, and in the second at least one position is necessarily excluded. The second set exchanges only with the first. The first set is the high power positions, whereas the second set is the low power positions.
- Equal power networks have one set of positions: in that set, all positions are isomorphic to each other. Following Borgatti and Everett (1992), isomorphic positions "have the exact same pattern of direct and indirect ties with others. . . . Structurally isomorphic nodes are absolutely indistinguishable except by name" (p. 291). Thus they must be power equals.

Figure 5.1
From Strong to Weak Power

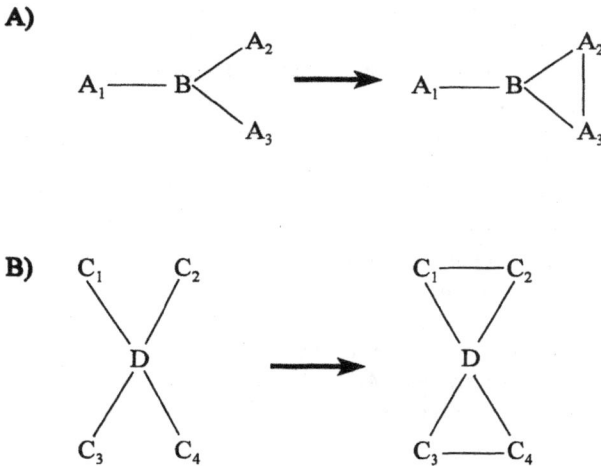

A)

B)

Because only strong power structures have two extreme power levels, only they have "high power positions" and "low power positions." Only equal power networks have a single power level, and their positions are called "equipower." Weak power structures can have two or more levels of power, but none is extreme; in weak power structures, positions are called "higher power" and "lower power."

WHAT IS WEAK POWER?

In this section I add and subtract relations in networks to show that the conditions of weak power structures fall between the conditions of strong power structures and the conditions of equal power structures. For brevity, I assume the default conditions: equal-sized resource pools are between each pair of positions, and all positions are limited to, at most, one exchange.

In Figure 5.1a, the 3-Branch to the left is a strong power structure. B, the high power position, is never excluded. Because B exchanges only once, two of the three As are necessarily excluded; the three As are low power positions. Since exchange relations only connect As to B, all exchanges must occur between the two sets. Resource divisions in the 3-Branch can be inferred in either of two ways. As seen in Chapter 3, resistance infers that resource divisions will move to the maximum favoring the high power B. Alternatively, assume that actors adjust offers as specified in the scope conditions of Chapter 4. Since the As are consistently excluded, they will raise their offers, while B, being consistently included, lowers its offers. These adjustments continue until resource divisions are maximally favorable to B, the high power position.

I now show how the 3-Branch can be transformed into a weak power network by adding one relation. The network to the right in Figure 5.1a is called the Stem. Relative to the 3-Branch, the A_2–A_3 exchange relation has been added. Because A_2 and A_3 are connected, no position is necessarily excluded; the Stem is not a strong power network. On the other hand, the positions of the Stem are not all isomorphic to each other; the Stem is not an equipower network. Only A_2 and A_3 are isomorphic, so only they will exchange equally. Other exchanges will be unequal, but they will not be extreme. They will not be extreme because B in the Stem is much weaker than B in the branch. B's power in the Stem is weaker precisely because no A is necessarily excluded. A_2 and A_3 can avoid B's power exercise by exchanging equally with each other. Since A_2 and A_3 each gain one-half of the resource pool when exchanging with each other, they will not bid against A_1 for the opportunity to exchange with B. Therefore, B–A_1 resource divisions will not move to the extreme.

At issue then is exactly how A_1 and B will divide resources. The theoretical tools to predict resource divisions in weak power networks are developed in the next two chapters. Although exact predictions cannot be offered here, formulations already in hand suggest the range within which B–A_1 resource divisions should fall. First, I infer the upper bound of B's power. Assume that resource pools contain 24 points and that B can always gain 12 when exchanging with either A_2 or A_3. Treating 12 as a fixed outside offer as in Chapter 2:

$$R_{\text{B}} = \frac{23 - P_{\text{B}}}{P_{\text{B}} - 12} = \frac{12 - P_{\text{A1}}}{P_{\text{A1}}} = R_{\text{A1}}$$

and $P_{\text{B}} = 17.7$ while $P_{\text{A1}} = 6.3$. But we know that this division is too extreme to be the A_1–B rate which should be expected. It is too extreme because B is not assured of a 12–12 exchange. When A_2 and A_3 exchange, B has no alternative to A_1 and thus has no power over A_1. Let $P_{\text{B}} = 17.7$ be the upper bound of B's power and note that the upper bound in the Stem is substantially lower than the $P_{\text{B}} = 23$ which is predicted for B in the 3-Branch.

The lower bound of B's power is $P_{\text{B}} = 13$. That is the lower bound because, by offering 13–11, A_1 should never be excluded. A_1 should never be excluded because B cannot gain more than $P_{\text{B}} = 12$ when exchanging with A_2 or A_3. The 13–11 division is the lower bound and not the expected B–A_1 rate. The 13–11 division is too low. At that rate, the costs of confrontation for A_1 and B are very unequal. If B exchanges with another A, B will lose only one point, but A_1 will assuredly lose eleven. Thus 13–11 is not the theoretically expected rate but the lower bound. Therefore, B–A_1 exchanges should fall between 17.7–6.3 and 13–11.

In Figure 5.1b, the 4-Branch to the left is transformed into the "Kite" to the right by adding two C–C exchange relations. Here power conditions are changed more radically than they were when the Branch was changed into the Stem. Being connected to each other in pairs, it is possible for all C positions to avoid exclusion. So the Kite is not strong power. But now the D can be excluded and

Figure 5.2
From Equal to Weak Power

A)

A—B   B—A ———▶ A—B—B—A

B)

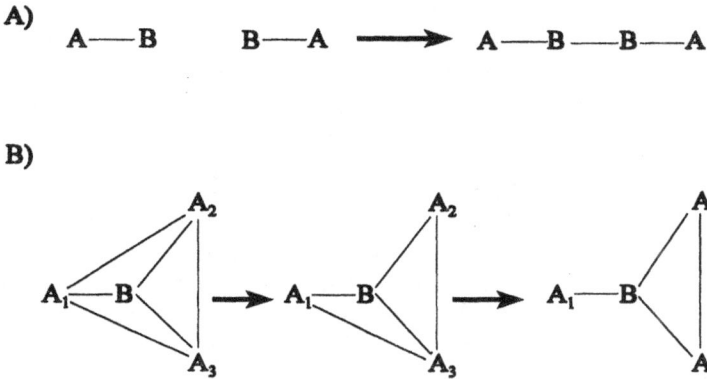

will be excluded when pairs of Cs exchange. Nevertheless, the Kite is not an equipower network because its positions are not all isomorphic. Thus the Kite must be weak power. But procedures at hand say little or nothing about its distribution of power. Is the D higher in power than the Cs? Perhaps. If so, what are the upper and lower bounds of that power? But it is not clear how to infer those bounds for the Kite. Certainly new theoretical tools are needed.

Weak power structures can also be built beginning with equal power structures like the networks to the left of Figure 5.2 and modifying them to eliminate isomorphism of positions. Because dyads and the "All-to-all" network to the left of Figure 5.2b are symmetrical, all positions must be power equals. In 5.2a I introduce power differences by adding the B–B exchange relation that connects the two dyads at the B positions giving L4, the A–B–B–A network. In L4, the Bs are higher in power than the As: Bs are never excluded but, if they exchange with each other, the As will be excluded.

I introduce power differences in Figure 5.2b by removing relations, one at a time. Beginning with the equipower All-to-all network and removing the A_1–A_2 relation gives the network in the middle. This change weakens both A_1 and A_2 because, if B and A_3 exchange, both will be excluded. By contrast, neither B nor A_3 can be excluded. Now remove the A_1–A_3 exchange relation which weakens both A_1 and A_3. This change gives the network to the right which is the Stem. Finally, we come full circle; removing the A_2–A_3 relation gives the strong power 3-Branch of Figure 5.1a, which was the point of departure of this discussion.

HOW WEAK POWER WAS DISCOVERED, 1987–1991

It may be difficult now to see why weak power was not immediately self-evident and why it had to be discovered. One reason why it was not self-evident was that many of us engaged in exchange network research were busy with other projects. For example, Patton and I became interested in inclusive branches where the central position must complete all exchanges in order to benefit from any one (Patton and Willer 1990). Following that study, Skvoretz and Willer (1991) experimentally investigated L4, the A–B–B–A network now known to be weak power. But in its Markovsky et al. (1988) form, $GPI = 1$ for all positions in L4, predicting power equality. Two experimental settings were used in the investigations, ExNet, a system of networked PCs, and Face-to-Face. Earnings by position observed in the experiments were significantly different from equal power earnings only in the ExNet setting. ExNet found a mean difference of 12.54–11.46 for B–A exchanges. Though significant, this difference is not convincingly distinct from 12–12 of equal power. Thus GPI's prediction of equal power was supported in one setting and marginally not supported in another. During much of this time, Markovsky was developing X-Net into a user-friendly network exchange simulator. Subsequently, X-Net proved to be important in the discovery of weak power.[3]

Toshio Yamagishi showed the Stem to Markovsky and me at the 1987 American Sociological Association meetings in Chicago. Barry and I had just presented the paper that was to become Markovsky, Willer, and Patton (1988) and, in showing us the Stem, Toshio suggested that GPI did not accurately cover that network. Toshio was quite right, but that was not obvious for the following reason. Figure 5.3a gives GPI values for the Stem: $GPI_A = 1$, $GPI_B = 2$, and $GPI_C = 2$. Applying the Axioms given in Chapter 4, we find that B will seek to exchange only with A and that the network breaks into two equal power dyads. Comparing Figures 5.3a, 5.3b, and 4.1, we can see that the Stem's break is not like the break in the "T"-shaped network. After the "T" breaks, D still seeks to exchange only with E because B remains a high power position. By contrast, in the Stem, the break produces two dyads where all positions are of equal power. Therefore B now seeks exchange with the Cs, and the network reconnects only to (presumably) break again. At the time, Barry and I believed that the oscillation of the Stem indicated that B–C exchanges would occur infrequently. More importantly, when the Stem was not broken, $GPI_B > GPI_A$. When Toshio showed me the Stem, I said that $GPI_B > GPI_A$ suggests a small B–A power difference favoring B. Beyond that, I saw nothing of theoretical interest. Barry remembers Toshio suggesting a 16–8 division favoring B and was struck by the lack of any explicit model generating that prediction.[4] In fact, no one then had a model to predict exchange ratios in the Stem.

By the spring of 1989 Markovsky was using his X-Net simulation to explore a number of networks. The simulated actors in X-Net closely follow the scope conditions of Markovsky et al. (1988). Actors included in exchange in the previous round make lower offers to others, whereas actors then excluded make higher offers. Simulated actors who can make more than one exchange per round differentiate relations in which they were included from relations in which they were excluded and adjust accordingly.[5] Simulation runs reliably showed small power differences between As and Bs favoring the latter in L4. Nevertheless,

Figure 5.3
Temporary and Permanent Network Breaks

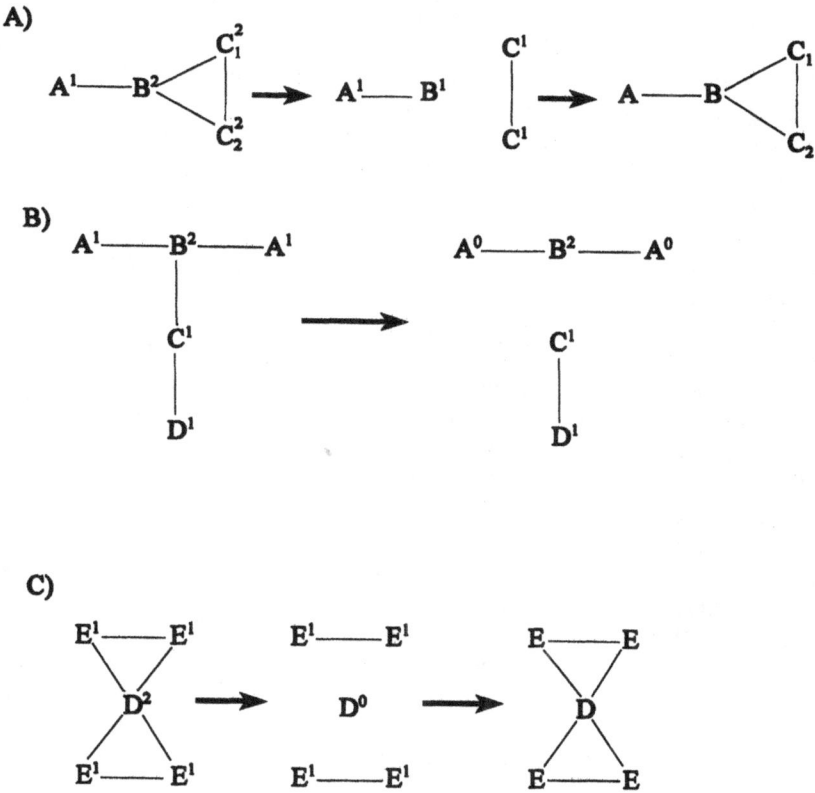

A)

A^1—B^2< C_1^2 / C_2^2 → A^1— B^1 C^1 | C^1 → A—B< C_1 / C_2

B)

A^1——B^2——A^1 A^0——B^2——A^0

C^1 C^1

D^1 → D^1

C)

E^1—E^1 → E^1——E^1 → E——E
D^2 D^0 D
E^1—E^1 E^1——E^1 E——E

X-Net results are not empirical data. Running X-Net is an exploration in theory; its output is a theoretical prediction. Thus X-Net outcomes indicating weak power differences are not empirical proof of the existence of weak power.

By late Fall of 1989, the Yamagishi and Cook (1990) *Comment* on Markovsky et al. (1988) was in hand and we were preparing our response. At one point in their *Comment*, Yamagishi and Cook reported simulation outcomes for Stem and Kite. They found B's profit in the Stem to average 14.02 and D's in the Kite, 12.89. But simulation results were mentioned only in passing. Having dropped Vulnerability which Markovsky et al. (1988) falsified (see Chapter 4), Yamagishi and Cook's *Comment* highlighted " 'informal' predictions based on Emerson's original power-dependence principles" (1990, p. 299). Because particular power-dependence principles were not explicitly stated or even named, their claim is empty.[6] To confuse matters, they misapplied both GPI and the Axioms. Thus much of our reply was spent in correcting their applications and explaining that, whatever GPI's limitations, it was an explicit and formal theory.

Relative to our predictions, Yamagishi and Cook's "informal predictions" were intuitions with no scientific standing. Insofar as weak power is concerned, their *Comment* and our *Response* resolved nothing. On the other hand, their simulation results turned out to be reasonably good predictions. Three years later, Skvoretz and Willer (1993) reported experimental results $P_B = 15.29$ for A–B exchanges in the Stem and $P_D = 14.05$ in the Kite.

Michael Lovaglia and Barry Markovsky named weak power and, because that naming began the study of weak power as phenomena distinct from strong and equal power, it must count as its discovery. In May of 1990, an E-mail correspondence developed between them in which the small power differences which were showing up in simulations were examined. Michael, still a graduate student at Stanford, was completing a Ph.D. preliminary examination on Vulnerability and GPI. Adopting the terms "strong force" and "weak force" from physics, he held that "weak force" power differences were real enough and should be found in experiments. By summer 1990, everyone working on NET recognized the existence of intermediate power levels as an important problem for theory. In 1991 the paper that was to become Markovsky et al. (1993) was presented at the American Sociological Association meetings in Cincinnati. That paper shortened "weak force power" to "weak power." It also extended GPI by introducing a new procedure analyzing "exchange seeks" to infer the probability that positions will be excluded. (I explain that method in the next section.)

Nevertheless, Toshio Yamagishi also has a sound claim as the discoverer of weak power. He was the first to draw attention to a network—the Stem—which was believed to produce intermediate resource divisions. Subsequent experiments have shown that Yamagishi was right; the Stem is a weak power structure. Since simulation runs are theory work, arguably his simulation runs were the first theoretical predictions for exchange outcomes in such structures.

PREDICTING WEAK POWER

With the discovery of weak power, it was realized that the GPI of Markovsky et al. (1988) failed to offer predictions for it. Here I explain the "random-seek" method as developed by Markovsky and adopted by NET. Random seek assigns likelihoods of exclusion to each position such that positions less likely to be excluded are predicted to be more powerful than positions more likely to be excluded. Actually, the random-seek method calculates "one minus the likelihood of exclusion" which is the likelihood of *being included*.[7]

I now explain how the application of the random-seek method is triggered by specific GPI outcomes. With the discovery of weak power, the 1988 GPI becomes the first of a two-step process; the random-seek method is the second. Now GPI's function is to find strong power networks, including strong power components in larger networks, locate their high and low power positions, and find breaks. After GPI is applied, for networks where no power differences are found, the random-seek method is applied. Random seeks determine the relative power of each position and, indeed, indicate whether the network is weak power or equal power.

The random-seek method is applied when the GPI values for all connected positions are equal. For example, in Figure 5.3a, the initial values of the Stem are not the same, but after its break into dyads, $GPI_A = GPI_B$ and $GPI_{C1} = GPI_{C2}$. That is, all positions that remain connected have the same GPI values as their partner's. These equalities signal that the random seek method should be applied to find the likelihood of being included for each position. Because GPI values are equal, positions will seek exchange with all partners so that all exchange relations are reconnected. In effect, this reconnection asserts that there are no breaks here or in any weak (or equal) power network.[8]

Application of GPI to the Kite in Figure 5.3c similarly produces the conditions for application of random seeks. Since the D has the higher GPI value, the Es seek exchange only with each other, and the Kite breaks temporarily into two dyads and the isolated D. As shown in the network to the left in Figure 5.3c, all positions that remain connected have the same GPI values as their partner's. These identical values mean that the network is either weak or equal power. Since breaks do not occur in weak or equal power networks, all exchange relations of the initial network are restored.

The random-seek method calculates the likelihood of being included in the following way. First, it assumes that each position's interest in exchanging with each partner is the same: that is, each position seeks exchange randomly with all connected others. If the position has only one connection, it seeks exchange with that partner with the likelihood of 1.0. If the position has two partners, it seeks exchange with each .5 of the time and similarly for more connections. The likelihood that any pair of positions will exchange is the *joint probability* of their seeking each other. For example, if one position has three partners and a second has only two, the joint probability of the two exchanging is $.333 \times .50 = .167$.

Calculating the likelihoods of being included for A–B–B–A is quite simple. The As seek exchange with the Bs all of the time, so the Bs are always included. At issue now is only how frequently the As are excluded. As are excluded only when Bs exchange with each other. Each B has two partners, so each seeks exchange with each other .5 of the time. It follows that the joint probability of a B–B exchange is $.5 \times .5 = .25$. Therefore, the As are excluded .25 of the time and included $1 - .25 = .75$ of the time. Thus the L4 likelihoods of being included are:

$$A^{.75} - B^{1.0} - B^{1.0} - A^{.75}$$

More generally, exchange-seek likelihoods are calculated using a Tree diagram such as that of Figure 5.4 which is drawn for the Stem. That particular Tree diagram begins with the B position, but the point of departure is arbitrary: exactly the same probabilities result from beginning with A or either C. The

Figure 5.4
Tree Diagram for Computing GPI$_3$ for the Stem Network

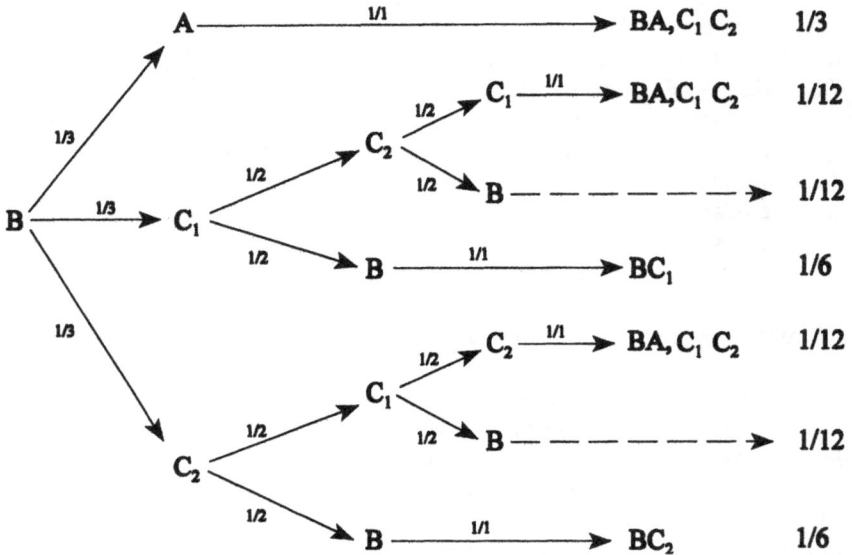

Tree traces joint probabilities as above by multiplying the likelihoods that adjacent positions seek each other. It is assumed that actors continue to seek until the maximum number of exchanges possible for the network has been completed. For example, tracing from B to A, it is concluded that they exchange one third of the time. Given that A and B exchange, the Cs will continue to seek a partner until they find each other. That is the A–B exchange implies the C–C exchange, and the two exchanges are displayed together in the diagram. The likelihood that each position is included is found by summing the likelihoods for it, which are given at the right of the Tree. Summing, we find that $p_B = 1.0$, $p_A = .60$, and $p_C = .80$. The exchange-seek values for L4, Stem, and the Kite are given in Figure 5.5.[9]

In Markovsky et al. (1993), exchange-seek likelihoods were put to two uses. The first use was to find power relations within networks. Here exchange seeks have been very successful. Exchange-seek values predict that $P_B > P_A$ in L4 and Stem and $P_D > P_E$ in the Kite. Referring to Table 6.2 in the next chapter, we see that these predictions are supported. The second use for exchange-seek values is to predict power levels between networks. For example, the predicted power difference is greater in the Stem than in the Kite: that is $P_B - P_A > P_D - P_E$, and reference to Table 6.2 again supports this prediction. The prediction that power differences in the Stem are greater than those in L4 is also supported. But B–A power differences in L4 are predicted to be larger than D–E differences

Figure 5.5
Exchange-Seek Values

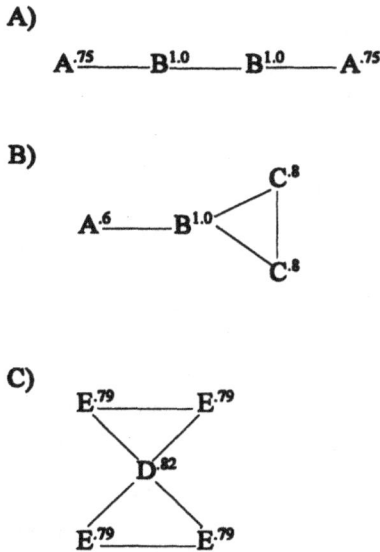

A)

$$A\underline{^{.75}}\underline{}B\underline{^{1.0}}\underline{}B\underline{^{1.0}}\underline{}A^{.75}$$

B)

$$A^{.6}\underline{}B^{1.0}$$

with $C^{.8}$ and $C^{.8}$ forming a triangle with B.

C)

$$E^{.79}\underline{}E^{.79}$$
$$D^{.82}$$
$$E^{.79}\underline{}E^{.79}$$

in the Kite, but Table 6.2 shows that $P_B = P_D = 14.05$; the predicted difference was not found. So the record of predictions across networks is mixed.

Exchange-seek values are intended to represent a structural quality determining relative power of positions: they are not intended to predict how likely positions are to engage in exchanges. The prediction of relative power and the prediction of the likelihood of exchanging are separate and distinct tasks: why the two cannot use the same likelihood is easily seen. Assume that the values given for L4 in Figure 5.5 reflect actual power differences. If they do, As are weaker than Bs, and Bs will always prefer to exchange with the As and avoid each other. As long as the As recognize their weakness and exchange accordingly, the Bs will never exchange with each other. In that case, the frequency of B–B exchanges is zero. Thus, if the seek likelihoods reflect relative power of positions, they cannot reflect the likelihood that positions will exchange.[10]

EXPECTED VALUE AND THE CORE

Expected value and the core apply to exchange networks, as well as to other phenomena. Expected value has been applied to interpersonal influence, the flow of information, and social support, whereas the core has been applied to the formation of coalitions. Broad scope makes these two theories particularly attractive. This discussion is too brief to be complete or balanced. My purpose is only to show the reader the most basic ideas of each, the ideas that are the point of departure from which predictions flow. More details are found in the next chapter.

Friedkin's expected value theory assumes, as does NET, that actors are rational and that the configuration of networks is stable. Networks are opportunities to exchange and, by assigning a given number of exchange opportunities to each position, we can infer all possible exchange configurations. We can call each exchange configuration a subnetwork and the set of all configurations the sample space. Only maximal subnetworks are considered: that is, those in which all feasible exchanges occur (Friedkin 1992, p. 217). For the sample space of Figure 5.6, I assume the 1-exchange rule: that each position may exchange maximally once. To the left are all maximal subnetworks for L4, the Stem, and Kite. For example, L4 has only two maximal subnetworks: either the two A–B pairs exchange or the B–B exchange occurs. By contrast, as seen in Figure 5.6b and c, the sample space of the Stem contains three subnetworks and the Kite contains five. Friedkin's baseline assumption is that each subnetwork is equally likely.[11] From that assumption, the likelihood of being included can be inferred for each position. Expected value likelihoods are given as superscripts in the networks to the right.

Exchange-seek and expected value likelihoods of being included are not the same. For example, in L4, the exchange seek likelihood for A is .75, whereas the expected value likelihood is .5. Here and elsewhere—with the exception of positions never excluded—the two give very different values. Although the two methods both depart from an equal likelihood assumption, the referent of "equal likelihood" is different. The exchange seek method is "position centered": each position seeks each partner with the same likelihood. Friedkin's expected value is "network centered": the incidence of each subnetwork is equally likely. There is no doubt that Friedkin's likelihoods are easier to calculate than those of the exchange seek method. Is Friedkin's the better method?

As a likelihood calculator to predict resource divisions, the head-to-head test in the next chapter gives the exchange seek method the edge.[12] But the comparison is confounded. The two theories use different equations to infer from likelihoods of being included to resource divisions: only exchange seek uses resistance, and that may be the reason for its edge. Looking at specific networks, exchange-seek predictions for the Kite are better: it predicts the power differences found, but expected value does not. Theories are not static, however. Friedkin (1995), not covered here, offers formulations allowing D–E power *and* the D–E frequency of exchange to be predicted.

Furthermore, currently the best predictor for weak power networks is the GPI–RD method of Chapter 7, *and*, if GPI–RD used Friedkin likelihoods, it would predict power differences in the Kite. Here is the reason. GPI–RD predicts power differences from two conditions: the likelihood of being included and the position's "degree." Degree means the number of exchange relations connected at a position. For GPI–RD, as degree increases, even holding the likelihood of being included constant, a position's power increases. Friedkin assigns exactly

Figure 5.6
Expected Value Likelihoods for a Sample Space Restricted by the 1-Exchange Rule

A) L4

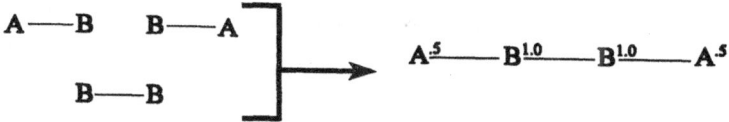

B) Stem

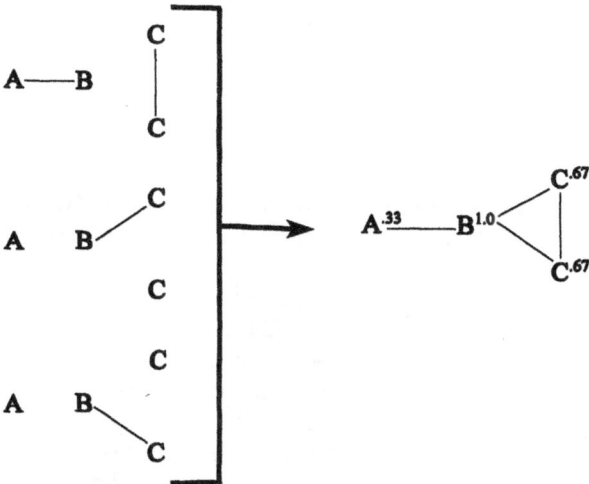

C) Kite

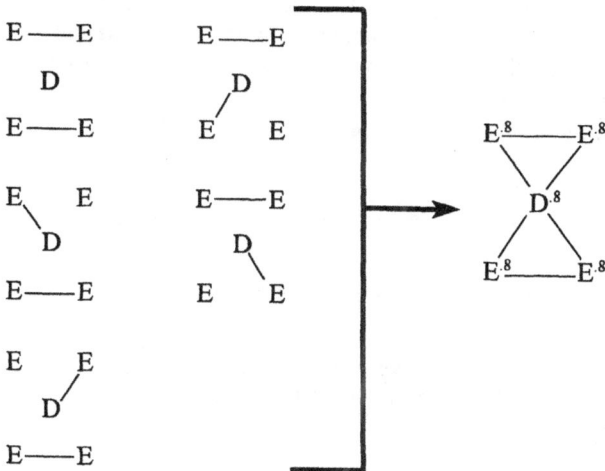

Figure 5.7
Expected Value Likelihoods for the "T" Sample Space Restricted by the 1-Exchange Rule

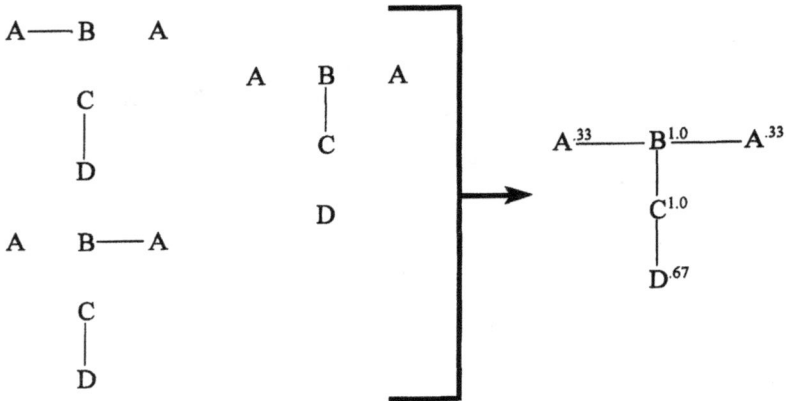

the same likelihood of being included to all Kite positions. But four relations are connected at D for degree = 4, whereas each E has only two connections for degree = 2. Therefore, GPI–RD predicts that D is advantaged, even if likelihoods are equal as in Friedkin's expected values.

For strong power networks, however, NET predicts breaks which expected value does not. When breaks affect resource divisions, NET offers better predictions, predictions that have substantial support. For example, as shown for the "T" in Figure 5.7, expected value's likelihood calculation includes a $B–C$ exchange. When B and C exchange, D is excluded and, because D is excluded it is predicted to be lower in power than C. As seen in the last chapter, NET predicts the $B–C$ break in the "T"-shaped network. Because of the break, C always exchanges with D, D is never excluded, and C and D are power equals. Experiments support NET predictions, not those of expected value.

Bienenstock and Bonacich (1992) adapt the core from game theory where it was developed by Shubik "to capture in a single numerical index the potential *worth* of a coalition" (1982, p. 129). They apply Rappaport's three levels of rationality (1970, pp. 88–90), which are:

- *Individual rationality*: "No individual in a coalition will accept less than what he can earn alone."

- *Coalition rationality*: "No set of actors S will accept less in total that what they can earn in a coalition together."

- *Group Rationality*: "The set of all actors in the grand coalition will maximize their total reward." (Bienenstock and Bonacich 1993, p. 124)

The sets of payoffs possible in each network, called characteristic functions, are listed together with contingencies linking them. For example, in the A–B–C branch, under the 1-exchange rule, when resource pools = 24 points:

$$\{P_A + P_B = 24\} \quad \text{or} \quad \{P_B + P_C = 24\}$$

and the only payoff value satisfying the statement is $P_B = 24$. Therefore, B gains all of the pool (or all minus ε). In this way, the core identifies what NET calls strong power payoffs. But now assume that C is connected back to A, turning the branch into a triangle. Then

$$\{P_A + P_B = 24\} \quad \text{or} \quad \{P_B + P_C = 24\} \quad \text{or} \quad \{P_C + P_A = 24\}$$

and no payoff value satisfies the core. Because the core is empty and, recognizing that any agreement can be bettered by the excluded partner, Bienenstock and Bonacich predict that the triangle is unstable.

Now consider the core applied to the Figure 5.6 networks. For L4,

$$A_1 + B_1 = A_2 + B_2 = 24; \ B_1 + B_2 \geqslant 24.$$

Whereas A–B transactions could be equal, it is also possible that they favor the Bs. Furthermore, the B–B exchange will not occur because it is *suboptimal*. Maximally, two exchanges can occur in L4, but if the Bs exchange, only one is possible. Thus the B–B exchange is suboptimal. Suboptimal exchanges do not occur because the postulation of Group Rationality asserts that total reward is maximized. As we will see, ruling out suboptimal exchanges has important implications. For example, in the Stem both B–C exchanges are suboptimal. Therefore, only A–B and C–C exchanges are predicted. Any C–C division is in the core; for A–B, equal divisions or divisions favoring B are in the core. By contrast, the Kite has no core, and Bienenstock and Bonacich predict that its behavior is like the triangle: agreements will be unstable.

For weak power networks, NET and core predictions are quite different. NET offers point predictions, whereas the core only designates a range of possible rates. For strong power networks, however, the two are quite similar. For example, applied to the "T"-shaped network, like NET, the core finds the B–C break. For the core, however, the break occurs because the B–C relation is suboptimal. The core predicts that, in exchanging with the As, the B will gain all points (or all less ε). NET's prediction is similar: the B is high strong power and will gain maximally. Only for the C–D relation are core and NET predictions different: all C–D payoffs are in the core, but NET, finding C and D to be equipower, predicts equal divisions.

For equal power and weak power networks, the core predicts a range of possible exchange ratios; it does not offer point predictions. Because it does not and to further comparisons between theories, Skvoretz and Willer (1993) (see Chapter 6) use an averaging method to force the core to make point predictions. Bienenstock and Bonacich object to this procedure (Personal Communication). To them, averaging the range of possible resource divisions is meaningless. Nevertheless, the core predicts interestingly different ranges of possible exchange ratios for equal and weak power relations. For example, applied to A–B–B–A, the core predicts the range from equal division to the division where B receives all, but for the equipower A–B dyad, the full range of divisions is predicted. For many networks these differing ranges allow the core to differentiate weak power from equal power relations.

NET differentiates strong, weak, and equipower networks, finds breaks, and makes point predictions for all three types. The core differentiates strong power networks from other types and frequently differentiates weak and equal power. It finds breaks but makes point predictions only for strong power. Expected value makes point predictions for all networks but does not find breaks and does not differentiate types. Taken together, the core and expected value make an array of predictions much like NET. But the core and expected value are not used together; they are not one theory but two. Each is elegantly simple. In the case of the core, that simplicity is bought at the price of making point predictions only for strong power networks. In the case of expected value, that simplicity is bought at the price of not differentiating the network types and not finding breaks.[13]

NET is the more complex theory, but that complexity is used to predict network types, predict breaks, and make point predictions for exchange ratios. Not predicting all three has important practical implications. For example, expected value does not differentiate network types but predicts exchange ratios from likelihoods alone. For both the 2-Branch, A–B–A and the L4, A–B–B–A, expected value likelihoods are the same: $p_A = .5$ and $p_B = 1.0$. Therefore expected value predicts the 21.1–2.9 division for B–A relations in both networks. But the A–B–A Branch is a strong power structure. The distribution of exclusions means that the As will bid against each other, moving the B–A division to 23–1. By contrast, L4 is weak power, there is no bidding, and experiments show that B–A divisions are far less extreme, averaging 14.05–9.95.

CONCLUSION

Unlike strong power networks, where resource divisions are always extreme, and equal power networks, where all divisions are equal, weak power varies in degree. Since metric predictions are possible, inevitably theories will be evaluated by how closely their predictions correspond to observed resource divisions. The Markovsky et al. study (1993) shows that the exchange-seek method effectively orders exchanges within networks Since that method gives smoothly varying likelihoods, it can be the basis for metric predictions. The two chapters that follow combine exchange-seek likelihoods and resistance to make metric predictions of resource divisions. The two combine likelihoods and resistance in very different ways.

Chapter 6, which is Skvoretz and Willer (1993), offers the first method devised for relating exchange-seek likelihoods to resource division outcomes. An important drawback of their method is that it loses the distinction between strong and weak power which, as we have just seen, is important for accurate predictions across types. That distinction is lost because, unlike the two-step application of Markovsky et al. (1993), the Chapter 6 theory has only one step. In that one step, both weak and strong power resource divisions are predicted from seek likelihoods. Lovaglia et al. (1995a), which is Chapter 7, offers two advances. First, it reestablishes the strong power–weak power distinction. Second, its method of predicting power outcomes is substantially more precise. Yet Skvoretz and Willer (1995) should not be dismissed. That chapter offers the first and only head-to-head experimental test of four theories in the history of sociology, and undoubtedly it is the only one ever in any of the social sciences.

NOTES

1. In Willer (1987), I used the terms "strong structure" and "weak structure," but these terms do not correspond to current usage. The strong structures that I investigated were, in fact, strong power structures. But the weak structures were equal power structures: they were called "weak" because their exchange relations were not affected by being (null) connected in the structure. Their exchange ratio outcomes remained medial as they were in dyads. "Strong structures" were called strong because exclusion transformed interactions and pushed exchange ratios toward the extreme.

2. When I first wrote this paragraph, I wrote that "The discovery of weak power drew forth new theories" but this proved to be mistaken. Bonacich explained (Personal Communication) that his interest in exchange networks went back to the mid-1980s. While reviewing a paper by Markovsky, he concluded that game theory, especially the core, was the best way to solve networks. Friedkin's interest stems from a somewhat later period. He explained (Personal Communication) that, having just finished his paper on influence and centrality (Friedkin 1991), he was intrigued that conventional measures of centrality did not effectively locate power positions. Friedkin insists that the term "weak power" is specific to the GPI approach. His theory sees, not qualitative differences like strong and weak power, but only "more and less pronounced inequalities of power." Nevertheless, the strong power–weak power differentiation is not limited to the GPI approach. It is also used by Bonacich and Bienenstock (1995).

3. X-Net is a simulation program developed by Markovsky. ExNet is an experimental system of networked computers, each of which serves as a subject station. ExNet was designed by Willer and Skvoretz and programmed by Skvoretz.

4. Nevertheless, Toshio's intuition was excellent. The A–B rate found by Skvoretz and Willer (1993) was 15.29–8.71.

5. The simulation which is designed to run on PCs is available from Markovsky on request (Department of Sociology, University of Iowa, Iowa City, IA 52242). Further information is given in Markovsky (1995).

6. Although power-dependence papers frequently cite Emerson's power-dependence

principles, to my knowledge no listing of these principles has been given. If by Emerson's principles is meant Emerson (1972a&b), there is a serious problem. In that paper, power differences are produced by satiation alone and not by structural conditions like exclusion. Willer et al. (1989) demonstrates that satiation cannot explain or predict the exercise of power in network exchange experiments.

7. In some publications (Markovsky et al. 1993), "being included" is unfortunately rendered as "inclusion." This rendering is unfortunate because the term "inclusion" was preempted by Patton and Willer (1990) to name a type of network connection; Willer and Skvoretz (1997) continue this use of the term. The "likelihood of being included" and "inclusive connection" are not the same phenomenon. They do not occur in the same type of network. The former occurs in "exclusive networks," while inclusive connection occurs in "inclusive networks." See Chapter 8, which is Willer and Skvoretz (1997), for the inclusive-exclusive-null typology of network connection.

8. The rule cited here for applying the random seek method is not the more restricted one of Markovsky et al. (1993), but the more general one of "Iterative GPI" in Lovaglia et al. (1995b), which is Part 1 of Chapter 10 in this volume.

9. More generally, before summing likelihoods for each node, sum exchange seek likelihoods for the network as a whole. The likelihood for the network as a whole is given by summing the column to the right in Figure 5.4. For the Stem, the likelihoods sum to 1.0. For some networks, however, likelihoods will sum to a value smaller than unity. If so, take the reciprocal of that sum and multiply each of the column values by that reciprocal to get the corrected exchange seek likelihoods. A program to calculate exchange seek likelihoods is available by request from John Skvoretz (Department of Sociology, University of South Carolina, Columbia, SC 29208).

10. Two methods predicting the occurrence of exchanges are Friedkin (1995) and Skvoretz and Lovaglia (1995).

11. Alternatively, exchange ratios can be calculated from observed frequencies as in the next chapter. Also see Friedkin (1995).

12. When observed frequencies of being included are used to infer power levels, Friedkin's theory has an edge over NET. The use of observed frequencies, however, means that neither exchange seek nor expected value likelihoods enter into the inference. The use of observed frequencies also means that power levels are not predicted. They are not predicted because frequency of exchange is observed *at the same time* as the exchange ratios which indicate power levels.

13. Chapter 10 discusses problems in the application of GPI. Part 2 of that chapter offers a new procedure for locating power relations which borrows from the core to find breaks by identifying suboptimal relations.

Chapter 6

Exclusion and Power

Preface
David Willer

This chapter tests four exchange theories against each other and is, to my knowledge, the first test of as many as four competing theories in sociology. Because it is very unusual for four theories to offer competing predictions within the same scope, this may yet be the only such test in any social science. These four theories were published together in a special edition of the journal *Social Networks* in 1992, one year before this test first appeared in the *American Sociological Review*.

When I edited that special edition, I commented that the appearance of these four competing theories represents a notable advance for sociological theory. Their appearance is a notable advance because, taken together, they give a pattern of theory growth to sociology—or at least to network exchange—like that of the advanced theoretic sciences. In less advanced sciences, knowledge simply accumulates: particularistic findings and ill-grounded speculations stack one upon another like cordwood. Today most parts of sociology are still marked by that kind of accumulation. Advanced sciences do not accumulate findings and speculations. Advanced sciences have theories and, as the scope of theory widens, knowledge "cumulates." By knowledge cumulation, I mean that more and more empirical information is rationally organized by theory and explained by it.

In the special edition of *Social Networks*, I explained the importance of this development in the following way:

When the status of a theoretic science is fully attained, theory competition advances the science, extending its scope and increasing its precision. The contributions of this volume all have explanatory and predictive power. When their scopes overlap they are in competition. Contributors expect competition among the theoretic formulations to be resolved by their scope and precision. Through appeal to these objective criteria, the contributors institute a pattern of theory growth that propels network exchange theory forward to the status of a theoretic science. (Willer 1992, p. 188)

This chapter tests only the precision of the four theories. I will comment on the scope of the competing theories in the concluding chapter of this book.

The appearance of this test only one year after the four theories were published represents a five-fold increase in the pace of scientific development. The only previous test of exchange theories against each other was Markovsky et al. (1988); as seen in Chapter 4, it followed, not one year, but five years after Cook et al. (1983) presented Vulnerability.

Exclusion and Power: A Test of Four Theories of Power in Exchange Networks
John Skvoretz and David Willer

We evaluate four theories that predict the distribution of power in exchange networks. All four theories—core theory, equidependence theory, exchange-resistance theory, and expected value theory—assume actors rationally pursue self-interests. Three of the theories add social psychological assumptions that further place the pursuit of self-interest in an interactive context. Predictions of exchange earnings by the four theories are evaluated against data from eight experimental networks, including types of networks not previously studied. These networks vary conditions that affect the chances that a position can be excluded from exchange. We find that when the theories base predictions on a network position's structural potential for exclusion, exchange-resistance theory provides the best fit, but when predictions are based on actual experiences of exclusion, expected value theory fits best. Our discussion focuses on the distinction between the a priori potential for exclusion versus experienced exclusion as factors in the genesis of power.

INTRODUCTION

The problem of power distribution in exchange networks has captured the attention of a variety of theorists. The appeal of the problem derives from the combination of the formal representation of social structure as network (Wellman and Berkowitz 1992) and sociology's perennial concern with power. A growing body of experimental studies now permits researchers to test various theoretical formulations. How does location in a network confer advantages on a person or a corporate body in their dealings with others? Consider the promotion prospects of two senior accountants, Andy and Bob. Because Andy's work involves accounts at various regional offices, his coworkers typically do not know each other. Bob, on the other hand, deals with corporate accounts, so his coworkers typically associate with each other. Thus, Andy and Bob are surrounded by two very different networks, and it is not obvious that Andy's network favors him for promotion (Burt 1992). In a second example, a university department searches for a chairperson who can negotiate with the college dean for support for the department. The common intuition that outsiders are more desirable is grounded in a belief that outsiders' network ties (or lack of them) provide alternatives that insiders cannot match. These ties strengthen the outsider's hand, giving an outsider more power to negotiate favorable levels of support. The strategic considerations quickly expand as alternatives distant in the network impact on the bargaining power of the dean and the leading candidate. Such considerations lead to the problem of power distribution as it has been addressed in the network exchange literature. This literature investigates the general properties of networks that influence the allocation of valued resources and focuses on how alternative positions remote in the network affect earnings from exchange in the network's ties.

We use experiments to evaluate four recent theories that predict power distribution/resource allocation in exchange networks. The four theories are game-theoretic core analysis (Bienenstock and Bonacich 1992a), the equidependence principle (Cook and Yamagishi 1992), the expected value model (Friedkin 1992, 1993b), and network exchange-resistance theory (Markovsky, Willer, and Patton 1988; Willer, Markovsky, and Patton 1989; Markovsky et al. 1993).

The key question is, Which of the four theories best predicts observed power distributions? This evaluation of the theories' relative predictive powers contributes to a long-standing process of theory competition in this research field that is necessary to a field's development into a theoretic science (Wagner and Berger 1985; Lakatos 1970). We are also concerned with the theories' absolute predictive power: How well does the best fitting theory account for observed power distributions, and how could its fit be improved? Our investigation uncovers new understandings about exclusion as a source of power in networks.

Our evaluation of the four theories is comprehensive—we examine resource distributions in eight different networks. These networks vary along three dimensions: (1) shape, as defined by the connections among positions; (2) number of exchanges available to each position; and (3) number of exchanges per connection. All previous studies have varied the first dimension; three studies have varied the second dimension (Brennan 1981; Markovsky et al. 1988; Skvoretz and Willer 1991); and none has varied the third. Varying the three dimensions allows us to extend the scope of each theory.

This extension of scope is valuable for two reasons. First, the applicability of theories to networks outside the laboratory is improved. Individuals are seldom limited to one exchange per partner, as most previous experiments have assumed. Furthermore, an experimental network that allows multiple exchanges per connection more closely resembles naturally occurring exchange structures.[1] Investigation of these experimental networks shows how to modify the principles developed for simple structures to apply to the more complicated circumstances found in natural settings. Second, the extension of scope allows us to examine further the fundamental distinction between "strong power" and "weak power" networks that has recently emerged in the literature (Markovsky et al. 1993).

Power differences are measured by differential earnings per exchange.[2] In strong power networks, earnings favor the advantaged position to an extreme degree: The advantaged position appropriates about 90 percent or more of the available resources, leaving 10 percent or less to the disadvantaged position. In weak power networks, earnings per exchange favor the advantaged position to a moderate degree: The advantaged position typically appropriates about 60 to 75 percent of available resources. Why do networks differ so strikingly in the distribution of power?

Current thinking suggests that the critical factor is the potential for exclusion associated with a particular position in a network structure, that is, the ways in which exchanges by some positions can preclude exchanges by other positions. For instance, if each position can exchange only once, the A–B–A network is a strong power network—B is never excluded, but one A is always left out. If each A offers increasingly better exchanges to B to avoid exclusion, extreme differences in resource distribution result. On the other hand, the four position A–B–B–A network is a weak power network—the Bs are never excluded, but exclusion of one or both of the As is not inevitable. Each B has only another B as an alternative to its A, and so each A needs only to better the other B's offer to avoid exclusion. In this network, moderate resource differentiation is expected.

The four theories agree, at least implicitly, that exclusion determines power. However, their predictions differ because each theory makes different assumptions about the effects of exclusion. Underlying these differences is the question of whether exchange outcomes are determined by the a priori potential for exclusion or the *actual* experience of being excluded. We address this question and thus carry the investigation of network exchange one step further than previous studies.

FOUR THEORIES OF POWER IN EXCHANGE NETWORKS

The concept of power has a precise meaning in the literature on exchange networks. Exchange usually is an agreement between two actors on the division of a pool of resources or "profit" points.[3] Power is indicated by a division of resources that significantly favors one actor over another: The actor with the larger share is said to be *exercising* power over the actor with the smaller share (cf. Cook and Emerson 1978; Willer 1992). The interpretation that power is being exercised is consistent with the idea that actors rationally pursue self-interests and, therefore, would not voluntarily agree to a small share if a larger share were possible.

The four theories share one fundamental assumption: Power differentials between actors are related to differences in actors' positions in the network of exchange relations. That is, the determinants of power, as revealed through "exchange outcomes of power use" (Molm 1990), are actors' structural locations rather than their strategic actions.[4] The key theoretical problem is identifying the structurally advantaged positions in a network, that is, the positions that will exercise greater power in exchange relations.

Proposals range from simple measures (e.g., positions connected to many other positions are more advantaged than those connected to few other positions) to more complicated graph-theoretic attributes like "Vulnerability" (Cook and Emerson 1978; Cook, Gillmore, and Yamagishi 1986; Willer 1986). The measure with the widest empirical support is the Graph-theoretic Power Index (GPI) of Markovsky et al. (1988). The four theories we examine go beyond the ordinal predictions of these efforts to the more difficult task of predicting exact earnings from exchanges between pairs of positions. All four theories assume actors are rational—they attempt to maximize their payoffs from exchanges. All but core theory make some additional social psychological assumptions about an actor's propensity to agree to particular terms of exchange. Core theory is a "strategic" theory because it emphasizes the purely strategic determinants of the terms of exchange. The other three theories are "social psychological" theories because, while they do not ignore strategic determinants, they augment them with social psychological considerations. (Details of each theory are presented in the Appendix to this chapter.)

Core Theory

Core theory views exchanges in networks in terms of cooperative N-person game theory. Because exchanges provide value to actors, a set of exchange agreements assigns a payoff vector to the set of actors. Vectors that meet three "rationality" conditions constitute the "core" of the exchange network *qua* game. These conditions are individual, subgroup (coalition), and group rationality. Individual rationality demands that each actor's payoff be equal to or greater than the payoff he or she can earn as a one-member coalition (which is zero by definition in exchange networks). Coalition rationality requires that the sum of the payoffs to any subset of actors is equal to or greater than the sum of payoffs that the subset can obtain by exchange agreements only among its members. Group rationality is coalition rationality at the network or complete group level.

The core of an exchange network *qua* game may contain one, many, or no outcomes; that is, the network may be strategically determined, underdetermined, or undetermined. In general, the payoff schedule will favor some positions over others.[5] In most cases, the actual payoffs to a particular position in the core outcomes can vary widely. In one core outcome, a position may get 100 percent of the resources, while in another core outcome, that position may get 0 percent. As a theory of exchange outcomes, core analysis simply predicts that some core outcome will occur. Because no specific social psychological principle is assumed, rationality considerations alone cannot always single out a particular outcome from this set. This indeterminacy makes comparisons with approaches that make point predictions difficult. To compare core theory with the other three theories, we follow Skvoretz and Fararo (1992) and assume that each core outcome is equally likely. Predictions are the average payoffs to the various positions, calculated over the core outcomes. For exchange networks that have no core outcomes (i.e., are strategically undetermined networks), core theory makes no prediction, although Bienenstock and Bonacich (1992) suggested that exchanges will be concluded but the bargaining will be unstable; "groups . . . should take longer to arrive at their agreements and the patterns should be more variable" (p. 11).

Equidependence Theory

In equidependence theory, ego evaluates potential exchanges with a particular alter with two considerations in mind: How much ego will get in an exchange with this alter, and how much ego could get in an exchange with some other partner. The possible payoff from an alternative partner is ego's comparison level for exchanges with a given alter. The difference between this level and alter's offer determines how dependent ego is on exchanges with alter for favorable outcomes. Meanwhile, alter is evaluating exchanges with ego in a similar fashion and is thus evaluating his or her dependence on ego for favorable outcomes. When ego and alter are equally dependent on their relation for relatively favorable outcomes, the relation is said to be equidependent. Given ego's and alter's comparison levels, equidependence depends on the payoffs the two earn from exchange with each other.

An example given by Cook and Yamagishi (1992) illustrates the idea. Suppose i and j are negotiating over a 24-point pool and i has another partner who guarantees i 10 points, while j has no other partner. If i and j divide the pool at 13 for i and 11 for j, actor i gets 3 points more than her next best alternative (10), while j gets 11 points more than her comparison level of 0. Thus, j is more dependent on i than i is on j and j "will be more willing to give up resources in order to conclude a successful transaction" (Cook and Yamagishi 1992a: p. 3). In this example, equidependence is achieved when i gets 17 points and j gets 7 points because then i and j make 7 points more than their next best alternatives. In networks larger than the dyad, this interdependent evaluation process goes on simultaneously in each of the network's ties.[6] Equidependence theory's basic claim is that exchange earnings are determined when all ties in the network have achieved equidependence by appropriate adjustment of the terms of exchange in each of the network's ties. At this point, actor i's structural power is defined as the maximum profit i can get from any of his or her partners. Observed earnings from exchanges are expected to be proportional to structural power.

Expected Value Theory

Friedkin's (1986) expected value theory follows from his general conceptualization of network effects. A structure defines a space of potential networks, each of which can be realized on a particular occasion. Predictions about a structure's outcomes are then expected values—outcome values of a particular network weighted by the probability of its occurrence. In the present context, a particular exchange network constitutes a structure, and a maximally complete exchange pattern, that is, one in which no further exchanges are possible, constitutes one element in the space of potential networks.[7]

The basic property of interest for each pair of actors i and j is whether actor i's failure to exchange with actor j implies that actor i is excluded from any exchange. Taken over all maximally complete outcomes, this property—the degree to which actor i is excluded from any exchange because he or she fails to exchange with actor j—defines the dependency of i on j. Dependency is the operative social psychological consideration for expected value theory. Ego's aspirations depend on ego's dependency on alter: If ego's dependency on alter is low, ego's aspirations are high, and if ego's dependency on alter is high, ego's aspirations are low. Calculating the dependencies of actors on one another requires an assumption about the likelihood of a particular maximally complete exchange pattern. Friedkin's baseline assumption is that all maximally complete patterns associated with a network are equally likely.[8]

Expected value theory assumes an offer-making function that translates a particular degree of dependency into an offer to alter. The predicted earnings from exchange then are a function of the reciprocal offers as modified by compromises when the offers are inconsistent. Unlike equidependence theory, there is no explicit assumption that these predicted terms of exchange equalize or balance out, in a psychological sense, the differential dependencies of actors on one another. Nevertheless, differential dependency focuses the aspirations of actors on a range of terms of exchange that are sensitive to their dependency on one another.

Exchange-Resistance Theory

The original network exchange theory assigned a GPI score to each node in a network. GPI sums "nonintersecting" paths from a node by adding odd-length paths, which are advantageous, and subtracting even-length paths, which are disadvantageous.[9] Relative GPI scores and three axioms predict with whom a position's occupant will seek to exchange. Agreements are assumed to occur only if actors mutually seek to exchange. The original theory made only ordinal predictions of earnings: if two positions have equal GPI scores, an equal division of points is expected, whereas if i has a higher GPI score than j, i is expected to receive a larger share. Subsequent work (Markovsky et al. 1993) identified $GPI_i > GPI_j$ as leading to strong power differences—extreme differentiation in earnings—and extended the theory to predict "weak power" differences—moderate differences in earnings—in networks in which structurally dissimilar positions have the same GPI score. Weak power occurs when the pattern of exchange-seeking differentially affects a node's likelihood of being included in an exchange. This extension of the theory is also limited to ordinal predictions.

To make this approach comparable to the other three theories, we propose a parsimonious model that unites the strong power and weak power analyses. To produce point predictions, we blend the exchange-seeking assumptions of GPI analysis with an actor's resistance to a particular set of terms of exchange (Heckathorn 1980; Willer 1981).[10] An actor's resistance to a set of terms declines as these terms become increasingly favorable (see Appendix). In our unified model, the exchange-seeking activity implied by GPI analysis and its extension modify resistance such that a high probability of exclusion lowers resistance to a particular set of terms. GPI calculations are necessary to apply this model—the relative scores determine the pattern of exchange-seeking activity and the resulting likelihood of exclusion. However, resistance is the relevant social psychological consideration for actors that makes point predictions possible. Actors make, accept, or reject offers based on their resistance to the proposed terms of exchange and converge on a set of terms to which both parties are equally resistant. This point of equiresistance exists and is uniquely specified for all connected pairs in a network.[11]

Summary

The theories of equidependence, expected value, and exchange resistance are social psychological theories because they assume actors are guided by more than simple rationality in their negotiations with a particular alter. Actors are assumed to be sensitive to their alternatives (or lack thereof) and thus to the possibility that they can "exit" from a particular relationship. Equidependence theory emphasizes the payoff from exit (the comparison level); expected value theory highlights the opportunities to exit without incurring costs (the probabilistic concept of dependency); and exchange-resistance theory combines both considerations through a resistance function that is modified by an actor's probability of being excluded. These assumptions enable the theories to "solve" network structures that core theory, which is based solely on the assumption of rational actors, leaves strategically underdetermined or undetermined.

METHODS AND EXPERIMENTAL NETWORKS

Subjects are undergraduates at a large university who participated for pay. All subjects received general information on the nature of the experiments, in particular, that the aim was to study the effects of network structure on negotiation. They were told that each resource pool consisted of 24 points, how each profit point would be translated into money, and how exchanges were to be made.

Subjects negotiated through ExNet, a system of networked PCs, in a "full information" design. The experimental network was displayed at each subject station, and the screen displayed and continually updated the status of all offers and completed exchanges. Before the experiment, subjects were shown how to read the screen and how to make, accept, or reject and confirm offers. A short training session tested their understanding of these directions, followed by a practice session in which subjects negotiated with simulated others. The practice rounds used a different network than the experimental network, and the randomly generated actions of the simulated actors were purposely unrealistic to avoid cuing effects.

Each experimental run was divided into periods and rounds with periods. Each run of a particular network involved a different group of subjects. The run typically had as many periods as positions in the network. Each period was divided into four rounds. Each round had a five-minute time limit on negotiations. Subjects changed locations in the network between periods in a manner designed to permit the estimation of the effects of particular subject pairs. At the end of each round, subjects were told their earnings in that round. At the end of the experimental run, subjects were paid an amount based on the points they earned. Subjects earned an average of $10.00.

The eight experimental networks are diagrammed in Figure 6.1 and are identified by simplified labels. The number of circles around a position indicates the number of exchanges the position can make per round. The number of lines connecting positions indicates the number of exchanges per round that can occur between the pair. Six networks are "unique-exchange" regimes because, as indicated by the single lines between nodes, only one exchange per connection is allowed per round. In these networks, positions that can make $N > 1$ exchanges per round must make them with N others.

Two networks are nonunique-exchange regimes. In NBranch2, A and B can make two exchanges per round and C can make one, whereas A and B can exchange with each other twice per round. In NT2, all positions can make two exchanges per round, and all pairs can exchange with each other twice per round. In these networks, negotiations for a pair's second exchange begin after the first exchange is completed; pairs cannot simultaneously negotiate the terms of the first and second exchanges.[12] In all networks, actors connected to several others can negotiate simultaneously with each partner. The derivation of predictions from each of the four theories is straightforward for the unique-exchange networks, whereas each theory must be extended to cover the nonunique networks. (Details are found in the Appendix.)

To compare predictions with observations, we estimated the effects of network position from the observed points earned by exchange. Because particular agreements could involve the same pair of subjects, point earnings are analyzed as a variant of a repeated measures, correlated observations problem (Skvoretz and Willer 1991; Winer 1962). The units of observation are particular subject pairs that can complete a series of exchanges. A particular pair can contribute

Figure 6.1
Experimental Networks Used in the Analysis

Unique-Exchange Networks

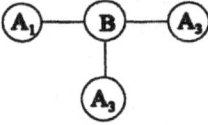

Branch 31

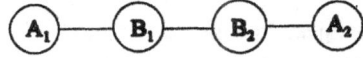

Line 4

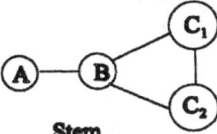

Stem

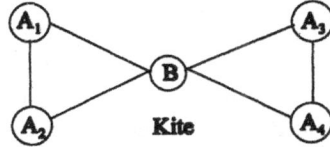

Kite

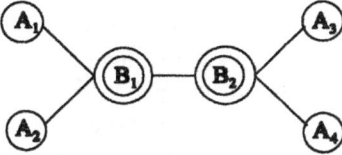

D Branch 2

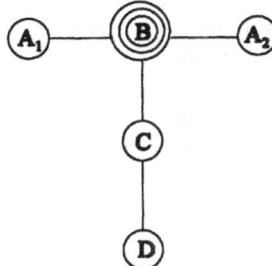

TB3

Nonunique-Exchange Networks

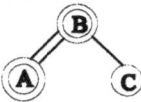

N Branch 2

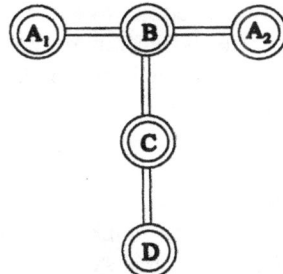

NT 2

more than one exchange agreement to the total set of observations. A constrained regression technique is used to estimate the effects of network position and, where possible, the effects of particular subject pairings. The analytical procedure is a variant of a procedure used in previous research (Skvoretz and Willer 1991; Markovsky et al. 1993).

In the original procedure, Y_i refers to the number of points earned by one member of the pair that completes the ith agreement. The earnings of the same subject in a pair must be used to code all agreements made by that pair. We index subjects by numerals so that Y_i refers to the earnings of the subject with the higher index number in the pair making the ith agreement. For each pair that could complete an agreement, there is a 0/1 variable denoted $V(x,y)$. For the ith agreement, $V(x,y) = 1$ if that agreement is between subjects x and y and otherwise, $V(x,y) = 0$. For each structurally distinct exchange relation involving structurally distinct positions, there is an indicator variable Z_k. For the ith agreement, $Z_k = 1$ if the subject with the higher index value occupies the advantaged position; $Z_k = -1$ if he or she occupies the disadvantaged position; and $Z_k = 0$ otherwise (i.e., when the ith agreement is between persons not in the kth structurally distinct exchange relation). The choice of which position is advantaged is arbitrary but must remain constant over the coding of agreements. (If a position initially coded as advantaged is, in fact, disadvantaged, then the effect of Z_k will be negative.) Structurally distinct positions are denoted in Figure 6.1 by different letters, and so structurally distinct exchange relations must involve different pairs of letters. The basic estimation equation is:

$$Y = 12 + \sum \pi_{xy} V(x,y) + \sum \tau_k Z_k + \varepsilon, \qquad (6.1)$$

in which a linear relation is assumed between the various independent variables and the exchange earnings.

The parameter π_{xy} represents the effects of the individual pair of subject x with subject y and the parameter τ_k represents the effect of structural position in the kth structurally distinct exchange relation. The intercept is constrained to the baseline rate of 12 points. This allows subject pair effects and position effects to be interpreted as additions to or subtractions from the even split of 12/12. In certain cases (e.g., when few exchanges occur between particular positions), it may not be possible to disentangle the effects of network position from the subject pair effects. In such cases, simple means are reported.

We used a variation on this procedure that calculates, for each subject pair, the mean values of Y for each combination of structural conditions indexed by the Z_k variables. We then estimated a constrained regression equation weighting each data point by the number of agreements that entered into its calculation. This procedure gives the same estimates of the structural parameters τ_k, but yields larger standard errors for these estimates.[13] Larger standard errors are appropriate at this early stage of theoretical predictions of exact exchange rates

Table 6.1
Number and Types of Exchanges by Network Structure

Network	Number of Periods	Number of Groups	Number of Exchanges	Type of Exchanges
Branch31	4	5	80	80 AB
Line4	4	5	134	120 AB, 14 BB
Stem	4	4	116	53 AB, 8 AC, 55 CC
Kite	5	4	158	47 AB, 111 AA
DBranch2	6	5	423	410 AB, 13 BB
TB3	5	4	218	140 AB, 34 BC, 44 CD
NBranch2	6	4	236	143 AB, 93 BC
NT2	5	4	307	155 AB, 4 BC, 148 CD

where the danger lies more in premature rejection of valuable ideas than in the acceptance of an incorrect hypothesis.

RESULTS

Table 6.1 lists the number and types of exchanges observed in each of the experimental networks. Each group was composed of subjects who had prior experience negotiating with other subjects (rather than simulated actors) in other network structures.[14]

Table 6.2 compares predictions from the four theories with observations. The general pattern of experimental results is consistent with previous research. Power advantage is extreme in strong power relations, such as the A–B relation in the Branch31 network. Only a modest advantage is found in the weak power networks, Line4, Stem, Kite, and DBranch2. Changing B's permitted number of exchanges from one to three in TB3 changes the relative advantage of all positions in a way Markovsky et al. (1988) anticipated for a seven-person network. The NT2 network behaves much as did the simple T network also studied by Markovsky et al. (1988). Finally, although the results from NBranch2 have no precedent in the literature, the general intuition that B has an advantage in both relations is confirmed.

The exchange-resistance model is the best fitting model—it has the smallest mean deviation from estimated advantage, 1.37 points, when deviations are weighted by the number of exchanges. Equidependence is the better of the two remaining social psychological theories, with an average deviation of 2.66 points. Expected value theory has an average deviation over 3 points. The place of core theory depends on the value assigned to its "no rate" cells. If core

Table 6.2

Points Earned by Advantaged Positions, by Network Relation: Predictions from Four Theories Versus Estimates from Experiments

| Network | Network Relation[c] | Theory (Predicted Points) | | | | Number of Exchanges | Estimated Points (SE) |
		Core	Equi-dependence	Exchange-Resistance	Expected Value		
Branch31	B/A	24.0	24.0	21.2*	22.0*	80	21.63 (.49)
Line4	B/A	16.0	16.0	16.0	21.1	120	14.05 (.40)
Stem	B/A	20.1	18.0	18.3	22.0	53	15.29 (.82)
	B/C	NA[a]	14.4*	15.2*	19.5*	8	16.49 (2.64)
Kite	B/A	NA[a]	12.0	12.5	12.0	47	14.05 (.77)
DBranch2	B/A	16.8	16.0*	14.6	20.2	410	15.50 (.41)
TB3	B/A	12.0	12.0	12.0	12.0	140	13.53 (.45)
	C/B	24.0	24.0	21.8	21.1	34	17.88 (1.01)[b]
	C/D	24.0	24.0	16.0*	21.1	44	17.72 (.93)
NBranch2	B/A	18.0	24.0	17.9	18.3	143	16.12 (.53)
	B/C	24.0	24.0	16.0	21.1	93	17.76 (.67)
NT2	B/A	24.0	24.0	19.6	21.8	155	20.67 (.49)
	B/C	NA[a]	16.0*	12.0*	12.0*	4	16.50 (2.40)[b]
	C/D	12.0*	12.0*	12.0*	17.4	148	12.86 (.70)
Weighted average absolute deviation from estimate[d]		2.40 (2.88)	2.66	1.37	3.54		

*The null hypothesis that the estimated points equal the predicted points cannot be rejected at the .05 level.

[a]No prediction because the network has no core outcome as in Kite or no exchange is possible between the two positions. To compute the deviation, a value of 12 or (0) is assigned to these cells.

[b]Simple estimate from mean values; all other estimates control for the effects of particular subject pairs.

[c]First position is the advantaged position.

[d]Weights are the number of exchanges.

theory is penalized by assigning these cells a score of 0, it has the second worst fit (2.88 points), but if these cells are assigned a score of 12, it is second best at 2.40 points. If we consider the number of predictions that fall within two standard errors of the estimated advantage, core theory fits worst (regardless of how empty cells are handled)—only one of its 11 predictions falls in this range. Exchange-resistance theory has 5 of 14 predictions within this range, equidependence theory has four, and expected value theory has three. That core theory fits least well is not surprising—it makes fewer assumptions than the other three. That exchange-resistance theory fits best is also, perhaps, to be expected because it uses exit costs and opportunities to make its predictions, whereas the other two social psychological theories use only one of these factors.

Although of the four theories exchange-resistance theory fits best, 9 of its 14 predictions are *outside* two standard errors of the estimated advantage. Because there is room for improvement, we propose some variants of the present models. These variants explore the idea that better fits can be obtained by taking into account the actual frequencies of exclusion experienced by actors.

REFORMULATION OF THE THEORIES

We drop core theory from further consideration and focus on the three theories that employ social psychological principles because they make explicit point predictions for all networks. The three theories emphasize the importance of exclusion and its consequences in the determination of exchange rates. However, there are two different paths by which network structure can affect exchange earnings differentials through exclusion.

In one path, earnings differentials are produced by the built-in *potential* for exclusion which varies among network positions. For example, in the Line4 network, the Bs, confident of never being excluded, bargain harder than the As who recognize the risk of demanding too much. Thus, As make concessions, Bs make demands, and terms of exchange come to favor the Bs even if no exclusion occurs. Because differential power is a consequence of possibilities of the network structure, it is independent of actual exclusion. Therefore, a priori probabilities of exclusion are the best predictors of positions' earnings from exchanges. This model is most compatible with an actor who rationally infers consequences, a "forward-looking actor" in Macy's (1990) terms.

In a second path, earnings differentials result because actors who are excluded adjust their offers upward whereas actors who are consistently included adjust their offers downward. Here both concessions and demands are direct consequences of *actual* events. In the Line4, Bs are never excluded and thus they never make concessions, but the As are excluded and, when they are excluded, they make better offers to the Bs. As a result, the terms of exchange between an A and a B will favor the B position. Because differential power is a consequence of actually being excluded or included, its best predictors are the observed frequencies. This model is most compatible with an actor who rationally adjusts to past experience, a "backward-looking" actor in Macy's (1990) terms.

The analysis of the previous section examined the network-specific "exclusion potential" version of the three social psychological theories. The exchange-resistance and expected value theories clearly base their predictions on assumptions about a priori probabilities. Exclusion-resistance theory uses the probabilities of being included to modify the resistance function, while expected value theory uses the exclusion probabilities to calculate dependency scores. In equidependence theory, the relevant a priori assumption is the setting of an actor's comparison level; that is, actors face an a priori dichotomous probability of being excluded of 0 (if they have alternatives) or 1 (if they have no alternatives).

We now consider the "actual exclusion" version of these theories to predict power differentials produced by different network structures. If the *potential* for exclusion reduces power, the theories will predict best when using a priori probabilities. If *actual* exclusion reduces power, the theories will predict best when using observed frequencies of exclusion. If both factors reduce power, then each theory's predictions may or may not be improved, *depending on which mechanism is implicit in the theory*. Using observed frequencies of exclusion will give different predictions if they (or related quantities) differ from their corresponding a priori values. Table 6.3 presents, for exchange-resistance theory, observed and a priori probabilities of being included; Table 6.4 presents, for expected value theory, observed and a priori dependency scores. For both tables, observed values can differ substantially from a priori calculations. Clearly, for those positions that have alternatives, the probability of exchange with one of these alternatives is almost never 1—the a priori assumption of equidependence theory.

Predictions from the structural potential for exclusion version of exchange-resistance and expected value theories are easily modified to take observed frequencies into account. Because both have terms that refer to the relative frequencies of various events related to observed exclusions, we simply substitute the observed values for the a priori values. Predictions from equidependence theory are modified by weighting what ego would receive from any alternative by the observed relative frequency that the particular alter exchanges with ego.[15] Table 6.5 presents these modified predictions.

The effect of using actual frequencies of exclusion varies substantially among theories. For exchange-resistance theory, the average deviation increases from 1.37 to 1.88 points, but two more predictions (for a total of seven) are within two standard errors of the estimated advantage. For equidependence theory, improvement is made on both counts—5 rather than 4 of the 14 predictions are within two standard errors of the estimated advantage, and the average deviation decreases from 2.66 to 2.38 points. The expected value model shows striking improvement: The average deviation decreases dramatically from 3.54 to 1.36 points, and 9 of its 14 predictions fall within two standard errors of the estimated advantage. These results suggest that (1) exchange-resistance theory emphasizes the structural potential for exclusion as a cause of power; (2) expected value theory emphasizes experienced exclusion; and (3) equidependence theory uses both the structural potential for exclusion and experienced exclusion. The general conclusion is that both forms of exclusion can produce power differentials.

This conclusion is supported by the data in Table 6.5, which show that all three theories have difficulty accounting for earnings advantages in the weak

Table 6.3
Potential and Observed Probabilities of Being Included by Position in the Network: Exchange-Resistance Theory

Network	Position in Network	Probability of Being Included	
		Potential	Observed
Branch31	A	.333	.333
	B	1.000	1.000
Line4	A	.750	.750
	B	1.000	.925
Stem	A	.600	.828
	B	1.000	.923
	C	.800	.922
Kite	A	.795	.841
	B	.821	.588
DBranch2	A	.833	.872
	B	1.000	.908
TB3	A	1.000	.875
	B (in A/B)	1.000	.875
	B (in B/C)	.250	.400
	C	1.000	.975
	D	.750	.575
NBranch2	A	.625	.578
	B	1.000	.938
	C	.750	.719
NT2	A	.500	.484
	B	1.000	.994
	C	1.000	.950
	D	1.000	.925

power networks (Line4, Kite, DBranch2 and, to a lesser degree, Stem). In these networks, no position is systematically excluded from exchange.[16] As expected, the estimated advantages are relatively modest, but even so the "experienced exclusion" models consistently predict less advantage than is observed—13 out of 15 predictions. Furthermore, for the Kite network, all three "experienced exclusion" models predict, contrary to observation, that the *B* position is at a disadvantage in exchanges with the *A*s. This pattern of underprediction and misprediction suggests that advantage in weak power networks is sensitive to differences in positions' *potential* for being excluded and that experienced exclusion is not necessary to produce such advantage.

Table 6.4
Potential and Observed Dependency Scores by Network Relation: Expected Value Theory

| Network | Relation | Dependency Score | |
		Potential	Observed
Branch31	AB	.667	.667
	BA	.000	.000
Line4	AB	.500	.250
	BA	.000	.075
Stem	AB	.667	.172
	BA	.000	.047
	BC	.333	.078
	CB	.000	.047
Kite	AB	.200	.159
	BA	.200	.412
DBranch2	AB	.400	.146
	BA	.000	.092
TB3	AB	.000	.125
	BA	.000	.083
	BC	.500	.200
	CB	.000	.025
	CD	.000	.025
	DC	.500	.425
NBranch2	AB	.250	.422
	BA	.000	.063
	BC	.000	.005
	CB	.500	.281
NT2	AB	.600	.513
	BA	.000	.006
	BC	.000	.006
	CB	.000	.050
	CD	.000	.050
	DC	.200	.075

CONCLUSION

We evaluated four recent theories of power distribution in exchange networks, one purely strategic theory and three social psychological theories. We examined eight different networks and tested two different versions of the three social

Table 6.5
Points Earned by Advantaged Positions, by Network Relation: Predictions from Three Modified Theories Versus Estimates from Experiments

		Theory (Predicted Points)				
Network	Network Relation[b]	Equi-dependence	Exchange-Resistance	Expected Value	Number of Exchanges	Estimated Points (SE)
Branch31	B/A	24.0	21.2*	22.0*	80	21.63 (.49)
Line4	B/A	13.0	15.0	15.8	120	14.05 (.40)
Stem	B/A	12.5	14.1*	15.2*	53	15.29 (.82)
	B/C	12.6*	12.5*	12.9*	8	16.49 (2.64)
Kite	B/A	8.1	7.2	10.1	47	14.05 (.77)
DBranch2	B/A	12.3	12.6	13.4	410	15.50 (.41)
TB3	B/A	12.0	12.0	13.1*	140	13.53 (.45)
	C/B	18.9*	20.5	16.5*	34	17.88 (1.01)[a]
	C/D	13.8	18.4*	19.6	44	17.72 (.93)
NBranch2	B/A	19.1	18.0	18.5	143	16.12 (.53)
	B/C	14.2	15.7	18.5*	93	17.76 (.67)
NT2	B/A	19.8*	19.7*	21.0*	155	20.67 (.49)
	B/C	16.9*	12.7*	13.5*	4	16.50 (2.40)[a]
	C/D	12.1*	12.4*	12.7*	148	12.86 (.70)
Weighted average absolute deviation from estimate[c]		2.38	1.88	1.36		

*The null hypothesis that the estimated points equal the predicted points cannot be rejected at the .05 level.
[a]Simple estimate from mean values; all other estimates control for the effects of particular subject pairs.
[b]First position listed is advantaged position.
[c]Deviations are weighted by the number of exchanges.

psychological theories, a "structural potential for exclusion" version and an "experienced exclusion" version. The best theory is exchange-resistance theory when predictions are based solely on structurally determined *potentials* for exclusion, that is, on a priori calculations of differential probabilities of exclusion (and related quantities) faced by different positions in a network. When predictions use *observed* instances of exclusion (and related quantities), expected value theory is the best theory. Moreover, expected value theory is the only social psychological theory whose fit is substantially improved by taking into account the observed frequencies of exclusion. Our conclusion highlights (1) the role played by differential chances of exclusion in the genesis of power differentials; (2) the significance of weak power networks for further research on power distribution in exchange networks; and (3) information availability as a catalytic agent in the process by which a network's structural potential for exclusion impacts on exchange outcomes.

Our study strongly suggests that power distribution in exchange networks is sensitive both to the potential for exclusion and to actual exclusion. Generally, actors who are less often excluded earn more from exchange and, hence, exercise power in negotiations with actors who are more often excluded. But the influence of differences in the structural potential for exclusion cannot be ruled out: In weak power networks, differences in the potential for exclusion augment the differentiation in power derived from actual exclusion. In one exceptional case—the Kite network—*the structural potential for exclusion overrides the effect of differences in experienced exclusion.* Even though the central actor B is excluded from exchange more than twice as often as the peripheral A actors (41 percent versus 16 percent), B nevertheless earns moderately more points in exchange with actors in the A positions (14.05 versus 9.95 points).

Of course, this interpretation assumes that the structural potential for exclusion favors B. In fact, only exchange-resistance theory suggests that A has a slightly greater potential for exclusion than B and so provides a basis for B's greater earnings. (However, its prediction based on this difference in structural potential underestimates B's advantage.) Fortunately, other general theoretical arguments can be applied to this anomaly. Burt's (1992) concept of "structural holes" adds theoretical grounding for the expectation that a structural potential can override actual events in their joint determination of exchange outcomes. In the Kite network, Burt would argue, B's advantage derives from the fact that there are four structural holes in B's primary network (of six possible holes), while each A's primary network has no structural holes. The total constraint on the B position is substantially less than that on the A position (.56 versus .78), and the constraint that a particular A places on the B position is much less than the B position places on that A position (.14 versus .39). Therefore, following Burt, A's demands on B would be more negotiable from B's perspective than B's demands on A would be from A's perspective. Therefore, B's greater earnings from exchanges with an A are no surprise.

In general, the four theories do less well in accounting for power differentials in weak power networks than in strong power networks. Before the discovery of weak power, only two power conditions were recognized. Either there were power differentials—now termed strong—and earnings from exchange dramatically favored high power actors, or power was equal and so were earnings. Predictions were evaluated simply by testing whether earnings differed from the baseline of equal division. Furthermore, in strong or equal power networks, potential exclusion and actual exclusion could not be disentangled. In strong power networks, low power actors were potentially excludable *and* were necessarily excluded. In equipower networks (e.g., an isolated dyad), neither actor could exclude the partner without cost and so no exclusion occurred. Because earnings of actors in advantaged positions in weak power networks fall between these extremes and are different in different networks, weak power networks place greater demands on theory and theories must now supply point predictions. More important, however, unlike other types of networks, weak power networks permit a decoupling of the structural potential for exclusion from actual frequencies of exclusion. These networks enable researchers to investigate the conditions under which one or the other or both of these mechanisms account for exchange rate differentials.

Finally, future research should use weak power networks to systematically explore the relationship between information and the development of power. None of the four theories qualifies its predictions by considering information conditions. Yet theorists have long suspected that information available to actors can influence power differentials. For example, actors need more complete information to act on structural potentials for exclusion than on actual exclusions. Although our results suggest that either mechanism can produce power, our experiments were conducted in an open information context in which actors knew how their position was connected in the larger network. With this information, subjects could make a cognitive assessment of their chances of exclusion and calibrate their behavior accordingly. However, we have no evidence that they make such assessments or that the effect of a structural potential for exclusion requires such assessments. Perhaps other mechanisms underlie the effects of a structural potential for exclusion on power distribution in information-poor environments or in information-rich environments with unobservant subjects. Certainly, exploration of the role of information should be conducted using weak power networks, for they alone allow the structural potential for exclusion to be decoupled from actual instances of exclusion and thus permit systematic examination of the catalytic effect of information.

APPENDIX

Core Theory

To identify the core in a network, each subset of positions is assigned a value based on the total number of exchanges possible in the subset and the size of the pool to be divided (typically 24 points). This mapping from a subset of positions to its value is called the characteristic function of the exchange network *qua* game. For instance, in the Branch31 network, any $\{A_i,B,A_j\}$ triple has the same value as an $\{A_i,B\}$ pair, namely, 24, because in both cases B can divide a 24-point pool with only one of the As. In the Line4 network, the complete set of actors $\{A,B,B,A\}$ has a value of 48 because two exchanges are possible within the set of four actors (two AB exchanges) and each exchange is worth 24 points. Once the characteristic function is defined, core payoff assignments are those assignments that meet the three rationality conditions. For instance, the Branch31 outcome in which B gets 22 points, A_1 gets 2 points, and A_2 and A_3 get 0 points is not a core outcome because the sum of B's payoff and A_2's payoff is less than 24, the value of the $\{A_2,B\}$ subset. In the Line4 network, the outcome in which the Bs divide the pool evenly at 12/12 and the As receive 0 is not a core outcome because the total payoff to each $\{A,B\}$ subset coalition is less than its value of 24.

Branch31's one core outcome occurs when B receives all 24 points and the As receive 0 points. This is the only payoff assignment that satisfies the three rationality conditions. B's strong advantage derives from its strategic location with respect to subset values—B must be included in any subset for the subset to have a positive value. This is not true for any A position. The B positions are advantaged in Line4 but in a more subtle way. Because the B positions are connected, any core outcome must have payoffs to the B positions that total 24 points or more. Because the A positions are not connected, their point total can be less than 24. B's advantage in Line4 derives from its strategic location with respect to coalition rationality—it has a nonzero alternative to its coalition with A. However, the advantage is not as extreme as in Branch31 because the group rationality condition ensures that the core outcomes give nonzero payoffs to the A positions.

The core outcomes for each of the unique-exchange networks are defined by a set of inequalities that payoff vectors for core outcomes must satisfy. Bienenstock and Bonacich (1992) specify the inequalities for the first four experimental networks. For DBranch2, the relevant inequalities are $B_1+B_2 \geqslant 24$; $A_1+B_1+A_2 \geqslant 48$; $A_3+B_2+A_4 \geqslant 48$; $A_i+B_1+B_2 \geqslant 48$ for $i = 1,2,3,4$; $A_1+B_1+B_2+A_i \geqslant 72$; and $A_2+B_1+B_2+A_i \geqslant 72$ for $i = 3,4$. There are 70,525 core outcomes that satisfy these inequalities—each A receives an average payoff of 7.2, and each B receives 16.8 points in an exchange with A. The TB3 network has 625 core outcomes because each A's payoff can vary from 0 to 24, determining B's payoff between 0 and 48, while C's payoff is fixed at 24 and D's at 0.

In the nonunique-exchange networks, our extension of Bienenstock and Bonacich's work assumes that the sequential aspect of the exchange protocol can be ignored. This means that a pair that can negotiate two 24-point deals per round is treated as if it is negotiating only one deal worth 48 points. For the NBranch2 network, the inequalities that define the core are: $A+B \geqslant 48$ and $B+C \geqslant 24$. B's average earnings are 36 points, A's are 12 points, and C earns nothing. For the NT2 network, the 1875 core outcomes are those in which $A_1 = A_2 = 0$, $B = 48$, and $C+D = 48$, so C and D each average 12 points.

Equidependence Theory

Actor i's profit in an exchange with actor j, denoted R_{ij}, is i's agreed share of the resource pool. Actor i's dependence on actor j, D_{ij}, is the difference between the profit i gets in an i-j exchange and the quantity A_{ij} which is the profit i gets from his or her mth best alternative where m is the number of exchanges i is allowed. If i has only one exchange, then A_{ij} can be defined by the equation:

$$A_{ij} = \max_{k \neq j} \{R_{ik}\} \tag{A.1}$$

The equidependence principle states that exchange rates are determined by the point at which the dependence of i on j equals the dependence of j on i throughout the network, that is, where $D_{ij} = D_{ji}$ for all connected pairs i and j. For the six unique-exchange networks, the equidependence point is easy to calculate using the basic algorithm described in Cook and Yamagishi (1992). The algorithm begins with each pool divided equally, calculates the A_{ij} values, then adjusts the R_{ij} values, then recalculates the A_{ij} values and adjusts the R_{ij} values and so on until they converge. For instance, for the Line4 network, the algorithm converges in 20 steps to the solution $R_{A1B1} = R_{A2B2} = 8$, $R_{B1A1} = R_{B2A2} = 16$ and $R_{B1B2} = R_{B2B1} = 8$ in which A has structural power 8 and B has structural power 16.[17]

To extend the principle to nonunique-exchange networks, unlike unique-exchange networks, some alternative exchanges are exchanges with the same partner. The question is whether such alternatives should be used in determining the comparison level for a particular exchange with that partner. The answer must be "no" otherwise actors could bid against themselves. The problem arises only when an actor's connection to another could have more exchanges per round than the actor is allowed. In that case, the "extra" exchange capacity of the connection is irrelevant and does not provide genuine alternatives. The algorithm is easily modified to take this restriction into account. The simplest procedure confines connections to the smaller of the total exchanges the partners can make. Then each partner's mth best alternative, necessarily, is exchange with some other partner.

In the NBranch2 network, A can make two exchanges, so A's comparison level to either one of these exchanges is determined not by the next best alternative but by the second best alternative, which is zero because A has no second best alternative. C can make one exchange, so C's comparison level is the next best alternative, which is also zero. B can make two exchanges but has three opportunities and so has a nonzero second best alternative to any one of the three. The equidependence point gives B 24 points in any of B's three exchanges—the dependence of A on B and B on A equal 0 and as do the dependence of B on C and C on B. (To be consistent with the sequential structure of the exchange regime, this prediction requires that B's first exchange be with A. If it were with C, the result is an isolated dyad whose equidependence point is a 12/12 division.) The NT2 network is solved similarly—B gets 24 points in an exchange with either A and 16 points in either exchange with C, and C gets 12 points in either exchange with D.

Expected Value Theory

In expected value theory, the dependency of actor i on actor j, d_{ij}, is defined as the joint probability that i is excluded from an exchange and i does not exchange with j.[18] The dependency of i on j affects the "offer" i makes to j in accord with the following equation (for a 24-point pool):

$$f_{ij} = 24 - 23^{1-d_{ij}}. \tag{A.2}$$

Thus, if $d_{ij} = 0$, i offers 1 point to j and claims 23 points, whereas if $d_{ij} = 1$, then i offers 23 points to j and claims only 1 point. Actor j's offer to i is determined in a similar manner. Further assumptions resolve situations in which the claims do not sum exactly to the pool size. In particular, (1) if the sum exceeds the pool size, actors "split the difference" and agree on the average of their two offers (so i gets one-half of the sum of his or her claim and j's offer); (2) if both actors claim less than one-half the pool size, they agree on a 12/12 division; and (3) if the sum is less than the pool size, but one actor claims more than one-half, they agree on a division in which that actor gets what he or she claims and the rest is allocated to the other actor. These assumptions produce a wide range of cases where a 12/12 division is predicted: All cases in which d_{ij} and $d_{ji} \geq .205$ and $d_{ij} = d_{ji}$.

For the nonunique-exchange networks, we generalize the dependency concept as follows: d_{ij} is the joint probability that "i fails to complete an allowed exchange" and, on that occasion, "i fails to exchange with j." The second clause recognizes the possibility that because multiple exchanges can be made with the same partner in a round, i may have exchanged with j on another occasion. The idea is that i's dependency on j reflects the fact that i is excluded from completing some potential exchanges as a result of the failure to complete as many exchanges with j as the connection allows. For all networks, we use the baseline assumption that all maximally complete outcomes are equally likely.

The NBranch2 network has two maximally complete outcomes: A exchanges twice with B and C has no exchange, or B exchanges once with each A and C. If these outcomes are equally likely, then $d_{BA} = d_{BC} = 0$ because B completes all allowed exchanges in both outcomes; $d_{AB} = .25$ because A fails to complete one exchange given four opportunities to exchange with B; and $d_{CB} = .50$ because C fails to complete one exchange given two opportunities to exchange with B. The NT2 network has five maximally complete outcomes. Because B and C always complete their allotted totals, their dependency scores are 0. The A positions complete only 40 percent of their potential exchanges and so have a dependency on B of .60, while D completes 80 percent of its potential exchanges and so has a dependency on C of .20.

Exchange-Resistance Theory

The baseline predictions of exchange-resistance theory use the concept of "resistance." In the work of Heckathorn (1980) and Willer (1981), an actor's resistance to an outcome is a function of the payoffs from that outcome, the "best hope" outcome, and the "conflict" outcome. Technically, the conflict outcome is the outcome given by the failure to reach agreement. Any outcome that yields payoffs for both actors that are just as good or better than the conflict outcome is in the "contract zone." An actor's best hope is the outcome in the contract zone that yields maximum payoff. In the experimental task of dividing a pool of M profit points, we assume (as do all other theories) that utility is a linear function of points (see Fararo and Skvoretz 1993). Therefore, the best hope of both i and j is M points, the conflict payoff is 0 points, and the resistances of i and j to a division in which i receives x_i points and j receives $M - x_i$ points are:

$$R_i = \frac{M - x_i}{M - 0} \quad \text{and} \quad R_j = \frac{M - (M - x_i)}{M - 0}. \tag{A.3}$$

Agreement is predicted to occur on the outcome to which i and j are equally resistant. This is the "equiresistance principle." In the absence of any further considerations, this outcome is an equal division of the pool.

To coordinate with previous research, we incorporate an additional consideration into the resistance equation and assume that the numerator is a function of the probability that an actor is included in an exchange. In particular, we assume a power function in which the difference between the maximum payoff and what the actor would receive from an offer is raised to the power determined by the probability of being included. Thus the baseline model for exchange-resistance theory assumes that the resistances of i and j are given by:

$$R_i = \frac{(M - x_i)^{p_i}}{M} \quad \text{and} \quad R_j = \frac{[M - (M - x_i)]^{p_j}}{M}, \tag{A.4}$$

where p_i and p_j are the probabilities of being included for i and j. Equating the resistances and simplifying yields an equation that can be solved for x and that provides the baseline predictions in Table 6.2:

$$\frac{\ln(M - x_i)}{\ln(x_i)} = \frac{p_j}{P_i}. \tag{A.5}$$

The probabilities of being included depend on the pattern of exchange-seeking. This pattern, in turn, is determined by the relative GPI scores following either Markovsky et al.'s (1988) Axiom 2 that "i seeks exchange with j if and only if i's power is greater than j's or if i's power relative to j equals or exceeds that in any of i's other relations" (p. 225) or the weak power random seek extension in Markovsky et al. (1993). For example, according to this analysis, A's probability of being included in Stem, a weak power network, is .60, whereas B's probability is 1.00. Therefore, the points that B should earn in exchanges with A is that value of x for which $\ln(24 - x) = .6x$, which is 18.3.

Extending this method to the nonunique-exchange networks is a simple matter because an actor cannot simultaneously negotiate multiple deals with another actor even if he or she can make more than one exchange per round with that alter. The only new element is that concluding a deal with such an alter may not eliminate that alter from the space of potential partners.

NOTES

1. Real networks—and the exercise of power in them—still differ in many ways from these experimental structures. In our view, extension of scope must continue in a stepwise fashion guided by a body of theoretical issues and concerns as formulated in ongoing research programs. In that context, permitting multiple exchanges per connection is a theoretically justified manipulation of a central initial condition of the research programs we evaluate.

2. We do not evaluate predictions about the relative frequency of exchanges between particular positions for three reasons. First, some of the theories do not make such predictions. Second, some predictions of frequency of exchange are imprecise, for example, "few" exchanges are anticipated (Bienenstock and Bonacich 1993). Third, precise predictions often are a priori assumptions of structural potential that are not necessarily intended to predict observed frequencies of exchange (Markovsky 1992; also see Lovaglia and Skvoretz 1993).

3. This task is formally equivalent to exchange formulated as an Edgeworth box problem (Edgeworth 1881). In Edgeworth's formulation, both actors can improve on their "initial" endowment by exchanging until some point on the "contract curve" is reached. At that point, any further exchange necessitates a decline in one actor's utility and an increase in the other's. Similarly, in the present task, both actors gain from any agreement because failure to reach agreement results in no payoff to either actor. However, any agreement that gives a larger share to one person necessarily gives a smaller share to the other, as do exchanges along the contract curve of the Edgeworth box.

4. Strategic action refers to how subjects use their potential power advantages. Although strategic action can affect the use of power, Molm (1990) showed that strategic action is unrelated to structural advantage.

5. For example, if all positions exchange only once when dividing a 24-point pool, the simple A_1–B–A_2 structure has a single-core outcome, namely, a payoff of 24 points to B and 0 to each of the As. Any other payoff assignment, say, 23 to B, 1 to A_1 and 0 to A_2 violates coalition rationality for some subset, in this case B and A_2, because the sum of their payoffs is 23, which is less than they could obtain by exchanging with each other.

6. For example, in the simple A_1–B–A_2 network, equidependence theory predicts that B gets all 24 points in an exchange with an A. Each A has no alternative and so has a comparison level of 0. Receiving 0 in an exchange with B makes A's dependence on B equal to 0. For B, A_2 is an alternative to A_1 in which B receives 24 points. This establishes the comparison level for the 24 points received from an exchange with A_1, making B's dependence on A_1 equal to A_1's dependence on B, namely, zero.

7. In the line network A–B–B–A, there are two maximally complete exchange patterns, one in which two AB exchanges occur and one in which the two B positions exchange. In the second exchange pattern, even though both A positions do not exchange,

the pattern is maximally complete because the two A positions are not connected and thus no further exchanges can be made.

8. In the A_1-B-A_2 network, the A_1-B and the A_2-B exchange patterns are equally likely. B's dependency on either A is zero because B is never excluded, while each A's dependency on B is .5 because A fails to exchange with B, and so is excluded 50 percent of the time.

9. Odd length indicates advantage because it means a node has alternatives or a partner's alternatives also have alternatives to one's partner, and so on. Even length indicates disadvantage because it means a node has one or more rivals for the attention of a partner.

10. Recent work has used resistance concepts (Lovaglia, Skvoretz, Willer, and Markovsky 1993). However, that work is not comparable to the other three theories because it was developed to predict weak power "equilibrium" rates only. Resistance in our analysis provides a "baseline" model chosen more with an eye toward simplicity of calculation and comprehensiveness of coverage than precise fit to a subset of exchange networks.

11. In the A_1-B-A_2 network, the exchange-seeking activity as determined by positions' relative GPI scores implies that B's probability of being included is 1.00 while A's is .5. In the unified model, an 18/6 exchange favoring B is one for which B's resistance is low at .25 but still greater than A's at .177. The point of equiresistance is a 19.6/4.4 division, at which point the resistances of A and B are equal at .183.

12. Several considerations motivated the choice of these networks. Four of the networks are of long-standing interest. The Branch31 and Line4 structures are among the simplest of the strong power and weak power networks, respectively; Stem and Kite are controversial weak power networks (Yamagishi and Cook 1990; Markovsky, Willer, and Patton 1990). The remaining four networks extend the scope of research in two ways: (1) they allow variation in the number of exchanges a position can make, and (2) they introduce networks that allow multiple exchanges per round between connected pairs. The T-shaped networks have played an important role in the history of network exchange research, motivating both theoretical and empirical work (see Cook, Emerson, Gillmore, and Yamagishi 1983; Willer 1986; Cook et al. 1986). The NBranch2 structure is the simplest nonunique network that has no unique-exchange counterpart. Finally, the DBranch2 structure is the first multiple-exchange network to be researched that should exhibit the effects of weak power. Previous investigations of this effect (Markovsky et al. 1993) have been limited to the Kite and Stem unique networks.

13. The standard errors increase because we are throwing out degrees of freedom identified with the multiple observations on a single pair in a particular combination of structural conditions.

14. Time and budget constraints necessitated using subjects in more than one network. Overall, 97 different individuals were used in the 35 different experimental groups listed in Table 6.1.

15. This modification follows an unpublished analysis proposed by Yamagishi (1993) that provides an algorithm for calculating equidependence predictions. The algorithm introduces a priori probabilities into the determination of an actor's comparison level and abandons the assumption that an ego and ego's next best alternative are sure to exchange. Our analysis uses observed frequencies in a way generally consistent with Yamagishi's algorithm.

16. These networks contrast sharply with a strong power network like Branch31 in which two of the three A positions are systematically excluded on each round.

17. This solution for the Line4 network makes some technically problematic claims. First, the payoff predictions for some pairs of positions are inconsistent with the pool division interpretation. In Line4, according to the R_{ij} values, B_1 earns 8 points in exchange with B_2 and so too does B_2, despite the fact that the pool size is 24 points. To circumvent this problem, Cook and Yamagishi invoke the structural power concept and assume that exchange earnings are proportional to structural power: the Bs are power equals and are predicted to divide at 12/12. But using that predicted rate as the operative R_{ij} value violates the equidependence principle: A's next best alternative to 8 from B is 0 for a dependence score of 8, while B's next best alternative to 16 from A is 12 from the other B for a dependence score of 4. The algorithm is easily modified to avoid these inconsistencies. However, to remain faithful to the published record, we use the original unmodified algorithm.

18. If actor i has only one exchange partner j, then the probability of the joint event is simply equal to the probability that i is excluded from an exchange. However, this equality may not hold when i has more than one exchange partner and i can make more than one exchange.

Chapter 7

Negotiated Exchanges

Preface
David Willer

This chapter extends the tests of theory against theory which began in the last chapter. In Chapter 6, four theories were tested against each other: the core, equidependence, exchange-resistance, and expected value. To that list, this chapter adds predictions from Coleman's "rational exchange" model as well as two new ways of predicting exchange ratios developed by the authors for Network Exchange Theory. Taken together, a total of seven theoretic procedures for predicting exchange ratios are compared. Here tests focus on four weak power networks where power is due to exclusion.

Network Exchange Theory maintains that strong and weak power networks are fundamentally different from each other. In strong power structures, exchange ratios go to the extreme because low power actors engage in bidding wars. Alternatively, high power actors iterate across low power actors demanding and getting better and better deals. Neither bidding nor iteration occurs in weak power networks. Like equal power networks, actors in weak power networks bargain to compromise. But unlike equal power networks, in weak power networks some positions are advantaged.

Because the Graph-theoretic Power Index of Chapter 4 cannot distinguish weak from equal power structures, a new procedure was devised called exchange seek analysis. For each position, i the exchange seek analysis calculates "l_i" which is the likelihood that a given position will be included. l_i reflects structural power differences because the likelihood of exclusion $= 1 - l_i$. For example, when l_i values of all positions are the same, the structure is equal power. In weak power networks, however, l_i values will differ across some connected positions; positions with larger l_i values are more powerful. In fact, l_i was already used in the previous two chapters.

The procedures of this chapter reflect the strong power–weak power distinction in the following way. Because all strong power networks have interaction processes that drive exchange ratios to the extreme, the predicted exchange ratio is the extreme favoring the high power position(s). Note that for predicting strong power exchange ratios, all that is needed is to identify strong power components and differentiate their high and low power positions. To predict weak power, however, this chapter introduces two new NET procedures, both using l_i and resistance. One of the procedures, GPI–RD, also uses "degree." Degree is the number of positions connected at a position.

Today the procedures introduced in this chapter are preferred to the exchange resistance formulation of the previous chapter. This preference rests on two grounds. First, exchange-resistance does not differentiate between strong and weak power networks. It uses one procedure founded in l_i to predict for both. But exchange ratios do not vary only with the l_i values of adjacent positions. Holding the l_i values of adjacent positions constant, strong power and weak power networks will have different exchange ratios. Therefore, the strong–weak distinction is essential for accurate prediction. Second, even when the investigation is limited to weak power networks, as it is here, one of the new procedures, GPI–RD is shown to be a more accurate predictor than exchange resistance.

This chapter has a second part. After the tests among the seven procedures of the first part, the second part critically reviews the use of degree in the prediction of weak power. In that review it offers an alternative procedure— one that uses l_i^2 instead of degree. The second part of the chapter concludes by proposing a justification for the use of the square of l_i.

Part 1: Negotiated Exchanges in Social Networks

Michael J. Lovaglia, John Skvoretz, David Willer, and Barry Markovsky

Network Exchange Theory predicts relative profits from negotiations among actors in social exchange networks (Markovsky, Willer, and Patton 1988; Markovsky, Skvoretz, Willer, Lovaglia and Erger 1993). Here we extend the theory to allow exact predictions, rather than merely ordinal, for actors' exchange profits. This is accomplished by integrating two important factors. First, a *resistance* model predicts bilateral negotiation outcomes within a given set of network constraints. It does so by weighing actors' interests in gaining the best possible exchanges against their desires to avoid the worst. Second, the resistance model predictions are modified by actors' *profit expectations*. In particular, we incorporate two factors that affect such expectations, both of which are common features of ongoing exchange relations: the number of other actors to whom one is directly connected in the network, and the likelihood of one's completing exchanges with them. We derive hypotheses from the theory and experimentally test them using data from four different network structures. We find that the theory's predictions are more accurate than those of previous versions of the theory and those of five alternative theories. One of the networks is also tested in a new *restricted information setting*. Despite numerous differences in procedures and conditions across the two experimental settings, findings from both settings are effectively equivalent.

INTRODUCTION

Social exchange theory grew from the application of the economic theory of exchange to social relationships. Sociology focuses on a problematic area for economic theory: the exchange of valued objects in relatively small groups, where actors seek to settle on one optimal outcome out of a range of possibilities. How can we predict that outcome? And how are such outcomes affected by social structure? Homans (1958, 1974) suggested that principles of behaviorist psychology would help to answer these questions. Blau's (1964) approach used rational choice and utility theory. Theoretical work on the problem since then has largely developed from one or the other perspective, sometimes combining the two.

Both Homans and Blau illustrated their ideas in the context of dyadic relationships. In work settings, for instance, an exchange may entail conferring some reward in return for a costly act. Giving prestige in return for expert help is a common example. Some of these illustrations were quite ingenious. Their very ingenuity, however, convinced critics that the social exchange perspective was tautological and scientifically vacuous. It seemed that any outcome could be explained by a judicious identification of the costs and rewards. This criticism was difficult to overcome as long as the theoretical context remained the isolated dyad. The key to theoretical advance in social exchange was to focus on the embeddedness of dyadic relations in broader contexts. The conceptual horizon has since expanded so as to incorporate broader relational structures. As a result, social networks have become the focus for rigorous tests of developing theories. These developments were led by Emerson's (1962) seminal work on power-dependence theory. He was the first to suggest specific ways to extend a model of dyadic exchange to larger networks of exchange relations (Emerson 1972). In 1983, Emerson and colleagues (Cook et al., 1983) introduced the concept of *vulnerability*, a measure that predicted which positions in a network structure had power. Vulnerability was based on the idea that some network positions are more important than others in determining the flow of resources through a network. If by removing itself from exchange a position could reduce the total resources available in a network, then that position has power. The amount of power depends on the disruption in resource flow.

The pace of research on structural power in social exchange networks quickened soon thereafter, spurred by Willer's (1986) critique of the 1983 vulnerability model and a reply by the power-dependence group (Cook, Gillmore, and Yamagishi 1986). It was another two years before an alternative formulation was developed that offered better predictions—the *network exchange theory* of Markovsky, Willer, and Patton (1988). To predict relative power levels for positions in exchange networks, it provided a *Graph-theoretic Power Index* (GPI) based on a network path-counting algorithm. The theory challenged some basic assumptions of power-dependence theory and withstood critical tests that corroborated GPI predictions and falsified those from the vulnerability model of power-dependence theory.

As this decade began, comments and responses pointed out limitations of the GPI (Yamagishi and Cook 1990; Markovsky, Willer, and Patton 1990). Soon thereafter, Markovsky (1992) introduced a further refinement, just as power-dependence researchers replaced vulnerability with a completely new algorithm

(Cook and Yamagishi 1992a). At the same time, three new theories were introduced: Friedkin's (1992) expected value theory, Bienenstock and Bonacich's (1992) application of the "core" from game theory, and Skvoretz and Fararo's (1992) application of Coleman's (1990) rational exchange model. In the next year, Markovsky et al., (1993) identified a new class of structural dynamics and additional refinements in the network exchange theory. Most recently, Skvoretz and Willer (1993) tested the first ratio scale predictions from four theories on a variety of networks. Now, it seems, theoretical developments that once required half a decade occur within a year's time.

Central to theoretical development today is a class of networks in which subtle power differences occur. This phenomenon is known as *weak power*. In these weak power networks, some positions may have advantages over others in acquiring resources through exchange. However, unlike the advantages in *strong power* networks, advantages in weak power networks are not progressive. Over a series of exchanges, a strong power advantage eventually results in one exchange partner receiving nearly all available resources. Weak power is limited in range and magnitude. This necessitates theoretical refinement because adequate assessment of power differences between positions in weak power structures requires more precise predictions of exchange rates at equilibrium.

Network exchange theory (Markovsky et al. 1988) and its weak power extension (Markovsky et al. 1993) generate ordinal predictions for profits accruing from exchanges among negotiating actors in social networks. The theory is supported primarily by data from experiments in which actors have full information about the shape of the network and know the offers and agreements of all other actors (Skvoretz and Willer 1991).[1] Although the theory is well-supported by empirical tests, we make two improvements in the present research. First, we make the theory more precise: By taking into account actors' expectations, we generate ratio-scale predictions. Our refinement predicts exact exchange outcomes. Second, we make the theory more general: We test the theory in a new restricted information setting. Correct predictions for this setting mean we expand the theory's domain of applicability. The theory could then potentially subsume within its scope more social settings in the field—buying a house, for example. When negotiating for a house, a buyer may have little information about the profit her offer will provide the seller and little information about the number and nature of the seller's alternative offers.

Below we review network exchange theory and then describe a new integration of two previous lines of theorizing: the GPI for network structures and the *resistance* model for bilateral negotiations. The extended theory also incorporates biases in actors' expectations induced by the number of their direct ties to other network positions. We first test this new version of the theory against five alternatives with data from full information experiments on four different exchange networks. Finally, the generality of the theory is tested by replicating one of the networks under a new *restricted information setting*.

NETWORK EXCHANGE THEORY

Network exchange theory uses GPI to predict power and profit rankings in exchange networks. Its scope includes networks in which actors in directly connected positions engage in a series of negotiations over divisions of resource pools. Most interesting are networks in which prevailing structural conditions prevent some actors from exchanging at certain times. Such conditions foster power.

GPI: Detecting Strong Power Differences

Network exchange theory assumes that GPI can predict power and profit rankings in exchange networks by detecting a position's structural advantage or disadvantage. Here we present an intuitive explanation of how and why it works.

GPI is calculated by counting paths out from a position in a network. It adds odd length paths which are advantageous and subtracts even-length paths which are disadvantageous. Odd lengths are advantageous because it means a position has alternatives or a partner's alternatives have alternatives and so on. For example, consider a simple network—three actors connected in a line: A–B–C. Actor A may exchange with B, B with C, but A may not exchange with C. If all actors may exchange only once in a round of bargaining, B gains power because the other actors compete for the single available exchange opportunity with B. We say that B has two 1-paths, while A and C have only one. Even-length paths are disadvantageous because it means that a position's potential partners have alternatives that vie with A for exchange with the partners. Actor A has a 2-path through B to C. This is disadvantageous and subtracts from A's GPI score. It means that B has an alternative to exchange with A. Actor B has no 2-paths. Thus the GPI for the positions in the three-actor line network are 0–2–0. B will have an overwhelming advantage in this network because B has a higher GPI score than A and C. We say that B has a strong power advantage.

Power changes dramatically with the addition of another actor to the above network making a four-actor line, A–B–C–D (Willer and Patton 1987). Actor A now has a 1-path, a 2-path, and a 3-path. Its GPI score is 1. Actor B now has two 1-paths and one 2-path. Its GPI score is also 1. GPI predicts no strong power advantage for B in the four-actor line network. The reason for this is that the addition of a fourth actor gave A an additional, advantageous, odd-length path; the addition also gave B an additional disadvantageous, even-length path.

GPI extends this analysis to exchange networks of any size and density of relations by counting only *nonintersecting* paths leading away from a position. Only nonintersecting paths are counted because intersecting paths do not seem to change fundamental power relations in a network. For example, suppose we add a fourth actor, Z, to the three-actor line A–B–C. Actor Z is connected only to B. Actor A now has two disadvantageous 2-paths, one through B to C and one through B to Z. But because these 2-paths intersect at B, the additional disadvantageous 2-path makes no qualitative difference in A's relationship with B. B is still A's only possible exchange partner, and B still has an alternative to exchanging with A. GPI ranks the two actors as in the three-actor line. B has a strong power advantage over A, but now GPI scores are more extreme. GPI for B is 3 because of the additional 1-path, while for A GPI remains 0.

GPI assumes that actors seek exchange with a potential partner who has a larger GPI only if no weaker alternative exists. (Here "to seek exchange" means to make competitive offers, a situation determined only by structural conditions.) Analysis of the Stem network (Figure 7.2) shows that both C_1 and C_2 have GPI scores of 1. They will seek exchange with each other but not with B who has a GPI score of 2. The theory assumes that when this happens, GPI is recalculated among the resulting subnetworks of actors who mutually seek exchange. Two subnetworks result in the Stem, $A–B$ and $C_1–C_2$; all positions now have a GPI score of 1. No position is predicted to have an overwhelming power advantage in the Stem.

Likelihood of Exclusion in Weak Power Networks

Markovsky et al. (1993) identify two kinds of power in exchange networks— strong and weak—distinguished by their structural bases and their consequences for exchange profits. The source of power in both types of networks is identical, however: exclusion from exchange. In strong power networks, one or more actors are excluded in every round of exchange by one or more others who, under given structural arrangements, need never be excluded. A position's GPI score encodes its potential to be excluded (or to exclude) relative to its partners. Immediate ties to partners—1-paths—provide alternatives that enhance a position's potential to exclude or avoid exclusion. This holds for all paths of odd length. But partners' immediate ties to others—2-paths—provide one's partners with alternatives to oneself and thus decrease a position's potential to avoid exclusion or to exclude. This holds for all paths of even length.

The idea behind weak power is that no position can consistently exclude another without incurring costs to itself (Markovsky et al. 1993). In most weak power networks, either all positions are prone to exclusion or no position is necessarily excluded.[2] That is, for each position there is some outcome in which it is excluded from exchange, or it is possible for all positions to be included in exchanges simultaneously. GPI registers these conditions by assigning the same score to all positions and thus predicts no strong power differences. However, GPI measures a position's susceptibility to exclusion on the basis of the pattern of ties alone. Markovsky et al.'s (1993) weak power extension to network exchange theory takes account of other factors, in particular, the pattern of activity in these ties that could induce differential susceptibility to exclusion.

In strong power networks, profit distributions approach maximum differentiation where the advantaged actors earn 90 to 100 percent of available profit. In contrast, profits in weak power networks are more sensitive to actors' strategies; and profits from exchange stabilize well short of maximum differentiation. Generally, the advantaged actor in a weak power network earns 51 to 75 percent of available profit. The differing levels of profit differentiation between strong and weak power networks reflect the different bases for excludability—that is, the pattern of ties versus the pattern of activity in those ties.

For example, the Stem is a weak power network. With strong power, profit distributions approach maximum differentiation. That is, if actors negotiate over the allocation of a resource pool containing P units, profits for high power actors will approach P, and those for low power actors will approach zero. In contrast, profits in *weak power* structures are more sensitive to actors' strategies, and profits from exchange stabilize well short of maximum differentiation, for example, at $(P/2) + 1$ for the advantaged actor and $(P/2) - 1$ for the disadvantaged actor. In general, structurally disadvantaged actors face more exclusions from exchange than advantaged actors; when excluded, they respond by making offers that slightly favor actors in advantaged positions.

The Markovsky et al. (1988) GPI model correctly identified strong power structures in all of its tests. That is, (1) unequal GPI values correctly anticipated unequal profits, (2) such profit inequalities were relatively large, and (3) whenever profit levels were equal, then so were GPI values. However, Skvoretz and Willer (1991) found that actors' profits may differ even when their GPIs are equal. Prediction of these profit differences required a *second step* taken in Markovsky et al. (1993): When all GPIs are equal, each position's likelihood of being included in exchanges, l (or of being excluded, $1 - l$), is calculated under the assumption that actors have no preferences among partners.[3] Then, in an i–j relation, actor i has weak power over j only if GPI values are equal and if $l_i > l_j$. Otherwise, $l_i = l_j$ and i and j are equal in power. Thus, likelihood of being included detects weak power in networks where GPI detects no strong power differences. The analysis of l_i is not applicable in strong power structures, but rather GPI is used to predict the very robust profit differences that occur there. In summary, we detect power differences in two steps. First, GPI is applied to find strong power differences. Second, where no strong power differences are found, likelihoods of being included are calculated to assess any weak power differences that may exist.

As an example, consider the four-actor line of Figure 7.1a. GPI $= 1$ for all positions. Because positions have equal GPI, no strong power differences exist. Therefore, we turn to calculation of l_i to check for any weak power differences. In this network, A_1 can negotiate and exchange with B_1; B_1 may do so with A_1 or B_2; and so on down the line. Assuming that each actor can exchange only once per round and is indifferent as to with whom, either B has a .5 probability of seeking exchange with an A and a .5 probability of seeking exchange with the other B. The probability that an A will seek exchange with a B is 1.0 because the As have no alternatives.

Figure 7.1b shows a probability tree used to calculate l for each position. Each branch of the tree shows an *exchange seek* and its associated probability.

Figure 7.1
Four-Actor Line and Its Likelihood

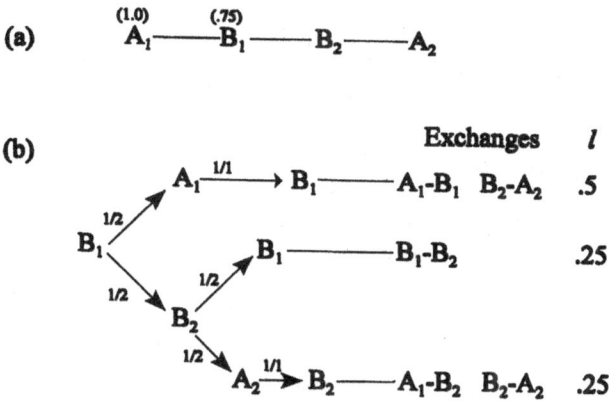

(a)

$$\overset{(1.0)}{A_1} \text{———} \overset{(.75)}{B_1} \text{———} B_2 \text{———} A_2$$

(b)

The "Exchanges" column shows mutual exchange seeks, and the "l" column shows the product of branch probabilities leading to each possible exchange. The likelihood of exchange between two actors is the sum of the probabilities associated with their mutual exchange seeks in the Exchanges column. An actor's likelihood of being included in (any) exchange is the sum of the probabilities associated with all exchanges that include that actor. From the tree we derive that $l_{AB} = .75$ for both A–B pairs; $l_{B1B2} = .25$; $l_A = .75$; and $l_B = 1$.

The foregoing procedure generalizes to more complex networks and to networks where actors can exchange more than once in a round of bargaining (Markovsky 1992; Markovsky et al. 1993). The distinction between single and multiple exchange is theoretically important because it determines the pattern of exclusions. This was first shown by Markovsky et al. (1988), where changing the number of exchanges allocated to positions altered the power exercised in every relation in the network. More recently, Skvoretz and Willer (1993) have shown similar consequences for a new array of networks. A real-world example will show why altering the number of exchanges has such a great impact on power. Auctions are a network exchange process. The seller has only a finite amount of time to sell any and all items at the best possible price. The finite period for the auction corresponds to a round of negotiation; that is, the period in which exchanges involving existing pools of resources must be completed. A resource pool might consist of a single item or several identical items, or there might be several resource pools containing a wide variety of items as in a real auction. Different items may appeal to some or all of a wide variety of bidders which determines the pattern of relations in the exchange network.

Consider two simple auctions. In both we have one seller and two buyers. In the first auction, only one item, an antique lamp, is of interest to both buyers. In the second auction, there are two such lamps. In the first auction, because there is only one lamp, the seller and each of the buyers can make only one exchange during the auction, but one of the buyers will be excluded from exchange. As the bidding opens, each buyer must try to provide the seller with the more lucrative offer. Because each buyer wants to make the higher bid, however, the offers "ratchet" higher and higher and become increasingly favorable to the seller. Eventually, one buyer backs down and the seller accepts a tidy profit.

In the second auction, each buyer (who wants only one lamp) still seeks exchange with the seller. But because there are two lamps, the seller now may exchange twice during the auction period—once with each buyer. The buyers do not need to outbid each other in order to obtain the lamp they desire, and so there is no structurally induced exclusion from exchange, nor is there any price-ratcheting. Ironically, the combined prices for the two lamps may end up being less than what the seller could have obtained by placing only one up for auction. Varying the number of permitted exchanges emphasizes the importance of exclusion as the generator of structural power in networks, as well as the generality of the theory (Skvoretz and Willer 1991).

Despite the theory's generality, the structurally induced exchange likelihoods that it generates have only been used to predict the *ordering* of exchange outcomes across positions in weak power networks. We now turn to the problem of predicting *exact* exchange rates in weak power networks.

PROFIT EXPECTATIONS

Network exchange theory depicts the generation of profit differentials in networks as an almost purely structural phenomenon. Profit differentials arise from differences in avoiding exclusion and from the sheer pattern of ties. The cognitions of actors play very little role in explanation. The strategy has been fruitful for two reasons. First, structural factors are often sufficient to accurately predict simple ordinal differences in earnings. Second, strong power networks have played an important developmental role in network exchange theory. In strong power networks, structural determinants are so powerful—as indicated by consistently extreme profit differentials—that actor cognitions can introduce only minor variation at best. But the study of weak power networks demands that more sources of variation be taken explicitly into account. In particular, we hold that more precise prediction requires that we extend network exchange theory to incorporate actors' profit expectations. We concentrate on possible sources of actors' expectations that might develop from initial network conditions and ongoing feedback that might result from them because our goal is to predict actor behaviors and exchange outcomes based on initial conditions.

In exchange networks, initial conditions and ongoing feedback provide actors with information they can use to estimate their potential profits, for example, the maximum amounts they could hope for, the minimum outcomes they fear, and the profit levels that might reasonably be expected to obtain. To the extent that such *profit expectations* are affected by situational factors, negotiations will be modified, and, in turn, actual exchange profits will be affected. The sensitivity of the negotiation process to contextual information should be especially evident in experimental settings. There, the simplicity of exchange conditions focuses attention on whatever minimal information is provided.

Our strategy is thus to employ a formal model that (1) accounts for the effects of profit expectations, (2) may be readily extended to accommodate situational factors that modify such expectations, and (3) may be integrated seamlessly with existing network exchange theory. In line with the existing theory's emphasis on the importance of exclusion and excludability, we assume that this factor also modifies actors' profit expectations. It would be surprising if it did not. We have all been excluded from social exchange at some time in our lives, whether it was not being invited to a party or having our application to a university rejected. These events certainly affect our cognitions. The following section, "Expectations and Resistance," incorporates the actors' experience of patterns of exclusion into our model. The second factor we will highlight in the section "Expectations and the Number of Direct Ties." Previous research (Marsden 1983) suggests the significance of the number of direct relations an actor has in the network. But more importantly, the number of direct relations is a highly salient and immediately apprehensible feature of the actor's environment even under conditions of highly restricted information.

Expectations and Resistance

The resistance model (Willer 1981; Heckathorn 1983) predicts rates of exchange based on each actor's beliefs or expectations about his or her own best and worst possible outcomes. Specifically, it assumes that the point at which actors agree to exchange is determined by balancing two interests: (1) Actors aspire to obtain the greatest possible profit from exchange; this is their "best hope." (2) Actors seek to avoid the worst possible outcome; this is their "worst fear." To decide whether to agree to exchange, actors balance their desire for maximum profit against their fear of receiving no profit or the profit that results if no exchange occurs.

In dyadic exchange, the scope of the resistance model overlaps the Nash equilibrium (1950, 1953), and under certain conditions the predictions of the two are the same. However, the scope of resistance is broader, extending beyond the dyad. It has been successfully applied to a wide range of exchange networks (Brennan 1981; Willer 1987; Willer, Markovsky, and Patton 1989). Its predictions have also been shown to hold in cross-national experimental research (Willer and Szmatka 1993).

We use the resistance model to formalize our claims about the effect of profit expectations on negotiations. It specifies how negotiators arrive at agreements based on each actor's beliefs or expectations about his or her own best and worst possible outcomes. Implicitly, the model may be interpreted as generating profit expectations for negotiating actors at a particular point in time, and these expectations then determine whether actors accept or reject offers.

Let P_i represent i's profit from exchange, M_i is i's maximum expectation or best hope for profit from exchange, and C_i is i's worst fear or "conflict outcome."[4] Actor i's interest in gaining her maximum expectation is $M_i - P_i$ and in avoiding her worst fear is $P_i - C_i$. Her resistance to a given exchange profit, R_i, is the ratio

$$R_i = \frac{M_i - P_i}{P_i - C_i}$$

Resistance is the ratio of $M_i - P_i$, the actor's interest in gaining a better outcome, to $P_i - C_i$, the actor's interest in avoiding disagreement. Because the ratio is small for favorable settlements and large for unfavorable settlements, the resistances of two actors in an exchange relation vary inversely for a given settlement. Network exchange theory asserts that agreements to exchange occur when actors' resistances are equal. Thus, compromise occurs when:

$$\frac{M_i - P_i}{P_i - C_i} = \frac{M_j - P_j}{P_j - C_j}$$

This is the *equiresistance* solution.[5] Knowing the number of resource units in the pool (P) such that $P = P_i + P_j$, we may algebraically solve for the values of P_i and P_j. More than a decision strategy, resistance is conceived as a potential limit of power use when actors use the best available strategies. Consequently, it holds promise of more general applicability than any particular decision strategy.[6]

To predict negotiation outcomes, M_i and C_i must be determined for each actor. In strong power structures such as A–B–A, we assume that each A's maximum expectation (M_A) is initially at or near P. However, given that B seeks only one exchange per round, M_A declines as A's are consistently excluded. M_A may begin at or near P, but this best hope will approach zero as exchanges continue to yield ever-declining profits. In contrast, because B has no rivals, M_B remains close to P. Over a series of rounds, all profit gravitates to the central, B, actor (Willer and Markovsky 1993).

C_i is determined by a position's best alternative (Willer 1987). Strong power structures such as A–B–A are characterized by bidding wars between rival As. Thus, when B negotiates with one A, C_B is the last offer from the other A. As the two As bid, however, C_B increases toward P. Because A has no alternative, C_A stays at zero. The result over a series of exchange rounds (derivable from the equiresistance model) is that P_A approaches zero and P_B approaches P (Willer and Markovsky 1993).

In weak power structures, an equilibrium exchange rate is reached such that neither actor gains the maximum available profit or is forced to accept almost none. To use resistance to predict exchange rates in these structures, it is necessary to determine the value of actors' maximum expectations and conflict outcomes, M_i and C_i, at equilibrium.

In weak power structures, actors do not initially have a realistic basis for estimating their maximum expectations and conflict outcomes, M_i and C_i. As a result, their initial expectations may be either optimistic or pessimistic. However, all equiresistance solutions assume that actors have expectations and that over a series of exchanges they come to be more or less realistic. Thus, we assume that during the interaction process actors learn more realistic expectations. For example, when initial expectations are too optimistic, actors are excluded by others and eventually adjust their expectations downward. If expectations are initially too pessimistic, then actors always gain agreements and eventually adjust their expectations upward. As a result, expectations become increasingly realistic. This model of actors' responses to inclusion and exclusion conforms to the scope specifications for offer adjustments first described by Markovsky et al. (1988). Here, however, we make the more specific suggestion that actors adjust their offers in response to changes in their profit expectations.

Below, we offer a solution for the problem of predicting exchange rates in weak power networks. It has two parts. First, we predict the equilibrium exchange rate. If actors adjust expectations as we assume they do, then expectations will come to correspond more closely to actors' likelihoods of being included in exchange. The result will be a fairly stable equilibrium exchange rate.

Second, we note that initial rates may not be like equilibrium rates. Because actors do not initially know their likelihood of being included in exchange, their expectations for maximum profit and their worst fears must have other bases. Initial expectations may or may not be realistic. We also offer a simple model for initial expectations from which actors, as a consequence of interaction, move toward equilibrium. These initial expectations likely have an enduring impact on exchange rates. In a final step, we complete our theory by combining the model of initial expectations with equilibrium exchange rate predictions. In effect, our predictions assume that actors' beliefs remain biased to some degree by initial expectations.

Resistance and the Likelihood of Being Included

We approach the problem of specifying the value of conflict outcomes and maximum expectations in weak power networks by first identifying theoretical restrictions for C_i and M_i. Within these theoretical limits, we then assume that C_i and M_i are proportional to an actor's likelihood of being included in exchange. That is, an actor's expectations for profit, her worst fears and best hopes, depend on how often she expects to be included in profitable exchange. The assumption of simple proportionality between inclusion probabilities and the likelihood of being included results in a modified resistance equation that can be used to make exact predictions of exchange rates between actors in weak power networks.

The conflict outcome, C_i, depends on the actor's expectations regarding available exchange alternatives, as noted above. For example in the four-actor line network, $A_1-B_1-B_2-A_2$, if B_1 knows that A_1 will agree to an equal division of profit at 12–12, then B_1 will not accept 11 from B_2. However, as Yamagishi and Cook (1990) noted, actors are not always certain of their alternatives. Nonetheless, weak power limits the range of conflict outcomes: the lower limit is zero— the amount an excluded actor receives—and the upper limit is half the total resource pool, as we will next explain.

In all weak power networks, actors cannot consistently exclude others from exchange without themselves suffering losses.[7] Still assuming 24-unit resource pools, this can be illustrated using four-actor line. Suppose that C_{B1} *is* greater than 12, an equal division of the profit pool. This means that B_1 would refuse offers of less than 13. That is, B_1 will refuse an equal division of profit and hold out for more. Because B_1 cannot consistently exclude B_2, however, B_2 will not be penalized for refusing to exchange with B_1 at this rate. As long as B_1 demands 13 from B_2, B_2 effects a temporary break in the network by exchanging with A_2 at no worse than 12–12. For B_1 to ever reestablish the possibility of exchanging with B_2 (and thus reestablish her weak power over A_1), C_{B1} must be reduced to 12, an equal division of the profit pool, or lower. Therefore, it is generally true that the "conflict" or worst-fear outcome in weak power structures is limited to the range from zero to half the size of the resource pool. Similarly, M_i is restricted to the range 12–24. M_i may be close to the total resource pool when exchange begins, but it cannot go below half the pool. Half the pool is always a competitive offer because no actor is ever consistently excluded.

At issue now is how to determine C_i and M_i from initial conditions within these theoretically determined ranges. We do so using l, the likelihood of being included, as derived from weak power calculations (Markovsky et al. 1993). Two assumptions integrate resistance with Network Exchange Theory. First,

Equiresistance Assumption: In weak power relations, actors' profits approach equiresistance solutions over a series of exchanges.

To the extent that actors use effective strategies to seek maximum profits, their profits should conform to the resistance predictions. For example, the behavior of more experienced actors or those with better training should conform more closely to resistance predictions than the behavior of less experienced or less well-trained subjects.[8] The idea that resistance predicts a profit limit reached at equilibrium after a series of exchanges allows application of the theory to exchange situations in which actors have different amounts of information and training.

Second, we theoretically link inclusion probabilities to actors' conflict outcomes and best hope outcomes in the resistance equation. We assume that an actor's perceived best hope and conflict outcomes are proportional to that actor's likelihood of being included in exchange. For example, an actor who is consistently included and who makes a profit would resist offers that are lower than she is accustomed to receive. The fact that she is very likely to be included in exchange has increased her point of conflict. Conversely, a frequently excluded actor, accustomed to receiving no profit much of the time, would accept a low offer. Her low likelihood of exchange has reduced her point of conflict. The same argument can be made for actors' best hopes. Actors consistently included in exchange should have higher aspirations for profit than should actors consistently excluded from exchange.

Markovsky et al. (1993) demonstrated that likelihood of being included (l_i) rank orders the power of positions in weak power networks. On this evidence, we assume that l_i will successfully rank order power positions even where power differences are very small. Further, we assume that larger differences in l_i identify larger differences in power between positions. That is, we assume that weak power is proportional to a position's l_i. If as we suggest, this occurs because likelihood of being included acts on points of conflict (C_i) and best hopes (M_i), then setting C_i and M_i proportional to l_i should provide a good indicator of an actor's power.

The following *Resistance-Likelihood Assumption* expresses the idea that C_i and M_i are proportional to l_i within their respective ranges. Our analysis demonstrated that C_i is limited to a range between zero and half the resource pool. Similarly, M_i is limited to a range from half the resource pool to the entire pool. This assumption predicts that the difference in profits for high power and low power actors in a weak power relation depends on their likelihoods of being included in exchange.

Resistance-Likelihood Assumption: The higher an actor's likelihood of being included in exchange, (a) the higher the actor's perceived conflict outcome, C_i; and (b) the higher the actor's maximum profit expectation, M_i. Formally,

$$C_i = \frac{P}{2} l_i$$
$$M_i = \frac{P}{2} (l_i + 1)$$

(7.1)

In words, the perceived worst-case exchange outcome (C_i) is a fraction of half the pool, and that fraction is larger for higher likelihoods of being included (l_i) and smaller for lower l_i. As explained above, C_i is limited to at most half the resource pool in weak power situations. Equation (a) expresses the assumption that C_i is proportional to l_i and ranges between zero and half the resource pool.[9] Similarly, an actor's maximum expectation for profit (M_i) is half the pool plus a fraction of half the pool. We also showed that M_i is restricted to be at least

Figure 7.2
Three Weak Power Networks and Likelihoods of Inclusion

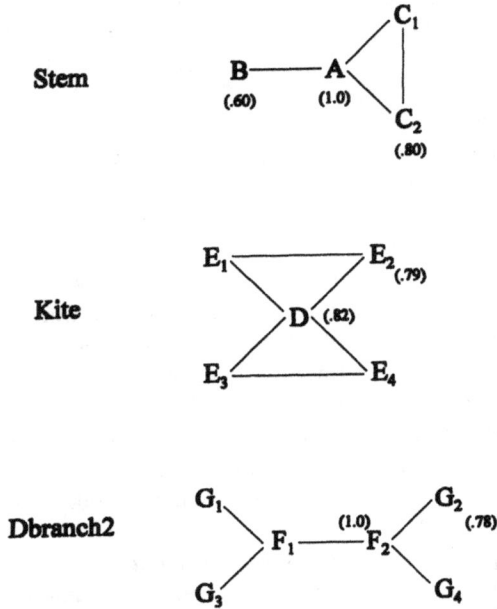

half the resource pool but not more than the total pool, P, in weak power situations. Equation (b) expresses the assumption that M_i is proportional to l_i on that range. In weak power situations at equilibrium, it follows from (a) and (b) that M_i is a direct function of C_i, that is, $M_i = C_i + P/2$. This feature pays considerable dividends in simplifying calculations and serves as a plausible assumption about perceived best- and worst-case outcomes.

The resistance model, resistance-likelihood assumption, and a little algebra yield the following prediction[10]

$$P_i = \frac{(P + C_i - C_j)}{2}$$
$$P_j = P - P_i.$$

In the "Stem" network (Figure 7.2), for example, likelihoods of being included for positions A and B are $l_A = 1$, $l_B = .6$. Assuming a typical 24-point resource pool, P, we can calculate profit distributions for the A–B relation. First, by the resistance-likelihood assumption, $C_A = (24 / 2) \times 1 = 12$, and $C_B = (24 / 2) \times .6 = 7.2$. Next, profits are calculated to be $P_A = (P + C_A = C_B) / 2 = 14.4$, and $P_B = P - P_A = 9.6$. Profits for any position in any weak power network can be predicted using this method if the network structure and total value of each profit pool are known. Likelihood of being included indicates the structural power advantage of a network position. By balancing two competing motives—the desire to increase profit and the need to reach agreement and avoid exclusion—actors reach an equilibrium level of profit that is proportional to their relative likelihood of being included.

Expectations and the Number of Direct Ties

In addition to the factors that we have previously related to profit expectations, there is good reason to assume that the number of an actor's direct relations in the network may also play an important role. In the parlance of network analysis, this refers to the actor's *degree*. Marsden (1983, p. 704) employed a similar idea in his theory of power in exchange networks. Where t_i is the number of actor i's direct network ties, he defined $\log(t_i/t_j)$ as one of several factors affecting i's "price-making" behavior in exchanges with j. Although some of his model's predictions diverge from experimental test results, the notion that degree biases actors' price negotiations in weak power situations has not been tested directly and may still be sound. Further justification is found in the judgment heuristics literature (e.g., Kahneman, Slovic, and Tversky 1982). In a wide variety of judgment contexts, informational *anchors* have been shown to bias judgments of such properties as magnitude, numerosity, value, weight, color, loudness, and pitch. For example, a *contrast* anchor effect occurs when yesterday's 95 degree temperature (the anchor) makes today's 78 degrees seem cool. Today's judged temperature is biased *away* from yesterday's. The *assimilation* anchor effect is often found in negotiation settings where an initial offer (the anchor) may be blatantly unrealistic, but subsequent offers and counter-offers are still pulled *toward* that initial offer. (For more detailed examples and applications, see Helson and Kozaki 1968, and Kahneman, Slovic, and Tversky 1982.)

Assuming that human actors cannot fully evaluate the ramifications of their location in a network structure—especially when lacking systemwide information—it is reasonable to presume that information of a more localized nature becomes especially salient. The number of one's direct ties is just such a piece of information. An actor with more direct network relations will probably expect to have more successful negotiations than an actor with fewer direct relations. It seems plausible that an actor with many potential exchange partners would think she has a better chance of being included in exchange than would an actor with only one or very few exchange partners. Of course, network exchange theory shows that this expectation is not necessarily justified. The extent to which alternative partners can benefit an actor depends on broader network patterns, for example, the alternative relations of each of one's alternative relations. Nevertheless, an actor's degree is a highly salient piece of information in network exchange contexts and should thus bias profit expectations via an assimilation effect.[11] This idea is captured in the following:

Degree Assumption: The higher an actor's degree, the higher the actor's expected profit.

An actor with higher profit expectations is assumed to adopt a tougher bargaining stance, for example, to make lower offers to others, and to have higher thresholds of acceptability for incoming offers. If negotiating actors have equally high degrees, however, degree would not provide special advantages to either. Therefore, our index of relative degree (d_{ij}) for actor i in the i–j relation must be based on the *relative* number of ties (t) for each actor. This is accomplished in the formula

$$d_{ij} = \frac{t_i}{(t_i + t_j)}.$$

This specification standardizes the index to a 0–1 scale, a useful property when we combine d with other components of the theory. As a structural measure, d_{ij} does not depend on actors knowing one another's degree. It captures what might be called the expectation advantage of one actor relative to another—a condition that will then manifest itself in the dynamics and outcomes of the negotiation process.

Resistance and Degree

Degree is assumed to bias profit expectations. Therefore, in the model, we incorporate the relative degree index as a biasing factor for best-hope and worst-fear outcomes. Given that we have already defined M (the maximum hoped-for profit) to be a function of C (the conflict or worst-fear outcome) in weak power networks, we only need to show how relative degree affects the latter. We assume that, in the same manner as the likelihood of being included, the higher the degree, the greater the inflation of the actor's worst-fear outcome:

Resistance-Degree Assumption: The higher an actor's relative degree, the higher the actor's perceived conflict outcome.

Combining this assumption with the Resistance-Likelihood Assumption yields

$$C_{ij} = \frac{P}{2} l_i d_{ij}.$$

We now subscript C by both i and j, because the inclusion of the biasing factor, d_{ij}, in the equation implies that i's expected conflict outcome may be different for each actor with whom i negotiates.[12] Again using the Stem network as an example and using the earlier formulas for P_i and P_j with a 24-point resource pool, $d_{AB} = 3 / (3 + 1) = 3/4$. Substituting the values for variables in the equation, $C_{AB} = 24 / 2 \times 1 \times 3 / 4 = 9$; $C_{BA} = 24 / 2 \times .6 \times \frac{1}{4} = 1.8$. Then we can solve for the prediction that incorporates both resistance and relative degree into the GPI model, $P_A = (24 + 9 - 1.8) / 2 = 15.6$, and $P_B = 8.4$. We label this elaborated model, GPI–RD.

Higher relative degree is thus assumed to bias the effects of the likelihood of being included. However, because advantages in relative degree are based only on actors' expectations and not on actual structural advantages, there is a potential cost to actors who try to exploit degree advantages. Although an actor with more potential exchange partners may negotiate tougher and receive more resources from completed exchanges, such exchanges may be less frequent than for actors of lower degree. This is because higher-degree actors are prone to negotiating tougher than warranted by their actual structural positions. The result would be higher profit when exchange occurs but a higher likelihood of being excluded from exchanges. In addition, actors with fewer potential exchange partners still seek more favorable alternative agreements whenever possible. In networks where all actors can be excluded—l_i less than 1.0 for all actors—a situation could arise where an advantaged actor is excluded from exchange so frequently that he or she can actually acquire fewer resources than the disadvantaged actor over a series of exchanges. Markovsky et al. (1993) report this phenomenon in the "Kite" network (Figure 7.2). Subjects in the D position have an advantage over those in E positions both in likelihood of being included, .82 to .79, and relative degree, 4/6 to 2/6. For experienced subjects, despite the very small advantage in likelihood of being included, D position subjects averaged a 14–10 profit point advantage in exchanges with E partners. However, for D these victories were Pyrrhic. Ds were excluded—and earned no profit— on 41 percent of rounds, while Es were excluded on only 15 percent of rounds.[13] Es preferred to exchange with each other over the more aggressive D. It seems strange that a high power actor can actually earn less overall than a low power partner. Incorporating degree into the theory explains this result—a result that previously had been considered anomalous. Although frequency of exchange can also be predicted using likelihood of being included and degree (Lovaglia and Skvoretz 1993), here we focus on testing the model's predictions for exchange profits.

METHOD

We tested the model's predictions using experimental data from four networks. Subjects in the test setting had full information on the network structure and on all other actors' exchange outcomes. We also replicated the test on one of these networks using a restricted information setting where each subject knew only his or her own dealings with potential exchange partners and his or her own profits from exchanges.

Experiment 1: "Full Information" Networks

Skvoretz and Willer (1991) described in detail the experimental setting used for these tests. Custom software ("ExNet") was used to configure networked PCs into "virtual" exchange networks. ExNet can establish networks of any shape and size, limited only by the number of PCs. Subjects in experiments know the network structures and their positions within them. In an initial session, assistants explain how to make offers and counter-offers, what it means to divide the 24-point resource pool, the dollar value of profit units, and that exclusion from exchange yields no points for that round. A practice session familiarizes subjects with the operation of the system. Subjects then return at a later date to participate in the actual research. In the experiments, each subject rotates through all network positions, negotiating for a total of four rounds at each position. The computer records the timing and content of all communications.

We investigated four different experimental structures of theoretical import (Figure 7.1a and Figure 7.2). The Double Branch 2 is a simple, weak power network that allows two positions multiple exchanges. It was converted from a strong to a weak power structure via a 2-exchange rule: The central Fs could exchange up to twice per round. Actors are only allowed one exchange per round in the other structures. These networks also have interesting theoretical properties that warranted our attention: The 4-Line is the simplest weak power network; the Stem and Kite sparked a debate between competing research programs over the validity of the GPI (Yamagishi and Cook 1990; Markovsky, Willer, and Patton 1990); and in the Kite, no position is guaranteed inclusion.

Five alternative theories are capable of generating ratio-scale profit predictions for positions in weak power networks. Most of these were presented in a special issue of *Social Networks* (Bienenstock and Bonacich 1992; Cook and Yamagishi 1992a; Friedkin 1992; Skvoretz and Fararo 1992). Bienenstock and Bonacich's *core* theory takes a game-theoretic approach. Cook and Yamagishi's *equidependence* theory extends the power-dependence program originated by Emerson. Friedkin's *expected value* theory developed out of his work on network analysis in general. Skvoretz and Fararo (1992) apply Coleman's *rational* exchange theory to these *exchange* structures. In addition, Skvoretz and Willer (1993) present *exchange-resistance* theory, a model that incorporates resistance into the GPI but does not include degree. These five theories are briefly described below. Except for Coleman's rational exchange model, Skvoretz and Willer (1993) provide details for using each to calculate predicted exchange outcomes.

Core Theory

Core theory (Bienenstock and Bonacich 1992, 1993) models network exchange in terms of cooperative game theory.[14] Three rationality criteria establish the "core" of an exchange network. First, agreements are individually rational when each actor's profit is equal or greater than the profit she could earn by not exchanging. That is, actors are assumed to exchange only when they receive at least as much profit from agreement as they do from being excluded from exchange. Second, agreements are rational for the coalition of exchange partners when the sum of the profit of both actors is at least as much as could be obtained if they exchanged with other partners. Third, group (or network) rationality obtains when the total profit of all positions of the network is at least as large as the total profit available from some other pattern of exchange agreements.

The core of an exchange network usually narrows the range of preferable exchange rates but does not necessarily predict a single ratio-scale exchange outcome. To make predictions when this occurs, we follow Skvoretz and Fararo (1992) in assuming that each core outcome is equally likely, then average the payoffs to various positions. In some cases, networks contain no core at all, which precludes a prediction.

Rational Exchange Theory

Coleman's (1973, 1990) rational exchange model is not easily applied to our exchange networks because it operates under scope conditions that differ from those of other network exchange theories. It assumes, for instance, that every actor may exchange with any other actor in a network. Marsden's (1983) model solves the problem by adding network restrictions and a variety of additional assumptions. However, he noted that some predictions ran contrary to data previously published. Coleman partially solved the problem by assuming that there are transaction costs between actors. When transaction costs are high, they effectively prohibit exchange from occurring, thus setting the stage for structural power to emerge. As it stands, however, Coleman's conception of power is not relational. Power manifests in an actor's resource holdings rather than in her relative ability to extract resources through exchanges. Also, it does not speak to the situation where one actor's exchange is contingent on whether or not another actor exchanges. Skvoretz and Fararo (1992) have modified and added assumptions to Coleman's theory to make it applicable in the kind of exchange networks discussed here. Predictions for the Coleman model are based on their analysis. A technical description of the method and a computer program that calculates predictions are available from the second-named author on request.

Equidependence Theory

Equidependence theory (Cook and Yamagishi 1992a) assumes that actors compare how much they will receive in exchange with a potential partner against how much they could get in exchange with some other partner. The difference between what an actor can obtain from this exchange relation and that of an alternative relation is deemed to be the dependence of the actor on the potential partner. This comparison process goes on simultaneously with all of an actor's direct ties. Actors are assumed to exchange at a point where their dependence on the relation is equal to the dependence of their potential partner. In other words, exchange occurs when actors are equidependent, and each actor can get no more profit by some alternative exchange. An actor's reward from exchange is given by the equation $R_{ij} = (P_{ij} + A_{ij} - A_{ji})/2$, where R_{ij} is the profit that actor i obtains in exchange with partner j; P_{ij} is the pool size; and A_{ij} is the best alternative available to i.

Cook and Yamagishi use the example of two actors, i and j, negotiating over a 24-point resource pool. Actor i has another partner who offers i 10 points, while j has no other partner. If i and j were to divide the pool at 13 for i and 11 for j, actor i gets 3 points more than her best alternative (10), but j gets 11 points more than her alternative (zero). Thus equidependence between i and j has not been reached. Negotiation is assumed to continue until i gets 17 points and j gets 7 points. Here, equidependence has been attained because both i and j get 7 more points from exchange with each other than they would outside the i–j relation. Actor i's power is defined as the maximum profit she can obtain from any of her partners.

Expected Value Theory

Friedkin's (1992) expected value theory first identifies all potential subnetworks that can result from different patterns of exchanges. Expected values are predictions about a structure's outcomes determined by weighting the value of a predicted outcome by the probability of its occurrence. For example, in the four-actor line network, A_1–B_1–B_2–A_2, there are two possible exchange patterns. Either each B exchanges with its related A, or the two Bs exchange with each other. To make predictions based on initial conditions, Friedkin assumes that either pattern is equally likely to occur. Actor i is dependent on actor j if failure to exchange with actor j results in i's exclusion from exchange. Dependency is an actor's likelihood of being excluded, calculated over all possible exchange outcomes. An offer-making function translates a particular degree of dependency into an offer to a potential exchange partner. Predicted earnings from exchange are a function of reciprocal offers modified by compromises when offers are inconsistent.

Exchange-Resistance Theory

Skvoretz and Willer (1993) use the likelihood of being included and the resistance model to make "baseline" predictions for exchange in both strong and weak power structures. Their goal is a simple formula that can be used in a single step to yield predictions in all exchange networks. We give their formula for predicting the profit of actor i using the notation for our own resistance-likelihood assumption:

$$\frac{\ln (M_i - P_i)}{\ln (P_i)} = \frac{l_j}{l_i}$$

Skvoretz and Willer assume that conflict points and maximum expectations for profit for all actors remain constant. The conflict point for all actors is assumed to be zero, and their maximum expectation for profit is assumed to be the entire profit pool. A power function is then applied in which the difference between the maximum expectation for profit and what an actor would receive from an offer is raised to the power of that actor's likelihood of being included in exchange. The equiresistance equation can then be reduced to the above equation using natural logarithms.

All five theories make ratio-scale predictions for at least some of the network relations we examined. Next we compare our predictions to those of the five alternative theories and to experimental results.

Results

Four different groups of subjects participated in Stem and Kite experiments, and five groups in the 4-Line and Double Branch 2. All were university students who signed up to participate in paid experiments. In Table 7.1, the column headed GPI–RD shows the predictions for our new model that integrates GPI, resistance, and degree. The column headed GPI–R shows the predictions for our resistance model without the biasing effects of degree. Also shown are the predictions from five alternative models and the observed means by network relation. Because we assume that the profits approach predicted equilibria over a series of negotiations, we use data from the final experimental periods.[15]

Observed profits conform well to GPI–RD predictions. The largest discrepancy between a predicted and an observed value is less than one profit unit. One-sample t-tests determined the probability that the differences between predictions and observed means were due to chance. No GPI–RD prediction differed significantly from its corresponding observed mean at or below the .40 probability level. The *smallest* probability that a prediction *did not differ* from the observed value was .47 for the Kite network. Two predictions from Coleman's rational exchange model, though not as close, were better than those of other alternatives. The probability that rational exchange predictions did not differ from observed values was .13 for the 4-Line and .11 for the Stem. In contrast, significant differences were found between observed means and the predictions of other alternative theories. For the Kite network, Skvoretz and Willer's exchange-resistance model, GPI–RD, Cook and Yamagishi's equidependence model, and Friedkin's expected value model all make acceptably close predictions. However, both the equidependence and expected value models predict no difference in power between D and E actors in the Kite—a difference that did occur in an empirical test and was statistically significant (Markovsky et al. 1993).

Table 7.1

Goodness of Fit[a] for Predicted and Observed Profits in Exchange Networks

Structure, Relation	Models and Predictions							Observed Means
	Core	Rational Exchange	Equi-dependence	Expected Value	Exchange Resistance	GPI-R	GPI-RD	
4-Line								
B–A[b]	16.0	15.0**	16.0	21.0	16.0	13.5	14.5****	14.4
t(29)	4.27	1.54	4.27	13.01	4.27	-2.54	0.18	
Stem[c]								
A–B	20.1	17.2**	18.0	22.0	18.3	14.4*	15.6****	15.9
t(13)	5.46	1.72	2.76	7.91	3.15	-1.88	-0.33	
Kite								
D–E	unstable	15.2*	12.0****	12.0****	12.5****	12.2****	13.7****	12.8
t(7)		1.95	-0.61	-0.61	-0.20	-0.46	0.77	
Dbranch2								
F–G	16.8***	13.8	16.0****	20.2	14.6	13.3	16.3****	16.4
t(63)	0.93	-5.68	-0.82	8.38	-3.89	-6.69	-0.14	

[a]One-sample t-tests were used to estimate the probability of *no difference* between prediction and observation. Larger p values suggest an *increased* likelihood that prediction and observation are identical. Degrees of freedom are in parentheses.

*p > .05; **p > .10; ***p > .20; ****p > .40.

[b]Predictions are for profits of the first position listed in a relation, here for example, actor A in A–B.

[c]The A–C relation is also of interest in this network. However, during the last period of the experiment, A exchanged with C only twice, both times at 14–10. This precludes meaningful comparison. With that caveat, we report only for completeness that the GPI–RD prediction of 13.7 for this relation was closest among the models, though the equidependence and rational exchange models were also close.

Establishing a GPI–RD prediction for the Double Branch 2 network requires some interpretation. Calculating degree as for a 1-exchange network, Fs have three direct ties and Gs have one. The GPI–RD model then yields predicted profits for F of 15.33, about 1 profit point away from the observed value. A one-sample t-test also finds this difference significant: $t(63) = 2.29$, $p = .03$. However, degree can be calculated differently when two exchanges are allowed. Fs exchange twice per round, while Gs exchange only once. At the beginning of a round, F has three potential exchange partners. If Fs first exchange in a round is with a G, then there are two actors left with whom to attempt a second exchange. If Fs first exchange with each other, then they have three actors left with whom to attempt a second exchange. Fs then have either five or six direct ties, while Gs have only one. If F's first exchange is with a G on two-thirds of the rounds (i.e., F is indifferent between the other F and its two Gs), then Fs effectively have 5.33 direct ties. This produces a GPI–RD prediction for F in exchange with G of 16.31. A t-test finds no difference between this value and the observed mean, 16.36, $t(63) = -.14$, $p = .89$. Although this is the closest prediction of any model, Table 7.1 shows that the Bienenstock and Bonacich core and Cook and Yamagishi equidependence models also make acceptable predictions for the Double Branch 2.

In sum, the GPI model incorporating resistance and degree formulations produced very accurate predictions for exchange outcomes. These predictions were superior to alternative models in their goodness of fit to experimental data: Only GPI–RD makes acceptably close predictions ($p > .40$ of *no* difference between predicted and observed values) for all four experimental networks.

Experiment 2: "Restricted Information" Networks

There is a theoretical distinction between full and restricted information settings used for network exchange experiments. Full information settings more closely model rational, forward-looking actors who use whatever information is available. Restricted information settings conform better to backward-looking actors who adjust their response based only on their experience in the situation. Our model requires that, minimally, three information conditions must be satisfied for negotiated social exchanges to occur:[16] (1) An actor in the network must be informed of, and have access to, other actors with whom it is possible to exchange. We assume that actors negotiate separately with each potential partner and are thus aware of each partner as a distinct person or organizational unit. Implicitly, then, actors also know the number of others with whom it is possible to exchange. (2) The actor must be informed of whether or not an exchange has been completed with each potential partner. (3) The actor must be informed of the magnitude of his or her profits from exchanges. In order to evaluate an offer, it must be at least ordinally scalable. This requires information on the offer's relative magnitude. In a typical experiment, this takes the form of an agreement between two partners to allocate a pool of resources at the conclusion of a given negotiation round. Implicitly, if actors know the magnitude of the offer on which agreement was reached, then they also know the magnitude of their own shares of subsequent resource allocations stemming from the agreement. Knowledge of others' profits is not essential. Therefore, to examine the empirical scope of our model, we examine data from experiments in a new, limited information setting that differs in several ways from the full information setting described earlier. The new setting restricts information to the minimum necessary for the operation of factors deemed important in the model.

As our theory evolves, refinements in its predictions demand that we study increasingly subtle network exchange phenomena. Consequently, our experimental setting must be made increasingly sensitive to predicted phenomena, and it must exert more stringent controls over potentially extraneous factors such as equity concerns. We have attempted to accomplish this by creating a new experimental setting that spreads the negotiation process across a larger number of rounds and limits information to the minimum necessary for negotiation and exchange. Each subject has information only on his or her *own* (1) negotiations and exchanges, (2) potential profit vis-à-vis particular offers received from others, and (3) realized profit when an exchange occurs. In addition, subjects negotiate for many more rounds because a subject's intra-round negotiations with a partner are simplified to a choice of three options: increase or decrease the previous offer by one "profit point" or do not change the previous offer. Cook et al. (1983) limit information in a similar fashion but allow subjects to select their offers from a wide range of possibilities on each round. The new setting then makes possible tests of our theory under information conditions similar to those of earlier restricted information exchange experiments.

Custom software was used to configure networked PCs.[17] Subjects were isolated in separate rooms and knew only the coded designations for their own potential exchange partners. They were informed that the shape of the full network would not be revealed and that their potential partners might have other potential partners of their own. An interactive tutorial guided subjects through the mechanics of conducting negotiations via the computerized system. On each round, subjects sent messages to a central computer telling it the lowest amount of profit they were willing to accept from each potential partner. If an agreement was reached, the subject was informed of this fact but did not know the amount of profit received by the partner; only his or her own profit was reported. Subjects completed a total of 60 rounds at the same network position. Each relation contained 30 profit points at the outset of each round, although subjects did not actually know the pool size. At the outset of negotiations, each partner could receive 15 points from an agreement, which was awarded as a 15-cent "bonus" for reaching an agreement. Subjects could raise or lower the amount they were willing to accept from each partner by one point or leave the amount unchanged. Each one-point change resulted in a one-cent change in the amount of bonus for agreement. The computer declared an agreement when the sum of the profits for which two potential exchange partners were willing to settle did not exceed

30 points. If the sum was less than 30 points, the computer split the excess and awarded half to each subject in addition to the amount on which she or he had settled.

Because subjects made offers to all potential partners on each round, some could reach provisional agreements with more than one partner. Because subjects were only allowed one agreement on each round, the central computer used the following algorithm to prioritize agreements: (1) Assign zero profit to subjects who do not reach any provisional agreement. (2) For those who remain, declare agreements for pairs of subjects whose best deals are with each other. (3) Select a subject randomly from those remaining and award her or his best deal. (4) Repeat the random selection until no more deals are possible.

This restricted information setting differs from the full information setting in several important ways.[18] Nevertheless, the settings are identical in several respects crucial to our model. First, in both settings the number of direct relations a subject has to others is immediately apparent and obvious. Therefore, degree can influence profit expectations. Second, in both settings, actors can over time get a sense of the range of acceptable terms through experiencing rounds in which they are excluded from exchange and rounds in which they are included. (This is true in the restricted information setting even if some inclusions have a chance element based on computer intervention when multiple provisional exchanges could be made.) Therefore, excludability can influence expectations. On the basis of these essential similarities, we make the same predictions for profit differentials by position at equilibrium in the new limited information setting. That is, exhange rates in the last rounds of an experiment should be comparable across settings.[19]

Results

Eleven groups participated in the Stem network. We treated the last 10 agreements in a session for each relation as an indicator of its equilibrium exchange rate. This provides sufficient cases for a stringent statistical test and roughly corresponds to our use of last-period results in the full information experiments. For the A–B relation, the last 10 agreements varied by no more than a few points in all groups, allowing us to conclude that equilibrium had been reached. The maximum range over which agreements varied was 4 ($M = 2.0$; $sd = 1.05$).[20] In exchanges with B, the subject in the A position achieved mean profit of 20.13 ($sd = 4.29$) out of a pool of 30 points, compared to the GPI–RD predicted level of 19.5. A one-sample t-test found no difference between prediction and observation, $t(10) = -.49$, $p = .64$. Profit of 20.13 on a 30-point scale is equivalent to 16.10 on a 24-point scale, and thus very close to the 15.86 observed in the full information experiment.

In previously reported experiments using the Stem network (Markovsky et al. 1993; Cook et al. 1992), A–C exchanges were infrequent. We had hoped that with 60 rounds in the new setting, we could establish an equilibrium value for this relation. This was not the case. *A–C* exchanges were still infrequent, especially during the final 30 rounds of a session. Two groups had no *A–C* exchanges during the last 30 rounds, and only four groups had 10 or more. With such limited data, we lack confidence that equilibrium was reached. However, we attempted to test our prediction for *A* in the *A–C* relation by taking the overall mean for all *A–C* exchanges that occurred in the last half of a session ($M = 17.46$, $sd = 3.77$). GPI–RD predicts that *A* will receive 17.10 profit units at equilibrium, a difference of less than half a profit unit from the observed mean. A *t*-test found no difference between predicted and observed values, $t(82) = -.88$, $p = .38$. Although this result does support the GPI–RD model, the variability in frequency of exchange argues against giving it much weight.

A significant difference was found in the C_1–C_2 relation. As with the *A–B* relation, we were able to use C_1's mean profit for the last 10 exchanges for each group as an indicator of the equilibrium exchange rate in C_1–C_2 ($M = 18.18$, $sd = 4.31$). This difference in profit between isomorphic network positions is puzzling; all models predict an equal, 15–15, division of profit. Comparing this predicted value to the observed mean, we find that $t(10) = -2.45$, $p = .03$. The anomalous finding may be a chance occurrence or an artifact of the experimental setting: The program treats C_1 and C_2 identically, with the one exception being that C_1 appears above C_2 as a potential partner on *A*'s video screen. Possibly because of simple ordering, *A* pays more attention to C_1 than to C_2, thereby impacting C_1's negotiations with C_2 in C_1's favor. Although this might not affect the *A–C* or *A–B* equilibrium values (and thus show how robust GPI–RD predictions are for these relations), it could impact the C_1–C_2 value. For the present, we regard this finding as a spur to additional research rather than as a disconfirmation of GPI–RD because the finding is completely unanticipated by any alternative model.

To summarize, we replicated our test of the GPI–RD model using the Stem network in an information-restricted exchange situation. The key hypotheses were again supported.

DISCUSSION AND CONCLUSIONS

We developed a theory to explain how actors in social exchange networks reach agreements on particular divisions of resources. This model incorporates previous ideas about the effects that network structure has on the power of individual positions, specifically, the Graph-theoretic Power Index of network exchange theory and its weak power extension (Markovsky et al. 1988, 1993). To this model we added theoretical ideas borrowed from several areas of sociology.

From elementary theory's concept of resistance, we borrowed the idea that actors balance two competing interests to reach agreement in exchange: (1) their ''best hope'' for maximum profit, and (2) their ''worst fear'' of being excluded from exchange entirely. We combined this with an idea from network exchange theory: Likelihood of being included in exchange ranks the power of network actors. This resulted in a new assumption: Actors' best hopes and worst fears are proportional to their likelihood of being included in exchange. Actors who are frequently excluded from exchanges (and profit) are likely to lower both their maximum and minimum aspirations for profit. Conversely, actors frequently included in exchanges become accustomed to receiving profit and raise their expectations accordingly. Integrating these previous theoretical strands yielded a model that generates ratio-scale predictions for the outcomes of negotiating actors in exchange networks.

The fact that actors adjust their expectations through negotiation implies that structural power differences emerge over time. In strong power networks identified by network exchange theory, these differences never reach an equilibrium point short of the point of extreme differentiation. They continue until powerful actors receive all (or nearly all) available resources from exchange with less powerful actors. In weak power structures, an equilibrium point is reached well short of maximum differentiation. It is this equilibrium point that we attempt to theoretically predict and experimentally measure.

We felt that the equilibrium point eventually reached will likely be affected by actors' initial expectations formed on the basis of prominent features of their structural context. From network analysis we borrowed the idea that an actor's degree, the number of her direct ties to other actors, would influence her initial expectations for success in exchange. That is, actors with more direct ties would be biased toward resisting exchange offers that they would otherwise accept. We included degree as a biasing factor in predicting the equilibrium exchange point that experimental subjects would eventually reach. Results of an experimental test in a setting specifically designed to measure the equilibrium point suggest that our theoretical integration was successful. This brings up potential avenues for future research. The theory suggests that actors' expectations have significant effects on resource distribution only in weak power networks. What effects, if any, do expectations have in strong power networks? Also, certain expectations about the social structure were shown to have important effects in weak power networks. Do other kinds of cognitions have important effects? And under what conditions are cognitions likely to be more or less important?

Our extension of network exchange theory provides a number of advantages over earlier versions and current alternatives. By highlighting the ways that actors' profit expectations interact with structural properties of their locations in the network, it generates predictions for all positions in weak power networks on a ratio rather than an ordinal level of measurement. Moreover, these predictions are more accurate than those of alternative theories, and the theory generalizes across experimental designs. Our predictions closely approximate experimental results from the full information experiments of Skvoretz and Willer, the restricted information experiments of Cook et al. (1992), and the results reported here for equilibrium rates in both full and restricted settings. In addition, results reported by Bienenstock and Bonacich (1993) for two weak power networks, the four-actor line and Kite, are extremely close to our predictions. Their experimental setting has features quite different from either the Skvoretz and Willer or Cook et al. designs. This remarkable convergence of experimental results in different settings demonstrates both the increased precision of the theory and its enhanced generality.

The empirical results also suggest that equity concerns are not inextricably woven into social exchange network settings. This is not to say that equity effects are unimportant, but rather that equity is a distinct process that may or may not be activated in a given social context, depending on whether or not certain conditions are satisfied (Markovsky 1985). In developing our restricted information setting, we struggled with the powerful effects of subjects' equity concerns when they felt they were receiving less than a partner who in other ways was their status equal. In some cases, subjects would refuse to exchange in as many as 50 out of 60 rounds because another subject would receive more profit than they would. That is, subjects would refuse five or six dollars in pay to avoid receiving a few pennies less than their partner in exchange. This study demonstrates that once equity concerns are controlled, different experimental settings produce comparable structural effects on resource distributions resulting from exchange. Structural positions have an effect on power independent of equity concerns. An interesting area for further inquiry is exactly how equity effects combine with the effect of structural position under different conditions to produce power and profit differences in social exchange networks.

We also wish to note that the equation for actor profit, P_i, converges with part of Cook and Yamagishi's (1992) theory—their equation $R_{ij} = (P_{ij} + A_{ij} - A_{ji})/2$. In this model, R_{ij} is the profit that actor i obtains in exchange with partner j and corresponds to our P_i; P_{ij} is the pool size and corresponds to P; A_{ij} is the best alternative available to i which corresponds to C_{ij}, i's expected conflict outcome. That is, i's best alternative is the least amount of profit i expects if exchange with j does *not* occur. A_{ji} is j's best alternative, that is, C_{ji}. Despite these similarities, our model diverges from Cook and Yamagishi's in significant ways. Unlike A_{ij}, which refers to the objective profit under "conflict," C_{ij} is assumed to be a subjective assessment or expectation of long-range profit from failure to reach agreement. We believe that one reason for our model's predictive success stems from this incorporation of the actor's point of view. This allows the new model to generate contrasting predictions that are here shown to be significantly more accurate than alternatives.

Although the predictions that we derived are accurate for the networks tested, these findings only tell us that the model is developing in potentially fruitful directions. Establishing its broader generality will require continued testing in a wider variety of networks. Further enhancements will also be required to allow predictions with theoretical restrictions further relaxed. Of course, these have been our goals all along: to generate increasingly precise and accurate predictions for network exchange outcomes under increasingly robust conditions. With the theoretical and empirical developments reported here, we have worked toward achieving these goals.

Part 2: l_i^2, An Alternative for Predicting Weak Power
Michael J. Lovaglia and David Willer

INTRODUCTION

Part 1 of this chapter introduced two methods for predicting power differences in weak power networks called GPI–R and GPI–RD. Both methods use l_i, the likelihood that the position i will be included in exchanges. In fact, GPI–R used l_i alone, whereas GPI–RD used l_i and degree. Degree is the number of relations connected at a node. As will be remembered from Table 7.1, GPI–RD is the better predictor. Despite its success at predicting power differences, and despite our justification of its use, degree raises problems, which we discuss in the following section.

GPI–RD is a more successful predictor than GPI–R, because substantial differences in profit are associated with very small differences in l_i. For example, l_i for position D in the Kite Network of Figure 7.2 is .82, while for the E positions it is .79. The percent difference of the two l_i values is $(.82 - .79)/(.82 + .79) = .0186$. D in the Kite, however, averages 14.05, whereas each E averages 9.95 (Skvoretz and Willer 1993 [Chapter 6]; also see Markovsky et al. 1993 and Bienenstock and Bonacich 1993). The percent difference of D's and E's payoffs is $(14.05 - 9.95)/24 = .171$. That these profit differences are not proportional to differences in l_i suggests that payoff differences are not a linear function of l_i.

If payoffs are related to l_i, but the function is not linear, the theorist has two options. The first option, which is the one pursued in Part 1 of this chapter, is to find a second factor, D, such that payoff differences are a joint function of D and l_i. Note that, for many networks, D and l_i are closely related. For example, in the Stem of Figure 7.2, the two are ordered identically. That is, when D_i is the degree of i, $(D_A = 3$ and $l_A = 1.0) > (D_C = 2$ and $l_C = .80) > (D_B = 1$ and $l_B = .60)$. When D varies with $_i l$, using them together is equivalent to using l_i^2.

The second option, which is the one considered here, is to predict payoffs using a nonlinear function of l_i. We propose that payoffs vary with the square of l_i. Later we will generate the l_i^2 predictions and compare them to GPI–R and GPI–RD.[21] First, we consider two objections to using degree to predict weak power differences.

OBJECTIONS TO DEGREE

There are theoretical and empirical objections to using degree to predict weak power. In theory the objection is as follows. Network Exchange Theory asserts that exclusion is the structural condition that produces power differences in weak power networks. l_i is a measure of exclusion. That is, the likelihood of exclusion $= 1 - l_i$. Therefore, NET asserts that power differences—and thus exchange ratios—are a function of l_i.

Degree is not a structural condition producing power in weak power networks. Arguably, degree is an *invalid* theory of power in exchange networks. As shown below for branch networks, power does not vary with degree. Since degree does not produce power, NET must assert that power differences are *not* a function of degree.

Introducing degree into the prediction of weak power comes perilously close to introducing a contradiction into the theory. It would seem that since degree does not produce power differences, it is wrong to use degree to predict power differences. Nevertheless, the use of degree can be justified and contradiction can be avoided. In doing so, however, the conditions under which degree can be used for prediction are sharply limited.

As will be remembered from the first part of this chapter, degree is not claimed to be a structural power condition. Degree is claimed to bias actors' perceptions such that, when degree is large, actors expect high profit and, when degree is small, actors expect low profit. Since degree is not a structural condition of power, however, these biasing effects have no structural foundation. In effect, they are mistaken beliefs. It follows that the effect of degree must be to make actors *overconfident* when degree is large and *underconfident* when degree is small. At issue is the question of how long these mistaken beliefs will be supported.

A model that sees the effect of degree as transitory easily avoids contradiction. If exclusion is the sole structural condition of power, the interaction processes of exchange networks will correct mistaken beliefs based on degree. An actor who is initially overconfident will be unpleasantly surprised. Because structural conditions are not as favorable as judged, exchanges are not as favorable as hoped. As a result, expectations fall. The actor who is underconfident will be pleasantly surprised to find that exchanges are more favorable than hoped. As a result, expectations rise. As beliefs come to reflect structural conditions, exchange ratios approach equilibrium values, values that are determined by exclusion alone.

The empirical objection to using degree to predict power differences is that there are exclusionary networks in which degree has no effect. Looking ahead at Table 8.3 in the next chapter, we find exchange ratios reported for three null connected branch networks, Br331, Br551, and Br771. It will be remembered that, in branch networks, one central position is connected to N peripherals which are connected only to the center. In Br331, there are three peripherals, and the central position exchanges with all three. In Br551, there are five peripherals, and the central position exchanges with all five—and similarly for Br771. In these networks no position is excluded, and Network Exchange Theory asserts that all relations are equal power.

Branch networks are unilateral monopolies and, in the social sciences, it is frequently believed that monopolists are power advantaged—a belief that rests firmly on the false theory of degree as a structural power determinant. That monopolists are powerful is also a folk belief which is particularly prevalent among college students, and it is from the population of college students that we recruit our subjects.

Nevertheless, as shown in Table 8.3, degree does not produce power differences in the three null connected branches. We make that flat assertion in spite of the fact that earnings of the central position in two of three branches are significantly larger than equipower. While statistically significant, the differences are slight, and we do not believe they are substantively significant. Other research shows means for the central actor which are as far below equipower as these are above.[22] Furthermore, comparing across the null connected branches, we find that power differences do not increase as the size of the branch increases. Exactly the opposite is seen. Power differences decline as degree increases. That degree is not a structural power condition argues against any but the most restricted use of it to predict power differences.

In the next section we dispense with degree and use l_i^2. Nevertheless, degree may affect initial power differences, and whether it does so is an empirical question that should be investigated.

USING l_i^2 TO PREDICT POWER IN EXCHANGE NETWORKS

Calculations using l_i^2 to predict profit in exchange relations are a straightforward extension of the GPI–R formula in Lovaglia et al. (1995), which is the first part of this chapter.

An actor's perceived conflict outcome, C_i, and the actor's maximum profit expectation, M_i, vary with the square of the actor's likelihood of being included in exchange, l_i^2. As Lovaglia et al. (1995) showed, this assumption results in the elimination of M_i from the profit equation. The formula for predicting profit using l_i^2 follows:

$$C_i = \frac{P}{2} \, l_i^2$$
$$P_i = (P + C_i - C_j) / 2$$
$$P_j = P - P_i$$

Here, P is the size of the profit pool. P_i is actor i's predicted profit from exchange, and P_j is actor j's predicted profit from exchange.

In the Stem network of Figure 7.2, likelihoods of being included for positions A and B are $l_A = 1.0$, $l_B = .6$. Assuming a typical 24-point profit pool, P, we now calculate profit distributions for the A–B relation. First, by the resistance-likelihood assumption, $C_A = (24/2) \times 1^2 = 12$, and $C_B = (24/2) \times .6^2 = 4.3$. Next, profits are calculated to be $P_A = (P + C_A - C_B)/2 = 15.8$, and $P_B = P - P_A = 8.2$. Just as with GPI–R and GPI–RD, if the network structure and total value of each profit pool are known, profits for any pair of positions in any weak power network can be predicted using l_i^2. Table 7.2 shows that predictions using l^2 are more accurate than those using l_i alone. Further, there is little to choose between l_i^2 predictions and predictions from GPI–RD but for the Double Branch 2 network.

ISSUES OF JUSTIFYING l_i^2

We have a strong preference for simple explanations over complicated ones. Had l_i directly predicted profit, the question of mathematical form would probably not have been raised. But it did not. Interestingly, the earliest version of Part 1 of this chapter, when read at the American Sociological Association meetings (Lovaglia et al. 1993), used l_i^2, not degree. But using l_i^2 to predict profit bothered some reviewers because NET does not explain why l_i^2 worked rather than some other mathematical transformation. Why not l_i cubed (l_i^3), for example? Some of the authors, taking the instrumentalist philosophical position, assert that l_i^2 works and the fact that it does work is sufficient justification. Others of us are less sure.

In thinking about squaring l_i our reflections come to this. In the physical sciences, good reasons are offered for squaring terms. For example, the energy of sound at a distance is expressed as an inverse square law. The underlying reason is that the area of a sphere is proportional to the square of its radius. Sound expands as the surface of a sphere from its source. Distance is the length of the radius from the source to the sphere on which the sound energy is distributed. Distance is squared because a given quantity of sound energy is being spread across an expanding spherical surface. As a result, sound energy, at any point, declines to the square of the distance. All this was known when the inverse square law was introduced.

But good reasons do not always accompany a term's introduction. Reasons may follow some time after squared terms are introduced. For example, gravity is also expressed as an inverse square law, but a model like that for sound does

Table 7.2

Goodness of Fit[a] for Predicted and Observed Profits in Exchange Networks

Structure, Relation	Models and Predictions			Observed Means
	GPI- l_i	GPI-l_i^2	GPI-RD	
4-Line				
B–A[b]	13.5	14.6****	14.5****	14.4
t (29)	-2.54	.64	0.18	
Stem[c]				
A–B	14.4*	15.8****	15.6****	15.9
t (13)	-1.88	.02	-0.33	
Kite				
D–E	12.2****	12.3****	13.7****	12.8
t(7)	-0.46	-0.36	0.77	
Dbranch2				
F–G	13.3	14.4	16.3****	16.4
t(63)	-6.69	-3.70	-0.14	

[a]One-sample *t*-tests were used to estimate the probability of *no difference* between prediction and observation. Larger *p* values suggest an *increased* likelihood that prediction and observation are identical. Degrees of freedom are in parentheses.

*$p > .05$; **$p > .10$; ***$p > .20$; ****$p > .40$.

[b]Predictions are for profits of the first position listed in a relation; here for example, actor A in A–B.

[c]The A–C relation is also of interest in this network. However, during the last period of the experiment, A exchanged with C only twice, both times at 14–10. This precludes meaningful comparison. With that caveat, we report only for completeness that the GPI–RD prediction of 13.7 for this relation was closest among the models, though the equidependence and rational exchange models were also close.

not apply. One reason for the early acceptance of Einstein's special relativity was its explanation for the inverse square law of gravitation, an explanation that Newton's theory lacked.

We offer the following justification for the use of l_i^2. First, only $l_i < 1$ values, and not $l_i = 1$, are affected by squaring. Further, all $l_i < 1$ are disadvantageous relative to $l_i = 1$. That is, all $0 < l_i < 1$ values are bad news to actors, and the news is increasingly bad as l_i declines. They are all bad news because only $l_i = 1$ positions are secure against exclusion; all others are insecure. Second, there is a long tradition in psychology and social psychology that negative payoffs have disproportionally greater utility effects than positive payoffs (cf. Kahneman, Slovic, and Tversky 1982). While $l_i < 1$ values are not themselves payoffs, l_i values stand in theory for the experiences of actors who gain payoffs and fail to gain payoffs because they are excluded. Since l_i values are experienced by actors as payoffs and exclusion from payoffs, and since all $l_i < 1$ values are negatives, l_i^2 expresses disproportional effect of negatives on actors' utilities. In so doing, only l_i, which is a power condition, and not degree, which is not a power condition, enters into calculations.

NOTES

1. However, network exchange theory predictions also generally agree with data from exchange situations with greater information restrictions, for example, Cook and Emerson (1978), Cook et al. (1983), and Cook, Donnelly, and Yamagishi (1992), and also from the setting used by Bienenstock and Bonacich (1993).

2. These conditions are probably sufficient but not necessary to determine if a network is strong power. In general, casual inspection often fails to classify networks properly as strong power or weak power. Full application of the GPI method is required.

3. Theoretical integration requires integration of notation systems as well. Markovsky et al. (1993) use the notation, $p\{i\}$, to denote the probability of inclusion of position i in an exchange network. But the letter p also occurs in resistance equations to denote profit. To avoid confusion and simplify our notation, we switch to l_i (actor i's likelihood of exchange).

4. C_i is similar to Thibaut and Kelley's (1959, p. 21) "comparison level for alternatives" or C_{alt}, that is, "the lowest level of outcomes a member will accept in the light of available alternative opportunities." M_i and C_i define the range of possible offers. The model does not assume that actors have objective knowledge of their values. "Best hopes" and "worst fears" need not be reasonable, though actors are likely to refine their estimates as they interact. We have again simplified the notation of earlier presentations of the theory: for example, Willer, Markovsky, and Patton (1989) use $P_{MAX}(A)$ to represent M_i and $P_{CON}(A)$ to represent C_i.

5. Assumptions are evaluated on the basis of their effectiveness in producing testable hypotheses that conform well with observation. The assumption that actors exchange when their resistances are equal has been very fruitful in previous studies (Willer 1987; Skvoretz and Willer 1993), including cross-national comparisons (Willer and Szmatka 1993).

6. Cook and Yamagishi (1992) also suggest that the idea of a limit to power use in networks holds promise for a general formula to predict resource distribution. Willer (1987) demonstrated such generality when he applied the resistance model to a wide variety of network situations both inside and outside of the laboratory.

7. Individuals participating in experiments or acting in natural exchange situations will exhibit a range of "best hopes" and "worst fears." This in no way interferes with the model's ability to predict exchange *rates*. Coalitions among actors are ruled out by the scope conditions of the theory, though they may often occur in exchange situations. Erger (1993) has extended the theory to include the effects of coalitions.

8. Markovsky et al. (1993) provide support for this idea. They found that ordinal predictions for weak power networks based on the likelihood of being included were more strongly corroborated for experienced than for inexperienced subjects.

9. Although simple proportionality is a straightforward way to incorporate likelihood of being included into the resistance model, other specifications are possible. For ex-

ample, Skvoretz and Willer (1993) take the difference between M_i and P_i and then raise it to the power of l_i. Our model is the simplest expression we could devise of the theoretical idea that actors' worst fears and best hopes in the exchange situation depend on—and are proportional to—the likelihood of their being included in exchanges.

10. The mathematical derivation is available on request from the first author.

11. Markovsky (1988) specifies the conditions under which anchoring will occur: judgments are indeterminate, an anchor is available, and anchors are salient. These conditions are satisfied in experimental tests of network exchange theory. Markovsky's "anchoring proposition" predicts when assimilation as opposed to contrast effects will be observed. According to this proposition, assimilation would be predicted in the present context because degree informs best-hope and/or worst-fear outcomes, each of which appears *on the same scale* as the "response" variable, that is, expected profit. (An anchor on the stimulus scale—as in the temperature example—produces a contrast effect.)

12. An actor's maximum expectation for profit may differ among exchange partners in the same way.

13. In a replication using a different experimental exchange setting, Bienenstock and Bonacich (1993) obtained similar results.

14. Some readers of earlier versions of this part of the chapter noted the similarity between network exchange and noncooperative game theory (e.g., see Nash 1951; Harsanyi 1980; Rosenthal and Rubinstein 1984; Rubinstein 1982, 1991; and Osborne 1990). Also, the few experimental tests of noncooperative game theory use experimental situations similar to those used in network exchange experiments but without the complication of network structure (e.g., see Nydegger and Owen 1974). Though intriguing, these similarities mask very real difficulties in applying noncooperative game theory to network exchange. Rubinstein (1982, p. 97) states the bargaining problem in noncooperative game theory as: "Two individuals have before them several possible contractual agreements. Both have interests in reaching agreement but their interests are not entirely identical. What 'will be' the agreed contract, assuming that both parties behave rationally?" (97). He goes on to distinguish this problem from two others: "(i) the positive question—what is the agreement reached in practice; (ii) the normative question—what is the just agreement" (97). Perhaps because of these distinctions, noncooperative game theory places little emphasis on theory testing through experimental or field research and does not fare well in experimental tests. Network exchange theories place more emphasis on the "positive question," on how subjects behave in controlled settings. Experimental results are then used to inform theoretical development in cumulative research programs. Bienenstock and Bonacich have made the most successful use of game theory to analyze network exchange structures.

15. Markovsky et al. (1993) and Skvoretz and Willer (1993) analyze data from these full information experiments. Markovsky et al. (1993) use data from the Stem and Kite networks; Skvoretz and Willer (1993) use data from all four experiments. Their analyses are based on all rounds of the experiments. Here we use data from just the last period, which is four rounds long. Although suitable for testing ordinal predictions, using the mean of all rounds in an experiment as an indicator of power is problematic for testing exact predictions. For example, exchange may begin at an even split of the profit pool, 12–12, in early rounds and then progress to a stable pattern of 20–4 exchanges. In this case, 20–4 is a good estimate of the power difference in the relationship. The mean exchange rate for all rounds (about 16–8) would seriously underestimate the magnitude of the equilibrated power difference.

16. Our model requires these assumptions; we do not assume that all naturally occurring social exchanges satisfy these conditions.

17. This system was designed to be relatively "low-tech" and portable to other laboratories. The software is written in Microsoft QuickBASIC (4.5), and PCs are connected in a ring configuration via cables connected to standard serial ports. The ring consists of one Master Control PC and any number of subject PCs. The program is available from the authors upon request.

18. Equity concerns, for instance, are controlled in both settings in different ways. If actors feel the exchange situation is unfair, they may refuse to accept the best offer available to them. The full information setting described solves the potential equity problem by rotating subjects through all positions. Actors disadvantaged in one position know they will be compensated when they rotate through an advantaged position. Restricted information settings in which subjects typically do not change positions solve the problem by not telling a subject the earnings of his or her partner in order to prevent comparison of subject's rewards with partner's rewards.

19. Because of the differences in intra-round negotiation options and total number of rounds between the two settings, we would not expect averages from all rounds to be similar across settings. The restriction to equilibrium rates is essential to the "no setting difference" prediction.

20. In contrast, the first 10 A–B agreements for each group varied more widely; the maximum range was 9 ($M = 4.23$, $sd = 2.35$). The mean range of the first 10 agreements was significantly greater than the mean range of the last 10 agreements, $t(10) = 3.09$, $p = .01$.

21. Before the biasing effect of degree (Skvoretz and Lovaglia 1995) was proposed as an explanation for differences in profit among positions in exchange networks, a formula like l_i^2 proposed here was found to work quite well (Lovaglia, Skvoretz, Willer, and Markovsky 1993).

22. Our belief is based in part on experiments on the Branch33 network showing no power differences. These experiments were conducted in several settings. In 1981, Brennan reported the unexpected finding that peripheral, B, actors had a profit advantage over the central, A, actor. That experiment was conducted in a face-to-face setting in which the A actors may have been able to put social pressure on B to reduce profit demands. Later, Skvoretz and Willer (1991) replicated the experiment using a computerized exchange setting that isolated actors in separate rooms. They found no differences in profit among positions in the Branch33 network. Szmatka and Willer (1995) reported a cross-national replication in Poland. There, actors exchanged in a face-to-face setting. Just as in Brennan (1981), the face-to-face setting produced a profit advantage for the *peripheral* actors. None of the experiments showed a degree advantage for the central, A, actor.

Chapter 8

Network Connections

Preface
David Willer

This chapter substantially broadens the scope of Network Exchange Theory. The theory and research of Chapters 4, 5, 6, and 7 focused on the distribution of power in exclusively connected networks. But exclusion is not the only type of connection in exchange networks. This chapter asserts that there are five and only five types of connection. They are inclusion, exclusion, null, inclusion-exclusion, and inclusion-null. The chapter presents a procedure called the "Combined Analysis," which predicts the distribution of power in networks with the five kinds of connection.

The first part of this study investigates each of the five types individually; predictions are developed for branch networks in which only one type of connection is present. Not all of this is entirely new. Exclusively connected networks have been extensively investigated. Nevertheless, exclusively connected branches with different numbers of peripherals have not previously been compared. At issue is whether degree of the central actor affects power. Degree is also investigated for null and inclusion. As predicted by the Combined Analysis, the exercise of power in exclusively and null connected networks is not affected by degree. By contrast, the exercise of power in inclusively connected networks increases as degree of the central position increases. This effect is also predicted by Combined Analysis. By extending the investigation to inclusive-exclusive branches and inclusive-null branches, this first part of the investigation is exhaustive for branches.

In the second part of the study, predictions for the distribution of power in networks with more than one type of connection are tested. This part of the investigation is by no means exhaustive. Here only two networks are investigated, but the array of conditions now possible for exchange networks implies that far more are needed. For example, ignoring variations in shape, there are

10 kinds of networks in which each of two nodes has a different type of connection. Allowing three or more types of connection and allowing shape to vary result in a mind-boggling array of contrasting structures. But there is even greater variety. The extension of the theory to connections where relations are nonsubstitutable multiplies each possibility manyfold. Certainly the study of networks with multiple types of connection cries out for a major research initiative.

The theoretic procedure offered here is called the Combined Analysis because it combines resistance and the Graph-theoretic Power Index (GPI) with other formulations. Today one modification to the combined analysis is needed. Since this chapter was published, it has been found that the GPI does not give unique predictions for some networks. Chapter 10 gives two alternatives to GPI. Although either can be readily substituted for GPI in the Combined Analysis, the "Optimal-Seek" procedure of Part 2 of that chapter is simpler and appears to have broader scope. Substituting Optimal Seek for GPI in the Combined Analysis gives the broadest scope theoretic procedure thus far devised for prediction power in exchange networks.

This chapter does not offer tests pitting Network Exchange Theory's Combined Analysis against other theories because no other theory competes. No other theory competes because none covers networks with the whole array of connection types. In this important regard, Network Exchange Theory's scope is decisively broader than others.

Network Connection and Exchange Ratios: Theory, Predictions, and Experimental Tests
David Willer and John Skvoretz

In exchange networks, connections of exchanges at nodes include conditions that affect actors' behavior. Actors may be limited to exchanging with fewer partners than they can reach, or they may be required to exchange with a minimum number of partners. A recent typology identifies five types of connection, but most theories have been limited to as few as two of these types. When theories are limited to a few types of connection, applications outside the laboratory are highly restricted. Here scope is extended to any mixture of types of connection in networks of any shape. The scope extension is attained with a new theoretic analysis, which combines the Graph-theoretic Power Index and Resistance Theory. Beginning with simple networks, the combined analysis is extended to networks with any configuration and any mixture of connection. A series of experimental tests supports each step of this extension. New applications outside the laboratory are proposed.

INTRODUCTION

Over the last decade, network exchange theories have substantially advanced, but only for a narrow range. Formalisms have focused on networks where actors are restricted to exchanging in fewer relations than are incident at their positions. Positions so restricted are "exclusively connected." Four recently introduced theories offer metric predictions: GPI-resistance (Markovsky et al. 1993), expected value (Friedkin 1992, 1993), equidependence algorithm (Cook and Yamagishi 1992a), and the core (Bienenstock and Bonacich 1992, 1993). Skvoretz and Willer (1993) found that all have predictive success but that GPI–Resistance Theory is the best predictor.[1] These theories extend previous work to "weak power" networks (Markovsky 1992; Skvoretz and Fararo 1992) but, focusing on exclusive connection, fall well short of covering the full range of exchange network connections.

In exchange networks, actors negotiate seeking favorable resource outcomes, and their success is conditioned by type of connection at their own and others' positions. Actors in exclusively connected positions are restricted to exchanging with only some or one of their partners and may benefit from rivalries produced by that restriction. By contrast, positions not so restricted are null connected; actors in null connected positions are never advantaged by rivalries (Markovsky, Willer, and Patton, 1988). Alternatively, actors in inclusively connected positions are required to complete exchanges in two or more relations to benefit from any one. Because failure to complete some exchanges jeopardizes payoffs from others, actors in inclusively connected positions may be disadvantaged in their negotiations (Patton and Willer 1990). Positions which are exclusively or null connected may also be inclusively connected for a total of five connection types.[2] Any theory that is limited to only one or two of the five types of connection will be blocked from many important applications.

For example, industrial networks are exchange networks which can contain any mixture of connection types (Williamson 1981, 1986; Hakansson 1989; Johanson 1989). Consider a firm which assembles a complex product such as an automobile. The firm buys hundreds, even thousands of different kinds of parts, and, for production to be ongoing, quantities of each kind must be received and available for assembly into the product (Womack, Jones, and Roos 1990). Cars lacking parts like transmissions and lights cannot be sold. Therefore, the firm must complete exchanges for *all* these resources in order to profit. How does the need to complete all exchanges affect the bargaining position of the firm? If the firm's bargaining position is weakened, are prices paid to suppliers affected? If alternative sources of supply are found, will the firm's bargaining position be improved? Is the firm's position improved only if alternative sources are exclusive?[3] To answer these questions for industrial networks and other applications in the field, a theory must apply to networks with all five types of connection.

We offer a theory developed from GPI-Resistance which predicts exchange outcomes in networks of any mixture of connection types and any configuration (shape). The outcomes predicted are exchange ratios which indicate the division of valued resources in each exchange relation. This theory has two components: the Graph-theoretic Power Index (Markovsky et al. 1988) and "Resistance Theory" (Willer 1981; Heckathorn 1983; Skvoretz and Willer 1993). When introduced by Markovsky et al. (1988), GPI was limited to exclusive and null connected networks. The combination of GPI and Resistance Theory offered by Skvoretz and Willer (1993) was similarly in scope limited.[4] Here both components are extended, and experimental tests are offered at each step of the extension.

The first part of this chapter investigates the effect of number of relations (*degree*) on exchange ratios for each of the five connection types. Emerson

(1972) suggests that a monopolist's power is increased as the number of alternatives increases, whereas Markovsky et al. (1988) assert that a surplus of only one relationship is needed to produce power differences. Only Patton and Willer (1990) have investigated the effect of number of connected relations. They studied only inclusive connection and found that increasing the number of connected relations from three to five weakens the bargaining position of the connected actor. Since they studied inclusion at only one node connected in either three or five relations, they did not have enough variation in degree to determine the function relating size and exchange ratio. The only previous investigation to study more than two types of connection was Szmatka and Willer (1995) who studied four of the five types investigated here. Since they studied only one network of each type, they left open the question of the effect of degree on exchange ratios.

With the effect of degree for each type of connection determined, in the second part of the chapter we extend the GPI-Resistance analysis to networks with *any* configuration and *any* mixture of connections. The analysis is experimentally tested on two complex networks. By varying both connection and configuration, this extension and its test significantly transcend the scope of previous theory and research. For example, the four competing theories mentioned in the introduction apply to networks of any configuration, but only for networks with exclusive and null connections. Szmatka and Willer (1995) study four of the five types of connection, but their theory applies only to simple branch (unilateral monopoly) networks. This study offers the only theory which covers the full range of variations of connection which is not limited by configuration and the only test of a theory with scope that broad.

The organization of this chapter departs somewhat from the norm. Experimental results are given for predictions for degree and at each subsequent step extending the theory.

TYPES OF NETWORK CONNECTION

Due to the recent rapid growth of network exchange theory, technical terms for structural conditions are only now entering general usage. Here the terms for connection are introduced, and each type is examined using examples from experimental research and from the field, including the industrial network of the auto manufacturing firm mentioned in the introduction. We then differentiate "compound connections" and show how the typology guides selection of networks for experimental tests.

The Typology

Conditions which govern the maximum and minimum numbers of relations in which an actor at a node exchanges are called "conditions of connection." Here we differentiate five types of connection by comparing three quantities: N, M, and Q. N is the number of exchange relations connected to the node. M is the maximum number of relations in which the actor can benefit. Q is the minimum number of relations in which all exchanges must be completed to benefit from any one. Let i be the connected node. Then Q_i is a subset of M_i which is a subset of N_i and

i is inclusively connected if $N_i = M_i = Q_i > 1$.

i is exclusively connected if $N_i > M_i \geqslant Q_i = 1$.

i is null connected if $N_i = M_i > Q_i = 1$.

i is inclusive-exclusively connected if $N_i > M_i \geqslant Q_i > 1$.

i is inclusive-null connected if $N_i = M_i > Q_i > 1$.[5]

The five types are exhaustive: they cover all conditions in which two or more relations are connected at a node (see below). When only one relation is connected, $N = M = Q = 1$ and the node is *singularly* connected.[6]

Exclusive and null connection are defined by comparing the number of relations incident at i to the largest number in which i can *benefit*. That is, N_i is the number of i's potential exchange partners, and M_i, a subset of N_i, is the maximum number with which i exchanges. $N_i - M_i$ are necessarily excluded from exchanging with i. When $N_i > M_i$, at least one of i's partners must be excluded from exchanging with i and the connection is exclusive. When $N_i = M_i$ the connection is null and none of i's partners must be excluded. N and M are not new. Since Stolte and Emerson (1978) and Brennan (1981), either implicitly or explicitly, N and M have been set as initial conditions of experimental structures.

All of the theories mentioned in the introduction agree that, in simple networks like A–B–A, only exclusive connection advantages B; null does not. Because B is connected to two As, $N_B = 2$. When B exchanges with only one A, $N_B > M_B$ and the connection is exclusive. B is high in power and will gain most of the resources in each exchange. When B exchanges with both As, however, $N_B = M_B$, the connection is null, and power and resource divisions are equal. In more complex networks, exclusively connected positions may be high or low in power. The Combined GPI-Resistance Analysis introduced later in this chapter asserts that exclusive connection may advantage a position but that null connection never does.

Outside the laboratory a variety of circumstances determine the sizes N and M. When families seek bargains and check more than one food market before making a purchase, $N > M = 1$, but when hurried purchases are made at the first stop $N = M = 1$. For the firm, M is the number of current suppliers, whereas N is all suppliers with which the firm could exchange. Economic analyses of industrial networks evaluate "opportunity costs," which are costs associated with maintaining N potential exchange partners, and "transaction costs," which are costs associated with maintaining M ongoing relations (Coase 1937; Williamson 1986). If costs are high, a firm may seek to minimize both costs by minimizing the size of N and M. The result is $N = M = 1$, a single supplier for each part. If a single supplier minimizes both costs, why do firms have multiple suppliers and seek options beyond? The Combined GPI-Resistance Analysis introduced later in this chapter shows that a firm's improved bargaining position can offset the costs of multiple suppliers.

Inclusive connection occurs when Q_i, the minimum number of relations in which i must exchange, is larger than one. In experiments, $Q_i > 1$ is an initial condition produced by a "threshold effect." Subjects are required to complete exchanges with Q others. When fewer exchanges are completed, the subject in the inclusively connected position is not paid for resources gained in any exchange. Only the subject in the inclusively connected position is in jeopardy; all of that subject's partners (who are not themselves inclusively connected) benefit upon completion of their exchanges.

The effects of inclusive connection have not been as fully investigated as have the effects of exclusion and null. All four of the theories mentioned in the introduction apply to exclusively and null connected networks, but only GPI-Resistance applies to inclusive connection. Patton and Willer (1990) studied two inclusively connected networks and found for both that the bargaining position of the actor in the inclusively connected position was weakened. No network having inclusive, exclusive, and null connection at different positions has been previously studied.

Outside the laboratory, a variety of circumstances determines the size of Q. Threshold effects occurred in a case reported by Hansen (1981). Lars gained the help of three friends from his exchange network to move an object. Because it was too weighty for him and two others to transport, for Lars $Q = 3$. Alternatively, values of $Q > 1$ flow from a need to combine diverse resources. When families need food, clothing, and shelter and each is supplied separately, $Q = 3$ and the family is inclusively connected. A firm is inclusively connected when resources from *two or more* suppliers are needed for production and subsequent sale of the product. To predict the consequences of inclusion on the firm, a theory must predict from the size of Q to the size of effects produced.

Furthermore, the questions raised in the introduction about the strategic situation of the firm concerned whether the effect of Q_i changed when N and M took on values larger than Q. The manufacturing firm which is inclusively connected becomes *inclusive-exclusively* connected by finding suppliers, which are exclusive alternatives for each kind of part. Similarly, the inclusively connected firm becomes *inclusive-null* connected by finding and exchanging with two or more suppliers for each kind of part. Now we have reached the outer limits of knowledge about exchange networks. Of the four theories, only GPI-Resistance has been applied to either inclusive-exclusive or inclusive-null, and then only the inclusive-exclusive was studied. For one network five peripherals were inclusive-exclusively connected to a central, and it was found that exchange ratios were like those produced by exclusive connection alone (Szmatka and

Table 8.1
Branch Networks Investigated by Type

EXCLUSION: 311; 321; 531; 751.
INCLUSION: 222; 333; 444; 555; 777.
NULL: 331; 551; 771.
INCLUSION-EXCLUSION: 322; 533; 755.
INCLUSION-NULL: 332; 553; 775.

Willer 1995). Below we apply Resistance Theory while varying N, M, and Q to predict exchange ratios for all connection types in both simple and complex networks.

In light of the variety introduced by the five types of connection, it is easy to overlook the fact that it is possible for more than one type of connection to occur at a position. For example, a firm with single suppliers for each of six parts, but exclusive alternatives for ten others, is inclusively connected in six relations and inclusively-exclusively connected in the rest. In general, a connection is "compound" when more than one connection type occurs at a position, and, given the five types of connection, there are 25 possible compounds. Later in the chapter, the GPI-Resistance analysis is extended to predict exchange ratios in all kinds of compound connection.

Type of Connection and Organization of Experiments

For study of the effect of degree on connection, the typology helps in the selection of networks for investigation.[7] Table 8.1 specifies the 18 branch networks investigated using NMQ triples, which indicate number of relations and type of connection by place notation. For example, "321" means $N = 3$, $M = 2$, and $Q = 1$, indicating exclusive connection and 755 means $N = 7$, $M = 5$, and $Q = 5$, indicating inclusive-exclusive connection. Figure 8.7, presented later in the chapter, gives the complex networks investigated.

The branch networks maximize scope within size limits and facilitate crucial comparisons. There are six possible 3-Branches, and all are studied. For larger branches, the number of possible cases increases rapidly as N increases. There are 15 possible 5-Branches and 28 possible 7-Branches, numbers that preclude exhaustive study. For both we select one of each connection type. For the 5-Branch we study: (1) the only inclusion case (555), (2) one of four exclusion cases (531), (3) the one of six inclusion-exclusion cases most like the selected exclusion type (533), (4) the only null case (551), and (5) the one of three inclusion-null types most like the inclusion-exclusion type (553). Similar reasons govern selection of five 7-Branches for study.

Practical concerns also enter into the selection process. For structures containing only human subjects, a 7-Branch network is currently very near the maximum tractable size.[8] Nevertheless, Resistance Theory asserts that this maximum does not limit generality. As seen in the following sections, resistance predicts that number of relations affects exchange ratios only for inclusive branches. Furthermore, that effect increases at a decreasing rate. As a result, more than one-half of the maximum possible effect of size is found in Br777, the largest inclusive branch studied.

Figure 8.1 introduces conventions used to designate the five types of connection in the figures of this chapter. $N_A = 3$ is given directly by A's connection to B, C, and D. The number of concentric circles (dashed plus solid) equals M_A whereas the number of solid concentric circles indicates Q_A. In the top left diagram, A is connected to B, C, and D such that $N_A = 3$; and the A node has three concentric solid circles, $M_A = Q_A = 3$. Thus A is inclusively connected. In the bottom right diagram again $N_A = 3$, but there are two solid circles and one dashed, $M_A = 3$, $Q_A = 2$ and the connection is inclusion-null.

RESISTANCE THEORY, TYPES OF CONNECTION, AND EXCHANGE RATIOS

Resistance Theory predicts exchange ratios under a variety of structural conditions. It was first applied to null and exclusively connected networks (Willer 1981) and subsequently to inclusive connection (Patton and Willer 1990). Skvoretz and Willer (1993) and Lovaglia et al. (1995a) extended its application to "weak power" networks in which no exclusion is costless. Resistance Theory has also been applied to "strong" and "weak" coercive structures (Willer 1987) and for cross-national replications (Willer and Szmatka 1993).[9] We first review the application of resistance to the dyad and then present and test its predictions for varying-sized null, inclusive, and exclusive branches, and finally for the inclusion-exclusion and inclusion-null types.

In Resistance Theory, "P_i" is i's payoff, "$P_i$max" is i's best payoff and "$P_i$con" is the payoff at confrontation (disagreement)[10] Pmax and Pcon define the range of possible settlements for the two actors. According to Resistance Theory, the negotiation process is governed by two interests: $P_i$max $- P_i$, the actor i's interest in gaining its best payoff, and $P_i - P_i$con, i's interest in avoiding confrontation. i's resistance is the ratio of the two interests,

$$R_i = \frac{P_i \max - P_i}{P_i - P_i \text{ con}} \tag{8.1}$$

Principle two of the theory asserts that agreements occur at equiresistance (Willer 1981). Setting $R_i = R_j$,

Figure 8.1
The Types of Network Connection

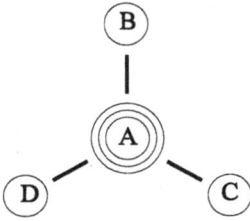

Inclusion (Br333)

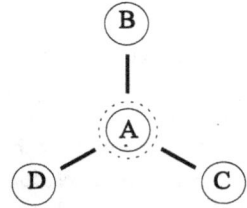

Exclusion (Br321)

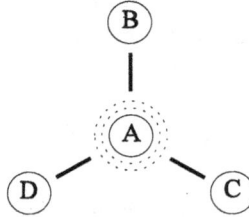

Null (Br331)

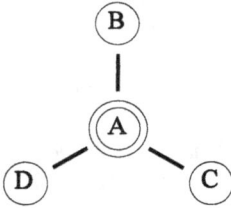

Inclusion-Exclusion (Br322)

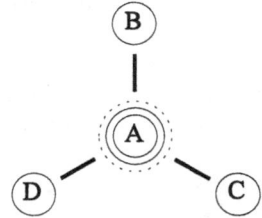

Inclusion-Null (Br332)

$$\frac{P_i \max - P_i}{P_i - P_i \text{ con}} = \frac{P_j \max - P_j}{P_j - P_j \text{ con}} \tag{8.2}$$

Note that i's resistance is smallest for P_i settlements that approach P_i max and largest for P_i settlements that approach $P_i$con and similarly for j. Since P_i and P_j vary inversely in exchange relations, i's resistance will be larger than j's for any ratio favoring j over i. Exactly the same is true of j. This suggests that the equiresistance agreements predicted for the dyad follow from a process of compromise.

More concretely, in all experiments we simulate exchange by the division of a pool of 24 resources.[11] The most unequal division possible is 23–1, and no resources are gained when actors do not agree: Pmax $= 23$ and Pcon $= 0$ for all actors and, for an A–B dyad,

$$R_A = \frac{23 - P_A}{P_A - 0} = \frac{23 - P_B}{P_B - 0} = R_B \qquad (8.3)$$

Thus $P_A = 12$ and $P_B = 12$ at equiresistance.[12] This division is the equipower baseline to which ratios in structures are compared.

The Effect of Degree in Null Connection

Figure 8.2 gives the three null connected networks that vary in degree from three through five to seven branches. According to Markovsky et al.'s Graph-theoretic Power Index, when null connected in a branch, each relation forms an independent dyadic domain (1988).[13] The assertion of independence has two important consequences, and the experiments to follow are the first to test both. First, the exchange ratio in the null branch is predicted to be completely independent from the number of connected relations. Second, the exchange ratio in every relation is predicted to be exactly the same as the exchange ratio predicted for the dyad. As shown above, for the 24-point resource pool that ratio is an equal 12–12 split. In Table 8.2 the resistance expression is given for the null connected branch. This expression is obtained by setting the initial value of Pcon $= 0$ in Equation (8.2). In fact, Pcon equals zero in the profit pool relation and in many exchange relations. We now turn to the test of this prediction.

The experiments of this chapter employ the ExNet system of networked PCs and use the same methods previously utilized (Skvoretz and Willer 1991, 1993). Briefly, undergraduate subjects were paid by points earned and interacted through networked PCs which displayed and updated all offers and completed exchanges. For each of the three null branches, there were five runs for a total of 15 experiments, each with a new group of subjects. To produce null connection, subjects in the central position were informed that they would earn payoffs for each exchange completed. The effects of connection are estimated from observed points earned in exchanges by the central position. Point earnings are analyzed as a variant of a repeated measures, correlated observations problem as employed by Skvoretz and Willer (1993).

The predicted 12–12 division is expressed in Table 8.3 as earnings of 12 for the central position. Here and elsewhere we follow the convention in network exchange research of giving earnings for each relation in which the position exchanges (Cook et al. 1983; Skvoretz and Willer 1993). Also listed are observed estimates for earnings of the central A position and the standard errors

Figure 8.2
Three Null Networks

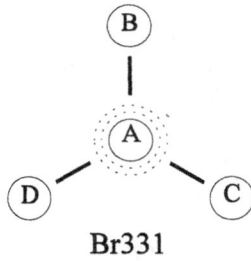

Br331

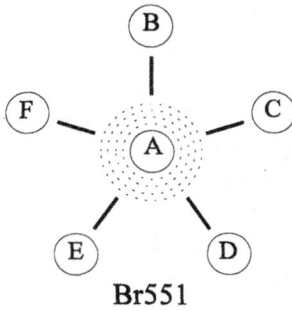

Br551

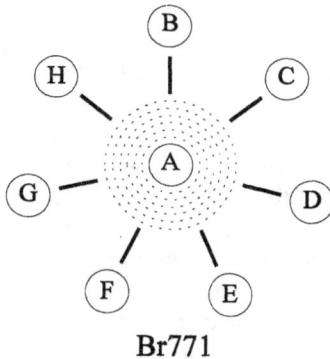

Br771

for the estimates. In all three branch networks, the A's earnings are slightly more than predicted, a difference that is significant in two of three branches. It is not clear to us why the adjusted means are inflated even slightly beyond 12. Neither Resistance Theory nor any of the three competing theories mentioned in the introduction suggest that null connected branches have any structural basis for

Table 8.2
Resistance Expressions for Three Types of Branches Where *i* Is Central and *j* Is Peripheral: For Relations Where Initially Pcon = 0

Type of Connection	Resistance Expression
NULL	$R_i = \dfrac{P_i \max - P_i}{P_i} = \dfrac{P_j \max - P_j}{P_i} = R_j$
INCLUSION	$R_i^i = \dfrac{P_i \max - P_i}{QP_i} = \dfrac{P_j \max - P_j}{P_j} = R_j$
EXCLUSION	$R_{ij}^e = \dfrac{P_i \max - P_i^t}{P_i^t - E_i^{t-1}} = \dfrac{E_j^{t-1} - P_j^t}{P_j^t} = R_{ji}^e$

power. Like resistance, all predict 12–12 divisions (Skvoretz and Willer 1993).[14] In spite of the inflation, experimental results do *not* indicate that increasing the degree of null connection produces increasing power differences favorable to the central position. If null connection had that effect, then the mean for the largest branch should be the highest and the mean for the smallest branch the smallest. *But exactly the opposite is the case.* The deviation is smallest for the 7-Branch, intermediate for the 5-Branch and largest for the 3-Branch. That comparison supports the conclusion for null connection that degree has no effect on power and exchange ratios.

The Effect of Degree in Inclusive Connection

The resistance expression for inclusion in Table 8.2 contains Q from the typology for connection, indicating that rates predicted for inclusion will be degree dependent. Since for inclusion $N = M = Q$, the expression in the table predicts that, as the size of the inclusively connected branch increases, the relative power of the central position will decline and exchange ratios will increasingly favor

Figure 8.3
Five Inclusive Networks

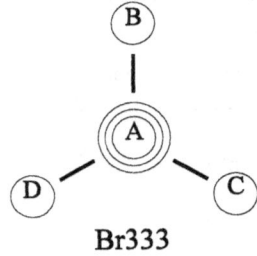

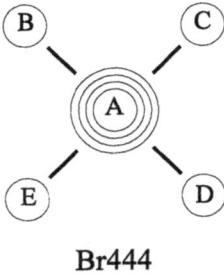

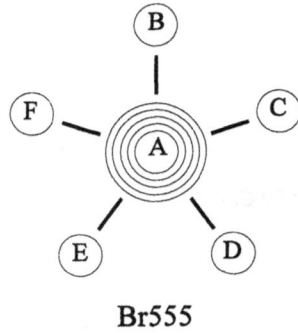

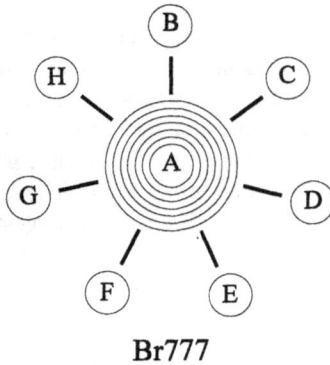

Br222

Br333

Br444

Br555

Br777

peripherals. The five inclusively connected branches of Figure 8.3 offer the first thorough test for the impact of the number of connections on power and exchange ratios.

We now explain how the resistance expression for inclusion is determined by identifying the Pmax and Pcon values which apply to the central position and to each of the peripheral positions. Both the central position and the peripheral positions are assumed to have the same Pmax value, receiving 23 points of the 24-point pool. For peripheral positions, the value of Pcon is the standard default value of 0; that is, if a peripheral fails to exchange with the central actor, then she or he earns nothing on that round. However, because the center's exchange relations are inclusively connected, the value of Pcon for that actor differs from the standard default value. The basic idea is that i's failure to exchange with a peripheral jeopardizes i's earnings from any exchange already arranged with other peripherals. Consequently, i's Pcon value should reflect this loss of earnings.

To illustrate the situation, consider the Br222 structure of Figure 8.3. If A fails to exchange with B, having already reached a tentative agreement with C of P_{Ac} points, then A not only earns nothing for the round but forgoes the payoff from the completed deal with C. Therefore, failure to exchange with B "costs" A, P_{Ac} points and we identify P_{Ab}con as equal to $-P_{Ac}$. Similarly, P_{Ac}con is identified as equal to $-P_{Ab}$. On grounds of symmetry, we assume earnings to be the same in both relations: $P_{Ab} = P_{Ac} = P_A$ and therefore:

$$R^i_{AB} = \frac{P_{AB}\text{max} - P_A}{P_A - P_{AB}\text{con}} = \frac{23 - P_A}{P_A - (-P_A)} = \frac{23 - P_A}{2P_A} \tag{8.4}$$

Here the function R is superscripted with "i" to indicate that this particular formula applies to inclusively connected positions. The resistance of the peripherals is given by the right side of Equation (8.3) above. Equating the two yields the following predictions for Br222: $P_A = 10.03$, $P_B = P_C = 13.97$.

Similar arguments apply to all other inclusively connected branches. We identify the central actor i's P_{ij}con vis-à-vis any peripheral actor j as the potential loss of earnings from each of the other $Q - 1$ negotiations. Therefore, as displayed in Table 8.2 under inclusion, the resistance equation has the factor QP_i in the denominator. Table 8.3 gives the predicted payoffs for the central A in the five branches. Note that the incremental effect of inclusive connection decreases as Q increases. For example, A is predicted to gain almost two points less in Br222 than in the dyad, but only 1.01 less in Br333 than Br222. Yet the payoff differential for the two steps between Br555 and Br777 is only .80. Thus inclusive connection will produce extreme ratios only when Q is very large.

We now turn to the experiments and results. For each of the five inclusive branches studied, there were five sessions for a total of 25 experiments, each with a new group of subjects. To produce inclusive connection, subjects in the central position were informed that they could earn payoffs if and only if exchanges were completed with all peripherals. Again, the effects of connection are estimated from observed points earned in exchanges by the central position. Table 8.3 also gives those estimates and standard errors. As predicted by Resistance Theory, the central position is low in power in all inclusive branches and its power declines as the number of relations (degree) increases. Resistance

Figure 8.4
Four Exclusive Networks

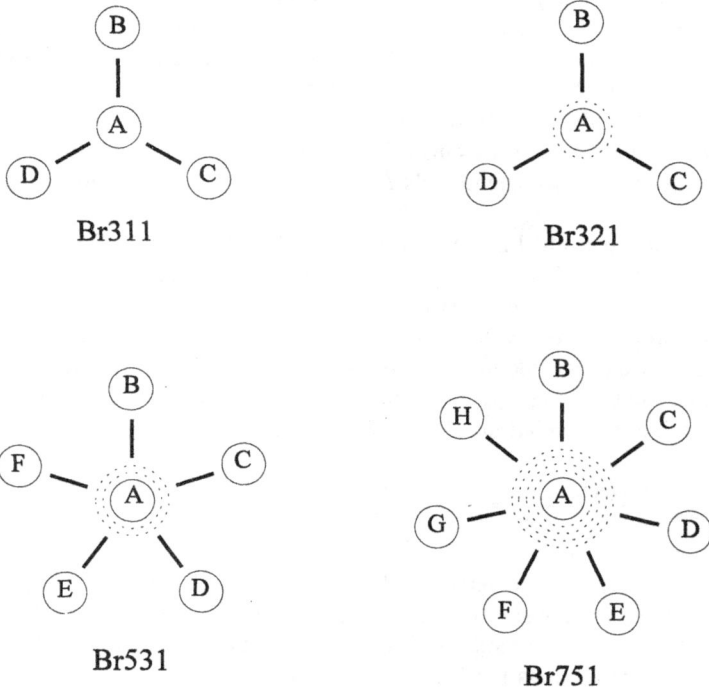

Br311

Br321

Br531

Br751

Theory successfully predicts point earnings in the three smaller branches but significantly underestimates the effect of inclusion in larger branches. In fact, for all but Br222, resistance predicts a weaker effect for inclusion than actually observed, but the deviation is small enough that it becomes significant only for the two largest branches. While the effect of inclusion increases with degree at a decreasing rate, experimental estimates indicate that the effect does not decrease as rapidly as predicted.[15]

The Effect of Degree in Exclusive Connection

Figure 8.4 displays the four exclusively connected branches studied. In the application of Resistance Theory to exclusively connected branches, Pmax and Pcon change from initial (default) specifications for both the central and the peripheral actors. (Cf. Willer 1981, pp. 125–6; Skvoretz and Burkett 1994.) For A in the central position, the value of P_{Ax}con vis-à-vis any particular peripheral position X is greater than 0 because, if A fails to exchange with X, points can be earned through agreement with one of the other peripherals. That is, upon failing to exchange with X, rather than earning nothing, A exchanges with another. From the peripheral X's point of view, failing to exchange and therefore earning nothing is sure to occur unless X matches or tops offers of other peripherals. More precisely, once the center has received offers from M peripherals, the next peripheral will fail to exchange unless it at least equals A's worst offer. In effect, prior offers set new upper limits on the best which X can hope for in an exchange with the central actor. Thus, for peripherals, P_{Xa} max declines from the initial (default) value of 23 and is a function of the outstanding offers of other peripherals to the central position.

As an example of the effect of these changes, consider the Br311 network in which the center, (1) negotiates tentative deals in turn with each of the peripherals and (2) the first deal, A with B, is at the 12–12 equipower division. Then the above argument implies that the A with C negotiation is governed by the following resistance equation:

$$R_{AC}^e = \frac{23 - P_A}{P_A - 12} = \frac{12 - P_C}{P_C - 0} = R_{CA}^e \tag{8.5}$$

which yields the solution $P_A = 17.74$ and $P_C = 6.26$. The function R is superscripted with "e" to indicate that this particular resistance formula applies to exclusively connected relations. Then the above argument says that the A with D negotiations are governed by the equation:

$$R_{AD}^e = \frac{23 - P_A}{P_A - 17.74} = \frac{6.26 - P_D}{P_D - 0} = R_{DA}^e$$

which yields the solution $P_A = 20.59$ and $P_D = 3.41$. Now B's position in the A–B negotiations has eroded even further. In general, if we let E_A^{t-1} and E_X^{t-1} be A's earnings and X's earnings at the $t - 1$th step of this imaginary process, the following equation describes the resistance formulas that apply to any exclusively connected branch:

$$R_{AX}^e = \frac{P_{AX}\text{max} - P_A^t}{P_A^t - E_A^{t-1}} = \frac{E_X^{t-1} - P_X^t}{P_X^t - 0} = R_{XA}^e \tag{8.6}$$

Since a similar scenario applies to all exclusively connected branches, even if $M_A > 1$, Table 8.2 gives Equation (8.6) for all exclusively connected branches simplified for relations where initially $P\text{con} = 0$. Note that when $M_A > 1$, a peripheral must match or top the outstanding offer that is Mth worst, and so it is this offer that determines his or her $P_{Xa}\text{max}$.

Since the end point of this imagined process is the same in all exclusively connected branches, exchange ratios are not affected by degree. By the conclusion of the process, resistance predicts that the center earns the 23-point maximum in each exchange with a peripheral regardless of the number of connected relations. Practically speaking, however, in experiments, this theoretically imag-

Table 8.3
Points Earned by the Central Position in Branches by Connection Type:
Resistance Predictions Versus Estimates from Experiments

Connection type	Network	Predicted	Estimated (SE)	p
Null	Br331	12.0	12.57 (.169)	<.01
"	Br551	12.0	12.53 (.455)	NS
"	Br771	12.0	12.38 (.153)	<.05
Inclusion	Br222	10.03	10.40 (.580)	NS
"	Br333	8.92	7.96 (.608)	NS
"	Br444	8.19	7.53 (.503)	NS
"	Br555	7.62	5.70 (.343)	<.01
"	Br777	6.82	5.09 (.231)	<.01
Exclusion	Br311	23.0	21.63 (.491)	<.01
"	Br321	23.0	17.48 (.553)	<.01
"	Br531	23.0	21.14 (.182)	<.01
"	Br751	23.0	19.49 (.254)	<.01

ined process of ever decreasing Pmax values for peripheral actors is likely to cut across rounds. If so, divisions observed in early rounds will occur early in the process and before the extreme 23–1 division is reached. Thus mean divisions will undoubtedly be lower than the extreme. Although the theoretical analysis is consistent with a power process, predicting rates of change are beyond the scope of this chapter. Thus, as given in Table 8.3, we simply offer the end point of the process, 23, as our prediction for all exclusively connected branches, recognizing that values observed across the experiment are likely to be lower.

As displayed in Table 8.3, estimated earnings in exclusive branches indicate that the central position exercises power in all exclusive branches. As expected, the estimated effect of exclusion is significantly less than the 23–1 extreme.[16] Although Br321 has the lowest estimated earnings of the four branches at P_A = 17.48, it is higher than the P_A = 15.81 earnings found by Skvoretz and Willer (1991) for the same type. Observed divisions lower than the 23–1 extreme could be due to an extended period of power development. To check we dropped the outlying Br321 and examined the last period means of the remaining three structures. For the test, the last four rounds were collapsed to 15 data points. Mean last-period earning was P_A = 22.45, which is slightly, but significantly, smaller than 23 (t = 2.41, df = 14, p < .05). These results indicate that power differences in exclusively connected branches do not increase with degree. In

Figure 8.5
Three Inclusive-Exclusive Networks

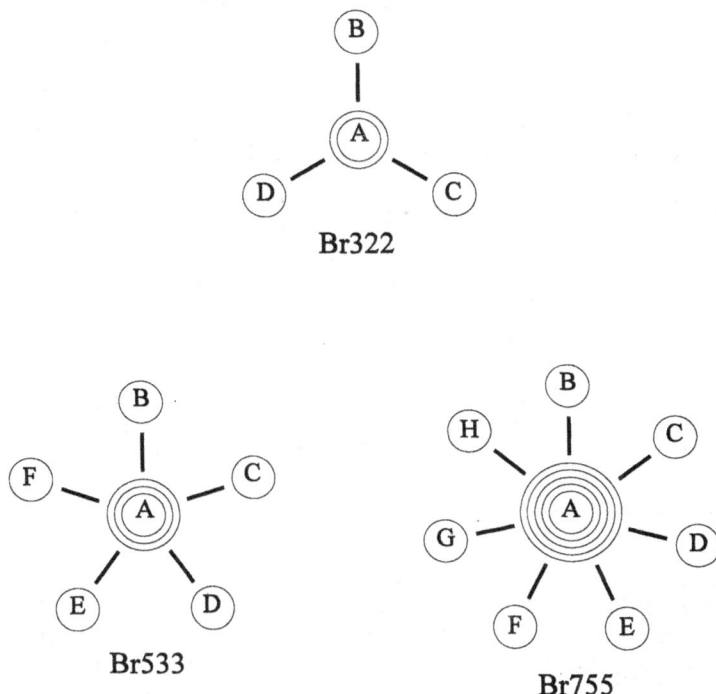

Br322

Br533

Br755

fact, one of the two smallest branches, Br311 had the highest rate in contrast to the largest branch, Br751 which had the second lowest rate.[17]

The Effect of Adding Inclusion to Exclusion and to Null

We now turn to the inclusion-exclusion and inclusion-null types. The analysis begins with inclusive-exclusive connection and Figure 8.5 gives the three branches investigated. For example, in Br533, A must complete three exchanges to benefit from any one, but has five alternatives within which to select the necessary three. In general, i is inclusive-exclusively connected when $N_i > M_i \geq Q_i > 1$. Since $N_i > Q_i$, inclusion cannot affect the first negotiation. Inclusion has no effect because failure in the first negotiation does not jeopardize earnings in subsequently negotiated relations. Earnings are not jeopardized because, were A to fail, there is at least one exclusive alternative in which to succeed.

With the completion of the first negotiation, $N_i - 1 > Q_i - 1$ and the second negotiation is not affected by inclusive connection for the same reason as the first—and similarly until $Q_i - 1$ are completed. For the Q_ith exchange and beyond, i is exclusively connected, but not inclusively connected. That is to

Table 8.4
Points Earned by the Central Position Estimates from Experiments: Inclusive-exclusive versus Exclusive Branches: Inclusive-null versus Null Branches

Network		Estimated (SE)		p
Inclusive-exclusive	Exclusive	Inclusive-exclusive	Exclusive	
Br322	Br321	19.62 (.359)	17.48 (.553)	<.01
Br533	Br531	19.71 (.296)	21.14 (.182)	<.01
Br755	Br751	16.45 (.247)	19.49 (.254)	<.01
Inclusive-null	Null	Inclusive-null	Null	
Br332	Br331	12.18 (.494)	12.57 (.169)	NS
Br553	Br551	12.96 (.222)	12.53 (.455)	NS
Br775	Br771	13.10 (.093)	12.38 (.153)	<.01

say, i has exclusive alternatives, and the resistance expressions employed in exclusive connection above apply. Thus, the settlement favors i, just as it does in a purely exclusively connected branch. More generally, the effect of exclusive connection eliminates the effect of inclusive connection, and therefore ratios in comparable branches should be identical.

Table 8.4 displays estimated earnings of the central A in each of three inclusive-exclusive branches and compares each to the exclusive branch to which it is most similar. There is unqualified support for the prediction that the effect of inclusion is eliminated by exclusion. The central A's estimated earnings indicate substantial power exercise in all inclusive-exclusive branches, exactly the *opposite* of that observed for the inclusively connected branches reported in Table 8.3. Mean exchange ratios are similar in inclusive-exclusive and exclusive branches, but they are not identical. That is to say, comparing similar-sized networks, exchange ratios are in the same neighborhood, and looking across the six networks, exchange ratios are not consistently higher for either type. For Br322, the central's earnings are higher than in the exclusively connected Br321 while, in the other two cases, the inclusive-exclusive earnings are lower than earnings in the corresponding exclusive branch.

Figure 8.6 gives the three inclusive-null branches studied here. For example, in Br553, A must complete at least three exchanges but has up to five exchanges with five different partners in which to complete the needed three. In general, i is inclusive-null connected when $N_i = M_i > Q_i > 1$. As in the exclusive branch, $N_i > Q_i$, and inclusion cannot affect the first negotiation. Inclusion has no effect

Figure 8.6
Three Inclusive-Null Networks

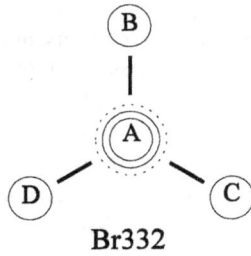

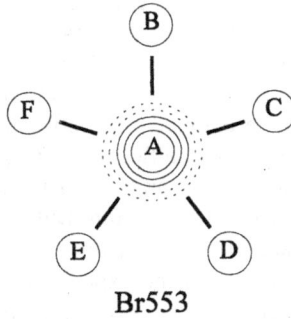

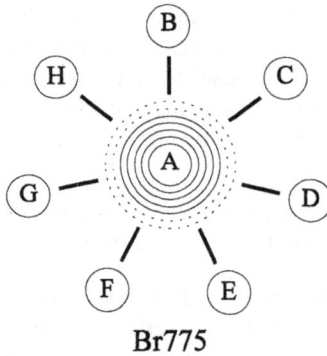

Br332

Br553

Br775

because failure in the first negotiation does not jeopardize earnings in subsequently negotiated relations. With the completion of the first negotiation, $N_i - 1 > Q_i - 1$ and the second negotiation is unaffected by inclusive connection for the same reason as the first. The next is also unaffected, and similarly until Q_i exchanges are completed and the remaining relations are only null connected.

Therefore, inclusion has no effect in inclusive-null connected relations for reasons parallel to those given for inclusive-exclusive connection.[18]

The conclusion that inclusion has no effect suggests that exchange ratios predicted for inclusive-null connected relations may be the same as predicted for null. Rates will be the same as predicted for null only if inclusive-null connected relations can be treated, like null connected ones as in independent domains. Because $N_i = M_i$ and $N_i > Q_i$ the first exchange is in an independent dyadic domain. Then, since $N_i - 1 = M_i - 1$ and $N_i - 1 > Q_i - 1$ for the second exchange, the exchange is again independent and the dyadic rate is predicted—and similarly until $Q_i = 0$. In other words, as each exchange is completed, i is only null connected in the next. Therefore, all exchanges are independent and, for inclusive-null branches, the same exchange ratios as in null branches are predicted.

Given in Table 8.4 are results for inclusive-null branches and comparisons of each to a similar null branch. The inference that null connection eliminates the effect of inclusion is supported. All adjusted means of inclusive-null branches are significantly higher than adjusted means for the inclusive branches given in Table 8.2. For two of the three comparisons between similar inclusive-null and null branches, the difference is not significant, giving partial support to the above analysis. That the central position's earnings in Br775 are significantly higher than in Br771 does not fit the point prediction. But the deviation is in the *wrong direction* to indicate any trace effect of inclusion.

This analysis and the results from the experiments extend resistance beyond the limits of Table 8.2. Since inclusive-exclusive connections behave like exclusive connections, the resistance expression for exclusion given in Table 8.2 applies *without modification* to inclusive-exclusion connections. Similarly, since inclusive-null connections behave like null connections, the resistance expression for null connection given in Table 8.2 applies *without modification* to inclusive-null connection. We now have resistance expressions that predict exchange ratios for all types of connection of any degree. With that foundation, we turn to complex networks where two or more types of connection are present.

THE COMBINED GPI–I–RESISTANCE ANALYSIS AND ITS APPLICATION TO COMPLEX NETWORKS

The Combined GPI–I–Resistance Analysis predicts exchange ratios for networks of any shape and any mixture of connections. In this section we introduce the combined analysis and test it in complex networks with more than one type of connection. As presented by Markovsky et al. (1988), the Graph-theoretic Power Index is a simple and effective guide to applying resistance expressions in exclusive and null connected networks. Together with its three Axioms, GPI also indicates in which relations exchanges will and will not occur.[19] We first extend the application of GPI to networks with any mixture of connections. As a part of this extension we introduce a second index, "I," and show how the two indexes govern the application of resistance to predict exchange ratios. In the second part of the section, the general analysis is tested on two complex networks.

GPI, I, and Resistance

We now give GPI and extend it beyond exclusive and null connection to networks containing all five types.[20] Briefly, the GPI value of a position i is the sum of nonintersecting paths m from i within its domain, d, divided by M.[21] In summing, advantageous odd-numbered paths are added and disadvantageous even-numbered paths are subtracted. Any two paths from i are nonintersecting when only i is common. Two positions are in the same domain if they are adjacent or if $N > M$ for all positions between them. Then,

$$GPI_{id} = [1/M]\sum_{k=1}(-I)^{(k-1)}m_{idk} \tag{8.7}$$

If $GPI_i > GPI_j$, i is higher in power than j. But if $GPI_i = GPI_j$, the two are power equals.

Applications of Resistance Theory and the experimental results above show that adding inclusion to exclusion or to null does not affect power exercised. *Therefore, GPI needs no modification to accurately reflect the structural power of network positions with inclusive-exclusive and inclusive-null connections.* Because inclusive connection at any position does not distort values calculated for other positions, GPI can be applied to networks in which any number of purely inclusively connected positions are mixed with other types. However, that application will not reflect power due to inclusion.

Since GPI does not register the effect of inclusion, we introduce the index $I = 1/Q$ only for inclusively connected positions. Unlike *GPI* which is applied within domains, "I" values are assigned independently from domains.[22] "I" values are given by locating all positions in a network for which $N = M = Q > 1$ and assigning $I = 1/Q$ to each. Then, for all positions to which an "I" value is assigned, the resistance expression for inclusion applies. For example, in Figure 8.7c there is one position that is inclusively connected; it is assigned $I = 1/3$. Here as elsewhere, the "I" value assigned reflects the quantitative effect of inclusive connection on the position's resistance. In the section that follows, we predict exchange ratios for the Figure 8.7c network.

Table 8.5 outlines the combined GPI–I–Resistance analysis. (For the remainder of the chapter numbers for resistance equations refer to Table 8.5.)[23] For exclusively *and* inclusive-exclusively connected positions, if $GPI_i = GPI_j$ then Equation (8.1) applies and if $GPI_i > GPI_j$ then Equation (8.2) applies. But for null *and* inclusive-null positions always $GPI_i = GPI_j$ and only Equation (8.1) applies. If an "I" value is assigned, Equation (8.3) applies. For null, exclusive, and inclusive branches only, Table 8.5 reduces to Table 8.2: When $GPI_i > GPI_j$

Table 8.5
The Combined GPI–I–Resistance Analysis: Index Values and Resistance
Expressions for Relations Where Initially *P*con = 0

Index Value	Resistance Expression	
$GPI_i = GPI_j$	$R_i = \dfrac{P_i\,\max - P_i}{P_i} = \dfrac{P_j\,\max - P_j}{P_i} = R_j$	(1)
$GPI_i > GPI_j$	$R_{ij}^{\bullet} = \dfrac{P_i\,\max - P_i^t}{P_i^t - E_i^{t-1}} = \dfrac{E_j^{t-1} - P_j^t}{P_j^t} = R_{ji}^{\bullet}$	(2)
$I_i = \dfrac{1}{Q_i}$	$R_i^i = \dfrac{P_i\,\max - P_i}{QP_i} = \dfrac{P_j\,\max - P_j}{P_j} = R_j$	(3)

the central *i* is exclusively connected. When $GPI_i = GPI$, and no "I" value is assigned, the central *i* is null connected. When $I_i < 1$ the central *i* is inclusively connected. This reduction fits the applications above and offers a preliminary check of the combined analysis.

Conversely, Table 8.2 does not accurately govern the application of resistance to complex networks where $N > 1$ for more than one position—even when connections are limited to null and exclusive. For example, when adjacencies are both exclusively connected, Table 8.2 implies that the "exclusion" expression applies, which suggests that one position is higher in power than the other. But the general analysis asserts that, if $GPI_i = GPI$, Equation (8.1) applies and the two positions are power equals. We now turn to applications and tests of the general analysis.

Testing the Combined Analysis in Complex Networks with Mixed Connections

Given in Figure 8.7 are networks with mixed connections. We begin with the Figure 8.7a network called "MEI." The positions *A* and *B* are similar, but *A* is

Figure 8.7
Complex Networks with Mixed Connections

a. Complex network, exclusive-inclusive at B and exclusive at A

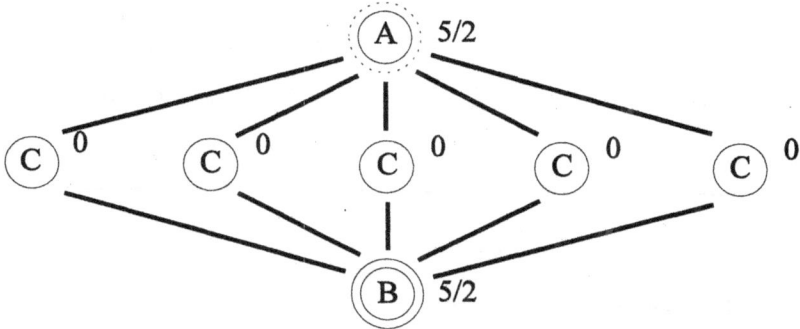

b. Complex network, exclusive at C, inclusive at D

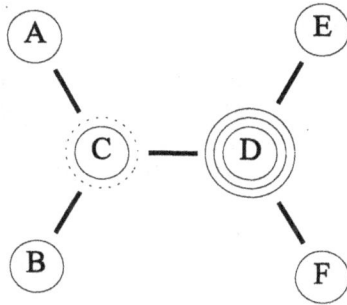

c. Domains and power scores of network B

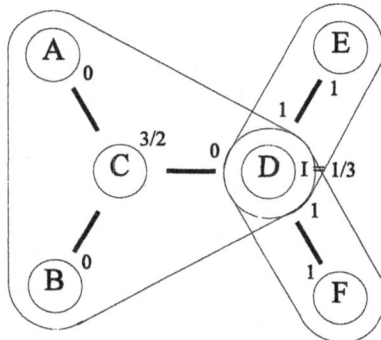

Table 8.6
Points Earned by Positions in Complex Networks: Estimates from Experiments

Network	Relations	Predicted Earnings	Estimated (SE) by Position	p
MEI	A - C vs. B - C	A = B	A = 17.89 (.227) B = 18.20 (.225)	NS
DBr	C - D vs. C - A(B)	$C_D > C_{AB}$	C_D = 20.69 (.475) C_{AB} = 19.39 (.355)	<.05
DBr	D - C vs. D - E(F)	$D_{EF} > D_C$	D_C = 3.31 (.475) D_{EF} = 8.79 (.307)	<.01

exclusively connected with $N = 5 > M = 2 > Q = 1$, whereas B is inclusive-exclusively connected with $N = 5 > M = Q = 2$. All Cs are exclusively connected with $N = 2 > M = Q = 1$. GPI values given in the figure indicate that A and B are high in power and the Cs are low. GPI indicates that the exclusively connected C positions are as low in power as the peripheral positions of exclusively and inclusive-exclusively connected branches. Since no position is purely inclusively connected, no position has an "I" value. Therefore, resistance Equation 8.2 applies to A–C and B–C relations and predicts that earnings of A and B should be the same. Adjusted means for A and B given in Table 8.6 are not significantly different, which supports the application of the combined analysis.

Figures 8.7b and 8.7c give information about the "DBr" network in two ways. Figure 8.7b uses the same notation as earlier figures and indicates that $N_C = 3 > M_C = 2 > Q_C = 1$, while $N_D = M_D = Q_D = 3$. C is exclusively connected; D's connection is inclusive; and all other positions are singularly connected. The 8.7c figure indicates domains used in the calculation of GPI and gives GPI and "I" values. DBr has three domains. $GPI = 3/2$ for C, which excludes one of A, B, and D for which $GPI = 0$. $GPI = 1$ for E and F because they are each in a dyadic domain with D; in those domains $GPI_D = 1$. Only the D position is inclusively connected and $I_D = 1/3$. These index values indicate that resistance Equation (8.2) applies to the A–C and B–C relations and Equation (8.3) applies to D–E and D–F relations. The C–D relation introduces something new to the analysis. C is high and D is low in power because C is exclusively connected and D is inclusively connected.

The application of Resistance Theory to this relation is a straightforward extension of the combined analysis. As in the expression to the right of Equation (8.2), $P_D$max shrinks because C is exclusively connected *and*, as in the expression to the left of Equation (8.3), $QP_D = 3P_D$ occurs in the denominator. That is, D is lower in power relative to C than either A or B, which are not inclusively connected. As shown in Table 8.6, the resistance prediction is supported. C's earnings in $C–D$ exchanges are significantly higher than C's earnings when exchanging with A or B. It also follows that D is lower in power relative to C than relative to E or F. As shown in Table 8.6, D's adjusted mean earnings reflect that power difference.[24]

Experimental results for the two complex networks offer important new tests for the Combined Analysis. The MEI network shows that exclusion eliminates the effect of inclusion in complex networks just as it did in simple branches. The similar earnings of the differently connected A and B *in the same network* provide important further support for resistance's treatment of inclusive-exclusive relations. The results for DBr indicate that applications of GPI within domains and "I" across domains are effective guides for Resistance Theory and that even subtle differences in exchange ratios are correctly anticipated by GPI–I–Resistance analysis.

THE APPLICATION OF THE COMBINED GPI–I–RESISTANCE ANALYSIS TO NETWORKS WITH COMPOUND CONNECTIONS

Two different kinds of conditions produce values of $Q > 1$: threshold effects and nonsubstitutability.[25] For the experiments, inclusively connected subjects were required to complete at least Q exchanges to be paid for any one. $Q > 1$ was produced by a threshold effect only. Because resources in all exchanges are identical, *exchange relations are substitutable*. Given substitutability, when inclusion is mixed with exclusion or null, every one of the $N–Q$ relations can serve as an alternative for the needed Q.

The connection is *compound* when at least some resources received are nonsubstitutable. Nonsubstitutable resources produce nonsubstitutable exchanges. Thus, if a connection is compound, at least some exchange relations are nonsubstitutable. To apply GPI–I–Resistance, first relations must be sorted into sets that are substitutable within and nonsubstitutable between. For example, assume that i must complete four exchanges for four different resources and has exclusive alternatives for only two. Then the connection is compound because i is inclusively connected in two relations and inclusive-exclusively connected in the rest. We now show how the Combined Analysis is applied to compound connections.[26]

Figure 8.8 provides a running example in which overall $N_A = 6$, $M_A = 5$, $Q_A = 4$, but A does not have substitutable alternatives for all Q of its relations. Let substitutability be a property identifiable *a priori*. We now extend the typology to connections that contain x nonsubstitutable sets of relations $nij \geq 1$, $nik \geq 1, \ldots nix \geq 1$. That is, the relations are substitutable within each n-sized set but not between. The figure shows A connected to four sets, each of which is designated by the letter of the position(s). Thus B_1 and B_2 form a set, as do the two Cs, the one D, and one E. The next step designates N, M, and Q values

Figure 8.8
A Compound Connection

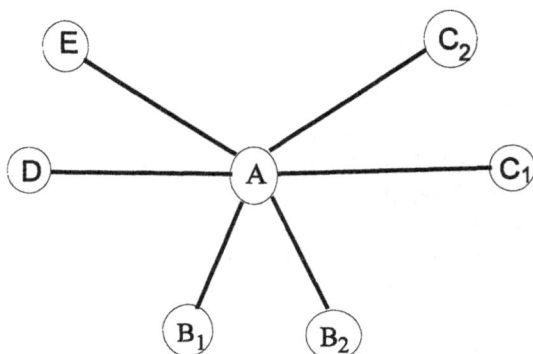

within each set with two or more relations. These values are given using terms "n, m, and q," respectively. For the Bs, $n = 2$, $m = 1$, $q = 1$. For the Cs $n = 2$, $m = 2$, $q = 1$. Therefore, within sets, Bs are exclusively connected and Cs are null connected. The D and E are inclusively connected to each other and to the other sets. At issue now is how to apply the Combined Analysis.

According to the Combined Analysis, when $N > Q$, exchange ratios are unaffected by inclusion. By extension, any set for which $n > q$ is unaffected by inclusion. Therefore, in A's relations with the Bs, since $n > m = q = 1$, the A–B exchange ratio is affected only by exclusive connection. A is high in power relative to the Bs and gains favorable exchange ratios. Since $n = m > q = 1$ in A's relations with the Cs, the A–C exchange ratios are determined only by null connection and will be equal in power. Furthermore, if the B set was inclusive-exclusively connected or the C set inclusive-null connected, exactly the same predictions would follow for each. Now let us turn to D and E.

Because the D and E are only inclusively connected, the settlement in either relation lowers A's resistance in the other. Furthermore, failure to complete exchange in either the D or E relation means that value received in the A–B relation and the two A–C relations will be lost. *Thus the A–B relations and A–C relations also affect A's resistance in the A–D and A–E relations, but not conversely.*[27] Therefore, $Q = 4$ applies to A–D and A–E exchanges, just as it does in any case where there are no alternative relations.

Now settlements vary across relations; therefore, the form of the resistance equation will be more complex than it was when Q was substituted in the denominator. For example, P_{Ab} from the A–B exclusively connected relations will be quite large and will have a corresponding large effect on the A–D exchanges. In fact, $P_D\text{con} = -(P_{Ab} + 2P_{Ac} + P_{Ae})$ and similarly for $P_E\text{con}$. Other compound connections are analyzed similarly.

The extension to nonsubstitutable relations has produced a great diversity of kinds of compounded connection. Even ignoring degree, there are 25 ways that the five types of connection can be compounded, and thus 25 kinds of compound connection to be investigated. But even greater diversity is implied. For networks with two or more nodes, each node can be compounded differently. Call networks with compound connections "multipathed." To apply GPI, paths are divided into sets of substitutable relations and then counted. GPI is applied within sets producing multiple GPI values for positions. Multiple GPI values were already seen in Markovsky et al. (1988), but now they are keyed to sets of substitutable relations. For example, in Figure 8.8, A's index value relative to the Bs is $GPI_{Ab} = 2$, but relative to each of the Cs it is $GPI_{Ac} = 1$. Although extension of the Combined Analysis to multipathed networks is straightforward, its full explication and test are beyond the scope of this chapter.

CONCLUSION

In this chapter, a formal theory of network exchange is extended to networks with any mixture of the five types of connection and then tested in both simple and complex networks. Previously, theories of network exchange were limited to networks with one or at most two types of connection. The extension here has shown that, of the five types, only inclusion is affected by degree—that is, by the number of relations connected at a position. It has also shown that the effect of inclusion is eliminated when it is mixed with either exclusion or null. Thus exchange ratios at inclusive-exclusively connected positions are like those at exclusively connected positions, and ratios at inclusive-null connected positions are like those at null connected positions. These results allow us to answer questions posed in the introduction.

The investigation began by asking whether a firm is disadvantaged because it is buying many different kinds of parts, all of which are needed to produce a saleable product. We also asked whether the existence of alternative suppliers affects the bargaining position of the firm and whether, to have an effect, the alternatives have to be exclusive. At issue are: (1) whether a position is weakened by inclusive connection and (2) the effects of adding inclusion to exclusion and null. Application of the GPI–I–Resistance analysis shows that the firm *is* disadvantaged by inclusive connection and that exchange ratio predictions estimate the amount of that effect. Application of the GPI–I–Resistance analysis also shows that the existence of alternative suppliers favors the firm *even if the alternatives are not exclusive*. The firm is no longer disadvantaged by inclusion because *both* exclusion and null eliminate the effect of inclusion.

The combined analysis also sheds light on why firms frequently prefer multiple suppliers for each component in spite of higher opportunity and transaction costs. At issue is the effect of inclusion across the set of all the firm's relations. Moving to single suppliers for each component minimizes both costs, but shrinks N and M to the size of Q. As a result, the firm that was inclusive-exclusive and inclusive-null connected becomes only inclusively connected and becomes disadvantaged in all its exchanges. These applications are supported by the experiments where the GPI–I–Resistance analysis was tested in both simple and complex networks.

Experiments show that the effect of inclusion is substantial but brittle. In fact, the effect of inclusion increased somewhat more with Q than was anticipated by Resistance Theory. This more powerful effect might be due to the experimental setting. Since each negotiation period was maximally five minutes long, as the number of connected relations increased, the time available for negotiation in each relation decreased. Only further research can test whether time pressures amplified inclusion's effect, however.[28] On the other hand, the brittleness of inclusion was amply demonstrated. For example, in the inclusively connected Br555 structure, the central position received, on the average, less than 25 percent of the divided resources, but when exclusion was added as in Br755 and Br533 structures, the inclusive-exclusively connected positions gained (respectively) almost 70 percent and more than 80 percent of the resource divisions. Adding null connection also eliminates inclusion's effect. In Br333, the inclusively connected position averaged slightly less than one third of resources, but in Br553, the inclusive-null connected position averaged slightly more than one-half of all resources divided.

According to Toulmin (1953) and Lakatos (1970, 1978) the confidence with which we hold theories increases with their scope. By that rule, extending the Graph-theoretic Power Index and Resistance Theory to networks with any configuration and any mixture of connections should add substantially to our confidence in future applications. That rule also suggests that the Combined Analysis (GPI–I–Resistance) should be held with more confidence than other network exchange theories as long as their scope is more limited.

This research extends applications of the Graph-theoretic Power Index and Resistance Theory to important new classes of networks. Now GPI–I–Resistance can be applied to predict power and exchange ratios in networks with any configuration and any mixture of connections. While further research focusing on compound connection is suggested, this study has substantially extended the scope of exchange theory to new networks of exceptional diversity and richness. By removing long-standing limitations, application of network exchange theory in the field is substantially furthered.

NOTES

1. When observed rates of exclusion were used for calculating exchange ratios, however, expected value fit observations best. The rapid development of these theories and their subsequent testing was due, at least in part, to theory competition (Berger and Zelditch 1993; Wagner and Berger 1985).

2. The five types of connection are formally introduced in the section immediately below.

3. The types of connection in the example industrial network are given in the fol-

lowing section. The example auto assembly firm is a composite drawn from Womack et al. (1990) and Johanson and Mattsson (1988). Studies of firms making other products in Engwall (1984) indicate that conditions of industrial networks are not unique to a single-product area like auto manufacturing.

4. When first introduced, applying GPI at the structural level together with simple assumptions about strategy at the actor level differentiated high and low from equal power positions (Markovsky et al. 1988). Subsequent extension of GPI to predict ratios in weak power networks uses Resistance Theory, a somewhat more complex and considerably more powerful predictor of actor strategy (Skvoretz and Willer 1993; Lovaglia et al. 1995a).

5. The five types specify *a priori* conditions that are related to, but not identical with, the *a posteriori* effects of negative and positive connection found in the power-dependence research tradition (Willer 1992). According to Emerson: "Two exchange relations, *A; B* and *A; C* are *connected at A* if the frequency or magnitude of transactions in one relation is a function of transactions in the other relation" (1972, p. 70 [italics in original]). According to Cook et al. (1983, p. 277): "(a) The connection is positive if exchange in one relation is contingent on exchange in the other. (b) The connection is negative if exchange in one relation is contingent on nonexchange in the other." Barron and Smith-Lovin (1990) suggest formulating negative connection in terms of probabilities: let *XeY* be the event "*X* exchanges with *Y*." Then the relation *AB* is negatively connected to the relation *AC* if $P(AeB/AeC) < P(AeB/\text{not-}AeC)$; that is, the *AB* relation is less likely if *A* exchanges with *C* than if *A* does not exchange with *C*. Positive connection is somewhat more difficult to define. An example given by Emerson (1981, p. 50) suggests the following interpretation: *AB* is positively connected to the relation *AC* if $P(AeB/AeC) > P(AeB/\text{not-}AeC)$; that is, the *AB* exchange is more likely if *A* exhanges with *C* than if *A* does not exchange with *C*. In this formulation the phrase "contingent on is taken to mean "affects likelihood of."

6. Allowing "=," ">," and "≥" connectives among *N, M,* and *Q* results in $3 \times 3 \times 3 = 27$ connective types, fully 21 more than the 5 plus singular given here. Other possible partitions group dissimilar cases, however. For example, both past research and research offered here clearly show that $N > M$ is very different from $N = M$. Therefore, the typology of this chapter eliminates all possible $N \geq M$ types because they group together cases that should be treated separately. Extensive research here and elsewhere also shows $N > M = Q = 1$ and $N > M > Q = 1$ connections are similar. Therefore, exclusion is defined as $N > M \geq Q = 1$, and similarly for the remaining possible types.

7. Therefore, the study of connection can be more systematic than the study of configuration where no theory designates networks for test.

8. Size is not a difficulty insofar as running experiments is concerned. Our experimental system of networked PCs has 10 nodes and, once subjects are trained and begin an experiment, we experience no difficulties when as many as 8 nodes are used. Instead, scheduling and subject payments set practical limits. Each 7-Branch has 8 subjects and, for at least 8 to appear, requires that at least 12 be scheduled. Because 7-Branches take about two and one-half hours, a payment of $12 for each subject is needed. As a result, each of the 25 runs costs $96, or a total of $2,400 in subject payments for 7-Branches alone!

9. Resistance Theory was first applied by Heckathorn (1980) but only to dyads; his equation takes a different form that will not be used here. Resistance Theory and the

Nash (1950, 1953) solution ($\Delta\mu_i \times \Delta\mu_j$ = max) can give similar predictions for the dyad, but Nash has not been applied under the conditions of connection considered here.

10. Since a payoff always stems from exchange with a particular partner, i's payoff when exchanging with j is Pij. We index the exchange partner only when its conditions are unique relative to those of other partners. In our experiments, subjects initially know Pmax and Pcon values, but application of Resistance Theory need not be so limited. Lovaglia et al. (1995a) use Resistance Theory for limited information experimental structures in which subjects do not initially know Pmax, and they report exchange ratios that are effectively identical to ratios found in more open information conditions. At issue is not simply knowledge initially available for actors. In attempting to improve their payoffs, actors will seek the limits of the range of possible payoffs and those limits are Pmax and Pcon.

11. The payoff matrixes of exchange and profit pool relations are similar. Each defines a mixed-motive game in which agreement results in a positive payoff for both actors, the size of which is inversely related, and confrontation results in no payoff to either actor from the relation.

12. Equating R_A to R_B, we find there are two unknowns, P_A and P_B. Since it is also true that $P_A + P_B = 24$, this and later resistance equations are solved by substitution.

13. Markovsky et al. (1988) use the term e^- to designate $N = M$ null connections.

14. Lovaglia et al. (1995a) suggest, for weak power networks, that actors' expectations vary with numbers of connected relations. If that idea applies to null branches, central positions should, as observed, earn more than peripherals.

15. For remarks on time pressure, see the Conclusion.

16. When "E" is earned by the central position, Skvoretz and Willer (1993) derive the equation $E^{pi} + E^{pj} = 24$ from resistance which they propose as an "equilibrium" solution. pi is the probability of being included in exchange, which is one for any central position and M/N for any peripheral. Thus for Br311, $E + E^{1/3} = 24$ and $E = 21.25$, which is not significantly different from observed 21.63. The equilibrium prediction also fits Br321 (17.33, NS) but underestimates the larger branches, Br531 (18.37) and Br751 (16.61), both of which more closely approach the 23–1 extreme than is predicted by the equilibrium solution.

17. Assuming that observed means are depressed below 23 due to an extended process through which rates are increasing toward that extreme, these results give partial support to Brennan's hypothesis that the increase of power over time is proportional to N/M. That order of the N/M ratio is 3/1 > 5/3 > 3/2 > 7/5, while the ordering of estimated mean exchange ratios is 3/1 > 5/3 > 7/5 > 3/2.

18. This presentation follows the insight of Michael Macy that the effect of $N > Q$ in inclusive-null is parallel to its effect in inclusive-exclusive connection ($P.C.$).

19. Chapter 10 revises GPI in response to critiques offered by Noah Friedkin (Personal Communications). Those revisions that extend the predictive power of GPI can be incorporated directly into the Combined Analysis offered here. They do not change the equation for GPI or applications offered below.

20. None of the networks investigated here is weak power, so this discussion of GPI omits the weak power extension of Chapter 7. The expression of GPI that follows substitutes "M" from our analysis of connection for their "e." In fact, $M_i = e_i$.

21. Two nodes are in the same domain if they are adjacent or if $N > M$ for all nodes on any path between them (Markovsky et al. 1988). For example, the exclusive branches

form a single domain because $N > M$ for the central position, but null and inclusive branches have as many domains as peripherals because $N = M$ for the central position.

22. Examples below show how domains are drawn and interpreted.

23. For simplicity of expression only, the table assumes that initially Pcon $= 0$ for all connected relations. For exchange relations where Pcon $\neq 0$, see corresponding equations earlier in the chapter.

24. The inclusive connection at D has one further effect that is also captured by the Combined Analysis. DBr has also been studied when both C and D were only exclusively connected, each exchanging twice (Chapters 6 and 7). Under that condition, DBr is a weak power structure such that C (and the now identical D) adjusted mean earnings were 15.50, which is substantially *less than* the 19.41 earned by C here when exchanging with A and B. Because C is identically connected to A and B in the two conditions, this increased power is surprising, but it is easily explained by GPI–I–Resistance. When inclusively connected, D's resistance is very low, even for very unfavorable offers from C: a C–D exchange should occur with minimal delay. After that exchange, C is central in a strong power 211 branch in which very favorable divisions are gained. That is, C's earnings here are higher than those in the earlier study because inclusive connection at D changes C's status relative to A and B from high weak power to high strong power.

25. In neoclassical microeconomics, substitutability magnitudes are ratios of utilities that are graphed as indifference curves (Samuelson 1947; Newman 1965). Industrial networks do not behave like markets because the substitutability of products is very limited (Johanson 1989), which is related to ever increasing product specialization (Williamson 1981, 1986). When manufacturing cars, there are thousands of parts which, like lights and transmissions, are nonsubstitutable.

26. In Szmatka and Willer (1995), "compound connection" refers to all inclusive-exclusive and inclusive-null connections: thus it is distinct from the meaning given that term here.

27. The converse is not true because A is exclusively connected to Bs and null connected to Cs.

28. The impact of time pressure could also explain an anomaly present only in the largest inclusive-exclusive branch. Unlike smaller branches, Br755 averaged fully three points less than Br751.

Chapter 9

Power and Influence

Preface
David Willer

The two parts of this chapter begin something that is new to sociology. Each draws connections between two theoretic research programs in order to make inferences that are not possible from either program taken alone. The two programs are Elementary Theory and Status Characteristics Theory. Work in Elementary Theory was first published in Willer and Anderson (1981), but Status Characteristics Theory, when traced to Berger et al. (1966), is a decade and a half older.

The two parts of this chapter connect quite different parts of Status Characteristics Theory to Elementary Theory. Stated somewhat differently, two quite different bridges are being proposed. These two are parallel developments in theory which overlap in time. Part 1 of this chapter was published in *Social Forces* late in 1997. Part 2 was specially written for this book. Experiments supporting Part 2 were carried out prior to the publication of Part 1.

Connecting two theoretic research programs can be quite difficult. Elementary Theory and Status Characteristics Theory are not about the same phenomenon. As a result, they have no common terms. Furthermore, each has its own image of social situations. Status Characteristics Theory makes reference to "social groups," while Elementary Theory makes reference to social relations and structures. Can precise relations be drawn between the groups of Status Characteristics Theory and the relations and structures of Elementary Theory? Neither part of this chapter seeks to answer that question. Finally, each program has its own scope conditions and the scope of the two are different, perhaps even exclusive. Are the two so different that there is no legitimate bridge from one to the other? That is yet to be determined.

Much work in formal theory is incremental. This book traces the development of Network Exchange Theory, showing how each new problem in theory is taken up only after the previous one is solved. Similarly, this chapter shows that integrating across programs is incremental and gives the first steps toward integration. Here is the distinction between bridging and integrating. Bridging does no more than connect implications from the two programs. By contrast, integration requires that the terms of the two programs be rationalized with each other and that the mechanisms through which the two generate predictions be fitted together. Bridging, being simpler and incremental, should precede integration. Bridging allows testable inferences to be drawn jointly from the two programs. Only if those inferences are supported should the larger task of integration go forward. In fact, supported inferences will guide integration of the two theories.

Part 1: Power and Influence: A Theoretical Bridge

David Willer, Michael J. Lovaglia, and Barry Markovsky

Frequently, social theorists conflate power and influence, often subsuming influence under a broad conception of power. Two contemporary theories separate them. Elementary Theory has investigated power, Status Characteristics and Expectations States Theory has investigated interpersonal influence, and neither theory has considered the phenomenon of the other. We use the two theories to explain how power produces influence and how influence produces power. We develop a theory that shows how the emotional reactions of group members mediate the influence produced by power and examine some new data. We also hypothesize that influence produces power, and we trace the consequences when power and influence are opposed within a single relationship. Implications outside the limitations of the laboratory are discussed along with new hypotheses to be tested.

INTRODUCTION

Conceptions of "power and "influence" are fundamental to the understanding of society. Consider the ways in which power and influence can occur in a social situation. A successful executive with a legendary work ethic asks a salaried employee to stay late to complete an important proposal. The employee agrees and cancels her plans for the evening. We would say that the executive used her influence to convince the employee to stay. Or the exchange could have been more direct. The executive might have told the employee that if she stayed late, the executive would recommend her for promotion. The executive has offered a reward in exchange for the employee's compliance (and implied a threat if she failed to comply). We would say that the executive used power to induce the employee's compliance. Of course, power might be operating in the first scenario as well. Because of the executive's position as her superior, the employee might have perceived a threat or promise of reward, though none was stated.

Conceptions of "power" and "influence" are also fundamental to sociology. Both terms are used in many ways by diverse researchers. Influence, for example, is sometimes considered an aspect of power. However, more narrow definitions clearly separating the two concepts may have important advantages for social analysis. Recently, research programs have progressed by defining the domain of power phenomena more narrowly and analyzing it more rigorously. Network exchange theories of power have limited their definition to differences in network position that advantage certain actors when negotiating for resources.[1] Limiting the definition of power in this way excludes most forms of influence. In studies of status characteristics and expectation states, influence derives from expectations group members have for each other's competence.[2] Influence occurs when the *advice* of competent members is followed. Limiting influence in this way excludes the conditions of power studied by network exchange theories.

Although research programs investigating power have developed independently from those investigating influence, some theoretical connections have been made. Here we build on previous work to explicitly link the Elementary Theory (ET) of structural power (Willer 1981a, 1981b; Willer 1987; Willer and Markovsky 1993) and Status Characteristics and Expectations States Theory (SCT) as it applies to interpersonal influence (Berger et al. 1966; Berger and Conner 1974; Berger et al. 1985). Both theories are good examples of cumulative research progams (Szmatka and Lovaglia 1996); both have been tested in experimental programs as extensive as any in sociology; both have also been applied in the field.[3] Their unusually high degree of development makes it possible to apply the theories jointly, once explicit links between them have been found.

This chapter does not seek to integrate ET and SCT into a single theory. Instead we bridge between the theories so that the two can be applied together. These joint applications relate power and influence in ways that are not possible when either program is taken alone. We ask whether power produces influence and whether influence produces power. The answers we seek have implications that are more general and richer than inferences from either theory taken alone. We offer hypotheses which, if supported, will contribute to the growth of both programs while overcoming limits of each. While not attempting an integration here, we do not reject theory integration as a long-term goal. To the contrary, these joint applications can serve as a feasibility study before the larger task of theory integration is taken up.

BACKGROUND AND THEORY

We define "power" as the structurally determined potential for obtaining favored payoffs in relations where interests are opposed. It is the executive's position that gives her power over the employee, rather than anything intrinsic to the person occupying the position. We define "influence" in a way that clearly distinguishes it from power. Influence is the socially induced modification of a belief, attitude, or expectation effected without recourse to sanctions.

The theoretical distinction between power and influence may or may not be warranted. Wrong (1979) adapts Russell's (1938) philosophical ideas to fashion a definition of power that encompasses influence: *"Power is the capacity of some persons to produce intended and foreseen effects on others"* (Wrong 1979, p. 2; emphasis in original).[4] Psychological definitions of power can be even more inclusive. For Heider (1958) power is a person's ability to accomplish something, to alter the environment—whether human or nonhuman—in some way, whereas social power is a person's ability to cause another to do something. On the other hand, the concept of influence can include power. Zimbardo and Leippe (1992, p. 2) define social influence as "the changes in people caused by what others do." Wrong (1979:4) asserts that "Power is identical with *intended* and effective influence," and French and Raven (1968, p. 260) "define power in terms of influence and influence in terms of psychological change." These uses result in a diffuse concept expressed in two different ways, depending on the context. When power and influence are identical, that A influences B's activity by changing B's beliefs is an example of power, whereas influence would be A changing B's behavior through threat of force.[5] Although a delimited conception of power has proven easier to approach empirically, the broader view of power continues to spawn some research.[6]

Other theorists have sought to demarcate power and influence. For Parsons, power derives from "positive and negative sanctions" through which "ego may attempt to change alter's intentions" (1963a, p. 338), whereas "Influence is a way of having an effect on the attitudes and opinions of others" (1963b, p. 38).[7] This distinction is like that drawn earlier by Bierstedt, for whom "influence and power can occur in relative isolation from each other." For Bierstedt, Karl Marx was influential upon the twentieth century, but he was not powerful. "Stalin, on the other hand, is a man of influence only because he is first a man of power" (1950, p. 732). Zelditch (1992, p. 995) draws the distinction more sharply, "What distinguishes power is that it involves external sanctions . . . Influence, on the other hand, persuades B that X is right according to B's own interests." Mokken and Stokman's distinction is similar: "The exercise of influence takes place mainly by means of persuasion, information and advice" (1976, p. 37), but, for power, "force, coercion and sanctions are *sufficient*" (1976, p. 35, emphasis in original).[8]

A theoretical distinction between power and influence will prove useful only if it entails empirical consequences. Table 9.1 shows the different antecedents and consequences of power and influence as the terms are used in the theories on which we focus, and the empirical tests in which those theories have been applied. Briefly, ET locates power in the structure of exchange networks and, when power differences occur, predicts different payoffs for exchanging actors. SCT locates interpersonal influence in the status (prestige) order of a group.

Table 9.1
Structures and Predicted Events for the Two Theories

Theory	Type of Structure	Events	Predictions
Elementary Theory	Exchange Network	Power Exercise	High vs. Low Payoffs
Status Characteristics Theory	Status Order	Interpersonal Influence	Stable vs. Changed Beliefs

When status differences occur, low-status actors alter their behavior to conform with advice of high-status actors because that advice is expected to be competent and beneficial to the group.

The two theories do not cover all kinds of influence and power. For example, SCT does not deal with the effects of persuasion, and ET does not predict power from negotiation styles. Furthermore, here we will focus only on the network exchange theory component of ET.[9] ET's applications to coercive relations with negative sanctions are not considered. Nevertheless, the definitions that the two theories provide for power and influence apply to a broad base of literature. In defining power, Weber ([1918] 1968) and Aron (1988) focus on the gain to the high power actor, while Dahl (1957, 1968) and Lukes (1974) focus on the loss to the low power actor. Because the larger payoffs of high power actors result from low power actors' smaller payoffs, power in exchange networks links gains to losses. Wrong's and French and Raven's definitions of power quoted earlier emphasize control. ET is more specific and deals with control only as it relates to valued outcomes. In regard to the belief change brought about by influence, we mean an expectancy regarding a property of an object or event (Rotter 1972). By implication, expectations need not be consciously recognized by those who hold them. To detect influence, it is sufficient to note behavior change in the absence of sanctions for that behavior. In experiments, the acceptance or rejection of influence is measured by the difference between the initial and final decision of a subject, given disagreement with another actor when that actor is not capable of rewarding or punishing the subject (Berger et al. 1977).

Having two hitherto independent theories, ET and SCT, which have not investigated the central phenomena of the other, we begin with power and influence sharply demarcated. Our initial treatment of power and influence as distinct phenomena will not dictate our conclusions, however. Because we bridge between the two, a convergence is possible. For example, if power and influence freely produce each other from similar conditions, the terms should be merged. Alternatively, relations may be asymmetric requiring power and influence to be kept distinct but understood as related phenomena.

As our argument unfolds, it will become apparent that the distinction between power and influence is useful and that the relationship between them is complex.

For example, whether power confers influence depends in part on emotional reactions, and we offer new formulations to explain these mediating factors.

STATUS AND INTERPERSONAL INFLUENCE

Influence occurs when actors change their behavior because they expect that change to benefit them or the group to which they belong. When a group forms to accomplish a task—for example, a rescue team trying to find a lost child, a research and development group developing a product, or a corporation out to make profit—it is necessary for members to coordinate their behavior. They do so by following the suggestions of group members who are expected to be most competent at accomplishing tasks valued by the group. The rescue team might turn to an expert tracker, the research and development group to the person who recently invented a successful process, and members of a corporation might willingly follow a new CEO known to have successfully turned around several failing companies. The likelihood of success increases when group members follow the advice of those competent at valued tasks. The differing expectations which members have for each other's competence create a status hierarchy with prestige, honor, and deference accorded those whose contributions are expected to be most valuable (Berger et al. 1980). Status Characteristics Theory (SCT) explains how status hierarchies are created and maintained in task-performing groups (Berger and Conner 1974; Berger et al. 1966, 1972; Berger et al. 1977; Berger and Zelditch 1985). A key consequence of a member's status is the influence she or he has over group decisions.

Status characteristics are differentially valued qualities associated with actors. These characteristics can be either diffuse or specific, and they have the capacity to establish and/or alter actors' expectations regarding another's competence. The existence of competence expectations need not have a rational basis. For example, in some cultures light skin is preferred over dark. In the United States, light skin has been associated with competence in a wide variety of situations. Thus race is a diffuse status characteristic. In contrast, chess playing ability is a specific characteristic associated with competence at chess but not necessarily with other abilities. SCT proposes that group members form expectations for each other's competence based on observable status characteristics. These expectations then produce a status hierarchy in which high-status members (a) are given more opportunities to perform, (b) perform more, (c) are given higher evaluations for their performances, and, most importantly for the present discussion, (d) have more influence over group decisions.

The theory asserts that group members aggregate information about different status characteristics when forming expectations about each others' competence. For example, suppose that a city council appoints a three-person citizen's subcommittee whose members were strangers prior to their first meeting. The members include a male doctor, a female doctor, and an unemployed woman brought together to work collectively to solve a certain problem. Initially, these people know nothing else about one another. Assuming that the council is in a culture that values males more than females, and doctors more than the unemployed, the theory predicts how these actors will rank themselves in terms of expectations for task competence. In the absence of information pertaining directly to specific task competence, the unemployed woman will be lowest and the male doctor highest.

Unless their status characteristics are explicitly dissociated from the task at hand, it does not matter that the task may have nothing to do with medicine or gender. The group's competence expectations manifest in behaviors during interaction: when diffuse status characteristics are decisive, the male doctor will have influence over the female doctor, and both will influence the unemployed woman. Although this example is simple, it suggests the complex and subtle implications of the theory when multiple and sometimes inconsistent status characteristics are salient. The theory has been extensively tested and supported with research both in and out of the laboratory (Berger et al. 1977; Moore 1985; Berger et al. 1992; B. Cohen and Zhou 1991; E. Cohen and Roper 1985; E. Cohen 1993).

Although status affects the potential for influence, other factors may intervene. Emotional reactions also play a role. Research has demonstrated a wide variety of mood-congruent social judgments (Bower 1991; Forgas and Bower 1987 1988; Mackie and Worth 1991; Shelly 1993). In particular, Baron (1987) found that interviewers in a negative mood evaluated job applicants more negatively than did interviewers in a positive mood. This suggests that mood alters expectations for competence. We evaluate others more highly when we are in a positive mood and more negatively when we are in a negative mood. Recently, Lovaglia and Houser (1996) showed not only that emotional reactions produce differences in influence congruent with emotion, but also that the effects of emotional reactions on influence combine with the effects of status characteristics. A theory that takes into account the combined effects of emotional reactions and status characteristics will be useful in showing how power differences affect influence (Lovaglia 1994, 1995, 1997).

REWARD EXPECTATIONS, POWER, AND INFLUENCE

The reward expectations branch of SCT (Berger et al. 1985) suggests that power differences should lead in a straightforward manner to corresponding differences in influence. Recall Bierstedt's (1950) comment that Stalin was influential because he was first powerful. We examine this relation below. That power can lead to influence agrees with Homans' (1974) contention that power is the fundamental process in society. We do not assert, however, that power necessarily leads to influence. To explain the path from power to influence requires that we also take scope conditions, actors' perceptions, and emotional reactions into account.

According to ET, the result over time of power exercise is the accumulation of resources by high power actors, whereas the smaller resource flows to low power actors make resource accumulation difficult or impossible (Skvoretz and Lovaglia 1995). It is the accumulation of resources that suggests increased influence for the powerful. Ridgeway's (1991) status value theory also concludes that resources are used to form expectations of competence. She adds that, because resources can be used to bring about group goals, those who hold resources are accorded high status by group members.

Reward expectations theory proposes that resources are related to status characteristics through cultural beliefs (Berger et al. 1985). For example, assume a capitalist society in which all actors accept the legitimacy of meritocracy. More competent performers should be paid more than less competent performers. Reward expectations theory asserts that the cultural belief that competence is rewarded becomes generalized in members' expectations that those who are highly rewarded are also more competent. From the belief that competence brings rewards comes the expectation that those rewarded are competent. It follows that highly rewarded actors will be judged more competent. They should then be accorded more influence by group members. This theoretical proposal has been tested and supported in empirical studies (Harrod 1980; Bierhoff et al. 1986; Stewart and Moore 1992).[10]

The fundamental assumption of SCT is that expectations for competence produce a status hierarchy in task groups. Members for whom the group holds expectations for high competence have higher status and influence than do members for whom the group holds expectations for low competence. We can now put ET together with reward expectations theory and SCT to specify the relationship of power to influence.

In ET, the exercise of power produces high rewards and an accumulation of resources for the powerful. In reward expectations theory, high rewards produces expectations of high competence for actors attaining them. Ridgeway's (1991) status value theory proposes that resource accumulation also produces expectations of high competence for resource holders. In SCT, expectations of high competence produce influence. Thus, high power should lead to increased influence for the powerful. Lovaglia (1995) tested this theory in the laboratory. He found some evidence of increased expectations for competence of a high power partner, but no difference in influence between high power and low power partners emerged. Instead, Lovaglia (1995) found that power exercise produced emotional reactions in subjects. Low power subjects had more negative emotional reactions than did high power subjects. This brings up problems of scope: Do the power processes described by ET fall within the scope of SCT?

Issues of Scope

SCT applies to situations in which group members are collectively oriented to a cooperative task. When the group achieves its goals, all members share in the success, although some may have contributed more than others. ET applies to mixed-motive exchange situations where outcomes are both cooperative and competitive. Because group members must agree to exchange before anyone can benefit, exchanges are cooperative. Because the more profit gained by one partner in exchange the less gained by the other, the terms of exchange are competitive. Since SCT does not mention competitive situations, application to exchange, though open to question, is not explicitly disallowed.[11]

Berger et al. (1977, p. 37) provide four scope conditions for SCT. (1) Group members must be task oriented. Their primary motivation is solving some problem. (2) They must expect that some characteristic is instrumental to that solution. Possessing a high state of the characteristic increases the likelihood of success. (3) The task is valued. A successful outcome is preferred over an unsuccessful one. And (4) group decisions are collective. It is necessary to consider the contributions of all members. Exchange relations satisfy conditions 1 and 3: negotiating an exchange is a problem with valued outcomes. Either an exchange occurs and both parties profit to some extent, or no exchange occurs and neither profits. Reward expectations theory satisfies condition 2 by linking the profit resulting from exchange to status characteristics. Condition 4, then, is decisive. That exchange agreements are collective is necessary, but is it sufficient? Does the fact that agreements are also competitive put them outside SCT's scope? Our answer is not global but contingent: only some, not all, exchange conditions are outside SCT's scope. We propose a scope extension for cases in which exchange is outside of SCT's present scope conditions.

Applying SCT and ET together raises two distinct questions, and issues of scope bear differently upon them: (1) does power produce influence? (2) does influence produce power? We first consider the path from power to influence in the following section; for that path there is evidence that the scope of SCT needs to be extended. Lovaglia (1995) found that high power actors were not more influential than low power actors. We use the theory of emotional reactions and status characteristics (Lovaglia and Houser 1996) to extend SCT and explain how power produces influence. Then we demonstrate how the influence resulting from power use sometimes is blocked by emotional reactions. Then we turn to examine the path from influence to power and show that, for that path, the scope of SCT need not be extended.

EMOTIONS MEDIATING THE EFFECT OF POWER ON INFLUENCE

A power advantage would likely produce an influence advantage for the powerful if influence were not blocked by the negative emotional reactions of those on whom power was exercised. However, since we are predicting that emotions mediate the effect of power on influence, demonstrating the process is difficult. Because negative emotional reactions engendered in low power subjects increase their resistance to influence of high power subjects, and positive emotional reactions of high power subjects reduce their resistance to influence of low power subjects, the direct effects of power on influence will be countered by the effects of emotional reaction on influence. Lovaglia (1997) proposed to overcome this difficulty through a series of studies. To demonstrate the effects of power on influence mediated by emotion, it is necessary to find that (1) power differences produce typical emotional reactions in those high and low in power, (2) these typical emotional reactions affect resistance to influence as predicted by the theory, and (3) the effects of emotional reactions combine with other status cues to affect resistance to influence. If it could be shown that low power actors have more negative emotional reactions than high power actors, that negative emotional reactions increase resistance to influence, and that the effects of emotional reactions combine with other status cues such as rewards, then we could infer that high power actors do gain influence, but that the negative emotions of those low in power could block that influence. Figure 9.1 models the theoretical elements relating power, emotion, and influence. The following section reports results that satisfy criterion (1) above and shows how previous research has satisfied (2) and (3).

Emotional Reactions to Power Use: New Research

In this section we present findings from new research connecting power to influence and relate those findings to related work already published. To complete the first study in the series proposed by Lovaglia (1997) above, we measured the effects of power differences in network exchange on the emotional reactions of participants. Following Lovaglia (1994, 1995, 1997), we predicted that low power actors in the exchange network would report more negative emotion than high power actors after a series of exchanges.

To test the hypothesis, subjects negotiated with each other in the 2-Branch, a strong power network, where they exchanged at most once in a round of bargaining. Subjects negotiated exchanges in a new variation on an exchange setting that has previously been used successfully to produce power differences (Lovaglia et al. 1995a). Like the old setting, it consists of networked personal computers. Because it is a "limited information setting," subjects were isolated in rooms and knew only the coded designations of their exchange partners. They negotiated exchanges in each of 60 rounds. Subjects did not divide a resource pool as in the older version. Rather, each attempted to trade units of one commodity for units of a second commodity. In each round, subjects sent a message to each partner declaring how much of one commodity they were willing to part with and the least amount of the other they were willing to accept. A central computer awarded agreements to pairs of subjects whose offers were compatible. Subjects began each round with 10 nuts and traded for bolts, and following exchange they were awarded 5 points for each nut and bolt combination and 1 point for each extra bolt or nut. For example, if an agreement was reached where

Figure 9.1
Modeling the Effects of Power Use on a Partner's Influence in an Exchange Relation

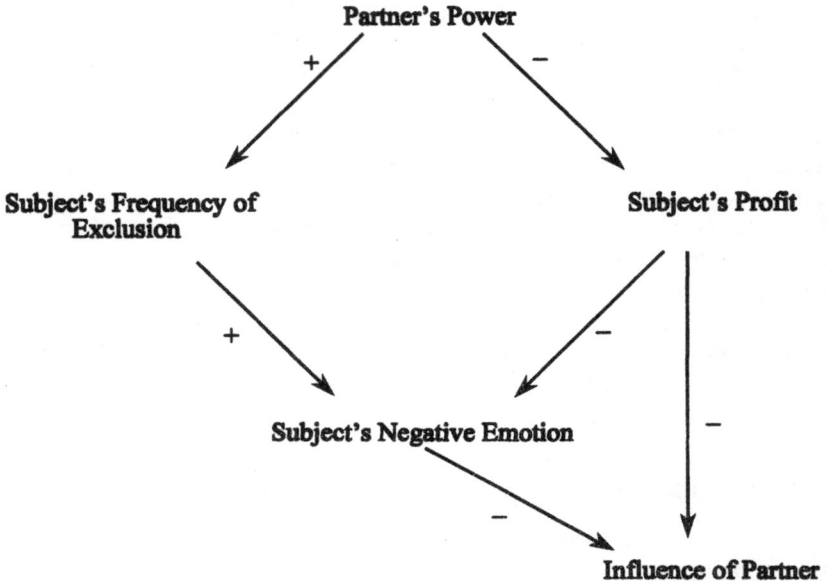

a subject traded 4 nuts for 7 bolts, the subject had 6 nut and bolt combinations worth a total of $6 \times 5 = 30$ points plus 1 extra bolt worth 1 point. The subject earned 31 profit points in that round. Subjects were told that the more profit points they earned, the more money they would be paid at the end of the experiment. As with the earlier setting, power is indicated by the average number of points earned in a round of bargaining. In reporting the results, we average earnings over the last 10 rounds of bargaining to allow power to approach its full potential. If, for example, the peripheral positions in the 2-Branch earn substantially less than the central position during the last 10 rounds of bargaining, we can infer that the central actor is in a high power position and has exercised power over the peripheral, low power, positions in the network

After 60 rounds of bargaining, subjects completed a questionnaire that asked them how they felt while trading with their partner(s). Subjects marked a 9-point scale anchored by the emotion items extremely happy–extremely unhappy, extremely angry–not angry at all, extremely satisfied–extremely dissatisfied, extremely disappointed–not disappointed at all, extremely resentful–not resentful at all, and extremely sympathetic–not sympathetic at all. Lovaglia and Houser (1996) found that subjects who rated themselves more negatively on these emotion items were more resistant to influence. We constructed a negative emotion scale by transforming the items so that the negative end of the scale was 9 and the positive end was 1, adding subjects' scores on the transformed items, and then dividing by the number of items. The resulting negative emotion scale ranges from 1 (very positive emotion) to 9 (very negative emotion). If the central, high power actor in the 2-Branch reports less negative emotion than the peripheral, low power actors, then we can conclude that power use produces negative emotions in those subjected to it.

In all, 60 undergraduate subjects—20 groups of 3 persons each—negotiated in the exchange setting. In each 2-Branch group, one person occupied the high power position, A, and two occupied low power positions, B and C. We first wanted to check that power was created in the experimental situation and that the negative emotion scale was sufficiently reliable before testing the hypothesis that power use would produce negative emotion in low power subjects. A substantial power difference between high power and low power positions is indicated by a t-test comparing the average number of profit points acquired in exchanges between A (mean profit $= 30.53$, $sd = 5.92$) and either B or C (mean profit $= 14.32$, $sd = 8.20$), $t(58)$ 7.87, $p < .001$. In addition, low power actors were excluded from exchange more often (5.75, $sd = 2.72$) than were high power actors (1.40, $sd = 1.23$) during the last 10 rounds, $t(58)$ 6.80, $p < .001$. The difference in profit indicates that a power difference existed between positions in the experimental setting. The difference in number of exclusions suggests that structural power operates through exclusion as predicted by ET. The negative emotion scale was also found reliable (Cronbach's alpha $= .90$).

To directly test the hypothesis that assignment to a low power condition increases negative emotion, we compared mean scores on the negative emotion scale for subjects in the high power position (3.41, $sd = 1.26$) and the low power position (5.55, $sd = 1.57$).[12] This difference is significant, $t(58)$ 5.29, $p < .001$ and supports the hypothesis. Subjects in the low power position reported more negative emotion during bargaining than did subjects in the high power position. Taken individually, each emotion item showed a significant difference in the predicted direction. Further, the negative emotions produced were exactly those shown by Lovaglia and Houser (1996) to increase resistance to influence. Thus we have demonstrated the first finding necessary to show that power produces influence mediated by emotion, while Lovaglia and Houser (1996) have demonstrated the second.

Lovaglia and Houser (1996) develop a theory whereby the effects of status characteristics and emotional reactions on influence can be combined. The theory uses Kemper's (1984, 1991) conception of positive emotions as "integrating" and negative emotions as "differentiating." That is, positive emotions promote behaviors that bind group members together, while negative emotions promote behaviors that drive group members apart. Thus, when a group member feels positive emotion, she is more likely to accept the influence of other group members than when she feels negative emotion. Recently, several studies have shown that negative emotions can block the influence effects of status characteristics (Lovaglia and Houser 1996; Lucas, Wynn, and Vogt 1995; Lovaglia 1995).

The fact that emotions can counter status processes explains why power differences may not produce differences in influence. While a power advantage may produce increased expectations of competence for the powerful, negative emotional reactions by those upon whom power is exercised may block the effect of those expectations. Lovaglia and Houser (1996) found that the effects of emotional reactions combine with other status information to affect resistance to influence. A partner's influence over a subject was lower when the subject had been induced to feel negative emotion than when induced to feel positive emotion. A partner who possessed several high status characteristics had greater influence over a subject than did a partner who possessed several low-status characteristics. But when emotion and status characteristics were combined, a partner who possessed several high-status characteristics had about the same amount of influence over a subject induced to feel negative emotion as a partner who possessed several low-status characteristics had over a subject induced to feel positive emotion. Lovaglia and Houser (1996) found that a partner with high-status characteristics decreased a subject's resistance to influence, the subject's negative emotion increased a subject's resistance to influence, and the effects of the subject's negative emotion counteracted those of the partner's high-status characteristics. This demonstrates the third and final finding necessary to show that power produces influence mediated by emotion. The conclusion possible from the three findings is that rewards and resources accumulated by those in positions of power may, but do not necessarily, produce increased influence, depending on the emotions generated by power use.

Experiments support the Figure 9.1 model in the following way. The experiment reported above showed that power use by a partner has two effects on a subject: (1) the subject is excluded more often and (2) the subject receives less profit from exchange. The experiment also showed that receiving less profit and being excluded more often are associated with a negative emotional reaction in the subject.[13] However, Lovaglia (1995) showed that receiving less profit also increased the subject's expectations for the partner's competence, which should increase the partner's influence. Countering this process, Lovaglia and Houser (1996) showed that the subject's negative emotion decreases the influence of the partner and that the effects of emotion combine with the effects of other status information. Thus, increased expectations of competence created by the partner's profit advantage are countered by increased resistance to influence caused by the subject's negative emotional reaction.

The role of emotion in power and influence processes has two important implications. First, the exercise of power in one group can produce influence in a second.[14] That is, even when all low power actors in one group reject influence because of negative reactions to power exercised over them, accumulated resources can produce high status and thus influence over a second group of actors. The Roman emperor influenced the Senate in part because of power exercised in the provinces (Antonio 1979). Second, the exercise of power can produce influence directly and in the same group of actors over which power has been exercised, but only if negative reactions are blocked. Let us assume, as does Weber ([1918] 1968) in his discussion of legitimacy, that low power actors can believe that high power actors deserve the fruits of power exercise. If that belief blocks negative reactions, then exercise of power produces influence directly and over the same group of actors. The following section addresses how influence may produce increased power.

CONVERTING INFLUENCE TO POWER

Analogous to the way power produces influence, it seems likely that influence can produce power. Weber asserted that high status frequently leads to increased power, but he provided little explanation (Weber 1958). Blau (1964, pp. 126–127) gave the classic description of the mechanism by which status and influence produce power:

Earning superior status in a group requires not merely impressing others with outstanding abilities but actually using these abilities to make contributions to the achievement of the collective goals of the group . . . , for example, suggestions that advance the solution of the common problem of a discussion group. . . . Having his suggestions usually followed by others is a mark of respect that raises an individual's social standing in a group, while others' social standing simultaneously suffers for two reasons, because they often follow his suggestions and because their own are rarely accepted. Initially, the high respect of the rest of the group may be sufficient reward for the contributions a group member makes. . . . [But] since the value of a person's approval and respect is a function of his own social standing, the process of recurrently paying respect to others depreciates its value. Hence, respect often does not remain an adequate compensation for contributions. Those who benefit . . . , therefore, become obligated to reciprocate in some other way, and deferring to the wishes of the group member who supplies the help is typically the only thing the others can do to repay him. As a result of these processes in which the contributions of some come to command the compliance of others, a differentiated power structure develops.

Our approach is more specific than Blau's. Below we hypothesize that status characteristics impact on the resistance of exchanging actors by altering the key parameters, Pmax and Pcon. Because the relation is drawn from SCT to *parameters* of exchange, not to the exchange relation itself, issues of fit between the mixed-motive conditions of the exchange relation and scope conditions of SCT are not relevant. Pmax and Pcon are expectations, and the only issue is whether these expectations, like others, are subject to alteration by status characteristics. If they are, exchange outcomes and thus power exercised will be affected. We cite evidence suggesting that status has effects on exchange outcomes, and we offer a formalization linking expectation advantage and resistance parameters.

The Effect of Influence on Exchange

To describe more precisely the effect of status and influence on an exchange relation, we link SCT and ET through their use of expectations. Recall from the section on resistance that Pmax and Pcon are expectations that actors hold with regard to the ongoing exchange context (Lovaglia et al. 1995a). Pmax, the actor's expected best payoff, and Pcon, the payoff at confrontation, can both change when power events occur in exchange structures. B, as a low power actor, has rivals whose offers to A set an upper limit on $P_B$max, B's expectations for a best possible payoff. When, as in the 2-Branch, a network structure induces power processes, this upper limit declines over time, reducing B's resistance. Conversely, the offers of B and its rivals become better and better alternatives for A, the high power actor. As a result, $P_A$con rises, increasing A's resistance. Thus A exercises power, gaining more from exchange than does his low power partner.

Power exercise occurs because high power actors believe they have alternative offers and because low power actors believe they must accept less or be excluded. These beliefs or expectations (the belief may not be consciously held) may or may not be well founded based on the existing power structure. It is only the beliefs, and not structures, that are necessary for exchange outcomes to manifest power differences. But for the effects of power to emerge fully, the beliefs of both high and low power actors must agree. For example, Willer (1987, p. 230) reports on an auction in which the only person bidding made better and better offers because he believed, owing to the methods of the auctioneer and his partner, that there were rival bids. The outcome depended not on the bids of others, but on the single bidder's belief that there were other bids, as well as on the auctioneer's belief that the bidder believed there were other bids. This is an example of power produced by influence alone. In terms of resistance, the auctioneer exercised power because the bidder's Pmax was declining.

SCT suggests that the production of power exercise through influence is common. An exchange relation with a high-status partner is likely to be valued more highly than one with a low-status partner. Thus we hypothesize that, when similar resources are offered, because the resources of high-status actors are valued more than those of low-status actors, actors will prefer to exchange with high-status actors. In terms of resistance, exchange with a high-status partner increases an actor's best hope for profit in the exchange independent of the resources available. Similarly, because actors expect that a high-status partner deserves more from exchange, a low-status actor's point of confrontation may decline independent of the resources available.

We hypothesize that, net of other factors, actors will expect to lose less when failing to exchange with a low-status partner than with one of higher status. Consistent with the idea from reward expectations theory that expected social outcomes correspond with social status, we hypothesize further that actors should expect to gain less when exchanging with a high-status partner than with one of lower status. If these hypotheses are supported, then as the status of any actor increases, the frequency of encountering lower-status actors increases as does influence. As influence increases, so does power, for resource accumulation favors the high-status actor.

Some research in economics supports these predictions. Two experimental studies have applied SCT to exchange to investigate the relation between influence and resource accumulation. Ball, Bennett, Eckel, and Zame (1995, p. 17) manipulated status in their study of six markets. They observed that high-status actors gained "the vast majority of the surplus." They note that "results so far indicate a surprisingly robust effect for the status treatment." (Also see Ball and Eckel 1993.)

SCT has a highly refined and empirically successful formal model from which an experimental test of the production of power through influence can be developed (Berger et al. 1977, 1992). For our purposes, SCT's coefficient of expectation advantage, calculated on the basis of differences in status characteristics, captures the biasing effect that status-based influence is assumed to exert on structural power.[15] To integrate this factor with the resistance model, we follow Balkwell's (1991) method for standardizing the presumed impact of expectation advantage on a 0–1 scale. Let d indicate the expectation advantage of one actor over the other and q be a scaling factor indicating the robustness of the effects of status differences in a given setting. (For the disadvantaged actor, d is negatively signed.) The effect of the expectation advantage is then

$$E = \frac{e^{qd}}{1 + e^{qd}}$$

where e is the exponential function. Because E ranges from 0 to 1, it readily integrates with the resistance model. That is, where P is the size of the resource pool over which actors are negotiating, and net of other factors that are known to affect resistance, $Pcon = EP/2$, and $Pmax = (E+1)P/2$. That is, an actor with the maximum status advantage would expect to receive, at worst, half the pool and, at best, the entire pool. It follows that an actor with maximum status disadvantage would expect to receive, at worst, nothing and, at best, one-half the resources.

To briefly illustrate the predicted biasing effect of a status advantage, assume that (1) two actors are differentiated by a single specific status characteristic, (2) they are in structurally equivalent network positions, and (3) they are negotiating over a pool of 10 resource units. Using values calculated by Berger et al. (1992), we find that $d = .990$ and q is approximately .40. By the assumption that actors negotiate to the point of equal resistance, we would predict that the higher-status actor's profit will be 5.6, and the lower-status actor's 4.4 when negotiated over a 10-point resource pool.

Working the coefficient of expectation advantage from SCT into ET's resistance model for negotiated exchanges constructs a bridge between two formal theories. (For resistance equations, see earlier chapters.) From our standpoint, the principal result of this bridge is a broadened array of testable hypotheses. In addition to making predictions for any network configuration under a variety of assumptions about exchange conditions and actor strategies, the two theories together generate explicit predictions for the biasing of exchange outcomes on the basis of differential status characteristics among network inhabitants. We view this as yet another step toward increasing the applicability of highly abstract theories to important real-world phenomena.

If, as hypothesized, influence can produce power in exchange relations in the absence of the structural conditions for power, if power conditions are present, then influence should amplify their effect. For example, weak power can become strong. Referring back to the Figure 7.2 Stem, B has a weak power relation with A, but assume that A is high status and can change B's belief to the effect that the $C–C$ relation does not exist. Then B believes that the Stem network is the Branch with A high power, and we hypothesize that exchange ratios in the $A–B$ relation should be like those in the strong power network. For example, when a manager's position is one of high status as well as high power over workers, those workers may expect increased costs for failure to comply with the manager's orders. The result is increased power for the manager. By using SCT and ET together, it may be possible to predict precisely the power gained by combinations of such factors.

POWER VERSUS INFLUENCE

Thus far we have focused on how power and influence can coincide. We first discussed how power produces influence. Arguably this is a common process. Powerful people in society seem to engage in a process that converts their power to high status, prestige, and increased influence. For example, Rockefeller, Ford, Getty, Carnegie, and Mellon all amassed great fortunes through sometimes ruthless methods. They then used their wealth to endow large projects dedicated to the public good, increasing their prestige considerably. We then hypothesized that influence produces power, cited limited evidence supporting the hypothesis, and drew formal relations for future investigations. None of this suggests that power and influence advantages will always coincide. What if power and influence vary in opposite directions for related actors?

We suggest that power and influence can be opposed in the same relationship. A's influence negates B's structural power when A changes B's Pmax or Pcon in a direction that produces favorable outcomes for A. Assume that an administrative assistant wants the boss to believe that a filing system cannot be understood by anyone but the assistant. If the boss attributes specific, task-relevant status characteristics to the assistant, and then believes that there are large costs associated with discharging him, the boss's Pcon becomes very large in a negative direction. The large absolute value of Pcon reduces the boss's resistance: The boss's power, which rests on the right to discharge, is countered. But for the clerk's influence attempt to succeed, he must be believed. His credibility will depend in large part on the assistant's status—perhaps he has a higher academic degree than his boss has. Higher status individuals are assumed to act in the best interests of the group (Ridgeway 1982), which in this case would include telling the boss the truth.

Whether an actor's statements are believed becomes important in exchange relations because actors' interests are opposed. If the clerk gets a raise based on his purported indispensability, he has used his influence to gain power at his boss's expense. However, should his boss discover his deceit, his influence will certainly decline. In a more basic exchange network, when the high power actor in the 2-Branch bargains aggressively to extract the last penny from his low power partners, the high power actor's status in the group may fall. His heedless pursuit of advantage will elicit disapproval. Thus the opposed interests present in exchange relations allow influence to be traded for power.

When organizations require expert knowledge and/or abilities in subordinate positions, they provide a basis for opposition between influence based on the specific status characteristic of expertise and power from higher to lower position. Influence based on expertness resembles what French and Raven (1968) call "expert power," but SCT finds its origin in the status order, not in power conditions like exclusion. Taken together, SCT and ET suggest that power struggles in organizations develop when structurally disadvantaged actors have specialized knowledge that is the basis for specific status characteristics. The theories also suggest that these power struggles will not be resolved as long as structurally advantaged actors do not share that knowledge. For example, consider the power struggles between managers of professional sports teams and their stars. It would be more accurate to call these power and influence struggles, for official position can operate as a generalized status characteristic within organizations. If so, power relations from higher to lower official positions are accompanied by influence flowing from higher to lower official statuses, which is opposed by influence flowing from expert qualifications.[16]

Universities provide an example of organizations with ongoing power and influence struggles. Deans, provosts, and chancellors hold formal power, especially in allocation of funds. They also exercise influence based on formal position, but they can have only a small fraction of the specialized knowledge held by faculty members. Thus the power and influence of central administration is potentially opposed by faculty influence, which tends to countervail that power. It also should follow that faculty members whose stature is most generally recognized will be more influential, while those with lower recognition will be more subject to administrative power. Therefore, we hypothesize that high-status faculty at research universities are more influential relative to their administrations than their counterparts at lower status universities and colleges.[17]

One way to resolve struggles when power and influence are opposed is for those who are in high power positions to eliminate the specialized knowledge required of those in low power positions, thus eliminating their basis for influence. Eliminating specialized knowledge of subordinates has the added advantage of increasing power directly by opening low power positions to less skilled labor markets where rates of exclusion are higher. Such "deskilling" of occupations is difficult to pursue in organizations like universities, where it would tend to make education and research impossible. But the tactic of separating subordinates from knowledge has succeeded elsewhere, for example, in the field of social work. The result has been declining prestige and pay for social workers.

The basic assumption of Taylorism is that workers' knowledge of jobs is unscientific and that only the new class of managers, in cooperation with capital, can organize work rationally (Taylor [1911] 1967). In fact, power in the steel industry had been centralized in 1892 by separating workers from knowledge of the labor process (Stone 1974). Taylorism, as in the Hawthorne studies, depicted workers as driven by irrational motives, further lowering their status relative to management (Roethlisberger and Dickson 1964). The scientific basis of "scientific management" is at best doubtful. Reexamination of evidence from the field experiments indicates that central conclusions of the Hawthorne studies were unsupported: workers were motivated by financial rewards (Cary 1967; Parsons 1974; Jones 1992). Antonio asserts that increasing power centralization reduces the organization's capacity to effectively complete tasks (1979). Certainly, the attempt to centralize power structurally at any cost by eliminating all bases for influence from below is now seen as typical of the inefficiencies of middle twentieth-century mass production. By contrast, "lean production" is said to gain efficiency by opening paths for influence throughout the organization (Womack et al. 1990).

Our analysis suggests that not only is it possible to find power and influence opposed in a single relationship, but also that considerable resources may sometimes be invested in eliminating the inconsistency between them. Thus, investigating relations where power and influence are opposed could be a promising research area.

CONCLUSION

This study began with power and influence sharply demarcated *and* isolated from one another. Elementary Theory investigates structural power, while Status Characteristics Theory investigates influence due to status. These were independent theoretical research programs, and neither investigated the phenomenon of the other. Power and influence are sharply demarcated because their meanings stem independently from the two programs, yet the two have not remained isolated from each other. The conceptual bridges built between the two theories show that power and influence are importantly linked. In some cases experimental studies support these links. When links have not been investigated, specific hypotheses foreshadow future experimental evaluations. At the beginning of this study, Elementary Theory and Status Characteristics Theory were independent research programs; but the conceptual bridges built here mean that they are separated no longer.

That power and influence were sharply demarcated initially would not prevent us from reaching the conclusion that the two terms should be combined. If power and influence produce each other and do so from similar conditions, the terms should be merged. In fact, the bridges between the theories imply that power produces influence and influence produces power. The two produce each other, but *not from similar conditions*. For example, the exercise of power can be produced directly by exclusion in power structures. It can also be produced indirectly: Bridging between theories, we hypothesize that influence produces power exercise through status-based expectancies. For both, the result is the same: a power exercise indicated by differential payoffs. But exclusion, which produces power directly, and status, which produces influence which then produces power, are very different conditions. Therefore, we conclude that power and influence should be distinct concepts.

Various conceptions of power and influence have long been contended, but our point of departure is different from that of our intellectual forebears: we began with two well-developed theoretical research programs. Each program is grounded in literally hundreds of experiments through which formulations have been tested and refined. The scope of each has been successively extended, and work now ongoing promises further substantial scope extensions. These are "structural social psychologies" (Lawler, Ridgeway, and Markovsky 1993) that locate power and influence in structures. But outside the limits of the laboratory, we expect power and influence to be found together in structures. When they are, application of both theories together increases explanatory power.

Our aim in linking the Elementary Theory of power to the Status Characteristics Theory of influence is to solve that problem—or at least begin its solution. The bridges between the theories uncover a new and broader phenomenal domain in which we are now able to make precise and subtle predictions about group processes. We have seen that power can produce influence and that influence can produce power. We have also seen that the two can be opposed in the same social relationship. In each case our aim has been to relate the two theories and their experimental grounding to some important structures and processes outside the laboratory. It is clear that the implications that can be derived from the two theories together are more general and richer than for either theory taken alone.

Part 2: Status Influence and Status Value
Shane R. Thye

In the first part of this chapter, Willer, Lovaglia, and Markovsky developed a theory which predicts that status characteristics lead to power in exchange relations. The theory begins at the point where culturally valued status characteristics activate performance expectations (Berger, et al., 1977; Wagner and Berger 1993). Performance expectations, in turn, are predicted to influence the perceptions negotiators develop for their highest expected payoff from exchange (Pmax) and payoff when no exchange is possible (Pcon). Because Pmax and Pcon affect exchange rations, high-status individuals can receive a greater share of the profit when exchanging with low-status individuals.

Although status characteristics influence the beliefs individuals develop, they can also invoke other cognitive processes. In the following pages I outline a *Status Value Theory of Power* that focuses on just such an alternative. This approach complements the Willer, Lovaglia, and Markovsky model in the sense that it provides a related, but distinct, mechanism for status-driven power. The two theories make the same basic prediction—that positive status characteristics lead to power—but differ in their explanation as to why. After briefly sketching the Status Value Theory of Power, I discuss how these two theories might be differentiated.[18]

STATUS LEADS TO VALUE

The Status Value Theory of Power uses the notion of *status value* to bridge the gap between status characteristics and power. Status value refers to the feelings of honor, esteem, or prestige that result from possessing a thing (Berger et al. 1972). Some things are given because they confer substantial status value, as when a soldier is given the medal of valor or a writer the Pulitzer Prize. Other status value effects can be subtle, as when a student is given dinner by her professor at the Faculty Club. The notion of status value is not new. Early discussions of this idea can be found in social critiques published nearly a century ago (e.g., Veblen 1899). More recently, status value has found application in a range of contemporary theories. For example, Berger and colleagues (1972) employ the notion of status value in a theory of distributive justice. Another set of investigators seeks to explain how nominal traits, such as race or gender, initially come to acquire status value in a society (Ridgeway 1991; Ridgeway and Glasgow 1996; Webster and Hysom 1996). They assert that when a trait is particularly associated with a valuable object, like wealth or political power, the value of the object can transfer to the trait. The result of this process is a newly formed status characteristic that carries a wide range of social advantages.

My Status Value Theory of Power asserts that the transfer of status value works in the opposite direction as well: the prestige or esteem associated with a high-status person transfers to things exclusively held by that person. (See Berger et al. 1972 for a related statement.) I call this transfer the diffusion of status value from person to thing. Exclusive ownership is sufficient for this effect but not necessary. For example, objects can also acquire status value when they are saliently associated with a high-status person. This effect is well known. Only the U.S. president awards certain military and civilian honors. The king of Sweden alone presents Nobel Prizes. Moreover, athletic shoe companies see to it that highly successful professional athletes are associated with their product lines. Similarly, celebrities attempt to ennoble bras, while racing teams are used to confer status to dangerous (but legal) drugs such as cigarettes and chewing tobacco.

Thus far, the status value theory of power has been tested only for the condition in which a high-status person has exclusive possession of an object to which value could spread. In one laboratory experiment, subjects were allowed to decide between exchanging with a higher status partner (who controlled purple poker chips) or a lower status partner (who controlled orange chips). The results showed that subjects tried harder to acquire the purple chips, assumed they were generally more important than orange chips, and were willing to accept less profit in exchange for them (Thye and Markovsky 1997). This tendency was observed even though all subjects knew that their pay was based only on numbers chips earned, not the type. That is, subjects understood that each orange and purple chip gave exactly the same payoff at the conclusion of the experiment, yet in the experiment they tried much harder to acquire the purple than the orange chips (see below).

This research is noteworthy for several reasons. First, it provides empirical support for the hypothesis that status value transfers from people to their possessions. Second, it demonstrates that individuals (1) attend to the status value of items that reside at various network locations and (2) factor these perceptions into the way they negotiate exchange. Outside of the lab, one need only price an authentic "Mickey Mantle" baseball to *really* feel the impact of status value on social exchange.

HOW GENERAL IS THE DIFFUSION OF STATUS VALUE?

Since experiments have shown the spread of status value from people to objects, the next question is to investigate the conditions of that spread and its breadth. I have no doubt that the spread of status value is more general than the theory currently assumes. The world of everyday experience can provide many examples where the diffusion of status value is not restricted to *exclusive ownership* by the high- or low-status individual. For instance, a baseball signed by Mickey Mantle will still hold status value even after it has been circulated among many, relatively lower status collectors. The next theoretical step is to precisely specify the relationship between person and object termed above "saliently associated with" such that its conditions can be systematically investigated.

Furthermore, status value may be transferred between people in much the same way it is transferred from people to things. It is not uncommon to see status value transferred from mentor to student, attorney to client, and parent to child. I adopt the term *associative status* to denote the interpersonal transmission of status value. Then positive associative status is any increment in prestige, esteem, or influence that is caused by a direct social relation to a higher status actor. Negative associative status is the decrement in status caused by a proximal low-status connection. Does status value diffuse through personal relations in the same manner it diffuses from persons to objects? This issue can be experimentally investigated and should be.

In the following section I return to more familiar theoretical territory. I discuss the spread of status value from people to their possessions and how this phenomenon converts status to power.

STATUS VALUE LEADS TO POWER

The diffusion of status value has direct implications for the development of power in exchange relations. In settings where high- and low-status individuals seek exchange with one another, the goods controlled by the high status negotiator will acquire status value. At the same time, the desirability of items held by low-status individuals will be reduced. The result of these concomitant processes is that the distribution of status characteristics will closely correspond to the distribution of status value in the system. Simply stated, high-status actors will control the most prestigious goods. The Status Value Theory of Power asserts that, all else being equal, the possession of valued goods leads to power. Other theories share this position (e.g., Emerson 1972a, 1972b, 1981; Willer and Anderson 1981), and recent experimental evidence supports it. Thye and Markovsky (1997) report that in dyads and fully connected triangles, the highest status negotiator received the greatest share of profit from exchange. The same research demonstrated that status effects can even countervail "weak power" advantages that stem from the pattern of exchange relations.

To briefly summarize, the Status Value Theory of Power links relative social status to the possession of valued goods and ultimately to power. Status produces power outcomes—differential exchange ratios—through the perceived value of goods held by status differentiated actors. The mechanism producing power from status in Willer, Lovaglia, and Markovsky is quite different. They suggest that status characteristics produce power because high-status individuals influence exchange-relevant beliefs held by lower status individuals. We can call these two formulations *status value* and *status influence*, respectively. The remainder of this chapter explores the possibility of differentiating these phenomena.

DEMARCATING INFLUENCE FROM VALUE EFFECTS

The amount of information available to exchange partners—such as the overall shape of the exchange network, the amount of profit available in each relation, and the magnitude of bargaining concessions—has different implications for the two theories. For the status influence proposed by Willer et al., there will be no status influence effects for actors with perfect information confidently held. Actors who have known Pmax and Pcon values will not change them given communications from higher status actors. Alternatively, actors inferring Pmax and Pcon when information is restricted are subject to influence by communications from higher status partners. By contrast, the effect of status value on exchange outcomes should be entirely independent from the actors' information.

What *is* most important for the emergence of status value effects is that high- and low-status negotiators possess things that are somehow distinct. For example, the theory currently applies to status-differentiated exchanges where apples are traded for oranges but not to settings where apples are traded for apples. Requiring that high- and low-status actors exchange things that are distinct is a structural condition that allows high-status value to be associated with one thing and low-status value with the other. By contrast, status influence can affect the division of a single resource. For example, the division of a resource pool by a pair of status-differentiated actors is predicted to favor the higher status actor when the conditions for status influence are present.

Power outcomes produced by status influence can be disentangled from power outcomes produced by status value by varying information and number of things exchanged. Table 9.2 depicts four conditions of a hypothetical experiment that disentangles status value and status influence. In Cell "a" of that table, only status influence should emerge: high- and low-status negotiators have a single resource to divide and exchange with restricted information. In Cell "d" only status value should emerge: high- and low-status actors have distinct items to exchange and full information about the other. In Cell "c" both effects are expected: high-status actors benefit from differential value and influence. By

Table 9.2
A Hypothetical Experiment

INFORMATION

		Restricted	Full	
NUMBER OF	*Single*	a	b	1
COMMODITIES	*Multiple*	c	d	2
		3	4	

contrast, in Cell ''b'' no status effects should be present. For all these cases, the dependent variable is movement of the exchange ratio in the direction favorable to the high status actor.

The possible outcomes include: (1) An information main effect (mean 3 > mean 4), (2) a commodity main effect (mean 2 > mean 1), or (3) a commodity by information interaction. The first outcome would demonstrate that status characteristics translate into greater relative power when information is restricted. Such a finding would be consistent with a status influence effect and would thus provide support for the Willer, Lovaglia, and Markovsky theory. The second outcome would suggest that status-based power is contingent on high- and low-status members possessing distinct commodities to exchange and would lend credence to the status value theory of power. Notice that this experimental design allows one, the other, or both status effects to emerge simultaneously. A significant interaction between information and the number of commodities would imply that status value and status influence aggregate in ways that are more complex than either theory currently suggests.

CLOSING REMARKS

My status value formulation is a new theory of power in exchange networks that complements the status influence theory of Willer et al. In many ways the theories are alike. Both connect culturally valued status characteristics to power in exchange networks. At the same time, however, there are important theoretical differences. One theory asserts that status produces influence; the other claims that status leads to differential perceptions of value. I have shown how the two are differentiated by varying information and numbers of things exchanged.

But differentiating these two phenomena is only the first step. Once it is shown that status value and status influence are empirically distinct, the next question is to determine whether the two combine, and if so, how. Perhaps either theory alone can exhaust the total effect of status on exchange. Alternatively, status influence and status value may have a joint effect that is additive or multiplicative.

Research relating status and power is just beginning. As status value, status influence, and the relations between the two are investigated, there is reason to hope that the relations between status and power, which once were murky, will become clear.

NOTES

1. Representative research on power includes Emerson (1962, 1972); Cook and Emerson (1978); Cook et al. (1983); Molm (1981, 1988, 1990); Bacharach and Lawler (1980, 1984); Lawler and Bacharach (1987); Willer and Anderson (1981); Willer (1987); Markovsky, Willer, and Patton (1988); Skvoretz and Willer (1993); and Markovsky et al. (1993). That some actors gain resource advantages undoubtedly implies that they control others more than they are controlled. Although this reseach on power does not rule out "power as control," the focus has been on power as measured by resource advantage.

2. See status characteristics and expectation states research, including Berger, Cohen, and Zelditch (1966, 1972); Berger et al. (1977); Humphreys and Berger (1981); Markovsky, Smith, and Berger (1984); Ridgeway (1981, 1982); and Ridgeway, Berger, and Smith (1985).

3. See, for example, application of the theory to create an effective school program (Cohen and Roper 1972, 1985; Rosenholtz 1985; Cohen, Lotan, and Cantanzarite 1988; Cohen 1986, 1993). For applications of Elementary Theory, see Willer and Anderson 1981; Willer 1987; and Willer et al. 1996.

4. The passage from Wrong does not assert that, for power to be exercised, people must intend to exercise power. It only states that power exercise is an intentional act. Since Wrong, considerable evidence has emerged supporting his assertion. Markovsky (1987) has shown that simulated actors who make and accept offers randomly do not exercise power under known structural power conditions, while Willer and Skvoretz (1977) show that power can be exercised over experimental subjects by a (minimally intentional) simulated actor that can do no more than accept its best offer.

5. Power and influence are used synonymously, according to Wrong, because of the absence, in English, of a verb form for power (1979, p. 6). According to Wrong, instead of "The boss powers the workers," we say "The boss influences the workers" and by "influence" we mean that the boss has exercised power. Exchange theories employ the terms "power use" (Cook and Emerson 1978) and "power exercise" (Willer and Anderson 1981). These terms allow the expression, "The boss exercises power over the workers," which makes it unnecessary to conflate power and influence.

6. See especially Friedkin's (1993a,b) extension and formalization of French and Raven's earlier theory. However, Friedkin's theory distinguishes structural bases of power from French and Raven's five original bases that include influence.

7. Because Parsons allows power to include the manipulation of symbols, his line between power and influence is not always clear. That he intends the two to be distinct, however, is evident from his postulation of two "circulating mediums," one for power and one for influence. Parsons' idea of circulating mediums, which he draws by analogy from money, is sharply criticized by Coleman (1963) and is not like the structural formulations employed by the two theories of this chapter.

8. Mokken and Stokman (1976:37) develop new formulations for power and influ-

ence that concern the control and selection of choice alternatives, respectively. Also see Stokman and Van den Bos (1992). While we believe that those formulations are compatible with those offered here, a detailed treatment of their work is beyond the limits of this chapter.

9. Research in social exchange has exploded in recent years. Several other social exchange theories are sufficiently developed that they may also be fruitfully related to SCT. Well-developed social exchange theories include the game theoretic approach of Bienenstock and Bonacich (1992, 1993), expected value theory (Friedkin 1992, 1993a), power-dependence theory (Cook and Emerson 1978; Cook and Yamagishi 1992a), identity theory (Burke 1997), and Yamaguchi's (1996) extension of Coleman's (1990) rational choice approach. For a comparison among most of these theories, see Skvoretz and Willer (1993) and Lovaglia et al. (1995a).

10. Since the link between power and influence in capitalist societies is resource accumulation, in a comment on an earlier draft, Phillip Bonacich suggested that resources accumulated by any means can produce influence. We agree, as does Ridgeway (1991). Furthermore, given the joint property system of the family (Willer 1985), resources accumulated by one spouse may produce status and thus influence for the other.

11. For scope conditions of an earlier application of ET, see Markovsky et al. (1988). In general, ET requires that self-interested actors recognize the value in lowering demands in order to be included in exchange or raising demands when inclusion is assured. These requirements do not appear to conflict with situations in which SCT applies. Thus, the problem of scope does not arise when using SCT and ET to explain how influence can produce power.

12. When two actors exchange, the profit of one actor determines the profit of the other. Similarly, when one low power actor is included in exchange, the other is necessarily excluded. Thus, observations for these variables cannot be considered independent. In addition, there are twice as many observations for low power actors as for high power actors, precluding a straightforward paired sample t-test. These problems can be overcome by analyzing data at the group rather than individual actor level. We replicated the analyses with one-sample t-tests that compared (1) whether the advantage in profit enjoyed by the high power actor over the average of the two low power actors was greater than zero, (2) whether the difference in number of exclusions between the average of the two low power actors and the high power actor was greater than zero, and (3) whether the difference in negative emotion between the average of the two low power actors and the high power actor was greater than zero. Results corroborated the independent sample t-tests in all three cases. For the 20 three-person groups, the high power actor's profit advantage was significantly greater than zero (mean = 15.96, sd = 10.95), $t(19)$ 6.52, $p < .001$. The high power actor's exclusion deficit was greater than zero (mean = 4.35, sd = .131), $t(19)$ 33.13, $p < .001$. In support of the main hypothesis, the high power actor's negative emotion deficit was greater than zero (mean = 1.95, sd = .154), $t(19)$ 5.67, $p < .001$.

13. Both exclusion and low profit are associated with negative emotion, but they are too highly correlated to determine whether each has an independent effect. In the future we intend to disentangle the two by investigating emotional effects in inclusively connected networks (Patton and Willer 1990) where inclusion, not exclusion, produces low profits.

14. Also worthy of study is the suggestion by Joseph Berger that bystanders who observe but do not engage in a power process, as in the e-state structuralism model of

Fararo and Skvoretz (1986), may also form expectations and thus influence or be influenced. This suggestion raises the possibility that power exercised over some members of a group may result in influence over others of that same group. The status of those subjected to power is important. Observers may not feel threatened by power use directed at a despised minority.

15. For more on biasing effects in exchange relations, see Skvoretz and Lovaglia (1995), Lovaglia et al. (1995a).

16. Power and influence struggles can also stem from subordinate status outside the organization. For example, the subordinate wealthy from outside income may influence the poorer boss, the male subordinate may influence the female boss, and so on.

17. In addition, the greater mobility of faculty at research institutions increases their power relative to central administration, as does their ability to provide resources through extramural granting.

18. The theory and empirical results discussed in Part 2 of this chapter were supported by funds provided by a National Science Foundation Doctoral Dissertation Improvement Grant to Barry Markovsky and Shane Thye (SBR 97–00766). I am also grateful to Barry Markovsky, David Willer, and Jeongkoo Yoon for their comments on an earlier draft of this manuscript.

Chapter 10

Recent Problems and Solutions in Network Exchange Theory

Preface
David Willer

The two parts of this chapter invite you, the reader, into our theory shop to tell you how we have dealt with problems in the Graph-theoretic Power Index (GPI)—or at least how we have dealt with them thus far. The GPI's problems were discovered by the author of a competing theory, Noah Friedkin. That they were discovered by a competitor points to the very important place of theory competition in science. Here I explain how objectivity and competition are related through the community of scientists engaged in advancing theory.

Scientific knowledge can be "objective," and it should be. By "objective" I mean, as Weber did, that the investigator keeps empirical facts distinct from her value judgments (Weber [1904] 1949). I also mean that the implications of scientific theory are logically and empirically accurate. Scientific objectivity is not just a property of individuals. Objectivity is produced by a community of scholars with the following norms. Scientists select theories that are broader in scope and more precise over competing theories with narrow scope and less precision. Theories with internal contradictions are not acceptable. Parsimonious theories are preferred over more complex formulations but not at the cost of scope of application.

The norms of science, like all norms, can be easily misunderstood—particularly by sociologists who have the fixed notion that norms work because of individual commitments. The ideals of the individual are not the central issue. More central for norms are the rules we apply to the behavior of others (Willer 1985). For example, regardless of how I am tempted, I want you to accept only those theories that are broader in scope and more precise. If every scholar in the community applies that rule to judgments made by all others, objective knowledge will result. The result will be objective knowledge in spite of biases individuals are tempted to pursue. Certainly, a scientific community is more effective when individuals internalize the norms. But it is enough that each apply the norms to all others.

Two qualities, one of theory and one of research, must be satisfied for the normative system of a community of scientists to produce objectivity. First, the theory must be "intersubjective." By intersubjective I mean that the theory must have the same implications to any reader. Intersubjectivity requires that theories reach some minimal level of formalism. Second, research that tests theory must be replicable: it must be possible for a test, once completed, to be exactly repeated by others. Most sociological work fails on both counts. The orienting perspectives that call themselves theory have very different empirical implications for different people. Most sociological investigations are, in principle, one-shot studies. Once a survey or case study is completed, it cannot be repeated. The only claims to objectivity that these kinds of work can make rest, precariously, on the good will of the investigator.

By the middle of the 1990s, network exchange theory had intersubjective theories and experimental designs that could be replicated—and a community of scholars looking closely at each other's work. As indicated by the last three chapters, issues of adding precision and expanding scope were at the center of attention of those of us engaged in NET study. GPI, though a core procedure, was not then being investigated. The experiments being run were concerned with extending NET's scope elsewhere. By contrast, it is entirely reasonable and right for competitors, in advancing their own theoretical program, to focus on finding GPI's faults. In fact, Noah Friedkin demonstrated a fundamental fault in GPI; for many networks, GPI produces more than one prediction. It was because GPI is intersubjective—that it can be applied by Friedkin in exactly the same way as it is applied by the authors of the procedure—that he could demonstrate this logical fault.

The work of this chapter follows from Friedkin's demonstration. Here three procedures to solve the problem found by Friedkin are offered. It is not yet determined which has greatest scope and precision, but the procedure offered in Part 2 is the simplest. The chapter offers another advance for network exchange research. Friedkin's discovery led the NET group to propose a new method of testing network exchange theories. Previously, theory had been tested in only a few networks; no general method of selecting networks for test had been proposed. The new method proposed here sorts among all connected networks up to a given size to find the best networks for experimental testing.

Part 1: An Automated Approach to the Theoretical Analysis of Difficult Problems
Michael J. Lovaglia, John Skvoretz, Barry Markovsky, and David Willer

INTRODUCTION

Research on exchange networks is some of the most theoretically formal and cumulatively progressive in sociology (Cook, Molm, and Yamagishi 1993; Knottnerus 1994; Molm and Cook 1995; Szmatka and Lovaglia 1996; Willer and Markovsky 1993). Rapid progress in network exchange research programs pushes theoretical growth, resulting in what Fararo (1984, p. 155) calls "the physics-like interplay between abstract theories, appropriate formalisms, and relevant data." This progress contrasts strongly with less formal and more static theories which may gain or lose favor but change little (Szmatka and Lovaglia 1996).

Recent problems that arose with GPI, the Graph-theoretic Power Index, and work done to overcome those problems represent a case study in the strategic development of a theoretical research program. Handling problems in a particular way often leads to progress well beyond the solution to immediate problems. It is the strength and the beauty of science that results can transcend the competence of individual scientists. This part of the chapter begins with the problems found with GPI and offers two new solutions, Iterative GPI and Iterative Likelihood Analysis (ILA). In seeking solutions to GPI's problems, we became dissatisfied with the way exchange networks theories are tested. Later, we explain a new procedure for selecting networks on which to test network exchange theories, an automated theoretical analysis.

GPI, ITERATIVE GPI, AND ITERATIVE LIKELIHOOD ANALYSES

Network exchange theory analyzes the power of network positions in three steps. Chapter 4 details how the theory first determines whether any positions have overwhelming advantages over one or more of their partners—a condition termed *strong power*—and finds breaks by determining which positions will exchange with each other. The first step uses GPI (Markovsky, Willer, and Patton 1988; and Chapter 4).

Second, the theory determines whether smaller *weak power* advantages and disadvantages exist between exchanging positions. This step of the analysis uses the exchange-seek procedure which finds li, the likelihood that a position will be included in an exchange (Markovsky et al. 1993; and Chapter 5).

Third, the theory predicts the exact profit a position will acquire through exchange at equilibrium. It uses a mathematical function derived from assumptions about actor behavior to transform the qualitative differences between positions identified in stage two into exact quantitative predictions of exchange power (Skvoretz and Willer 1993; Lovaglia et al. 1995a; and Chapters 6 and 7).

As this theory evolved, work at each step presumed that the foundation for earlier steps was solid. Yet, Friedkin (Personal Communication) showed the GPI of Markovsky et al. (1988) to be flawed. This problem sparked intensive collaboration among the authors, and, while the immediate problem was soon solved, a general solution proved elusive. Our aim was a method that gives unique solutions, allowing us to find breaks and correctly classify any network, no matter how large or complex, as a strong, weak, or equal power structure. Our work was a classic example of conjecture and refutation. Elaborations and revisions of the GPI path-counting method were proposed for specific problematic networks, and then new networks were painstakingly assembled to test the revised and elaborated procedure. The result is *two* theoretic procedures: Iterative GPI and Iterative Likelihood Analysis (ILA). ILA is based on the probability tree algorithm, which is already in use to analyze weak power structures (see Chapters 5 and 7). We present both methods below. Interestingly, the two give identical predictions for the power of positions in all networks of six or fewer positions and in the 105 7-position networks considered thus far. Furthermore, the predictions are consistent with results from Markovsky's X-Net simulations, a program in which earnings differentials emerge as simulated actors adjust offers based on their experience of being included or excluded from exchanges (see Markovsky 1995). Finding consistent predictions among theoretic procedures—and inconsistencies as well—is the idea behind the automated network analyzer considered later.

Recall from Chapter 4 that GPI uses a path-counting algorithm to identify how advantaged one position is in comparison to another. For example, for the network of Figure 10.1a, A has a single 1-path to B, a single unique 2-path to C, a 3-path through B and C to D, and a 4-path through B, C, D, and ahead to the other C. Adding 1 for the 1-path and 3-path while subtracting 1 for the 2-path and 4-path yields a GPI value of 0 for position A. In contrast, position B has four 1-paths, a 2-path through C to D, and a 3-path through C and D to the other C. Thus its GPI value is $4 - 1 + 1 = 4$. Similar counting procedures

Figure 10.1
Friedkin Network and GPI Scores

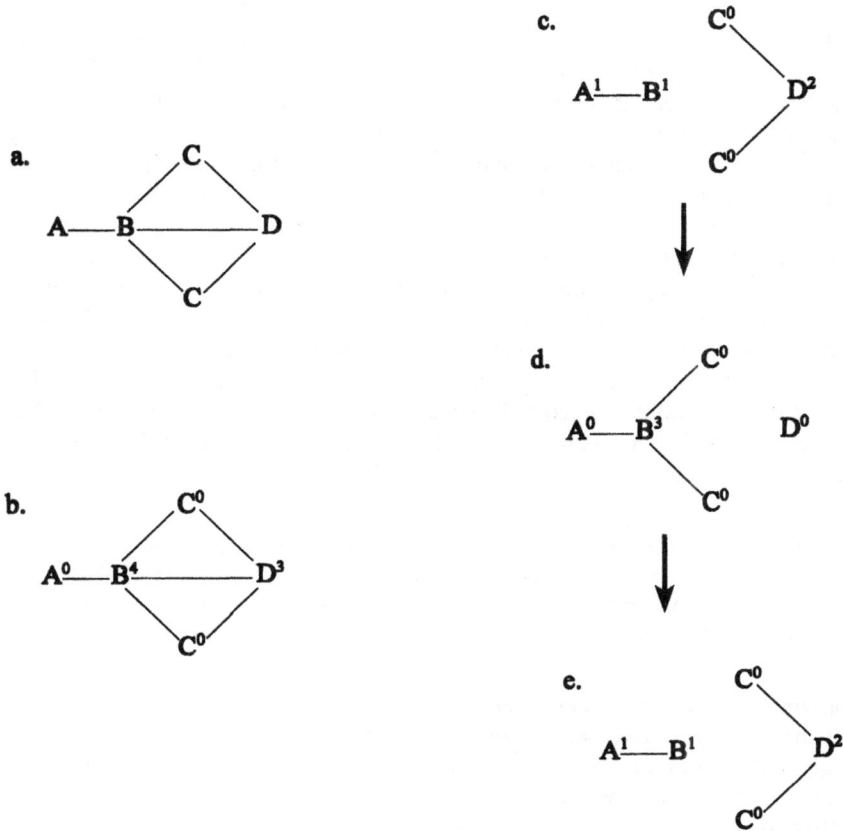

give $GPI_C = 0$ and $GPI_D = 3$. (See Markovsky et al. 1988 in Chapter 4 for details of GPI calculations.)

When GPI values differ for two positions, one has a strong power advantage over the other. Axiom 2 of Markovsky et al. (1988) asserts that actors seek exchange with partners whose GPI value is lower than theirs. Or, if all partners have a GPI value equal to or greater than an actor, the actor is assumed to seek exchange with the weakest partner(s) available. However, exchange is possible only when an actor and a partner mutually seek exchange with each other. Hence, if an actor and a partner do not mutually seek each other, that tie is broken. When such broken ties cause networks to break into subnetworks, GPI is applied iteratively to resulting subnetworks.

Using Axiom 2 to analyze the Figure 10.1 network gives the oscillations shown in that figure. Initially, C actors will seek exchange with D but not B.

The network breaks into an A–B dyad and a C–D–C 3-Line network. GPI equals 1 for the positions in the dyad. In the 3-Line, D's GPI equals 2, whereas C's equals 0. Axiom 2 then applies to these new subnetworks. Now Cs seek exchange with B, but not with D, thus leaving D isolated from the rest of the network. Applying GPI again produces the dyad and 3-Line. The analysis cycles indefinitely from one iteration to the next, making it impossible to find breaks, designate the power of positions, or determine whether the network is strong power or not. Nevertheless, simulation using Markovsky's X-Net program suggests that B and D are in fact strong power positions. (Markovsky 1995 describes the simulator.)

We soon found that the anomalous Figure 10.1 network proposed by Friedkin has a relatively easy solution, a modification of Axiom 2. Markovsky et al. (1988) assume that C actors will seek exchange with D while avoiding B because B is more powerful than D. When a strong power advantage exists, however, low power actors eventually lose nearly all available resources regardless of the size of the GPI values. Since a disadvantaged actor does not care whether the difference in GPI scores is large or small, a better specification of the exchange-seek assumption is:

> *Revised Exchange-Seek Assumption (Axiom 2)*: Actors seek exchange with those less powerful than they are. If no actors with less power are available, actors seek exchange with actors of equal power. If no actors of equal power are available, actors seek exchange with more powerful actors.

Applying the revised exchange-seek assumption to the Figure 10.1 network, we find that C actors seek both B and D and the network does not oscillate, so unique GPI values are given for each position. Now GPI values clearly indicate that Figure 10.1 is a strong power network. Furthermore, only the B–D exchange relation breaks. Therefore, the network does not break into subnetworks. Although this new axiom satisfactorily resolves the anomaly of the Friedkin network, exploring its implications soon revealed other networks that challenged GPI analysis.

Heuristics in the Construction of Test Networks

To further examine the implications of GPI, we built up complex networks from simpler structures using heuristics about the way power develops through exchange (Willer and Willer 1995). When predictions of the heuristics and predictions of an established theoretical formulation differed for a given network, we simulated the network using the X-Net program. In all cases so far, the X-Net simulator and analysis using the following heuristics agree. In reading the heuristics, it should be remembered that "low power positions" and "high power positions" occur only in strong power networks.

Heuristic 1: Adding a relation between a low power position and a high power position does not change the type of power (strong versus weak) of any position in the network.

Heuristic 2: Adding a relation between two high power positions does not change the type of power of any position in the network.

Heuristic 3: Adding a relation between two low power positions creates a weak or equal power structure or substructure.

Heuristic 4: Adding a relation between weak or equal power positions cannot create a strong power structure.

Heuristic 5: Breaks occur between high power positions or between high power positions and equal or weak power positions, not between equal or weak power positions.

(Cf. Willer and Willer 1995 for heuristics 1, 2 and 3.)

These heuristics have proven to be powerful tools for the development of theory beyond the current empirical knowledge base. We must caution, however, that they are neither deduced from the theory nor empirically inducted. They most closely resemble conjectures in the mathematical sense, theorems yet to be proved.

Our explorations discovered many networks for which GPI analysis produced repeating cycles of subnetworks that would not allow classification of positions as strong power in any simple way, even though simulation and heuristic analysis suggested that strong power was present. Thus, further analysis of the problem yielded a refinement of the GPI analysis called Iterative GPI. The method decomposes networks into strong power, weak power, and equal power components. The heuristics, computer simulation, and the empirical knowledge base serve as checks on the method's results in particular cases.

Iterative GPI

The general method for iterating GPI to decompose complex networks uses the following seven rules:

1. Iterate GPI using the new exchange-seek assumption until a stable solution—wherein GPI values of all positions remain the same in two consecutive iterations—or a repeating cycle of solutions emerges. A stable solution ends analysis.

2. (a) For a stable solution, inequalities between connected positions indicate strong power.

   (b) For a repeating cycle of solutions, draw the network that includes all relations across iterations in the cycle with two exceptions: (i) Breaks that occur in every iteration of a repeating cycle are considered permanent and are not redrawn. And, (ii) when a position has a GPI advantage over other connected positions in every iteration of a repeating cycle, the advantaged and disadvantaged positions form a strong power component that breaks off permanently. Then, reiterate GPI on the redrawn network until a stable solution or repeating cycle of solutions appears.

Figure 10.2
7p40 Network

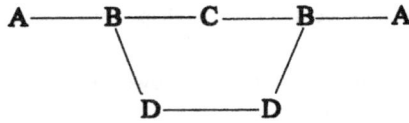

3. Reapply rule 2. Continue until the redrawn network is identical to the previous step's redrawn network or until a repeating cycle of redrawn networks appears.

Rules 1–3 above identify many strong power structures in exchange networks.[1] However, computer simulation reveals that some structures harbor strong power differences not identified by the first three rules. For example, consider the 7p40 network of Figure 10.2. (We started labeling networks sequentially for each size. 7p40 is the 40th network with seven positions.)

Because all positions in the 7p40 network have GPI values of 1, the network appears to be equal power and no breaks are predicted. However, computer simulation and our heuristics tell a different and convincing story. The *B* positions in the L5, *A–B–C–B–A*, are high strong power. In addition, each *B* is connected to one member of the *D–D* dyad. Our heuristics tell us that *D* actors will initiate a break from the *B* actors. *D* actors will prefer to exchange equally with each other rather than exchange at a disadvantage with the *B*s. In turn, *B* actors are indifferent to exchange with *D* actors because they have low power alternatives to exploit. X-Net simulation shows two *B–C* breaks, and the *B*s have a strong power advantage over *A*s and *C*.

The following rules 4–7 decompose networks such as 7p40 that have strong power hidden within them. The rules work by breaking down networks to their core structures to assure that no lurking potential for strong power remains undetected.

4. Look for a "stem-dyad" in all networks and subnetworks that have not been identified as strong power. A stem-dyad is a position of degree 1 (i.e., connected to only one other actor) and the position connected to it. The position connected to the degree 1 position has the potential to be high power. We call the degree 1 position the low power position and the other position the high power position in the stem-dyad.

5. Remove the stem-dyad from the network and examine the residual network.

6. (a) If the residual is strong power and the high power position in the stem can reconnect to a low power position in the residual, then the original structure is strong power.

   (b) If the residual is strong power and the high power position in the stem can reconnect only to high power positions in the residual, then the stem breaks from the residual as an equal power dyad.

   (c) If the residual breaks into strong and weak power components and the high power position in the stem connects to a low strong-power position in the residual, then the network breaks where the residual breaks.

7. For remaining structures not identified as strong power, reapply steps 4–6. Continue until no stem-dyads remain attached to a larger structure not yet identified as strong power. Then reconnect all relations among structures not identified as strong power.

Applying these rules to the 7p40 network gives the following analysis. Removing the *A–B* stem-dyad results in a five-actor T structure that we know breaks into a strong power 3-Line and a dyad (Markovsky et al. 1988). By rule 6c and symmetry, 7p40 breaks into a five-actor line and a dyad.

The Iterative GPI method solves a fundamental, though narrow, problem in network exchange theory. Rules 1–7 identify all strong power structures in networks of six or fewer positions and in the 105 7-position networks thus far considered without finding predictions at odds with simulations or ILA below. Having identified and broken out strong power structures, remaining networks can be analyzed using the probability tree method explained in Chapters 5 and 7. Thus the method classifies the fundamental power type (strong, weak, or equal) of all positions. Exact resource point predictions at equilibrium can then be made using the method of Lovaglia et al. (1995), which is Chapter 7 of this volume.

Furthermore, the heuristics developed as tools in the solution have general implications. For example, in exchange networks it seems impossible to gain a strong power advantage by opening channels of exchange to weak or equal power network members. Strong power can only be achieved by cutting off the alternative exchange opportunities of one's partners as in political oppression, or by establishing new connections to isolated individuals outside the network as in colonization.

Rules for the Iterative Likelihood Analysis (ILA)

At one point in the development of Iterative GPI, the problem seemed intractable. The difficulty prompted search for a solution that did not use the path-counting algorithm of the GPI. We found the alternative solution by extending the exchange-seek likelihood analysis given in Chapters 5 and 7, which was previously used only to determine the extent of weak power. First, we show that strong and weak power cannot be distinguished by differences of exchange-seek likelihoods between positions. Then we introduce the rules for ILA.

The Stem in Figure 10.3.b is known to be weak power, whereas the *A–B–C–B–A* L5 is known to be strong power. The *A–B* relation in the Stem is weak power because B does not have a surplus of lower power positions to exploit. Said somewhat differently, the *B*'s only alternative to exchanging with *A* is exchanging at equal power with one of the *C*s. So the *A* need offer only enough more than an equal power division to entice *B* away from exchange with one of the *C*s. But the conditions in L5 are entirely different. The *B*s need never be excluded. Either one of the As or the C must be excluded. To avoid exclusion, the three low power positions make better and better offers to the Bs who eventually garner maximum profit.

Nevertheless, the strong power versus weak power difference between relations in these two networks cannot be found by the size of li values or by the size of differences of li values between exchanging positions. In both cases the B(s) are never excluded: $l_B = 1$. In the Stem $l_A = .60$, but in L5 $l_A = .69$ and $l_C = .63$! These values mean that the A in the weak power Stem is *more likely to be excluded* than any of the low power positions in L5. Yet the A in the Stem gains much better deals than the As and C in L5. Therefore, strong and weak power differences cannot be differentiated by the size of li differences between positions.

The ILA rules that follow may appear complicated. In fact, each rule involves only simple procedures and is easily formalized in a computer program that automates application of the analysis.

A. Apply the exchange-seek likelihood analysis to the network as a whole in the first iteration or on identified substructures—if any—in subsequent iterations.

1. Potential low power positions have $l < 1$ and are connected only to positions with $l = 1$.

2. Potential high power positions have $l = 1$ and must be connected to at least two potential low power positions that satisfy 1 above.

3. Potential low power positions must be connected to at least one potential high strong power position and to nothing but potential high power positions.

4. Potential strong power structures must contain only potential low power and potential high power positions, and must have more low than high power positions.

B. Break out potential strong power structures and break any relations that occur between potential high power positions to test for strong power.

C. Repeat steps A and B until structures remain unchanged from one iteration to the next.

1. Strong power structures contain only potential high and low power positions, and have more low than high strong power positions.

2. Reconnect all original relations among positions not in strong power structures. These are potential weak power structures.

D. Decompose complex potential weak power structures to detect concealed strong power.

1. Check to see if the network has at least one position with $l = 1.0$; if not, then use likelihood analysis one last time to determine relative weak power.

2. Remove from the network one position with $l = 1.0$ along with the position connected to it that has the lowest l.

3 (a). If the residual network is strong power and the removed $l = 1.0$ position can reconnect to a low power position in the residual, then the original network is strong power. (b) If the residual is strong power and the removed 1.0 position can reconnect

only to high power positions in the residual, then the Stem breaks from the residual as an equal power dyad. (c) If the residual breaks into strong and weak power components and the removed 1.0 position connects to a low strong-power position in the residual, then the network breaks in that manner once the Stem has been reconnected.

4. For remaining structures not identified as strong power, apply steps 1–3. Continue decomposing until the residual network becomes trivial. Reconnect all relations among weak power structures. Use likelihood analysis a final time on potential weak power structures to determine weak power differences among connected positions.

At this point in the analysis, the procedure in Lovaglia et al. (1995) can be applied to obtain exact predictions for the resources that different positions will acquire in weak power networks at equilibrium.

An example will help to clarify the details of applying iterative likelihood analysis to a network. Consider the seven-actor line, $F–G–H–I–H–G–F$. Line networks with an odd number of actors have been predicted to be strong power structures (Willer, Markovsky, and Patton 1989). This is a good example of the ILA method because differences in l between high and low power positions become smaller as the length of the line increases. Inclusion likelihoods for positions in the 7-Line network are given below:

$$F \ - \ G \ - \ H \ - \ I \ - \ H \ - \ G \ - \ F$$
$$.70 \quad 1.0 \quad .76 \quad .92 \quad .76 \quad 1.0 \quad .70$$

Note that for the high strong power, I, position $l = .92$, and for the low strong power position, H, $l = .76$. The difference in l between high and low strong power positions is only .16. Compare this to the weak power 4-Line where the difference in l between high and low power positions is larger, .25.

To apply Iterative Likelihood Analysis, start with rule 1a. It tells us that F is a potential low strong power position in the network because it is connected only to a position with $l = 1.0$. However, rule A2 says that G cannot be a high strong power position because it is connected to only one potential low strong power position, F. Rule A4 tells us the 7-Line is not a potential high strong power structure because it contains positions (G, H, I) which are neither potential low strong power nor potential high strong power. Iteration following rules B and C produces no change because there is no identified strong power substructure to break out. Rule D1 tells us to decompose the network to check for concealed strong power because $l = 1.0$ for position G. Rule D2 tells us to remove an F and a G position from one end of the 7-Line, leaving a residual network—in this case, the five-actor line. We apply ILA to the residual network and find that it is strong power by rules A, B, and C. Then following rule D3a, we note that the residual network is strong power, and the removed $l = 1.0$ position, G, will reattach to the low strong power position on the end of the residual 5-Line. By rule D3a, we conclude that the 7-Line is a strong power network.[2]

Iterative GPI analysis and ILA give us two theories to predict the relative power of positions in exchange networks. Both are sufficiently formal to be operationalized in a computer program.[3] Both successfully explain existing research results.

AN AUTOMATED THEORETICAL ANALYSIS

In an automated theoretical analysis, a computer program generates test networks and applies the computer models of two or more theories to generate predictions for the test case. The program compares the exchange predictions of the two theories. When predictions of any pair of theories differ for a given network, a *strategic network* has been located. Such strategic networks have previously required years to discover. For example, Friedkin's Figure 10.1 network is a strategic network. Yet, in spite of ongoing research by numerous scholars using diverse approaches, seven years elapsed between the publication of the Markovsky et al. (1988) method and Friedkin's discovery of that network in 1995. Automation can cut that time to a few days, perhaps to a few hours.

The prerequisites of automated theoretical analysis are demanding, however. There must be (1) two or more competing theoretical models, both sufficiently formal that a computer can be programmed to make predictions in specific cases using them, and (2) a computer program to generate progressively more complex test networks on which to compare predictions of the competing theoretical models. Ideally, both theoretical models should explain the amassed body of empirical results. Little is gained by running unsuccessful theories through an automated theoretical analysis. Running two unsuccessful theories against each other does not usefully sort out strategic networks. Instead, we sort networks where the two theories' errors agree from networks where each theory is uniquely in error. Running one unsuccessful theory against a successful one will tell us little more. It will sort out a great many networks where the two theories disagree, but those networks have no general significance.[4]

It is unusual that two successful theories of similar scope will coexist after decades of cumulative research, so it is fortunate that we now have four NET theories. Two were presented here: Iterative GPI and Iterative Likelihood Analysis. In addition, we have Markovsky's (1995) X-Net simulation program and the Optimal-Seek procedure given in Part 2 of this chapter. We are also interested in running three other formulations through the automated analysis: Burke's (1997) identity model, Friedkin's (1992, 1993, 1995) expected value model, and Fararo and Hummon's (1994) discrete event simulator.

Beyond having at least two theories to compare, the key to the automated analysis is a program that generates only unique networks. The number of unique network configurations grows rapidly with the number of positions, but the number of isomorphic variants of each network configuration grows more rapidly still. For example, consider the three-actor line, *A–B–C*. One isomorphic variant is *A–C–B*, another is *C–B–A*. With networks larger than about seven positions, the number of isomorphic variants becomes astronomical. Even fast computers would not be able to analyze all networks of a reasonable size if isomorphic variants were included. John Skvoretz solved this problem using the method described by Read (1978) and has developed a working prototype program. The program systematically generates all networks with a given number of positions and excludes isomorphic variants, leaving a unique example of each network configuration.

CONCLUSION

We have traced a line of recent work that began when problems developed for GPI. GPI has long been a core procedure of NET, and once its faults were found, a solution was imperative. The line of work that began when Friedkin found GPI's shortcomings has had three results recounted here. We have developed not one but two procedures intended to solve the problems of GPI. Of the two, Iterative GPI directly attacks the problems found and adds new procedures to GPI to solve them. ILA, the Iterative Likelihood Analysis, dispenses with GPI by extending the exchange-seek analysis backwards to find strong power structures and substructures. Having two plausible theoretic procedures in hand, we needed a method to select between them. Thinking about that method led to the automated theoretic analysis.

Work on automatic theoretical analysis is beginning as this chapter is being written. No results are yet forthcoming. But the overall design of the Analyzer is clear; it finds strategic networks by generating all unique networks of size *n* or smaller to which two or more theoretic procedures are applied. Strategic networks, for which the theoretic procedures give different solutions, are sorted out by the Analyzer for further study.

In the future, new automated theoretical analyses may find application in other areas of sociology. As computer modeling becomes increasingly sophisticated, models of behavior in stratification, mobility, demography, and collective action can be compared using the large databases accumulated over years of study. The goal would be to find strategic cases which, like the strategic networks found here, are theoretically significant.

Part 2: A New Method for Finding Power Structures
Brent Simpson and David Willer

INTRODUCTION

Competition among rival theories has been crucial to the advances of Network Exchange Theory. This is especially apparent in Friedkin's (Personal Communication) demonstration that the theory's Graph-theoretic Power Index does not offer unique predictions for some networks. In Part 1 of this chapter, Lovaglia et al. propose both an extension and an alternative to GPI called Iterative GPI and Iterative Likelihood Analysis. Motivated by the problems discovered by Friedkin, and Lovaglia et al.'s proposed solutions, we offer Optimal-Seek, a new method for locating breaks and finding power structures. As in Iterative Likelihood Analysis, GPI is dropped altogether. We propose the Optimal-Seek method because (1) although Lovaglia et al.'s modifications solve the problems discovered by Friedkin as well as an array of further problems, the changes cost the theory its simplicity, and (2) despite the increased predictive power of the theory, there remain comparatively simple networks for which Iterative GPI and Iterative Likelihood Analysis do not give accurate predictions.

In establishing an alternative to Iterative GPI, we seek the simplest theory that can accurately find breaks and predict exchange ratios. By dispensing with GPI, we reduce the number of procedures used by Network Exchange Theory from three to two: as shown in later sections, only the Exchange-Seek Likelihood procedure and "resistance equations" (Willer 1981, 1987; Lovaglia et al. 1995b) are needed. To replace GPI, we extend the functions of the Exchange-Seek Likelihood procedure. Then we show how it is superior to Iterative GPI and Iterative Likelihood Analysis emphasizing parsimony and precision. (As stated in Part 1 of this chapter, Iterative GPI and Iterative Likelihood Analysis give the same predictions at least through networks of six or fewer nodes. Thus, for brevity, we can confine our comparisons to Iterative GPI.) In addition, our Optimal-Seek method uncovers power phenomena unrecognized by prior formulations of exchange network theories.[5]

Although Optimal-Seek extends the functions of the Exchange-Seek Likelihood procedure, it does not change how Exchange-Seek predicts exchange ratios in weak power networks. (For weak power networks, we predict exchange ratios using either the RD or li^2 method of Chapter 7.) After offering new definitions for strong, weak, and equal power networks, we show how the Exchange-Seek Likelihood procedure differentiates the three types. Then we use the Exchange-Seek Likelihood procedure to differentiate "optimal relations" from "suboptimal relations." These two extensions allow us to develop the Optimal-Seek method, a development that is grounded in six hypotheses. All six hypotheses are supported by evidence given later.

FINDING TYPES OF POWER IN NETWORKS

The Exchange-Seek Likelihood procedure (hereafter ESL) was developed to predict power differences in "weak power networks" and to differentiate weak power from networks where power is equal in all relations. Here we offer new definitions for the three network types and show how ESL can be used to differentiate strong power networks from the other two.

Strong power structures are networks that contain two and only two types of positions: one or more high power positions which are never excluded and two or more low power positions, at least one of which must be excluded; low power positions are only connected to high power positions. High power positions can be connected to each other or to other kinds of positions, but, for the latter, relations extend outside the strong power structure (see below).

ESL easily identifies strong power structures. For all high power positions l_i = 1.0, and for all low power positions $l_i < 1.0$. All $l_i < 1.0$ positions are connected only to $l_i = 1.0$ positions. Therefore, all paths through strong power structures have alternating $l_i < 1.0$ and $l_i = 1.0$ positions. Strong power structures and the strong power components of larger structures can be found by tracing those paths. Since low power positions are connected only to high power positions, resource divisions move to the extreme: Low power positions, seeking to avoid exclusion, make better and better offers to high power positions, or high power positions make greater and greater demands of low power positions or both.

Equal power structures are networks in which all positions have identical l_i values. There are two kinds of equal power networks central to concerns here, and ESL easily identifies both. First, there are equal power networks in which all positions are always included ($l_i = l_j = 1.0$). These include dyads and all-to-all networks with even numbers of positions. There are also equal power networks in which all positions face exclusion with some—identical—likelihood ($l_i = l_j < 1.0$). In an A, B, C triangle in which each position is connected to

Figure 10.3
Weak Power Networks

a. L4

b. Stem

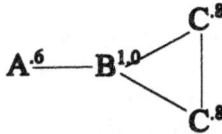

c. DBox

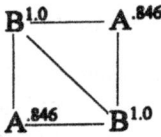

d. Kite

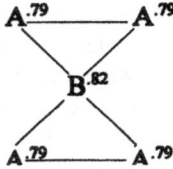

every other position, one must be excluded. Yet all positions must be power equals because they have exactly the same l_i values.

Networks that do not satisfy ESL conditions for strong or equal power networks are weak power. There are two types of weak power networks, and l_i differentiates them. In Type 1 at least one position is never excluded ($l_i = 1$), but other positions face exclusion with some likelihood ($l_j < 1$). The L4, Stem, and Dbox of Figure 10.3 are Type 1 weak power. In Type 2 weak power networks, all positions face the possibility of exclusion ($l_i < 1$) but not all with the same likelihood ($l_i \neq l_j$ for some i and j). The Figure 10.3d (Kite) network is a Type 2 weak power network.

Weak power is the only network type that contains both differential power and equal power relations. For example, the Bs in the L4 network of Figure 10.3a are never excluded, but the As are excluded when the Bs exchange with each other. As and Bs do not exchange equally because their negotiations are affected by the likelihood of being excluded. But the Bs have identical l_i values so they must exchange equally.

USING ESL TO FIND SUBOPTIMAL RELATIONS

In this section we show that the ESL procedure locates all suboptimal relations in the network being analyzed. Suboptimal relations are used to find breaks in the sections to follow. A relation is suboptimal iff exchanging in that relation necessarily reduces the number of exchanges from the maximum possible for the network. Interestingly, ESL was not developed to find suboptimal relations. It is fortuitous, but not accidental, that it does so.

The ESL procedure was given earlier in this volume for two weak power networks: in Chapter 5 for Stem (Figure 5.4) and Chapter 7 for L4 (Figure 7.1). As anticipated in the definition of strong power structures, ESL also applies to networks with strong power components. As will be remembered, ESL assumes that actors seek exchange randomly among those to which they are connected. Then l_i is i's relative proportion of mutual exchange seeks—the likelihood that i will be included; $1 - l_i$ is the likelihood that i will be excluded. l_i indicates the relative strength of a position and is not intended to predict the frequency with which i exchanges with other positions (Markovsky 1992; Markovsky et al. 1993; Lovaglia et al. 1995b).

An important quality of any ESL tree is that each branch is a series of consequential events, tracing from priors to all exchange events yet possible. For example, in Figure 10.4a, the top branch begins with the $B–A_1$ exchange and also includes the $C–D$ exchange. The tracing of events assumes, once B and A_1 exchange, that C and D will continue to seek partners until they link up. Taken as a whole, the ESL tree gives all joint events possible for the networks.

Since the ESL tree gives all possible joint events, it is not accidental that it gives all suboptimal relations. To find suboptimal relations, simply compare the number of exchange events across branches. Suboptimal branches have fewer exchanges, and the suboptimal relations in them are those that do not occur in any optimal branch. In Figure 5.4 it is seen that the Stem has two suboptimal relations, $B–C_1$ and $B–C_2$. In Figure 7.1, it is seen that the L4 has one suboptimal relation, $B_1–B_2$. In Figure 10.4a it is seen that the T network has one suboptimal relation, $B–C$, while the tree diagram of Figure 10.4b shows that the T' has no suboptimal relations.

LOCATING NETWORK BREAKS

To formulate the Optimal-Seek method, we must know the general qualities of breaks in networks; what kind of positions are divided by breaks and what kind of relations divide them. Relations in which rational actors have no interest in exchanging are said to break. Using a rational actor model and the typology introduced above, we now show that all such relations connect strong high power positions and positions that are never excluded. These inferences give testable hypotheses. Having found the conditions for breaks, we show that all breaks occur in suboptimal relations, but not all suboptimal relations necessarily break.

Rational actors always select their best offers and always prefer any offer to being excluded. Let i be rational and related to j plus k_n positions where $n \geq 1$. i will not exchange with j iff (1) k's offers are better than j's and (2) i is never excluded in the i–k_n relations. Since k's offers are better, j must be higher in power than k (i.e., $Pj > Pk$). Then i is never excluded in the network containing i and k_n iff (a) i is high power and the network is a strong power structure, or (b) i is highest power for a Type 1 weak power structure, or (c) i is in an equipower network where no position is excluded. That i is never excluded implies that i is never less than equal power with k (i.e., $Pi \geq Pk$). It follows that there are three power inequalities for which i and j will not exchange: (1) $\{Pj = Pi > Pk\}$, (2) $\{Pj > Pi > Pk\}$ and (3) $\{Pj > Pi = Pk\}$. Thus, if j is a strong high power position, three hypotheses exhaust the inequalities:

- H_1: If i and j are strong high power positions, they will not exchange: the network breaks at the i–j relation.
- H_2: If j is strong high power and i is the highest power position in a Type 1 weak power network, they will not exchange: the network breaks at the i–j relation.
- H_3: If j is strong high power and i is not excluded in an equal power network, they will not exchange: the network breaks at the i–j relation.

We now show for all three hypotheses above that the breaks are suboptimal. In strong power components, low power positions are connected only to high power positions. Therefore, the number of exchanges in any strong power component is the sum of the exchange opportunities across the high power positions. As hypothesized, let j be high power and i never excluded in relations with k_n. Make a compound network by connecting i to j and let the two exchange. Now there is one less exchange in the strong power component, and one exchange is precluded in the i–k_n component. Thus the one i–j exchange reduces the maximum number of exchanges of the compound network by two: the i–j exchange is suboptimal.

An exhaustive test of the rational actor model when a high power j is assumed requires two more hypotheses. First, the assertion that i will not exchange with j iff (1) k's offers are better than j's and (2) i is never excluded in the i–k_n relations also implies that, if j is strong high power and i is excluded in the i–k_n relations, the two will exchange. For this implication two hypotheses are exhaustive:

- H_4: If j is strong high power and i is ever excluded in a weak power network, they will exchange: the network does not break at the i–j relation.
- H_5: If j is strong high power and i is excluded in an equal power network, they will exchange: the network does not break at the i–j relation.

Hypotheses 4 and 5 are analogous to Hypotheses 2 and 3, but the lower power position is excluded and no breaks occur. Since high power positions are never excluded, there is no analogue to Hypothesis 1. Therefore, given a strong high power j, the above statements are exhaustive.

Now assume that j is not a strong high power position. Since j is higher in power than k, j must be a higher power position in a weak power network. But since i is not excluded, it must hold the highest power possible in the weak power component. Thus two inequalities, $\{Pj > Pi > Pk\}$ and $\{Pj > Pi = Pk\}$ are precluded. The remaining inequality, $\{Pj = Pi > Pk\}$, satisfies the conditions. The weak power x–j–i–k (L4) illustrates the inequality; j and i are equal in power, always included, and higher in power than k (and x). Furthermore, the i–j relation is suboptimal. At issue now is whether breaks occur in weak power networks like L4.

In order to determine whether weak power networks break, we must know whether the "network game" is played once or is repeated. The rational actor model asserts that, if the x–j–i–k game occurs only once, i's strategy space is restricted to two options: exchange at equal power with j or at equal or greater power with k. Let k prefer to offer i at least ε more than an equal power rate to any chance of being excluded. Therefore k's offer to i is better than j's offer to i, i and k exchange, and the suboptimal j–i exchange does not occur.

When the x–j–i–k network game is repeated, however, the strategy space for all actors is expanded by cross-game strategies.[6] Now if lower power x and k offer only ε more than the equal power division, i–j exchanges will impose large costs on the excluded k and x, leading them to raise their offers in future rounds. As shown in experiments by Thye et al. (1997), excluded actors adjust offers upward, producing power differences of the type discussed here. Thus, over a series of rounds, i can earn more by occasionally exchanging with j, which implies that there are conditions in which i–j exchanges are rational and will occur. Since network exchange experiments are repeated games, we conclude that:

- H_6: Weak power networks do not break.

Apparently, Bienenstock and Bonacich disagree with Hypothesis 6. In applying the core, they assert that no suboptimal relations are used, including those in weak power networks like the L4 (1993, p. 129; Bonacich and Bienenstock 1995, pp. 299–300). Driving the core's prediction is a group rationality postulate which asserts that total reward is maximized. This maximization requires that the optimum number of exchanges be made in each game, or round. In the L4 network, if j and i exchange, only 24 points flow through the network, but 48 points are distributed throughout the network if x exchanges with i and j with k. The core predicts only the latter configuration will occur, and similarly for other weak power networks containing suboptimal relations.[7]

OPTIMAL-SEEK VERSUS ITERATIVE GPI: THEORETICAL COMPARISONS

We now outline the Optimal-Seek procedure and test the method against Iterative GPI. Using only ESL to locate breaks and find power structures, Optimal-Seek is informed by the proofs of the previous section: all breaks occur at suboptimal relations that connect high power positions in strong power networks to positions in networks where they are never excluded. The steps of the Optimal-Seek method are:

1. Apply ESL to find (a) strong, weak, and equal power components, and (b) suboptimal relations. If no suboptimal relations are found, use ESL values to predict weak power exchange ratios (and stop).
2. Remove all suboptimal relations that connect high power positions to positions outside the strong power component. Recalculate ESL for the resultant subnetworks.
3. A suboptimal relation is a break iff the outside position is never excluded after the relation is removed. A suboptimal relation is not a break if the outside position is excludable after the relation is removed.[8]

We now demonstrate the method for several networks.

Consider first the T network of Figure 10.4a for which the predictions of Optimal-Seek and Iterative GPI do not differ. Both agree with GPI as originally given in Markovsky et al. (1988), which is Chapter 4. We now show how the break in the T network is found without reference to GPI's Axioms. Note that all branches of the ESL tree given in Figure 10.4a have two exchanges but for the $B \times C$ branch where only one exchange occurs. Since the $B \times C$ event does not occur in any two-exchange branch, the B–C relation is suboptimal. Next we determine whether the T network has a strong power component. Remember that, in strong power structures, low power positions ($l_i < 1.0$) are connected only to high power positions for which ($l_i = 1.0$). This finds A–B–A as T's only strong power component.

The high power B of the A–B–A strong power component is connected by a suboptimal relation to C. Remove that relation. Because C and D are now identically connected in the dyad, they are equal power and not excluded. We need not recalculate l_i for them to infer that the B–C relation is a break. ESL need not be recalculated for the A–B–A strong power structure either. Since it is already known to be a strong power structure, the exercise of power is predicted to go to the maximum favoring B and independent from the exact values calculated for l_A.

Now consider a similar structure, the T' network (Figure 10.4b), for which Optimal-Seek and Iterative GPI offer competing predictions. First consider Optimal-Seek's predictions. Note that all branches in the ESL analysis have two exchange events and none fewer, indicating that T' has no suboptimal relations. A–B–A is the strong power component. Remember that, in strong power struc-

Figure 10.4
Exchange-Seek Likelihoods Applied to T and T' Networks

a) ESL Tree for the T Network

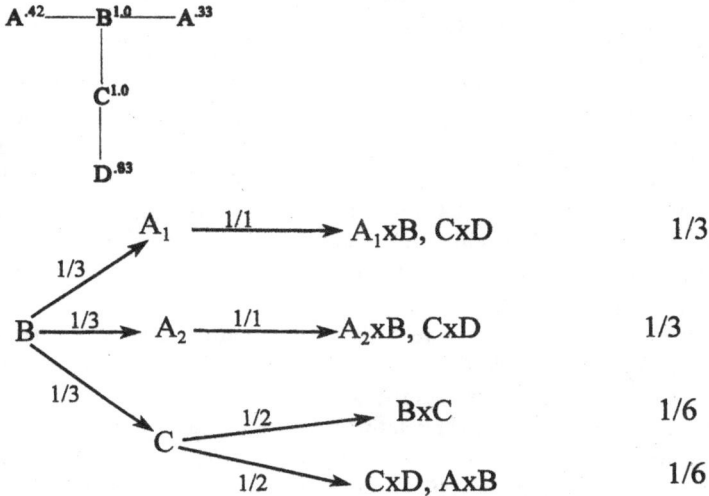

b) ESL Tree for the T' Network

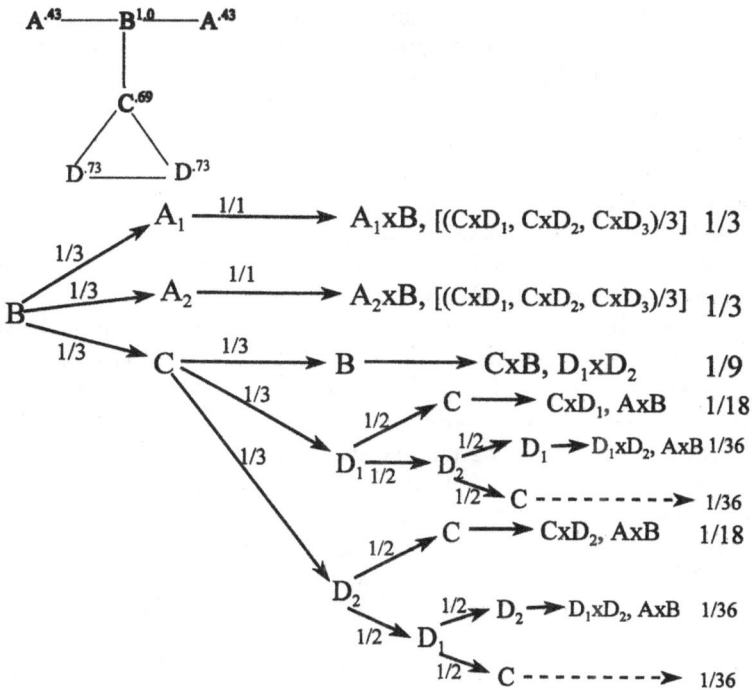

tures, low power positions are connected only to high power positions. Because C is also connected to the Ds, it is not a part of the strong power component. (Stated differently, only B's relations to the As make B a high power position.)

C faces exclusion when exchanging only with the Ds. Since rational actors prefer exchange at any rate to exclusion, C will exchange with B. But to do so, C's offers to B must be competitive with As' offers to the B; a rational B will not accept anything less than going rates. C also exchanges in the equal power triad with the two Ds. Thus application of Optimal-Seek predicts that there will be B–C exchanges at exchange rates like B–A exchanges and C–D exchanges at rates different from B–C exchanges. Conversely, Iterative GPI asserts that, since $GPI_C = GPI_D < GPI_B$, C will seek exchange with the Ds (and never with B) and the B–C relation will break. Said differently, Iterative GPI predicts the network will break into two independent subnetworks: a strong power 3-Line and an equal power triad.

Experiment outcomes provide support for Optimal-Seek over Iterative GPI for the T' network. The B–C relation does not break. Nine groups were run on the T' network.[9] The Ds exchanged with each other .439 of the time. As predicted, instead of breaking off relations with B, C avoids the exclusion threatened in the D, D, C triad by exchanging with B. When the Ds exchanged with each other, C exchanged with B .215 of the time. A z-test for proportions shows that this proportion is significantly different than zero ($p < .001$).[10] Thus experiments support Optimal-Seek over Iterative GPI.

Experiments also support Optimal-Seek's prediction that C's earnings in exchanges with B will be significantly different from earnings in exchanges with D. In the experiments, C averaged 5.48 when exchanging with B, which was not significantly different from the 4.84 averaged by the As ($t = .31$, NS). But C averaged 12.39 when exchanging with Ds, which is significantly different from C's earnings when exchanging with B ($t = 4.16$, $p < .01$). By breaking the network, Iterative GPI overlooks a crucial characteristic of the T' network and single-domain networks in general; positions may exchange at significantly different rates in different relations. Previously, disparate earnings for positions in different relations were observed only in multiple exchange networks with distinct "domains" (see Chapter 4). Thus, by discovering them in 1-exchange networks at relations previously believed to break, Optimal-Seek offers a useful scope extension to Network Exchange Theory.

Finally, consider Iterative GPI's and Optimal-Seek's solutions to the Figure 10.2 network. After applying the first three "rules" of Iterative GPI, all positions have $GPI = 1$ (see Lovaglia et al.; this chapter). But, as noted by Lovaglia et al., notwithstanding the identity of GPI values, the network is a composite of two well-known parts, a strong power 5-Line and an equal power dyad, and the two should break. To break this network at the B–D relations, Iterative GPI adds four additional steps, each of which further complicates the application of the theory.

Optimal-Seek arrives at the same conclusion but with fewer steps: Initial calculation of ESL gives the following values: $l_A = .52$, $l_B = 1.0$, $l_C = .52$, $l_D = .85$ and finds both $B-D$ relations are suboptimal. Both $B-D$ relations are removed and ESL is recalculated, revealing the $A-B-C-B-A$ strong power component and the $D-D$ equal power dyad. Since the Bs are strong high power and neither D is ever excluded, both $B-D$ relations are found to be breaks and the application is complete. Where seven rules must be applied iteratively to find the breaks using Iterative GPI, Optimal-Seek needs three steps. Furthermore, the steps of Optimal-Seek never iterate.

TESTING THE NETWORK BREAK HYPOTHESES

In this section we offer tests of Optimal-Seek's six hypotheses.

- Hypothesis 1: If i and j are strong power positions, they will not exchange: the network breaks at the $i-j$ relation.

The Figure 10.5a Double-Branch is the simplest network which tests the hypothesis. Applying ESL finds the $B-B$ relation suboptimal, $l_B = 1.0$ and $l_A = .50$. Since excludable As are connected only to positions never excluded, the two $A-B-A$ branches are strong power structures: the $B-B$ suboptimal relation is predicted to break. Table 10.1 reports the observed proportion of $B-B$ exchanges against a predicted value of 0 and tests for differences using a z-test for proportions. The observed proportion of .007 is not significantly different than zero. Thus we accept Hypothesis 1 and conclude that relations which connect high power positions will break.

- Hypothesis 2: If j is strong high power and i is the highest power position in a Type 1 weak power network, they will not exchange: the network breaks at the $i-j$ relation.

Consider the Branch-minus-L4 given in Figure 10.5b. ESL finds both $B-C$ relations suboptimal and recognizes B as high power in the strong power $A-B-A$ branch. Therefore, removing the two $B-C$ relations and reapplying ESL gives $l_C = 1.0$ and $l_D = .75$, confirming that the Cs are not excluded in the L4 component. As shown in Table 10.1, the proportion of $B-C$ exchanges, .031, is not significantly greater than zero. The $B-C$ relations are breaks. We accept Hypothesis 2 and conclude that breaks occur between strong high power positions and the highest power positions in Type 1 weak power networks.[11]

- Hypothesis 3: If j is strong high power and i is not excluded in an equal power network, they will not exchange: the network breaks at the $i-j$ relation.

The Figure 10.5c Branch-minus-dyad tests Hypothesis 3. Applying ESL again gives the strong power $A-B-A$ branch and finds both $B-C$ relations suboptimal. This network is an excellent test for the Optimal-Seek method. Initially $l_C = $

Figure 10.5
Networks That Break

a) Double-Branch

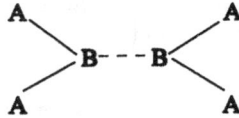

b) Branch-minus-L4

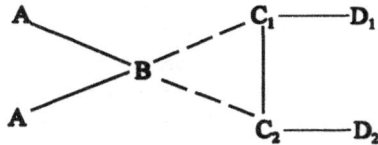

c) Branch-minus-dyad

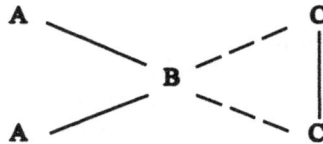

.857; the Cs can be excluded in the composite Branch-Dyad network. Nevertheless, the Optimal-Seek method removes both suboptimal $B–C$ relations, finding that $C–C$ is an equal power dyad in which neither C is ever excluded. Results in Table 10.1 support Hypothesis 3: the proportion of $B–C$ exchanges, .053, is not significantly greater than zero.

• Hypothesis 4: If j is strong high power and i is ever excluded in a weak power network, they will exchange: the network does not break at the $i–j$ relation.

Table 10.1
Suboptimal Relations That Are Predicted to Break

Structure	N	Relation	Predicted	Observed Frequency (Proportion)	p
Double-Branch	27[a]	B - B	0	(.007)	NS
Branch-minus-L4	27[b]	B - C	0	(.031)	NS
Branch-minus-Dyad	45[c]	B - C	0	(.053)	NS

[a]The 27 periods were obtained from nine groups participating in three periods, each consisting of 15 negotiation-rounds. Subjects were rotated through positions at the conclusion of each period.
[b]The 27 periods were obtained from nine groups participating in three periods, each consisting of 10 negotiation-rounds. Subjects were rotated through positions at the conclusion of each period.
[c]The 45 periods were obtained from nine groups participating in five periods, each consisting of 10 negotiation-rounds. Subjects were rotated through positions at the conclusion of each period.

The Figure 10.6 Branch-plus-L4 tests the hypothesis. The Optimal-Seek method first applies ESL to the initial network, showing that B–C relations are suboptimal and revealing the strong power A–B–A component. Remove the two suboptimal B–C relations and apply ESL to the 4-Line, which finds that $l_D = 1.0$ and $l_C = .75$. Since the Cs are excluded, the B–C relations are not predicted to break and they are restored to the network. The rational actor model asserts that since the Cs will gain more favorable rates when exchanging with Ds than B, each will first seek exchange with its D. But if the Ds exchange with each other, the Cs face exclusion. Rational actors prefer any offer to exclusion and will therefore seek exchange with B. As shown in Table 10.2, when the Ds exchange with each other, the Cs exchange with B .259 of the time, which is significantly greater than zero. Thus Hypothesis 4 is supported.

Like the C in the T' network (Figure 10.4b), the Cs in the Branch-plus-L4 exchange in two different kinds of power relations. Their relation to the B is strong power. Any offer that B accepts from either C must be competitive with As' offers; a rational B will not accept anything less than going-rates. Thus Cs' offers to B must not be unlike As' offers to B. But the Cs also exchange in weak power relations with the Ds. Since, as we have shown, these strong and weak power components have distinct exchange ratios, the Cs' exchanges with the strong high power B are predicted to be distinct from exchanges with the weak higher power Ds. In fact, the Cs' average 2.75 exchanging with B, which is not significantly different from the 1.97 averaged by the As ($t = .41$, NS), but C gains 10.73 exchanging with D, which is significantly different from its earnings when exchanging with B ($t = 4.53$, $p < .01$).

Figure 10.6
A Network That Does Not Break

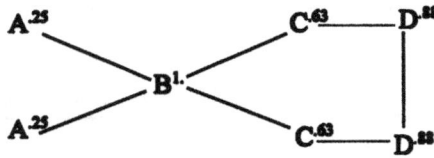

Table 10.2
Proportion of B–C Exchanges When Cs Are Threatened with Exclusion

Structure	N	D - D Exchanges Frequency (Proportion)	H_0 (Given D - D Exchange)	Observed B - C (Given D - D Exchange)	p
Branch-plus-L4	31[a]	(.177)	0	.259	< .001

[a] The 310 rounds were obtained from eight groups participating in four periods, each consisting of 10 negotiation-rounds. Subjects were rotated through positions at the conclusion of each period. A system failure in one of the groups resulted in the loss of 10 rounds.

• Hypothesis 5: If j is strong high power and i is excluded in an equal power network, they will exchange: the network does not break at the i–j relation.

This hypothesis was already tested and supported on the T' network. (See Figure 10.4b.) Those tests showed that the frequency of B–C exchanges was significantly greater than zero. Furthermore, C's resource divisions with B were like A–B divisions and unlike C's divisions with the Ds.

• Hypothesis 6: Weak power networks do not break.

Table 10.3 is offered as evidence. Hypothesis 6 was tested using three weak power structures: the Stem, D-Box, and L4 of Figure 10.3. All three weak power structures contain suboptimal relations, which we assert do not break. We test this hypothesis against the null hypothesis that no exchanges will occur at the suboptimal relations. (The null hypothesis is also the core's prediction.) Hypothesis 6 is supported for all three networks. Contrary to the core's prediction, exchanges do occur at suboptimal relations in weak power networks.

CONCLUSION

We have shown that efforts to overcome the difficulties associated with the Graph-theoretic Power Index (GPI) has led to an increasingly cumbersome procedure. Here we offer a method that preserves the useful understandings of

Table 10.3
Frequency of Exchange in Suboptimal Relations of Weak Power Networks

Structure	N	H_0	Observed	p
Stem	44	0	.170	$< .01$
D-Box	28	0	.152	$< .05$
L4	20	0	.175	$< .05$

Network Exchange Theory while reestablishing parsimony. At the same time, the method discovers power phenomena previously unrecognized by network exchange theories. Experimental support is offered for our method's assertion that, though all breaks are suboptimal, not all suboptimal relations necessarily break. This runs counter to the core's proposition that all suboptimal relations are breaks. In short, the head-to-head tests offered here support the new Optimal-Seek method over its competitors.

NOTES

1. A computer program for analyzing networks using these rules is available from John Skvoretz, Department of Sociology, University of South Carolina, Columbia, SC 29208.

2. A more complex network, the nine-actor line, would be decomposed in the same way. It would first be decomposed to a seven-actor line; from there by rule 4, the analysis is the same as for the seven-actor line.

3. Prototypes of both Iterative GPI and ILA computer programs are available on request from John Skvoretz. See note 1 for his address.

4. Automated theoretical analysis helps ensure that many of the criteria for good theory are met. For example, Cohen (1989) and Markovsky (1992) suggest the following criteria for scientific theories. Theories should be: (1) free of contradiction, (2) free of ambivalence, (3) communicable, (4) abstract, (5) general, (6) precise, (7) parsimonious, and (8) conditional. Programming theories usually free them of internal contradictions and ambivalence, and assure that they are communicable to anyone who uses the programming language. Furthermore, programming lends itself to parsimony.

5. In addition to Friedkin, the theory developed here owes much to Bienenstock and Bonacich (1993), who were the first to show that breaks can be found by removing "suboptimal relations," a technique also employed in our method. Their application of the core treats all suboptimal relations as breaks. But, as detailed below, Optimal-Seek disagrees, at least for the conditions under which exchange networks are normally investigated. Experimental support is offered in a later section.

6. The optimal strategy for a single game is not necessarily the optimal strategy for a repeated game. A well-known example of this distinction is found in the prisoner's dilemma game. When the prisoner's dilemma game is played only once, defection and not cooperation is rational. As a repeated game, conditional cross-game strategies such as tit-for-tat are possible.

7. Bienenstock and Bonacich may be implicitly assuming that the networks are played as a single game. If so, it may be that their predictions do not disagree with ours.

8. When excludable positions are reconnected to high power positions and ESL is recalculated, positions previously found to be nonexcludable may or may not retain that status. Nevertheless, the Optimal-Seek method does not produce oscillations. Consider the Figure 10.6 network, but now add exchange relations connecting both Ds to B. After calculating ESL for the initial network, the suboptimal $B–C$ and $B–D$ relations are removed. This leaves an L4 in which Cs, but not Ds, face exclusion. Since only the Cs can be excluded, the network is reconnected but only at the $B–C$ relations. After the reconnection, $l_D = .88$. However, we count this $l_D < 1$ as irrelevant because the Cs always prefer exchanging with Ds to exchanging with B. Because the Cs do not allocate their exchange seeks randomly, as assumed by ESL, the Ds are not threatened by exclusion. Therefore, it is sufficient for the $B–D$ break that the Ds not be excludable when the suboptimal relations are removed.

9. Each of the nine groups participated in four periods; each period consisted of 10 rounds of negotiations. To control for individual effects, subjects were rotated through network positions at the conclusion of each period.

10. Since the predicted proportion of exchanges is zero, a standard z-test for proportions would contain a zero in the denominator. To avoid division by zero, we treat the predicted value as the observed and vice versa. This means that we actually test the assertion that our prediction falls within the confidence limits of the observed.

11. Since the $C–C$ suboptimal relation does not have a high power position on either side, it should not break. A z-test for proportions confirms that the frequency of $C–C$ exchanges is significantly greater than zero ($p < .001$).

Chapter 11

Developing Network Exchange Theory

David Willer

INTRODUCTION

This chapter is focused on directions of development for Network Exchange Theory. For this exposition, there is one danger especially to be avoided: the foreshortened view. When one's day-to-day work is concerned with pushing theory forward one incremental derivation at a time, it is all too easy for vision to become myopic. When intellectual myopia sets in, the future shrinks down to the next derivation—the longer view is lost. In order to avoid the foreshortened view, this chapter begins with very general questions. What is a general theory of social structure? What is the point of departure for its development? Then the chapter moves to more immediate questions regarding directions for Network Exchange Theory development. Some of the immediate questions concern the next incremental derivations.

DYNAMICS AS A GENERAL THEORY OF STRUCTURE

Whereas the idea of social structure is at the core of sociology, for a long time that core had no theory. The idea of social structure which I have in mind is the understanding that society is composed of structured social relations, an idea that is reflected in the chapters of this volume. As seen in Chapter 1, Marx and Weber were the first to develop the understanding of society as structured social relations. Lacking a geometry, neither could draw diagrams of structures and, lacking diagrams, neither could develop theory formally.

Because diagrams for social structures were not drawn, by the middle of the twentieth century, the understanding of society as structured social relations was lost, at least to mainstream thinking. By then, the idea of social structure had become as varied as the scholars discussing it. Merton ([1949] 1968), Parsons ([1940] 1954), Nadel (1957), and Lévi-Strauss (1953) all had ideas about social structure. But they drew no diagrams and, therefore, formal theory did not develop. Only Heider drew diagrams (1946), and his were for cognitive structures. Yet only his work demonstrated what was possible when structures were actually drawn. The turning point came in 1965. Harary, Norman, and Cartwright's *Structural Models* joined other works on graph and network theory to give social science the geometry needed to represent social structure.[1] Without *Structural Models*, Network Exchange Theory could not have been developed.

In this section, I seek the point of departure from which a general theory for social structure can be developed. By a "general theory for social structure" I mean a theory that explains both the original development of social structures and their consequences. Of course, no social structure starts from nothing; all start from social structures that came before. Therefore, a theory of social structure links structure to structure over time. It is a theory of social structural dynamics. Network Exchange Theory is not currently a theory of social structural dynamics. It begins with a fixed structural configuration and infers its consequences on power outcomes.

Marx developed terms for social structural dynamics which are still helpful; social structures reproduce, or they are in transition. His idea of reproduction can be given the following meaning: a social structure reproduces when the structure at a later time is identical to its earlier form. A social structure is in transition when the structure at a later time is different from its earlier form. In Marx's theory the mode of inference was from structure at t_1 to structure at t_2.

Dividing Marx's mode of inference into two parts, we find that a general theory of structure must do two kinds of work: (1) it infers from structure at t_1 to resulting social conditions and (2) it infers, from social conditions, to structure at t_2. These can be called the two components of a general theory of structure. NET is the first of these components.[2] For example, from exclusively connected branches it infers that the central position will exercise power over the peripherals. The power exercise is the inferred social condition. Each of the studies included in this volume tested inferences from structure to resulting conditions. If NET can act as the first of the two components, we still need a theory for the second. A theory of structural dynamics must also infer from conditions to structure.

The goal of inferring from conditions to structures is not unknown to modern sociology. In fact, it was the goal of the social exchange perspective of Homans, Blau, and Emerson. As seen in Chapter 1, their avowed mode of inference was reductionist. They wanted to infer from the condition, "individuals' differential rates of satiation" to power structures. As seen in the first chapter, however, the reductionism of the social exchange perspective was falsified by Stolte and Emerson's first experiments. I will now show that, even if it could be rescued from falsification, the social exchange perspective cannot contribute to a general theory of structure.

At issue is whether structure at t_1 must be one of the conditions from which structure at t_2 is inferred. Because social exchange theory is reductionist, it must infer the structure at t_2 without including the t_1 structure at any point of the inference. To avoid reference to any prior structure, the social exchange perspective must assert either (1) that there is a time, t_1 at which no social structure exists or (2) that no structure existing at t_1 affects the behaviors that produce the later t_2 structure. But both assertions are assuredly wrong. Regarding the first, we know today that humans evolved as social animals.[3] Therefore, there has never been a t_1 for humans which was free of structured social relations. Regarding the second point, we know that behavior is always affected by the structured social relations in which it occurs. That behavior is always affected by structure is no longer a matter of opinion. Two decades of research—a portion of which is detailed in this volume—has detailed the effects of structure. Therefore, the reductionist approach is fundamentally flawed. It is not a useful point of departure from which to develop theory that infers from conditions to structure. A better point of departure is to work toward a theory that infers structure at t_2 from structure at t_1—toward a theory of structural dynamics.

Fortunately, we are not entirely ignorant of structural dynamics; some inferences can already be drawn. Consider the following problem. Assume a strong power structure with actors who are knowledgeable concerning the effects of structure. Allow these actors to periodically add new exchange relations to the structure. Can the resulting structure be inferred? Let us see.

1. Strong power structures contain only two kinds of positions, high power and low power. Exchange relations only connect across the two kinds of positons.

2. High power positions exchange only with low power positions and benefit greatly from such exchanges. Therefore, if any high power position is not connected to all low power positions, those connections will be added by the high power position. High power positions always prefer exchanging with low power positions to exchanging with each other. Therefore, no high power position will add an exchange relation to another high power position. As long as they are connected only to high power positions, low power positions will exchange with them, even though benefits to the low power positions are small.

3. Low power positions prefer any other exchange to an exchange with any high power position.[4] Therefore, all low power positions will add relations to each other. Adding a relation between any pair of low power positions will have one of two effects (Willer and Willer 1995). If, after the relation is added, the larger structure remains strong, the pair of connected actors will break off from that structure. The result is an isolated dyad in which the two exchange with each other at equal power. (Note that these equal power exchange outcomes are substantially more favorable to both actors than previous outcomes when the two were not connected.) Alternatively, the added relation may transform the larger structure from strong to weak or equal power. If so, no

break will occur. (Note again that exchange outcomes are substantially more favorable to the newly connected pair than they were when the structure was strong.)

4. As all low power positions connect to at least one other low power position, the structure can no longer be strong. Therefore, all breaks reconnect (Willer and Simpson 1997). Either the network is now equal power or there are weak power differences. If weak power, the two weakest positions will connect and exchange with each other to gain better deals than when exchanging in their other relations. When that relation is added, the power of the two weakest positions increases. This increase produces a new weakest pair which connects . . . and so on until the network is totally connected.[5]

Totally connected exchange networks are always equal power. Therefore, all strong power structures in which positions may add relations become equal power structures.

The solution to the foregoing problem has important implications for a theory of structural dynamics. A necessary condition for the reproduction of strong power structures is that low power positions have no alternative but to exchange with high power positions. Stated somewhat differently, strong power structures remain such only if their structural parameters are fixed. Structural parameters may be fixed by the environment.[6] If not, knowledgeable high power actors will seek to control them.

Examples abound of the control of structural parameters by the powerful. In the United States in the nineteenth century, factory owners successfully lobbied the federal government to place high prices on western lands. Land was then in far greater supply than demand. Without government price controls, land would have been effectively free. With free land, low power factory workers would have broken their exchange relations with high power capitalists and escaped to become farmers. But the high price of land blocked escape, and thus the power structure reproduced. Similarly, English laws of trespass can be traced to the industrial revolution. By denying land-use rights to others, owners eliminated alternatives to working in the mine and factory. And finally, without fugitive slave laws—the Dred Scott Case in the United States—slaves would have escaped and slavery could not have reproduced.

A general theory of structure, that is, a theory that deals with structural dynamics over time, now appears within reach. It is time to extend theory and, with that theory, to design research projects that will push NET toward a more complete comprehension of structural dynamics. Even today, without substantially extending NET, experiments can be designed to further our understanding of dynamics. For example, two similar laboratory structures can be designed, one that reproduces and the other that does not. In the first, an experiment is built in which relations can be freely added to a structure that is initially strong. A second experiment also begins with a strong power structure, but now adding a relation is costly. Let the cost of adding relations be adjusted so that only subjects in high power positions can afford to add them.

The dynamics of the two structures will be entirely different—even though the two are identical but for a single parameter, the cost of adding new relations. Following the earlier discussion, NET predicts that the first structure will be in transition, beginning strong and moving through weak power to equal power. For the second structure, high and not low power actors can add relations. NET predicts that the second structure will reproduce, remaining a strong power structure throughout the term of the experiment.

For the kind of structural dynamics considered here, reproduction and transition are inferred through power. In the second example structure, resources gained from power exercised in the structure at t_1 is itself the condition for producing the power structure at t_2. That is to say, the structure *reproduces itself*. Structures reproduce themselves, or are in transition, through their power relations. This is the same image for structural dynamics found in Marx and Weber, though now it is understood somewhat more formally. Certainly, this kind of structural dynamics is close at hand. With this in mind, let us turn to a major obstacle to broadening NET's scope, the experimental paradigm, and to the issues for investigation that require a new paradigm.

BREAKING OUT OF THE RESEARCH PARADIGM

The "research paradigm" used in most network exchange research up to now has biased the selection of issues for empirical investigation. This bias has moved research away from issues that can make the greatest contribution to expanding NET's scope. To investigate important new issues, NET must develop fundamentally new experimental designs.

The "research paradigm" is an experimental design in which (1) the configuration of exchange relations is fixed initially by the experimenter and cannot be altered by subjects' actions; (2) resource pool relations are substituted for exchange relations; (3) positions are routinely limited to maximally one exchange; (4) the value of all relations are the same; and (5) positions not connected by exchange relations cannot communicate. This is the research paradigm Stolte and Emerson developed and used in the first experimental study of exchange networks.[7] We owe much to them for developing the paradigm, for in using it, we have learned much about structure. The limitations of the paradigm discussed later in this chapter are not the fault of Stolte and Emerson. Rather, the faults can be attributed to the researchers following them who found it easier to slavishly follow than to innovate.

When an established experimental paradigm governs what will and will not be investigated, theory development becomes one-sided and research focuses on issues that have no importance or no known importance outside the laboratory.[8] Certainly, there are no social structures outside the laboratory which satisfy the five conditions just listed. Stolte–Emerson networks are quite artificial, but all experiments are to some degree artificial. At issue here is not artificiality alone, but whether a paradigm, which is avowedly artificial, is determining the direction of theory development and research.

When developing theory, only two criteria should govern the selection of new issues for investigation. Is the issue significant to the theory? Is the issue empirically significant? For much recent research, neither question can be well answered. For example, recently research has focused on weak power networks. But are they significant? Weak power networks offer a challenge to the theorist. Because the exchange ratios in them are difficult to predict, weak power networks pose more subtle problems for theory than do strong or equal power networks. Weak power networks are frequently encountered under Stolte–Emerson conditions. For example, fully one-half of all four node networks are weak power.

There is good reason to suppose that research has recently focused on weak power networks only because researchers use the Stolte–Emerson design. For the range of phenomena defined by that design, weak power is theoretically significant. But now look outside. Whereas weak power poses subtle problems for theory, the problems in theory posed by ''power-at-a-distance'' are at least as subtle. An example of power-at-a-distance is the exercise of power by A through B and C over D. But power-at-a-distance cannot be investigated within the Stolte–Emerson paradigm. Therefore, power-at-a-distance has long been ignored. Unlike weak power, there is no competition among theories predicting power-at-a-distance.

Now consider empirical significance. Are weak power networks empirically significant in the larger world outside the laboratory? No one has studied weak power networks in the field. Therefore, their empirical significance, even their empirical existence, is not known. By contrast, there is little doubt that power-at-a-distance occurs in large organizations every day and that it deeply affects our lives.

Studying Structural Dynamics

Because network structure is fixed initially by the experimenter, network dynamics cannot be studied within the confines of the Stolte–Emerson paradigm. The first step is to allow subjects to change the network structure—as in the examples analyzed earlier. But a thorough investigation of network dynamics will require changes beyond allowing relations to be added or subtracted by subjects. At issue is not just dynamics but the kind of relations that are dynamic.

Control of exchange structures through coercion by high power actors is an important condition for reproducing strong exchange structures. In an example given earlier, workers were kept in low power positions in factories by the U.S. government's coercive power to set high prices on western lands. More generally, for strong power structures to remain so, low power actors must be constrained to exchange only with high power actors. The normal condition of that constraint is coercion. It follows that, to study dynamics, we need an experimental paradigm in which coercive and exchange relations can be mixed. Coercive relations pair positive and negative sanctions. Exchange relations pair positive sanctions. But these relations cannot be studied in the Stolte–Emerson paradigm, for it has no sanctions. It has only resource pools.

Certainly, an experimental paradigm that can investigate structural dynamics must be almost entirely new. It will be a paradigm in which subjects can alter relations *and* in which exchange and coercive relations are paired sanction flows. The new experimental paradigm will have a further advantage over current practice. Its exchange and coercive relations, unlike resource pool relations, are much like social relations found outside the lab.

Power-at-a-Distance

An important scope limit that has been unknowingly introduced by use of the Stolte–Emerson paradigm is the restriction of power relations to pairs of actors that are immediately adjacent to each other. In modern organizations outside of the laboratory, orders start at the top and pass through many levels in order to determine the activities of those far below. That is, outside the laboratory, power relations extend far beyond adjacent pairs. Here I will first show that restricting power to adjacencies is a consequence of the substitution of resource pool relations. Next I will introduce a flow network and show how power-at-a-distance is predicted. Then I will contrast the distribution of power in that network to the distribution that would occur had a network with that configuration been investigated under Stolte–Emerson conditions.

In the Stolte–Emerson experimental paradigm, power exercise is always restricted to adjacencies. That power is always so restricted follows immediately from how the exercise of power is measured. The measure of power is one actor's gain at the expense of another. Only adjacent positions share a research pool. Therefore, only adjacent positions gain at the expense of the other. For example, in the A–B–C network, because B divides a resource pool with A or C, B can exercise power over either. Now consider the longer network, A–B–C–D–E. Again B divides resources with A and C. However, B cannot divide resources with D or E because neither shares a resource pool with B. Therefore, B can exercise power over A or C and cannot exercise power over D or E. For the same reason, D cannot exercise power over A or B and similarly for all nodes of the network. Therefore, resource pool networks restrict the exercise of power to adjacent positions. In contrast, exchange networks are not so restricted.

To understand the exercise of power in the exchange network of Figure 11.1, first trace payoffs as resources flow from A through B to C and the reverse. The payoffs per unit resource flow are given in the figure. Where no payoff is indicated, the resource has no value to that position. Initially, A has one α resource which I will call a "widget." The widget is valuable only to the Cs; for any C it is worth 20 points. Initially, each C has β resources which I will call money. Each unit of money has a payoff of one point to all positions in the network. For example, when B receives a unit of money the "$+1$" indicates a positive payoff of one, and when B pays a unit of money the "-1" indicates a cost

Figure 11.1
A Network with Power-at-a-Distance

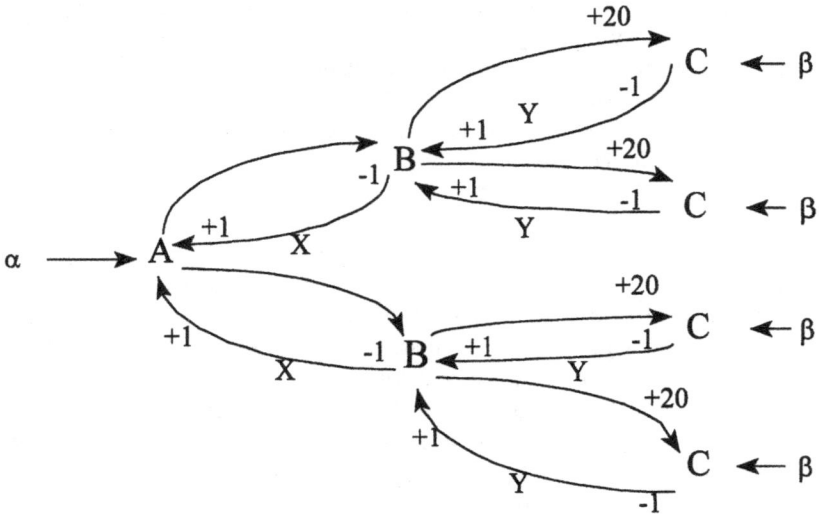

(loss) of one. B and C positions are initially allocated a quantity of money. At issue is what position or positions benefit most and at whose expense.

A straightforward extension of NET predicts that A will gain almost all of the value in the network at the expense of the Bs *and* the Cs. That is, A exploits the Bs, and A exploits the Cs. Note that NET predicts that A exploits the Cs even though there is no exchange relation directly connecting A to the Cs. To find this result: (1) determine the power of the positions relative to the immediate exchange partners, (2) find the payoffs of each position relative to resource flows, (3) write the resistance equations, and (4) solve. Interestingly, there will be two resistance equations with two unknowns, so the solution will be straightforward.

Because A initially holds only one widget, one of the Bs will be excluded. Therefore, the A will be high in power relative to the Bs. Because each B has two Cs, but at most one widget, the Bs are high power relative to the Cs. These inferences determine the form that resistance factors will take. In the A–B exchange, A's resistance factor is that of a high power position and B's is that of a low power position. For the B–C exchange, B's resistance factor is that of a high power position, and C's is that of a low power position.

To write resistance equations, the resource flows of Figure 11.1 are analyzed to determine "P" values, which are the payoffs by position. The α resource (the widget) begins at A, flows though B and is worth 20 points to C only. The β resources (money) initially held by Cs are each worth one point to each position. In the figure, the money flow from B to A is X, and the money flow from C to B is Y. Thus $P_A = X$, $P_B = Y - X$ and $P_C = 20 - Y$. That is, A's payoff is money received, B's payoff is the difference between money paid and money received, and C's payoff is the gain when buying the widget. In the absence of power differences, the best hope of each position is that others gain the minimum. Let that minimum approach zero; then Pmax $= 20$ for high power positions. For low power positions, however, there is a ceiling for Pmax which is the payoff of the previous exchange. For high power actors Pcon is the P of the previous exchange. Thus, when t is the time of the current exchange and $t - 1$ the time of the previous exchange,

$$R_{Ab} = \frac{20 - X^t}{X^t - X^{t-1}} = \frac{(Y^{t-1} - X^{t-1}) - (Y^t - X^t)}{Y^t - X^t} = R_{Ba}$$

$$R_{Bc} = \frac{20 - (Y^t - X^t)}{(Y^t - X^t) - (Y^{t-1} - X^{t-1})} = \frac{(20 - Y^{t-1}) - (20 - Y^t)}{20 - Y^t} = R_{Cb}$$

In the first equation, A's resistance factor is for a high power position, and B's is for a low power position. In the second equation, B's factor is for a high power position, and C's is for a low power position.

Let the payoffs be equally divided when $t = 1$. Then for $t = 2$, $Y^{t-1} = 13.33$ and $X^{t-1} = 6.67$. Now there are two equations with two unknowns and, upon solving, $X = 16.18$ and $Y = 20.95$. The power exercise has already overshot the maximum flow rate for Y. C will not pay 20.95 for a widget worth only 20 points. Assuming that C gains minimally such that $P_C = 1$, then $Y = 19$. Therefore, $P_A = 16.18$, $P_B = 2.82$ and $P_C = 1$. That is, at $t = 2$, A's power has moved close to the maximum; A is already exercising power over B and through B over C. Then, as t approaches t_n, P_A approaches $P_A$max. A series of recently completed experiments support these predictions from resistance.

To see that power-at-a-distance cannot be understood in the Stolte–Emerson paradigm, substitute resource pool relations for the exchange relations in Figure 11.1. Now each B has two Cs to exploit, and both Bs share the exploitation of A. Therefore, the Bs are high in power and gain most of the resources, whereas the Cs and A are low and gain minimally. This power distribution is entirely different from that of the exchange network. The distance over which power is exercised is also entirely different. Now the exercise of power is restricted to adjacencies.

Furthermore, the problems for theory in the two cases are entirely different. For the resource pool network, the problem is distal effects. To predict the Bs' power over A requires understanding the effect of the Cs on the A–B relation. In the exchange network, there are no distal effects. A's power over the Bs is unaffected by the configuration of the B–C end of the network and conversely. The problem in theory is to find the overall flow of resources. To find that flow, the network is solved as a whole by means of the simultaneous resistance equations. Certainly, nothing can be learned about power-at-a-distance by studying the resource pool network.

To gain a general understanding of power in exchange structures, it is necessary to study exchange structures and not the very different resource pool networks. When resource pool relations were substituted for exchange relations, it was thought that little was changed because the payoff matrixes for the pair of related actors could be made identical. That thought was wrong. The distribution of power that results from the substitution is entirely different, a difference that long went unnoticed. Two decades of research on resource pool networks has contributed nothing to our knowledge of power-at-a-distance. Therefore, our understanding of the large power structures of modern societies has not advanced.

Overcoming the Evils of the 1-Exchange Rule

The 1-exchange rule restricts positions to, at most, a single exchange. Today it is known to produce *exclusion*, the strongest power condition thus far discovered for exchange networks. It produces exclusion for the following reason. When two or more exchange relations are connected at a position—as they must be to build any structure beyond a dyad—the 1-exchange rule forces actors to choose to exchange with one of two or more adjacent positions. This forced choice produces exclusion in all but a handful of network shapes.

Although the 1-exchange rule produces exclusion, which is the single most efficacious condition of structural power, early experimental studies did not reflect an understanding of the rule's effect. For example, in Cook et al. (1983), the 1-exchange rule is not part of the discussion of how power is produced; it is mentioned only incidentally in the discussion of experiments (p. 290).[9] In that mention, no reason is given for limiting each position to a single exchange. Therefore, power differences were produced in the early exchange experiments, but not by conditions comprehended by theory. There is a reason why the production of power was not understood. For Cook, Emerson, and associates, power is produced by dependence, not by exclusion.

Today exclusion is understood, yet most research remains narrow, relying only on the 1-exchange rule to produce power differences. Exclusion does not require that rule. Let n be the degree of some node(s) in a network. Then it should be obvious, since Brennan (1981), that power differences due to exclusion are as readily produced by a "$n-1$" exchange rule as by a 1-exchange rule. There is no good reason for research to still focus on the 1-exchange rule. Its use has simply become embedded in a tradition carried by an outworn experimental paradigm.

Blind adherence to the 1-exchange rule further narrows the scope of investigation because it precludes the study of conditions of structural power beyond exclusion. For example, inclusion requires that positions complete at least two exchanges. Researchers who always use the 1-exchange rule cannot study inclusion. As a result, only three papers have studied inclusion: (1) Chapter 8 of this volume which was first published in 1997, (2) Szmatka and Willer (1995), and (3) Patton and Willer (1990). Patton and Willer (1990) were the first to demonstrate that inclusion produces power and to show that the effect of inclusion varies by degree. Szmatka and Willer (1995) were the first to show that exclusion wipes out the effect of inclusion. These three studies are only a beginning. It is a sad statement on the study of structure that inclusion has not been investigated further.

Even worse, no new condition of power has been discovered since Patton and Willer's 1990 discovery of inclusion. Are there more conditions of power waiting to be discovered? Of course there are. Here is one I call "ordering." Imagine a simple branch structure with one central position, A, and two peripherals, B and C. Let the stakes in the two exchange relations be of the same order of magnitude. Now impose an ordering such that A must exchange with B before exchanging with C.

Resistance shows why ordering produces power differences. Consider Pcon values for the A–B relation. For B, Pcon $= 0$. But for A, Pcon $= -P_{Ac}$. That is, A, failing to complete the exchange with B, will lose the value that would have been gained in exchanging with C. Therefore, B will exercise power over A. Does ordering actually produce power? Preliminary experimental studies support ordering as a power condition *and* suggest that resistance accurately predicts the power exercise. Outside the laboratory, ordering is a power condition that takes many forms and is frequently encountered. For example, gatekeeping is ordering. I leave it to the reader's imagination to discover other examples.

The focus on 1-exchange networks appears to preclude the discovery of new power conditions for two reasons. First, it is unlikely that any new power condition can occur under the 1-exchange rule. For example, ordering cannot occur under the 1-exchange rule because a single exchange cannot be ordered. In fact, no power condition discovered since exclusion can occur under the 1-exchange rule. Second, in the unlikely event that a new power condition can occur under the 1-exchange rule, it will be difficult to find because its effects will be masked by the confounding effects of exclusion produced by the 1-exchange rule. In either case, discovery demands that investigations pursue a broader scope, a scope that abandons the 1-exchange rule of the Stolte–Emerson experimental paradigm.

Differently Valued Relations

As this chapter is being written, a paper by Bonacich and Friedkin (1998) has arrived which predicts exchange ratios in networks where the value of all relations is *not* the same.[10] As they point out, previous work has focused on "a special case of exchange structure" (160) where the value of all relations are the same. They go on to say that

a general theory of exchange processes should predict patterns of exchange transactions and power inequalities in any exchange network, regardless of the values of the exchange relations. The scope of applicability of network exchange theory is a concern when it limits, rather than encourages an understanding of social exchange phenomena. (160)

Whereas Bonacich and Friedkin point out correctly that empirical work has been "unduly restrictive" (160), their discussion is inaccurate on two points. First, current theories of network exchange do not explicitly limit consideration to systems of equally valued relations. Second, it is not true that all previous investigations studied networks "in which all exchange relations are equally valuable" (1998, p. 160).

Early power-dependence experiments studied networks in which two different-sized pools were present.[11] For example, Stolte and Emerson's (1977) networks had 3- and 13-point resource pools, whereas Cook and associates' networks had 8- and 24-point resource pools (Cook and Emerson 1978; Cook et al. 1983). It was Markovsky et al. (1987) who began the tradition of studying networks where all pools are given the same number of resources. They claimed that the smaller pools of the power-dependence experiments add little or nothing. The smaller pools are too small to affect the distribution of power among positions connected by the larger pools. The only effect of smaller pools is to put a ceiling on the extent of power exercise. Their reservations do not hold, however, when differential payoffs across relations are of magnitudes that are more similar than those used earlier.

Bonacich and Friedkin claim that only three approaches can apply to networks with differentially valued relations; those three do not include NET (1998, p. 161). They are wrong. As will be shown here, resistance is easily applied to networks with differentially valued resource pools. As a part of that demonstration, I will show how networks with differentially valued relations are particularly sensitive to actor rationality and institutional conditions. Whereas only a single network will be used as an example, it should be obvious that the application of resistance is not limited to this simple network. By adding issues of actor rationality and institutional conditions, my example will show the greater generality of NET's multilevel approach as compared to the approaches in Bonacich and Friedkin.

Imagine the A–B–C branch where B is exclusively connected. Let B hold a widget valuable only to A and C. To A the widget is worth $23, and to C it is worth $11. I will first solve for the price under the conditions normally assumed in network exchange research. A and C will bid until C offers $11. C will offer no more. C's offer is $P_B$con. Furthermore, C's offer restricts the range of prices that A must pay. A's payoff is the value of the widget to A, $23 minus the price. C's final bid means that $P_A\text{max} = 23 - 11 = 12$. Therefore,

$$R_A = \frac{12 - P_A}{P_A} = \frac{23 - P_B}{P_B - 11} = R_B$$

NET predicts that the widget is sold for $17.50.

Now apply NET to a second institution which economists call a "first price auction." This institution is common outside the laboratory, and its conditions are quite different from those found in network exchange experiments. In the auction, only bidding is allowed. Actors do not bargain. The widget is sold to the highest bidder. Let the minimum differential between bids be $1.00. Then the widget is sold to A but now for $12.00. The price becomes $12 because C will make no bid higher than $11. In both cases, A is the buyer, but now the price paid is fully $5.50 less than for the first institution. Note that differences like these are masked when all relations have exactly the same value.

Interestingly, the contrasts between the two institutions can also be expressed by making different actor assumptions. In an earlier chapter, two types of rationality were introduced, strategic and parametric. Game theory uses strategic rationality; actors seek to maximize and take others' courses of action into account in their decisions. Economics historically has used parametric rationality; actors seek to maximize while treating the actions of others as given parameters. In ET and NET, the default actor is strategic, but parametric actors can also be deployed. Only strategic actors bargain. Parametric actors can bid but cannot bargain. Therefore, the first example, where the price is $17.50, assumes strategic actors. All applications of resistance assume strategic actors. The second example requires only parametric actors. If parametric actors are specified, the resulting price will be $12 under a wide variety of institutional conditions, including those normally found in network exchange experiments.

Either price outcome should be easily produced in the laboratory. To produce the first, simply run the usual experimental conditions. For the second, only one change is needed. Simulate B as a parametrically rational actor. Let B's decision rule be, ''Take the best offer.'' C will offer no more than $11. Thus, when A offers $12, B accepts. Note that it does not matter whether A and C are strategic or parametric. In either case, C will offer, at most, $11, A will offer $12, and B will accept it.

Competing theories have long been common in other sciences. But theories that make precise predictions that can be tested against each other are new to sociology. Certainly, competing theories are desirable. As seen in this volume, science advances more quickly when theories compete. But science can advance only when the capabilities of available theories are recognized and used. It is an important contribution of Bonacich and Friedkin to open research to networks with differentially valued relations. After Markovsky et al., the Stolte–Emerson paradigm was much too narrow. Nevertheless, it is unfortunate that Bonacich and Friedkin mistakenly excluded NET from their study. Because of its flexibility, NET has no difficulty with differentially valued relations. Furthermore, it offers multiple predictions for multiple conditions of institutions and actors.

Their exclusion of NET is particularly unfortunate. Only NET, not the theories they discuss, has a scope broad enough to apply to all the conditions of power thus far discovered and to the full array of other conditions considered in this chapter. If a theory is to be excluded from study, it is not good science to exclude the one with decisively broadest scope.

Communication, Collective Action, and Countervailing Power

Let us now turn to the last of the restrictions of the Stolte–Emerson experimental paradigm. The paradigm does not allow positions to communicate unless they are connected by exchange relations. This is not a neutral restriction. Its effect is to block low power actors from acting collectively to countervail power. Low power actors have an interest in countervailing the power of high power positions because to do so results in higher payoffs.

Communication is certainly necessary, but it may not be sufficient for successful collective action. Whether or not it is sufficient is simply not known. Surprisingly little has been done about understanding how collective action countervails power in structures. It is surprising because network exchange experiments offer an excellent venue for the investigation of collective action. The conditions of power in strong power structures are well known, interactions in strong power structures are well understood, and strong power structures can easily be produced in the lab.

Previously, only two studies experimentally investigated the effect of coalition formation and collective action on power. Cook and Gillmore (1984) assert that coalitions eliminate power differences through "consolidating positions" (p. 43). Let A_1, A_2, and A_3 be connected to B but not to each other. Then a coalition among A_1, A_2, and A_3 is said to consolidate the three A positions, leaving an A–B dyad. Since dyads are equal power, the coalition eliminates power differences. There is no doubt that the coalitions in Cook and Gillmore's experiments countervailed power, but the study has conceptual limitations. Power is countervailed when a coalition acts on a structural power condition. Their idea of "consolidating" means eliminating branching from a position. But branching is not a power condition. Therefore, consolidating positions is not a general mechanism for countervailing power.

Chapter 3 traced the effect of collective action in coercive structures and studied the effects of coalition formation in strong power and null branches. In the null branch, threats of a coercer in the central position produced power differences. These differences were due to the coercive relations alone; the structure did not affect power exercise. The strong power coercive branch also had structural power. Its structural conditions were analogous to those of strong power exchange structures. Two types of collective action were studied. In the first type, subjects could coordinate their actions only through communications and enlightened self-interest. In the second type, subjects could sanction free riders who did not help the coalition. Both types of coalitions countervailed structural power, but the one where free riders were sanctioned was more effective. Coalitions affected only power produced by structural conditions. For the null branch, the formation of coalitions had no effect on power exercised (Willer 1987). An important limitation of this study was that all subject interactions were face-to-face, a condition strongly favoring coalition formation.

Whatever their shortcomings, the great advantage of these two studies over more conventional studies is that collective action occurs in recognizable social structures.[12] By contrast, the conditions conventionally employed by game theorists and economists to investigate collective action do not include structured social relations. In their investigations, subjects are given resources that they may keep for a given payoff or contribute to a common pool. When resources are contributed to the common pool, their value is increased. Typically, their value is multiplied by 1.5. The value of resources kept remains constant. The pool is divided equally among all game players. Players who contributed gain exactly the same from the pool as those who did not. The design produces the payoffs of an n-person prisoner's dilemma, but it does not produce a recognizable social setting.

Because network exchange experiments are social settings, for many purposes, they offer better designs for investigation of collective action than the one conventionally employed. Network exchange experiments place people in social relations in social structures; the conventional design does not. In network exchange experiments, when collective action is successful, power is countervailed. This explicit link between collective action and countervailing power opens important opportunities for theory. Network exchange theory offers an array of proven designs for collective action and has the potential for more to be devised. For example, when the central actor in a strong power branch is simulated, the payoff matrix for peripherals is a virtual prisoner's dilemma game. (See Willer and Skvoretz 1997.)[13]

I have criticized the Stolte–Emerson paradigm, but primarily for the rigid and narrow way it has been employed, and not for the design as originally conceived. Almost unique among experimental settings in the social sciences, the Stolte–Emerson paradigm produces social relations in social structures—and has done so since Stolte and Emerson's first experiment. That capability gives it a decisive advantage over most designs, including the design conventionally used in the study of collective action.[14] The faults I have cited lie not in their first design, but in those following who have failed to break out of the narrow conditions first employed. I now turn to the problem of attaining a critical mass of scholars for scientific study and to the issue of connecting ET/NET to other theories in sociology and related sciences.

THE CRITICAL MASS AND CONNECTING THEORIES

In spite of many blind alleys, the development of a formal mathematical theory of structure has been marked by substantially improved scope and precision. The development of the theory has shown, contrary to popular myth, that there is no tradeoff between scope and precision; both can increase together. There is good reason to be optimistic concerning the future of Network Exchange Theory.

But there is also real cause for concern. Today, too few scholars are engaged in the development and application of Network Exchange Theory as well as other formal theories. Scientific knowledge can be objective and self-correcting only through the critical cooperation of a community of active researchers. Currently, the community of formal theorists is too small to ensure objectivity and self-correction. Beyond objectivity and self-correction, the number is also too small to ensure continuity of the enterprise of theory development. For example, when formal theorists meet annually at the "Group Process" meetings, fewer than one hundred are in attendance.

Here I cite two problems and propose solutions. The first concerns the expense of experimental research. As shown in this volume, theory development and experimental study go hand-in-hand. But experimental research has recently become so expensive as to block entry. I propose a "Web-Lab" as a solution. The Web-Lab, which is an active web site housing publicly available experimental software, will soon make the tools for experimental research cheaply and easily available to all.

Second, Elementary Theory and its exchange component, NET, have been criticized for being too isolated from other parts of the sociological enterprise. Presumably, isolation suppresses interest, thus restricting the numbers engaged in theory development. Contrary to this critique, I will indicate how Elementary Theory can become a focal point to which other theoretical work systematically connects. We have already seen some consequences of connecting across theories. Elementary Theory's experimental designs produce a social setting for the study of collective action—one in which people *interact* in relations in structures.

The Web-Lab and the Critical Mass

Today, the community of scholars who develop theory in interaction with experimental research is too small, and entry into that community is more and more closed by increased laboratory costs. Years ago, when a lab could be an egg timer and a box of poker chips, as mine was, entry into this important scientific community was open. Because the cost of entry today is over $80,000 for even a modest laboratory,[15] the vast majority do not have access to a "dedicated electronic laboratory." By a "dedicated laboratory," I mean a laboratory with instruments and space used only for research. Poker chips and egg timers are no longer good enough. Reviewers recognize that electronic laboratories are more precise, so experimental reports based on less sophisticated technology are strongly disadvantaged. Electronic laboratories, while displacing other kinds of laboratories, have not replaced them.

Yet, there is no doubt that electronic laboratories advance experimental research in the social sciences. Consider my ExNet II, a state-of-the-art Windows-based electronic laboratory system for the investigation of exchange networks. Subjects seated at PCs in separate rooms send offers and make exchanges using mouse control only. The design of ExNet II follows the rule, "Show, don't tell." The network being investigated is an active display on each subject's screen; subjects click icons to make offers and complete exchanges. With experimental conditions actively displayed, many uncontrolled effects of language on subjects are avoided. Compared to previous instruments, ExNet II is more intuitive; subject training time is much shorter, and subject errors are substantially reduced. But now consider the problem which electronic laboratories like ExNet II produces.

Today sociology faces a dilemma. Whereas electronic laboratories advance experimental research by offering levels of control that were not previously possible, they are expensive. Their expense threatens to reduce the size of the community of experimenters below the critical number needed to ensure the integrity of social science knowledge. For example, beyond my lab, only three electronic sociology laboratories study exchange networks in the United States: the University of Iowa (Lovaglia et al. 1995), UCLA (Bienenstock and Bonacich 1992, 1993; Bonacich and Bienenstock 1995), and the University of Washington (Cook et al. 1983, now inactive).[16] Only four advanced electronic laboratories study other theories in sociology.[17] In sociology there are perhaps 70 to 80 active experimenters, but at most 12 can access an electronic laboratory at their home schools. Not all of these are dedicated laboratories.

Furthermore, electronic laboratories have increasingly restricted the ability to conduct cross-national experiments that test theory for universality as well as the replications needed to ensure the integrity of scientific knowledge. Like all scientific theory, social science theory must claim universality; it must claim not to be conditioned by specifics of time and place (Lakatos 1970, Walker and Cohen 1985). Since theory is asserted to hold regardless of special conditions of cultures and nations, cross-cultural and cross-national experiments are an essential part of the production of social science knowledge (Foschi 1980; Faucheux 1976; Willer and Szmatka 1993). Before electronic laboratories became the norm, cross-cultural/cross-national experimental study was straightforward.[18] Because laboratories of networked desktop PCs are not portable instruments, however, cross-national studies, with few exceptions, are no longer feasible.[19] Furthermore, in sharp contrast to other sciences, in the social sciences replication of pivotal prior experiments is not routine. Replication should be a typical exercise for graduate students, but currently it is not.

With research concentrated in a handful of laboratories, the majority of experimenters are disenfranchised. High start-up costs imply that the future is equally bleak. Young investigators without electronic laboratories cannot build up the research reputation needed to justify funding the lab they lack. The result is a dangerous privatization of social science knowledge. Lacking laboratories, the next generation of scholars may well be forced into less rigorous areas of inquiry. To a significant degree, these problems are, at their root, technological; it is the cost of high-tech labs which restricts access. Fortunately, a technological solution is at hand.

The solution to these problems is a Web-Lab that is an active web site housing publicly available experimental software. The Web-Lab is not an adjunct to existing or proposed laboratory facilities; the Web-Lab is the Laboratory. The software developed for it will support multiple experimental designs such that scholars at any location with access to the Internet can use the Web-Lab to run experiments. Supported by NSF, I am now engaged in the first steps of building a Web-Lab. Soon after this book is published, we expect to have the software for ExNet II on the Web and available for network exchange research. Working with Lisa Rutstrom and a number of other sociologists and economists, there are plans to expand the Web-Lab as a tool for both sociology and economics.

Beyond housing software to support theoretically driven experimentation, the Web-Lab will be a multifunctional knowledge center. A library of simulation programs will be available for research and education. Data from current experiments will be recorded and automatically archived. In addition, the Web-Lab will archive data from prior experiments in a format compatible with that used for archiving current work. Innovative data retrieval and display systems will be developed. Because its publicly available software supports replications, the Web-Lab will increase the integrity and effectiveness of social science knowledge.

The goal is to solve the problem of critical mass by democratizing experimental research and strengthening the community of scholars engaged in developing theory. Instead of becoming increasingly expensive, experimental research will become one of the least expensive modes of enquiry. Local laboratories will have virtually no software costs. With user-friendly flexible shareware in place at the Web-Lab, local laboratories can use existing designs or build new ones from available modules. Furthermore, the hardware requirements of local laboratories are drastically cut. Because the Web-Lab Library connects subject PCs, local labs do not need hubs; they will require no more than a few computers. In many cases, no dedicated hardware or space will be needed. Existing computer classrooms can serve as settings for experiments.

Because experiments can be run on widely distributed subjects, the Web-Lab solves the problem of cross-national research while encouraging the formation of networks of cooperation among experimentalists distributed across states and nations. Local labs will be linked in an extensive knowledge network, allowing them to run experiments with large numbers of subjects. Local labs will become Super-Labs. Precisely because experimenters are widely distributed, these cooperative knowledge networks will build a strong community.

Technology is not a solution; it is an opportunity. As of today there is a Web-Lab, but only ExNet is available. It is technologically feasible, and it will be expanded. As a result, experimental research will be democratized, education in sociology will be revolutionized and laboratory components will be incorporated into mainline sociology courses. At issue now is what we make of these opportunities, and to an important degree, that is determined by the power and precision of the theories we deploy.

Focusing on Elementary Theory

Although Elementary Theory has been criticized for its isolation from the rest of sociology,[20] it can be a focal point connecting an important number of other theories. Two qualities of Elementary Theory give it unique potential. First, it is formulated out of simple elements using network geometry to display social relations and social structures. Its modeling procedure draws relational structures which, once drawn, can be analyzed in detail. No other social theory offers procedures like these to represent relational structures. Nevertheless, other theories would benefit from the use of Elementary Theory's modeling procedure.

Second, Elementary Theory is multilevel in the following sense. Formulations for relational structures and for social actors are introduced independently and the result is an unusual conceptual flexibility. For purposes of prediction and explanation, different kinds of social actors can be placed in the same structure. Alternatively, different kinds of structures can be peopled with the same kind of actor. The result is a rich array of contrasting formulations. Yet these formulations are coherent because exactly the same simple theoretic elements, which are employed when constructing relational structures, are also used in constructing actors. Indeed, the combination of flexibility and coherence of Elementary Theory encourage its connections to other theories.

Let us consider first connecting Elementary Theory and Status Characteristics Theory (hereafter SCT). The two parts of Chapter 9 describe two ways of connecting the theories. The first part focuses on influence whereby SCT relates status effects to belief change. In exchange relations, the effect of influence can be measured as an exchange ratio favoring the influencing actor. The second part of the chapter deployed the "status value" component of SCT. There Thye showed how SCT relates actors' statuses to the way resources are valued. Resources held by high-status actors are more highly valued than similar resources held by low-status actors. The effect of differential valuations is measured as an exchange ratio favoring the high-status actor. As seen in Chapter 9, the connection of these two theories gives substantially broader scope and much richer predictions than either theory taken alone.

Furthermore, connecting the two theories gives a better experimental setting in which to test SCT effects than what is typically used in SCT experiments. In SCT's experimental paradigm, there is an experimental task. Subjects are asked to judge whether each of a series of rectangles is more shaded than not. The task is ambiguous. Subjects make initial judgments and are given a judgment purporting to come from a partner of higher or lower status. Subjects then make final judgments. Subjects are being misdirected when they are told that they interact with another subject; in fact, they do not: No subject interacts with another; they are all cued by a machine. The machine produces a minimum number of disagreements. Change of judgment by the subject is the measure of the machine's influence.

By contrast, once SCT is connected to Elementary Theory, there is no need for misdirection because the experiment is actually what subjects are told it is. Subjects of different statuses, once informed of those differences, are linked by exchange relations. Then subjects actually interact in negotiating exchanges. SCT effects are seen when resulting exchange ratios are biased in favor of high-status subjects at the expense of low-status subjects. For example, in equal power structures, like dyads, the high-status subjects are predicted to exercise power and gain favored exchange ratios.

This design has a number of advantages. SCT effects now occur in a recognizable social setting, and the subjects are actually interacting in social relations in social structures. Furthermore, the resulting exchange ratio gives a quantitative expression to the size of the SCT effect. As status differences increase, payoff differences increase. Alternatively, the exchange ratio can also be used as a *derived measure*, through the SCT effect, for the size of status differences.

Experiments connecting the two theories do two things. Here I have emphasized the advantages of Elementary Theory's experimental design over the design long used by SCT. In addition, experiments connecting two theories test connections between them. For example, in equal power relations, we test whether SCT effects can produce a power exercise. As in other Elementary Theory experiments, we measure the power exercise by the exchange ratio resulting in the relation. Alternatively, when power and influence are opposed in a relation, we test whether influence can negate power in the relation and, if so, whether the direction of power exercise can be reversed.

Experiments linking Elementary Theory and STC suggest directions toward a full integration of the two. Experiments connecting the two are easily constructed because they place subjects in Elementary Theory's social relations and structures. SCT does not produce social relations or social structures in experiments because SCT has no modeling procedure. SCT contains terms designating "groups" and "relations," but, lacking a modeling procedure, models for groups and relations cannot be drawn. These observations strongly suggest that the integration of the two should begin with Elementary Theory's formulations for social relations and structures.

The advantages gained in connecting Elementary Theory to game theory are very like the advantages gained in connecting Elementary Theory to SCT. Like SCT, game theory has no modeling procedure for representing social relations and social structures. Lacking a modeling procedure, game theoretic experimental designs place subjects in contrived decision situations. Theoretically, those contrived situations are not like social relations and social structures. For example, as already seen in the discussion of collective action and countervailing power, game theory's experiments on prisoner's dilemma games are not like any recognizable social setting. By contrast, Elementary Theory uses strong power structures to produce a prisoner's dilemma game.

Using Elementary Theory designs when testing game theory has two advantages: (1) in Elementary Theory designs, unlike conventional designs, subjects are placed in relational structures, and (2) the use of Elementary Theory's designs allows connections between Elementary Theory and game theory to be investigated.

Experiments linking Elementary Theory and game theory suggest directions toward a more complete integration of the two. Not having a theory of relational structures restricts the utility of game theory. Social applications of game theory's many well-developed formulations for decisions would be both more precise and more general if they were linked through a procedure for modeling relational structures. Connecting game theory to Elementary Theory provides that procedure. It follows that connections across the two theories should begin with game theory's formulations for decisions and Elementary Theory's structural theory.

For too long, social events have been difficult to understand and have been beyond the social sciences' powers of explanation. In the past, the primary reason for that difficulty was the underdevelopment of structural theory. Today, formal theorists and experimentalists struggle to reach the critical mass needed for sustained progress. Yet the development of structural theory is well underway. Unfortunately, explanation has not advanced proportionately, and the reason is easy to see. For explanations, structural theories like Elementary Theory must be applied institutionally or historically. Very few of these applications have been carried out (cf. Willer et al. 1996; Bell, 1997). Applying formal theory outside the limits of the lab is a new specialization; thus far, only a handful of scholars have taken it up.

Nevertheless, the time for a breakthrough is upon us, and it will come in three ways. First, undoubtedly there are new structural conditions to discover. For example, norms are almost certainly produced by structures (Southard 1981). But how they are produced is little understood. Second, there are important new connections to draw among theories. As shown here, Elementary Theory's formulations for social structure are a common focal point to which Status Characteristics Theory and game theory can be connected. Third, as these discoveries and connections enrich experimentally grounded formal theory, explanatory power will rapidly increase. More scholars will take up historical and institutional applications. As a result, social events will no longer be difficult to understand or be beyond social sciences' powers of explanation.

NOTES

1. The late development of the social sciences may be due only to the late development of a geometry to represent its phenomena. Certainly, modern physical science dates back to Galileo's geometric representation of motion. The story is told that Hobbes visited Galileo to learn how to do science. If true, Hobbes' failure to fully emulate Galileo could have been due to the absence of a social geometry.

2. This discussion is not intended to suggest that NET is now a fully general theory. Of course it is not. It is subject to scope limits in its applications. I will address NET's

scope limits later in this chapter when focusing on the next steps to be undertaken in NETs development to make it more general.

3. Hobbes ([1651]1968) and others proposed the idea of a "state of nature" which contained no structured social relations. But they proposed the state of nature as a theoretic formulation, knowing full well that it did not exist anywhere, any time.

4. This assertion will be recognized as similar to Axiom 2 of the Graph-theoretic Power Index.

5. It has not yet been proven that when the two weakest connect they necessarily become stronger relative to others in the network. Perhaps someone will take on the proof (or disproof) as a useful exercise. As new connections are ongoing, it is possible for the network to assume an equal power configuration that is not fully connected. If so, there will be no weakest pair. Nevertheless, any position in the equal power network that is not fully connected can gain a higher power position by connecting to some other, and it is in the interest of that position to do so. Given that connection, the network is again weak power and the process given in the text restarts.

6. In Carneiro's theory of the origin of the state (1970), structural parameters are fixed by the environment. For states to develop, it is necessary that subordinated populations not escape from taxation by the powerful; that is, populations must be circumscribed. Carneiro's theory begins with environmental circumscription as produced by seas, deserts, and mountain ranges. Environmental circumscription blocks escape, keeping populations in place so that they can be taxed.

7. More accurately, the Stolte–Emerson design used relations with two differently valued resource pools. Because the value of one pool was trivial relative to that of the second, power distributions were the same as they would have been if the trivial pools had been omitted. See the discussion later in the chapter. Because they did not affect the distribution of power, more recent designs, like ExNet II, have dropped the small resource pools.

8. This volume is not entirely free of this bias; most of its studies were carried out within the confines of the Stolte–Emerson paradigm.

9. When looking over Cook and Emerson (1978) for this chapter, I did not find the 1-exchange rule. It may have been mentioned, but not prominently, or it would not have been missed.

10. My thanks go to Henry Walker for drawing my attention to Bonacich and Friedkin's error of excluding NET from the analysis of differentially valued relations and for helpful editorial comments. Any errors that remain are mine alone.

11. Henry Walker (Personal Communication) pointed out this prior use as well as Bonacich and Friedkin's error in ignoring it.

12. This point was explained to me by Brent Simpson (Personal Communication).

13. The simulated actor accepted its best offer(s) and, when offers were tied, chose randomly.

14. Also see the discussion of the designs conventionally employed by status characteristics theory below.

15. For a small laboratory, hardware costs total $45,000: 10 PCs at $3,000 each as subject stations, one server at $5,000, and a Hub at $10,000. Producing a windows-based system will require three years for a computer science graduate student at minimally $12,000/year, for a total cost of $81,000. In addition to these costs, the individual researcher should expect at least a two-year delay for software completion and minimally

six months for debugging. A 30 PC laboratory will cost more than $100,000 for computer hardware alone.

16. There are only two international electronic laboratories in sociology; they are at Groningen, The Netherlands and Krakow, Poland.

17. Beyond network exchange theory, two other theories in sociology have undergone intensive experimental investigation: status characteristics theory and legitimacy theory. Only four electronic laboratories investigate status characteristics theory: Foschi's lab at Vancouver, which developed the first software, and Troyer at Iowa, which developed the second (Troyer and Younts 1997). Ridgeway at Stanford (Ridgeway et al. 1998) and Ilardi at Rochester use these systems. Only Stanford uses an electronic laboratory to investigate legitimacy theory.

18. For U.S. results replicated cross-nationally in communist Poland, subjects in both settings negotiated over stacks of poker chips. Plywood boards as barriers between selected subjects set network structures, while an egg timer timed interactions. This kind of technology is easily moved or cheaply acquired. The only substantial problem faced by experimenters was standardizing payments of U.S. versus. Polish subjects (Willer and Szmatka 1993).

19. Cross-national study is still possible in the occasional case where laboratories at other locations have similar electronic capabilities.

20. For example, I recently submitted a research proposal to the National Science Foundation to extend NET's scope. The one critical comment consistent across reviews of the proposal was concern about the isolation of NET from the core of sociology. While I am not sure that sociology has a core, I think that the reviewers' comments are cause for concern.

Bibliography

Antonio, Robert J. 1979. "The Contradiction of Domination and Production in Bureaucracy." *American Sociological Review* 44:895–912.

Aron, Raymond. 1988. *Power, Modernity and Sociology*. Cambridge: Cambridge University Press.

Axelrod, Robert. 1984. *The Evolution of Cooperation*. New York: Basic Books.

Bacharach, Samuel B., and Edward J. Lawler. 1980. *Power and Politics in Organizations*. San Francisco: Jossey-Bass.

———. 1984. *Bargaining*. San Francisco: Jossey-Bass.

Bachrach, Peter, and Morton S. Baratz. 1962. "Two Faces of Power." *American Political Science Review* 56:947–52.

Balkwell, James W. 1991. "From Expectations to Behavior: An Improved Postulate for Expectations States Theory." *American Sociological Review* 56:355–69.

Ball, Sheryl, Elaine Bennett, Catherine Eckel, and William Zame. 1995. "Status in Markets." Paper presented at the Economic Science Association Meetings, Long Beach, CA.

Ball, Sheryl B., and Catherine C. Eckel. 1993. "Stars upon Thars: Status and Discrimination in Ultimatum Games." Working paper. Economics Department, Virginia Polytechnic Institute.

Baron, Robert. A. 1987. "Interviewer's Moods and Reactions to Job Applicants: The Influence of Affective States on Applied Social Judgments." *Journal of Applied Social Psychology* 17:911–26.

Barron, D. N., and L. Smith-Lovin. 1990. "The Interaction of Structure and Strategy in Negatively Connected Exchange Networks." Paper presented at Sunbelt X International Social Network Conference, San Diego, CA.

Bell, Richard. 1997. "Endorsement as Nonlegitimate Domination: An Application of Experimental Research to Historical Settings." Pp. 404–24 in Jacek Szmatka, John Skvoretz, and Joseph Berger (eds.), *Status Network and Structure*. Stanford, CA: Stanford University Press.

Berger, Joseph, Bernard P. Cohen, and Morris Zelditch, Jr. 1966. "Status Characteristics and Expectations States." Pp. 29–46 in Joseph Berger, Morris Zelditch, Jr., and Bo Anderson (eds.), *Sociological Theories on Progress*, vol. 1. Boston: Houghton Mifflin.

———. 1972. "Status Characteristics and Social Interaction." *American Sociological Review* 37:241–55.

Berger, Joseph, and Thomas L. Conner. 1974. "Performance Expectations and Behavior in Small Groups: A Revised Formulation." Pp. 85–109 in Joseph Berger, Thomas L. Conner, and M. Hamit Fisek (eds.), *Expectations States Theory: A Theoretical Research Program*. Cambridge, MA: Winthrop.

Berger, Joseph, M. Hamit Fisek, Robert Z. Norman, and David G. Wagner. 1985. "Formation of Reward Expectations in Status Situations." Pp. 215–61 in Joseph Berger and Morris Zelditch, Jr. (eds.), *Status, Rewards, and Influence*. San Francisco: Jossey-Bass.

Berger, Joseph, M. Hamit Fisek, Robert Z. Norman, and Morris Zelditch, Jr. 1977. *Status Characteristics and Social Interaction: An Expectations States Approach*. New York: Elsevier.

Berger, Joseph, Robert Z. Norman, James Balkwell, and Roy F. Smith. 1992. "Status Inconsistency in Task Situations: A Test of Four Status Processing Principles." *American Sociological Review* 57:843–55.

Berger, Joseph, Susan J. Rosenholtz, and Morris Zelditch, Jr. 1980. "Status Organizing Processes." *Annual Review of Sociology* 6:470–508.

Berger, Joseph, and Morris Zelditch, Jr. (eds.). 1985. *Status, Rewards, and Influence*. San Francisco: Jossey-Bass.

Berger, Joseph, and Morris Zelditch, Jr. 1993. "Orienting Strategies and Theory Growth." Pp. 3–19 in J. Berger and M. Zelditch, Jr. (eds.), *Theoretical Research Programs: Studies in Theory Growth*. Stanford, CA: Stanford University Press.

Berger, Joseph, Morris Zelditch, Jr., Bo Anderson, and Bernard P. Cohen. 1972. "Structural Aspects of Distributive Justice: A Status Value Formulation." Pp. 119–46 in Joseph Berger, Morris Zelditch, Jr., and Bo Anderson (eds.), *Sociological Theories in Progress*. Boston: Houghton Mifflin.

Bienenstock, Elisa Jayne, and Phillip Bonacich. 1992. "The Core as a Solution to Exclusionary Networks." *Social Networks* 14:231–44.

———. 1993. "Game-Theory Models for Exchange Networks: Experimental Results." *Sociological Perspectives* 36:117–35.

Bierhoff, Hans W., Ernst Buck, and Renate Klein. 1986. "Social Context and Perceived Justice." Pp. 165–85 in Hans W. Bierhoff, Ronald L. Cohen, and Jerald Greenberg (eds.), *Justice in Social Relations*. New York: Plenum.

Bierstedt, Robert. 1950. "An Analysis of Social Power." *American Sociological Review* 15:161–84.

Blalock, Hubert M., and Paul H. Wilken. 1979. *Intergroup Processes*. New York: Free Press.

Blau, Peter. 1964. *Exchange and Power in Social Life*. New York: Wiley.

Bonacich, Phillip. 1987. "Power and Centrality: A Family of Measures." *American Journal of Sociology* 92:1170–82.

Bonacich, Phillip, and Elisa Bienenstock. 1995. "When Rationality Fails." *Rationality and Society* 7:293–320.

Bonacich, Phillip, and Noah Friedkin. 1998. "Unequally Valued Exchange Relations." *Social Psychology Quarterly* 61:160–71.

Borgatti, Steve, and Martin Everett. 1992. "Graph Colorings and Power in Experimental Exchange Networks." *Social Networks* 14:287–308.

Bower, Gordon H. 1991. "Mood Congruity of Social Judgments." Pp. 165–85 in Joseph P. Forgas (ed.), *Emotion and Social Judgments*. Oxford: Pergamon.

Bredemeier, Harry C. 1978. "Exchange Theory." Pp. 418–56 in T. Bottomore and R. Nisbet (eds.), *A History of Sociological Analysis*. New York: Basic Books.

Brennan, John S. 1981. "Some Experimental Structures." Pp. 189–204 in David Willer and Bo Anderson (eds.), *Networks, Exchange and Coercion*. New York: Elsevier/ Greenwood.

Burgess, R. L., and T. L. Huston (eds.). 1979. *Social Exchange in Developing Relationships*. New York: Academic Press.

Burke, Peter J. 1997. "An Identity Model for Network Exchange." *American Sociological Review* 62:134–50.

Burt, Ronald S. 1992. *Structural Holes: The Social Structure of Competition*. Cambridge, MA: Harvard University Press.

Carneiro, Robert. 1970. "A Theory of the Origin of the State." *Science* 169:733–38.

Cary, Alex. 1967. "The Hawthorne Studies: A Radical Criticism." *American Sociological Review* 32:403–16.

Coase, Richard. 1937. "The Nature of the Firm." *Econometrica* 4:386–405.

Cohen, Bernard P. 1989. *Developing Sociological Knowledge*, 2nd ed. Chicago: Nelson-Hall.

Cohen, Bernard P., and Xueguang Zhou. 1991. "Status Processes in Enduring Work Groups." *American Sociological Review* 56:179–89.

Cohen, Elizabeth G. 1986. *Designing Groupwork: Strategies for the Heterogeneous Classroom*. New York: Teachers College Press.

———. 1993. "From Theory to Practice: The Development of an Applied Research Program." Pp. 385–415 in Joseph Berger and Morris Zelditch, Jr. (eds.), *Theoretical Research Programs*. Stanford, CA: Stanford University Press.

Cohen, Elizabeth G., Rachel Lotan, and Lisa Cantanzarite. 1988. "Can Expectations for Competence Be Altered in the Classroom?" Pp. 27–54 in Murray Webster, Jr. and Martha Foschi (eds.), *Status Generalization: New Theory and Research*. Stanford, CA: Stanford University Press.

Cohen, Elizabeth G., and Susan Roper. 1972. "Modification of Interracial Interaction Disability: An Application of Status Characteristics Theory." *American Sociological Review* 37:643–57.

———. 1985. "Modification of Interracial Interaction Disability." Pp. 350–78 in Joseph Berger and Morris Zelditch, Jr. (eds.), *Status, Rewards, and Influence*. San Francisco: Jossey-Bass.

Coleman, James S. 1963. "Comment on 'On the Concept of Influence.' " *Public Opinion Quarterly* 27:63–82.

———. 1973. *The Mathematics of Collective Action*. Chicago: Aldine.

———. 1990. *Foundations of Social Theory*. Cambridge, MA: Belknap.

Cook, Karen S. 1987. *Social Exchange Theory*. Newbury Park, CA: Sage.

Cook, Karen S., Shawn Donnelly, and Toshio Yamagishi. 1992. "The Effect of Latent Paths on Power in Exchange Networks." Paper presented at the annual meeting of the American Sociological Association, Pittsburgh, PA.

Cook, Karen S., and Richard M. Emerson. 1978. "Power, Equity and Commitment in Exchange Networks." *American Sociological Review* 43:721–39.

Cook, Karen S., Richard M. Emerson, Mary R. Gillmore, and Toshio Yamagishi. 1983. "The Distribution of Power in Exchange Networks: Theory and Experimental Results." *American Journal of Sociology* 89:275–305.

Cook, Karen S., and Mary Gillmore. 1984. "Power, Dependence and Coalitions." In Edward Lawler (ed.), *Advances in Group Processes*, vol. 1. Greenwich, CT: JAI Press.

Cook, Karen S., Mary R. Gillmore, and Toshio Yamagishi. 1986. "Point and Line Vulnerability as Bases for Predicting the Distribution of Power in Exchange Networks: Reply to Willer." *American Journal of Sociology* 92:445–48.

Cook, Karen S., Linda D. Molm, and Toshio Yamagishi. 1993. "Exchange Relations and Exchange Networks: Recent Developments in Social Exchange Theory." Pp. 296–322 in Joseph Berger and Morris Zelditch, Jr. (eds.), *Theoretical Research Programs: Studies in Theory Growth*. Stanford, CA: Stanford University Press.

Cook, Karen S., and Toshio Yamagishi. 1992a. "Power in Exchange Networks: A Power-Dependence Formulation." *Social Networks* 14:245–66.

———. 1992b. "The Effect of Latent Paths on Power in Exchange Network Structures." Paper presented at the American Sociological Association meetings, Pittsburgh, PA.

Dahl, Robert. 1957. "The Concept of Power." *Behavioral Science* 2:201–18.

———. 1968. "Power." In David Sills (ed.), *International Encyclopedia of the Social Sciences*, vol. 12. New York: Macmillan and Free Press.

Earls, Timothy, and Jonathon Ericson. 1977. *Exchange Systems in Prehistory*. New York: Academic Press.

Edgeworth, Frederik Y. 1881. *Mathematical Psychics*. London: Kegan Paul.

Ekeh, Peter. 1974. *Social Exchange Theory*. London: Heinemann.

Elkin, A. P. 1953. "Delayed Exchange in Wabag Sub-District, Central Highlands of New Guinea." *Oceania* 23:161–201.

Elster, Jon. 1979. *Ulysses and the Sirens: Studies in Rationality and Irrationality*. Cambridge: Cambridge University Press.

——— (ed.). 1986. *Rational Choice*. New York: New York University Press.

Emerson, Richard M. 1962. "Power-Dependence Relations." *American Sociological Review* 27:31–40.

———. 1972a. "Exchange Theory, Part I: A Psychological Basis for Social Exchange." Pp. 38–57 in Joseph Berger, Morris Zelditch, Jr., and Bo Anderson (eds.), *Sociological Theories in Progress*, vol. 2. Boston: Houghton Mifflin.

———. 1972b. "Exchange Theory, Part II: Exchange Relations and Networks." Pp. 58–87 in Joseph Berger, Morris Zelditch, Jr., and Bo Anderson (eds.), *Sociological Theories in Progress*, vol. 2. Boston: Houghton Mifflin.

———. 1976. "Social Exchange Theory." *Annual Review of Sociology* 2:335–61.

———. 1981. "Social Exchange Theory." In Morris Rosenberg and Ralph H. Turner (eds.), *Social Psychology: Sociological Perspectives*. New York: Basic.

Engwall, Lars. 1984. *Uppsala Contributions to Business Research*. Uppsala, Sweden: University of Uppsala Press.

Erger, Jeff. 1993. "Structural Cooperation in Exchange Networks." Paper presented at the American Sociological Association meetings, Miami, FL.

Fararo, Thomas J. 1973. *Mathematical Sociology*. Huntington, NY: Keiger.

———. 1984. "Neoclassical Theorizing and Formalization in Sociology." *Journal of Mathematical Sociology* 10:361–394.

Fararo, Thomas J., and Norman P. Hummon. 1994. "Discrete Event Simulation and Theoretical Models in Sociology." *Advances in Group Processes* 11:25–66.

Fararo, Thomas J., and John Skvoretz. 1986. "E-State Structuralism: A Theoretical Method." *American Sociological Review* 51:591–602.

———. 1993. "Methods and Problems of Theoretical Integration and the Principle of Adaptively Rational Action." Pp. 416–50 in J. Berger and M. Zelditch, Jr. (eds.), *Theoretical Research Programs: Studies in Theory Growth*. Stanford, CA: Stanford University Press.

Faucheux, Claude. 1976. "Cross-Cultural Research in Social Psychology." *European Journal of Social Psychology* 6:269–322.

Forgas, Joseph P., and Gordon H. Bower. 1987. "Mood Effects on Person-Perception Judgments." *Journal of Personality and Social Psychology* 53:53–60.

———. 1988. "Affect in Social and Personal Judgments." Pp. 183–208 in Klaus Fiedler and Joseph P. Forgas (eds.), *Affect, Cognition and Social Behavior*. Toronto: C. J. Hogrefe.

Foschi, Martha. 1980. "Theory, Experimentation and Cross-Cultural Comparisons in Social Psychology." *Canadian Journal of Sociology* 5:91–102.

French, John R. P., Jr., and Bertram Raven. 1968. "The Bases of Social Power." Pp. 259–69 in Dorwin Cartwright and Alvin Zander (eds.), *Group Dynamics*. New York: Harper & Row.

Friedkin, Noah E. 1986. "A Formal Theory of Social Power." *Journal of Mathematical Sociology* 12:103–26.

———. 1991. "Theoretical Foundations for Centrality Measures." *American Journal of Sociology* 96:1478–1504.

———. 1992. "An Expected Value Model of Social Power: Predictions for Selected Exchange Networks." *Social Networks* 14:213–30.

———. 1993a. "Structural Bases of Interpersonal Influence in Groups." *American Sociological Review* 58:861–72.

———. 1993b. "An Expected Value Model of Social Exchange Outcomes." Pp. 163–93 in E. J. Lawler, B. Markovsky, K. Heimer, and J. O'Brien (eds.), *Advances in Group Processes*, vol. 10. Greenwich CT: JAI Press.

———. 1995. "The Incidence of Exchange Networks." *Social Psychology Quarterly* 58:213–22.

Galaskiewicz, J. 1985. "Interorganizational Relations." *Annual Review of Sociology* 11: 281–304.

Galilei, Galileo. [1665] 1954. *Dialogues Concerning Two New Sciences* (trans. Henry Crew and Alfonso de Salvio). New York: Dover.

Gergen, Kenneth. 1969. *The Psychology of Behavior Exchange*. Reading, MA: Addison-Wesley.

Gilham, Steven A. 1981. "State, Law and Modern Economic Exchange." In David Willer and Bo Anderson (eds.), *Networks, Exchange and Coercion*. New York: Elsevier/Greenwood.

Goldhamer, Herbert, and Edward Shils. 1939. "Types of Power and Status." *American Journal of Sociology* 45:171–82.

Hakansson, Hakan. 1989. *Corporate Technological Behavior: Cooperation and Networks*. London: Routledge.

Hansen, Knud. 1981. " 'Black' Exchange and Its System of Social Control." Pp. 71–83 in D. Willer and B. Anderson (eds.), *Networks, Exchange and Coercion*. New York: Elsevier/Greenwood.

Harary, Frank. 1969. *Graph Theory*. Reading, MA: Addison-Wesley.

Harary, Frank, Robert Norman, and Dorwin Cartwright. 1965. *Structural Models: An Introduction to the Theory of Directed Graphs*. New York: Wiley.

Harrod, Wendy J. 1980. "Expectations from Unequal Rewards." *Social Psychology Quarterly* 43:126–30.

Harsanyi, J. C. 1980. "Analysis of a Family of Two-Person Bargaining Games with Incomplete Information." *International Journal of Game Theory* 9:65–89.

Heath, Anthony. 1976. *Rational Choice and Social Exchange: A Critique of Exchange Theory*. Cambridge: Cambridge University Press.

Heckathorn, Douglas. 1980. "A Unified Model for Bargaining and Conflict." *Behavioral Science* 25:261–84.

———. 1983. "Extensions of Power-Dependence Theory: The Concept of Resistance." *Social Forces* 61:1248–59.

Heider, Fritz. 1958. *The Psychology of Interpersonal Relations*. New York: John Wiley & Sons.

Helson, Harry, and A. Kozaki. 1968. "Anchor Effects Using Numerical Estimates of Simple Dot Patterns." *Perception and Psychophysics* 4:163–64.

Hobbes, Thomas. [1651] 1968. *Leviathan*. New York: Penguin Books.

Homans, George Caspar. 1958. "Social Behavior as Exchange." *American Journal of Sociology* 63:597–606.

———. 1971. "Commentary." In H. Turk and R. Simpson (eds.), *Institutions and Social Exchange*. Indianapolis, IN: Bobbs-Merrill.

———. 1974. *Social Behavior: Its Elementary Forms*, rev. ed. New York: Harcourt, Brace & Jovanovich.

Humphreys, Paul, and Joseph Berger. 1981. "Theoretical Consequences of the Status Characteristics Formulation." *American Journal of Sociology* 86:953–83.

Johanson, Jan. 1989. "Business Relationships and Industrial Networks." Pp. 65–77 in O. Williamson, S. Sjostrand, and J. Johanson (eds.), *Perspectives on the Economics of Organizations*. Lund: University of Lund Press.

Johanson, Jan, and Lars-Gunnar Mattsson. 1988. "Internationalization in Industrial Systems—A Network Approach." Pp. 287–314 in N. Hood and J. Vahlne (eds.), *Strategies in Global Competition*. New York: Croom Helm.

Jones, Stephen. 1992. "Was There a Hawthorne Effect?" *American Journal of Sociology* 98:451–68.

Kahan, James P., and Amnon Rapoport. 1984. *Theories of Coalition Formation*. Hillsdale, NJ: Lawrence Erlbaum.

Kahneman, Daniel, Paul Slovic, and Amos Tversky. 1982. *Judgement under Uncertainty: Heuristics and Biases*. Cambridge: Cambridge University Press.

Kanter, Rosabeth Moss. 1977. *Men and Women of the Corporation*. New York: Basic Books.

Kemper, Theodore D. 1984. "Power, Status and Emotions: A Sociological Contribution to a Psychophysiological Domain." Pp. 369–83 in Klaus R. Scherer and Paul Ekman (eds.), *Approaches to Emotion*. Hillsdale, NJ: Lawrence Erlbaum.

————. 1991. "Predicting Emotions from Social Relations." *Social Psychology Quarterly* 54:330–42.

Knottnerus, J. David. 1994. "Social Exchange Theory and Social Structure: A Critical Comparison of Two Traditions of Inquiry." *Current Perspectives in Social Theory, Supplement 1*, pp. 29–48.

Kornai, Janos. 1992. *The Socialist System*. Princeton, NJ: Princeton University Press.

Korpi, Walter. 1985. "Developments in the Theory of Power and Exchange." *Sociological Theory* 3:31–45.

Kuhn, Alfred. 1974. *The Logic of Social Systems*. San Francisco: Jossey-Bass.

Lakatos, Imre. 1970a. "Falsification and the Methodology of Scientific Research Programmes." Pp. 91–196 in Imre Lakatos and Alan Musgrave (eds.), *Criticism and the Growth of Knowledge*. Cambridge: Cambridge University Press.

————. 1970b. "History of Science and Its Rational Reconstructions." *Boston Studies in the Philosophy of Science* 8:91–136.

————. 1978. *The Methodology of Scientific Research Programmes*. New York: Cambridge University Press.

Lasswell, Harold, D. 1936. *Politics: Who Gets What, When and How*. New York: Peter Smith.

Laumann, Edward O., John H. Gagnon, Robert T. Michaels, and Stuart Michaels. 1994. *The Social Organization of Sexuality: Sexual Practices in the United States*. Chicago: University of Chicago Press.

Lawler, Edward J., and Samuel B. Bacharach. 1987. "Comparison of Dependence and Punitive Forms of Power." *Social Forces* 66:446–62.

Lawler, Edward J., Cecilia Ridgeway, and Barry Markovsky. 1993. "Structural Social Psychology and Micro-Macro Linkages." *Sociological Theory* 11:268–90.

Lévi-Strauss, Claude. 1953. "Social Structure." In A. L. Kroeber (ed.), *Anthropology Today: An Encyclopedic Inventory*. Chicago: University of Chicago Press.

Lind, Joan. 1987. "Exchange Processes in History." *Sociological Quarterly* 28:223–46.

Loukinen, Michael. 1981. "Social Exchange Networks." Pp. 85–94 in David Willer and Bo Anderson (eds.), *Networks, Exchange and Coercion*. New York: Elsevier/Greenwood.

Lovaglia, Michael J. 1994. "Relating Power to Status." Pp. 87–111 in Barry Markovsky, Karen Heimer, Jodi O'Brien, and Edward J. Lawler (eds.), *Advances in Group Processes*, vol. 11. Greenwich, CT: JAI Press.

————. 1995. "Power and Status: Exchange, Attribution and Expectation States." *Small Group Research* 26:400–426.

————. 1997. "Status, Emotion and Structural Power." Pp. 159–78 in Jacek Szmatka, John Skvoretz, and Joseph Berger (eds.), *Status, Network and Structure*. Stanford, CA: Stanford University Press.

Lovaglia, Michael, and Jeffrey Houser. 1996. "Emotional Reactions, Status Characteristics and Social Interaction." *American Sociological Review* 61:867–83.

Lovaglia, Michael, and John Skvoretz. 1993. "Predicting Frequency of Exchange in Networks: The Biased Seek Method." Paper presented at the Sunbelt Social Networks Conference, Tampa, FL.

Lovaglia, Michael, John Skvoretz, David Willer, and Barry Markovsky. 1995a. "Negotiated Exchanges in Social Exchange Networks." *Social Forces* 74:123–55.

————. 1995b. "Assessing Fundamental Power Differences in Exchange Networks." *Current Research in Social Psychology* 1:8–17.

Lucas, Jeffrey, Victor Wynn, and Anastasia Vogt. 1995. "The Effect of Status on Emotion in Face-to-Face Group Interaction." Paper presented at American Sociological Association meetings, Washington, DC.

Lukes, Steven. 1974. *Power: A Radical View*. London: Macmillan.

Mackie, Diane M., and Leila T. Worth. 1991. "Feeling Good But Not Thinking Straight: The Impact of Positive Mood on Persuasion." Pp. 201–20 in Joseph P. Forgas (ed.), *Emotion and Social Judgments*. Oxford: Pergamon.

Macy, Michael 1990. "Learning Theory and the Logic of Critical Mass." *American Sociological Review* 55:809–26.

Markovsky, Barry. 1985. "Toward Multilevel Distributive Justice Theory." *American Sociological Review* 50:822–39.

———. 1987. "Toward Multilevel Sociological Theories: Simulations of Actor and Network Effects." *Sociological Theory* 5:101–17.

———. 1988. "Anchoring Justice." *Social Psychology Quarterly* 51:213–24.

———. 1992a. "Network Exchange Outcomes: Limits of Predictability." *Social Networks* 14:267–86.

———. 1992b. "Building Theories in Structural Social Psychology." Paper presented to the Annual Meeting of the American Sociological Association. Pittsburgh, PA.

———. 1995. "Developing an Exchange Network Simulator." *Sociological Perspectives* 38:519–45.

Markovsky, Barry, David Willer, and Travis Patton. 1988. "Power Relations in Exchange Networks." *American Sociological Review* 53:220–36.

Markovsky, Barry, John Skvoretz, David Willer, Michael Lovaglia, and Jeffrey Erger. 1993. "The Seeds of Weak Power: An Extension of Network Exchange Theory." *American Sociological Review* 58:197–209.

Markovsky, Barry, LeRoy F. Smith, and Joseph Berger. 1984. "Do Status Interventions Persist?" *American Sociological Review* 49:373–82.

Marsden, Peter V. 1983. "Restricted Access in Networks and Models of Power." *American Journal of Sociology* 88:686–717.

———. 1987. "Elements of Interactor Dependence." In Karen S. Cook (ed.), *Social Exchange Theory*. Newbury Park, CA: Sage.

Marx, Karl. [1867] 1967. *Capital*. New York: International Publishers.

Merton, Robert K. [1949] 1968. "On Sociological Theories of the Middle Range." Pp. 39–72 in Robert K. Merton, *Social Theory and Social Structure*. New York: Free Press.

Mokken, Robert J., and Frans N. Stokman. 1976. "Power and Influence and Political Phenomena." Pp. 33–54 in Brian Barry (ed.), *Power and Political Theory: Some European Perspectives*. London: John Wiley.

Molm, Linda D. 1981. "The Conversion of Power Imbalance to Power Use." *Social Psychology Quarterly* 44:151–63.

———. 1988. "The Structure and Use of Power: A Comparison of Reward and Punishment Power." *Social Psychology Quarterly* 51:108–22.

———. 1990. "The Dynamics of Power in Social Exchange." *American Sociological Review* 55:427–47.

Molm, Linda D., and Karen S. Cook. 1995. "Social Exchange and Exchange Networks." In Karen S. Cook, Gary Alan Fine, and James S. House (eds.), *Sociological Perspectives on Social Psychology*. Stanford, CA: Stanford University Press.

Moore, James C., Jr. 1985. "Role Enactment and Self Identity." Pp. 262–315 in Joseph

Berger and Morris Zelditch, Jr. (eds.), *Status, Rewards, and Influence*. San Francisco: Jossey-Bass.

Nadel, S. F. 1957. *The Theory of Social Structure*. London: Cohen & West.

Nash, John F. 1950. "The Bargaining Problem." *Econometrica* 18:155–62.

———. 1951. "Non-Cooperative Games." *Annals of Mathematics* 54:286–95.

———. 1953 "Two-Person Cooperative Games." *Econometrica* 21:128–40.

Newman, Peter. 1965. *The Theory of Exchange*. Englewood Cliffs, NJ: Prentice-Hall.

Nydegger, R. V., and G. Owen. 1974. "Two Person Bargaining: An Experimental Test of the Nash Axioms." *International Journal of Game Theory* 3:239–49.

Osborne, Martin J. 1990. "Signaling, Forward Induction, and Stability in Finitely Repeated Games." *Journal of Economic Theory* 50:22–36.

Parsons, H. M. 1974. "What Happened at Hawthorne?" *Science* 183:922–32.

Parsons, Talcott. [1940] 1954. *Essays in Sociological Theory*. Glencoe, IL: Free Press.

———. 1963a. "On the Concept of Political Power." *Proceedings of the American Philosophical Society* 107:232–62.

———. 1963b. "On the Concept of Influence." *Public Opinion Quarterly* 27:37–62.

Patton, Travis. 1986. "A Theoretical Analysis of Positively Connected Networks." Paper presented at the annual meetings of the Midwest Sociological Society, Des Moines, Iowa.

Patton, Travis, and David Willer. 1987. "Power in Centralized Networks: The Conditions of Positive, Negative and Null Connection." Paper presented at the American Sociological Association meetings, Chicago.

———. 1990. "Connection and Power in Centralized Exchange Networks." *Journal of Mathematical Sociology* 16:31–49.

Peplau, Letita Ann. 1979. "Power in Dating Relationships." In J. Freeman (ed.), *Women: A Feminist Perspective*, 2nd ed. Palo Alto, CA: Mayfield.

Polanyi, Karl. 1957. *The Great Transformation*. Boston: Beacon Press.

Rapoport, Anatol. 1970. *N-Person Game Theory*. Ann Arbor: University of Michigan Press.

Rapoport, Anatol, and Melvin Guyer. 1966. "A Taxonomy of 2 × 2 Games." *General Systems* 11:203–14.

Read, Ronald C. 1978. "Everyone a Winner or How to Avoid Isomorphism Search When Cataloguing Combinatorial Configuration." *Annals of Discrete Mathematics* 2: 107–20.

Ridgeway, Cecilia. 1981. "Nonconformity, Competence, and Influence in Groups: A Test of Two Theories." *American Sociological Review* 46:333–47.

———. 1982. "Status in Groups: The Importance of Motivation." *American Sociological Review* 47:76–88.

———. 1991. "The Social Construction of Status Value: Gender and Other Nominal Characteristics." *Social Forces* 70:367–86.

Ridgeway, Cecilia, Joseph Berger, and LeRoy Smith. 1985. "Nonverbal Cues and Status: An Expectation States Approach." *American Journal of Sociology* 90:955–78.

Ridgeway, Cecilia, Elizabeth Boyle, Kathy Kuipers, and Dawn Robinson. 1998. "How Do Status Beliefs Develop? The Role of Resources and Interaction." *American Sociological Review* 63:331–50.

Ridgeway, Cecilia, and Kristan Glasgow. 1996. "Acquiring Status Beliefs from Behavior in Interaction." Paper presented at the annual meetings of the American Sociological Association, New York.

Roethlisberger, Fritz J., and William J. Dickson. 1964. *Management and the Worker*. New York: John Wiley & Sons.

Rosenholtz, Susan J. 1985. "Modifying Status Expectations in the Traditional Classroom." Pp. 445–70 in Joseph Berger and Morris Zelditch, Jr. (eds.), *Status, Rewards, and Influence*. San Francisco: Jossey-Bass.

Rosenthal, R. W., and A. Rubinstein. 1984. "Repeated Two-Player Games with Ruin." *International Journal of Game Theory* 13:155–77.

Rotter, Julian B. 1972. "Beliefs, Social Attitudes and Behavior: A Social Learning Analysis." Pp. 335–50 in Julian B. Rotter, June E. Chance, and E. Jerry Phares (eds.), *Applications of a Social-Learning Theory of Personality*. New York: Holt, Rinehart & Winston.

Rubinstein, Ariel. 1982. "Perfect Equilibrium in a Bargaining Model." *Econometrica* 50:97–109.

———. 1991. "Comments on the Interpretation of Game Theory." *Econometrica* 59: 909–24.

Russell, Bertrand. 1938. *Power: A New Social Analysis*. London: George Allen & Unwin.

Sahlins, Marshall. 1972. *Stone Age Economics*. New York: Aldine Publishing Co.

Samuelson, P. A. 1947. *Foundations of Economic Analysis*. Cambridge, MA: Harvard University Press.

Schelling, Thomas. 1970. *The Strategy of Conflict*. Cambridge, MA: Harvard University Press.

Shelly, Robert K. 1993. "How Sentiments Organize Interaction." Pp. 113–32 in Edward J. Lawler, Barry Markovsky, Karen Heimer, and Jodi O'Brien (eds.), *Advances in Group Processes*, vol. 10. Greenwich, CT: JAI Press.

Shubik, Martin. 1982. *Game Theory in the Social Sciences: Concepts and Solutions*. Cambridge, MA: MIT Press.

Skinner, Steven J., and Joseph P. Guiltinan. 1986. "Extra-Network Linkages, Dependence and Power." *Social Forces* 64:702–13.

Skvoretz, John, and Tracy Burkett. 1994. "Information and the Distribution of Power in Exchange Networks." *Journal of Mathematical Sociology* 19:263–78.

Skvoretz, John, and Thomas. J. Fararo. 1992 "Power and Network Exchange: An Essay Toward Theoretical Unification." *Social Networks* 14:325–44.

Skvoretz, John, and Michael J. Lovaglia. 1995. "Who Exchanges with Whom: Structural Determinants of Exchange Frequency in Negotiated Exchange Networks." *Social Psychology Quarterly* 58:163–77.

Skvoretz, John, and David Willer. 1991. "Power in Exchange Networks: Setting and Structure Variations." *Social Psychology Quarterly* 54:224–38.

———. 1993. "Exclusion and Power: A Test of Four Theories of Power in Exchange Networks." *American Sociological Review* 58:801–18.

Southard, Frank. 1981. "Normatively Controlled Social Exchange Systems." Pp. 55–70 in David Willer and Bo Anderson (eds.), *Networks, Exchange and Coercion*. New York: Elsevier/Greenwood.

Stewart, Penni A., and James C. Moore. 1992. "Wage Disparities and Performance Expectations." *Social Psychology Quarterly* 55:78–85.

Stokman, Frans N., and Jan M. Van den Bos. 1992. "Two-Stage Model of Policymaking with an Empirical Test in the U.S. Energy-Policy Domain." *Research in Politics and Society* 4:219–53.

Stolte, John, and Richard M. Emerson. 1977. "Structural Inequality: Position and Power in Exchange Structures." Pp. 117–38 in R. Hamblin and J. Kunkel (eds.), *Behavioral Theory in Sociology*. New Brunswick, NJ: Transaction Books.

Stone, Katherine. 1974. "The Origins of Job Structures in the Steel Industry." *The Review of Radical Political Economics* 6:22–33.

Szmatka, Jacek, and Michael J. Lovaglia. 1996. "The Significance of Method." *Sociological Perspectives* 39:393–415.

Szmatka, Jacek, and David Willer. 1995. "Exclusion, Inclusion and Compound Connection in Exchange Networks." *Social Psychology Quarterly* 58:123–31.

Taylor, Frederick W. [1911] 1967. *The Principles of Scientific Management*. New York: W. W. Norton.

Thibaut, John W., and Harold H. Kelley. 1959. *The Social Psychology of Groups*. New York: John Wiley & Sons.

Toulmin, Stephen. 1953. *The Philosophy of Science*. New York: Harper & Row Publishers.

Thye, Shane, and Barry Markovsky. 1997. "Power from Status in Exchange Networks." Paper presented at the annual meeting of the American Sociological Association, Toronto.

Thye, Shane, Michael Lovaglia, and Barry Markovsky. 1997. "Responses to Social Exchange and Social Exclusion in Networks." *Social Forces* 75:1031–49.

Troyer, Lisa, and C. Wesley Younts. 1997. "Whose Expectations Matter? The Relative Power of First- and Second-Order Expectations in Determining Social Influence." *American Journal of Sociology* 103:692–732.

Turner, Jonathan H. 1986. *The Structure of Sociological Theory*, 4th ed. Chicago: Dorsey.

Urban, Michael E. 1989. *An Algebra of Soviet Power*. New York: Cambridge University Press.

Von Neuman, John, and Oskar Morgenstern. 1944. *Theory of Games and Economic Behavior*. Princeton, NJ: Princeton University Press.

Wagner, David, and Joseph Berger. 1985. "Do Sociological Theories Grow?" *American Journal of Sociology* 90:697–728.

———. 1993. "Status Characteristics Theory: The Growth of a Program." Pp. 23–63 in Joseph Berger and Morris Zelditch, Jr. (eds.), *Theoretical Research Programs: Studies in the Growth of Theory*. Stanford, CA: Stanford University Press.

Walder, Andrew G. 1995. "Career Mobility and the Communist Political Order." *American Sociological Review* 60:309–28.

Walker, Henry A., and Bernard P. Cohen. 1985. "Scope Statements: Imperatives for Evaluating Theory." *American Sociological Review* 50:288–301.

Weber, Max. [1918] 1968. *Economy and Society*. Berkeley: University of California Press.

———. [1896] 1976. "The Social Causes of the Decay of Ancient Civilization." In Russell Kahl (ed.), *Studies in Explanation* (trans. R. Frank). Englewood Cliffs, NJ: Prentice-Hall.

———. 1958. *From Max Weber: Essays in Sociology* (trans. and ed. Hans H. Gerth and C. Wright Mills). New York: Galaxy.

Webster, Murray, and Stuart J. Hysom. 1996. "Acquiring Status Value." Paper presented at the Iowa Workshop for Theoretical Analysis, University of Iowa.

———. 1998. "Creating Status Characteristics." *American Sociological Review* 63:351–78.

Wellman, Barry, and Stephen D. Berkowitz (eds.). 1992. *Social Structures: A Network Approach*. New York: Cambridge University Press.

White, Harrison C. 1970. *Chains of Opportunity*. Cambridge, MA: Harvard University Press.

Willer, David. 1981a. "The Basic Concepts of Elementary Theory." Pp. 25–53 in David Willer and Bo Anderson (eds.), *Networks, Exchange and Coercion*. New York: Elsevier/Greenwood.

———. 1981b. "Quantity and Network Structure." Pp. 109–27 in David Willer and Bo Anderson (eds.), *Networks, Exchange and Coercion*. New York: Elsevier/Greenwood.

———. 1984. "Analysis and Composition as Theoretic Procedures." *Journal of Mathematical Sociology* 10:241–70.

———. 1985. "Property and Social Exchange." Pp. 123–42 in Edward J. Lawler (ed.), *Advances in Group Processes*, vol. 2. Greenwich, CT: JAI Press.

———. 1986. "Vulnerability and the Location of Power Positions: Comment on Cook, Emerson, Gillmore, and Yamagishi." *American Journal of Sociology* 92:441–44.

———. 1987. *Theory and the Experimental Investigation of Social Structures*. New York: Gordon & Breach.

———. 1992a. "Predicting Power in Exchange Networks: A Brief History and Introduction to the Issues." *Social Networks* 14:187–212.

———. 1992b. "The Principle of Rational Choice and the Problem of a Satisfactory Theory." In J. S. Coleman and T. J. Fararo (eds.), *Rational Choice Theory: Advocacy and Critique*. Newbury Park, CA: Sage.

Willer, David, and Bo Anderson (eds.). 1981. *Networks, Exchange and Coercion*. New York: Elsevier/Greenwood.

Willer, David, and Barry Markovsky. 1993, "The Theory of Elementary Relations: Its Development and Research Program." Pp. 323–63 in Joseph Berger and Morris Zelditch, Jr. (eds.), *Theoretical Research Programs: Studies in Theory Growth*. Stanford, CA: Stanford University Press.

Willer, David, Barry Markovsky, and Travis Patton. 1989. "Power Structures: Derivations and Applications of Elementary Theory." Pp. 313–53 in Joseph Berger, Morris Zelditch, Jr., and Bo Anderson (eds.), *Sociological Theories in Progress: New Formulations*. Newbury Park, CA: Sage.

Willer, David, and Travis Patton. 1987. "The Development of Network Exchange Theory." Pp. 199–242 in E. J. Lawler and B. Markovsky (eds.), *Advances in Group Processes*, vol. 4. Greenwich, CT: JAI Press.

Willer, David, and Brent Simpson. 1997. "Breaking Networks and Power Structures." Presented at the American Sociological Association Conference, Toronto.

Willer, David, Brent Simpson, Jacek Szmatka, and Joanna Mazur. 1996. "Social Theory and Historical Explanation." *Humboldt Journal of Social Relations* 22:63–64.

Willer, David, and John Skvoretz. 1997a. "Games and Structures." *Rationality and Society* 9:5–35.

———. 1997b. "Network Connection and Exchange Ratios: Theory, Predictions and Experimental Tests." Pp. 199–234 in Barry Markovsky, Michael Lovaglia, and Lisa Troyer (eds.), *Advances in Group Process*, vol. 14. Greenwich, CT: JAI Press.

Willer, David, and Jacek Szmatka. 1993. "Cross-National Experimental Investigations of Elementary Theory: Implications for the Generality of the Theory and the

Autonomy of Social Structure.'' Pp. 37–81 in E. J. Lawler, B. Markovsky, K. Heimer, and J. O'Brien (eds.), *Advances in Group Processes*, vol. 10. Greenwich, CT: JAI Press.

Willer, David, and Robb Willer. 1995. ''Exchange Network Dynamics and Structural Agency.'' Paper presented to the annual meeting of the American Sociological Association, Washington, DC, August.

Williamson, Oliver. 1975. *Markets and Hierarchies*. New York: Free Press.

———. 1981. ''The Economics of Organization: The Transaction Cost Approach.'' *American Journal of Sociology* 87:548–77.

———. 1986. *The Economics of the Institutions of Capitalism*. New York: Free Press.

Winer, B. J. 1962. *Statistical Principles in Experimental Design*. New York: McGraw-Hill.

Womack, James P., Daniel T. Jones, and Daniel Roos. 1990. *The Machine That Changed the World*. New York: Harper.

Wrong, Dennis H. 1979. *Power: Its Forms, Bases and Uses*. Oxford: Basil Blackwell.

Yamagishi, Toshio. 1993. ''PDP: Power/Dependence Predictions.'' Hokkaido University, Japan. Unpublished algorithm.

Yamagishi, Toshio, and Karen S. Cook. 1990. ''Power Relations in Exchange Networks: A Comment on 'Network Exchange Theory.' '' *American Sociological Review* 55:297–300.

Yamagishi, Toshio, Mary R. Gillmore, and Karen S. Cook. 1988. ''Network Connections and the Distribution of Power in Exchange Networks.'' *American Journal of Sociology* 93:833–51.

Yamaguchi, Kazuo. 1996. ''Power in Networks of Substitutable and Complementary Exchange.'' *American Sociological Review* 61:308–32.

Zelditch, Morris, Jr. 1992. ''Interpersonal Power.'' Pp. 994–1001 in Edgar F. Borgatta and Marie L. Borgatta. (eds.), *Encyclopedia of Sociology*. New York: Macmillan.

Zimbardo, Philip G., and Michael R. Leippe. 1991. *The Psychology of Attitude Change and Social Influence*. New York: McGraw-Hill.

Author Index

Subject Index

About the Editor and Contributors

DAVID WILLER is Professor of Sociology at the University of South Carolina. For the last two decades his research has contributed to the development and testing of Elementary Theory and its exchange component, Network Exchange Theory. His work focuses on extending Network Exchange Theory to cover an increasingly wide variety of structures. He is the author of *Theory and the Experimental Investigation of Social Structures* and co-editor (with Bo Anderson) of *Networks, Exchange and Coercion*. He has also authored and co-authored a number of papers on theory development and the theory of social structure.

MICHAEL J. LOVAGLIA is Associate Professor of Sociology at the University of Iowa. He founded the peer-reviewed scientific journal, *Current Research in Social Psychology*, in 1995 and continues as its editor. His research focuses on status and power. Recent publications include "Status Processes and Mental Ability Test Scores," co-authored with Jeffrey Lucas, Jeffrey Houser, Shane Thye, and Barry Markovsky, in *American Journal of Sociology* (1998) and *Knowing People*, a book on the personal use of social psychology (1999).

BARRY MARKOVSKY is Professor of Sociology at the University of Iowa and Director of the Center for the Study of Group Processes. In addition to his theoretical and empirical work on Network Exchange Theory, he has conducted research on a variety of group processes, including social influence, justice, and status processes. He also writes on methods for theory construction and analysis.

TRAVIS PATTON is Associate Director, Morehouse Research Institute. His previous research includes investigation of the effects of inclusive connection on power in exchange structures. Currently his work focuses on new modes of teaching social and economic theory to undergraduates.

BRENT SIMPSON is a Ph.D. candidate in sociology at Cornell University. His research areas include theory, methods, collective action, and social psychology. He co-authored ''Power in Exchange Networks'' in *American Sociological Review* (1997) and ''Social Theory and Historical Explanation,'' in *Humboldt Journal of Social Relations* (1996).

JOHN SKVORETZ is Professor of Sociology at the University of South Carolina. He is an associate editor of the *Journal of Mathematical Sociology* and serves on the editorial board of *Social Psychology Quarterly*. Professor Skvoretz has published over 60 books, book chapters, and papers, and has authored several computer programs used in network research and analysis.

SHANE R. THYE is an Assistant Professor of Sociology at the University of South Carolina. He is currently developing theoretical models that bridge theories of power and status, and is conducting experiments on the transfer of status value from people to commodities. With several colleagues (Edward Lawler and Jeongkoo Yoon), he is also investigating the emotional bases of commitment and solidarity in laboratory and organizational settings.